The Future of Risk Management

CRITICAL STUDIES IN RISK AND DISASTER

Kim Fortun and Scott Gabriel Knowles, Series Editors

Critical Studies in Risk and Disaster explores how environmental, technological, and health risks are created, managed, and analyzed in different contexts. Global in scope and drawing on perspectives from multiple disciplines, volumes in the series examine the ways that planning, science, and technology are implicated in disasters. The series also engages public policy formation—including analysis of science, technology, and environmental policy as well as welfare, conflict resolution, and economic policy developments where relevant.

The Future of
RISK MANAGEMENT

Edited by

Howard Kunreuther,

Robert J. Meyer,

and Erwann O. Michel-Kerjan

PENN

UNIVERSITY OF PENNSYLVANIA PRESS

PHILADELPHIA

Published by
University of Pennsylvania Press
Philadelphia, Pennsylvania 19104-4112
www.upenn.edu/pennpress

Printed in the United States of America
on acid-free paper
10   9   8   7   6   5   4   3   2   1

Library of Congress Cataloging-in-Publication Data

Names: Kunreuther, Howard, editor. | Meyer, Robert J. (Robert John),
   editor. | Michel-Kerjan, Erwann, editor.
Title: The future of risk management / edited by Howard Kunreuther,
   Robert J. Meyer, and Erwann O. Michel-Kerjan
Other titles: Critical studies in risk and disaster.
Description: 1st edition. | Philadelphia: University of Pennsylvania
   Press, [2019] | Series: Critical studies in risk and disaster | Includes
   bibliographical references and index.
Identifiers: LCCN 2018054752| ISBN 9780812251326 (hardcover: alk.
   paper) | ISBN 0812251326 (hardcover: alk. paper)
Subjects: LCSH: Risk management. | Risk (Insurance) | Insurance—
   Decision making. | Emergency management.
Classification: LCC HD61 .F88 2019 | DDC 368—dc23
LC record available at https://lccn.loc.gov/2018054752

CONTENTS

PART II. IMPROVING RISK ASSESSMENT

PART III. DEVELOPING BETTER RISK COMMUNICATION STRATEGIES

PART IV. ROLE OF RISK MITIGATION, RISK-SHARING, AND INSURANCE

Introduction

Howard Kunreuther, Robert J. Meyer, and Erwann O. Michel-Kerjan

Hurricane Katrina. Superstorm Sandy. Hurricanes Harvey, Irma, and Maria. Contaminated water in Flint, Michigan. Anthrax. 9/11 terrorist attacks. Earthquakes. Oil and chemical spills. Boston Marathon attack. Financial crisis. Refugee crisis. Ebola. Sea level rise. Devastating floods. Cyber-attacks. Geopolitical instability.

Whether man-made or naturally occurring, an unprecedented series of large-scale disasters and crises have caused a vast number of fatalities and injuries, destroyed property, devastated communities, savaged the environment, imposed significant financial and emotional burdens on individuals and firms, and challenged political leadership.

The Future of Risk Management

Thirty years ago, the study of risk management was viewed narrowly. Scientists and engineers provided estimates of the probability of specific types of disasters occurring and their potential consequences. Economists proposed risk management policies based on these experts' estimates with little thought as to how these data would be used by interested parties.

Today we live in a new age of catastrophe and increasing uncertainty. Besides the disasters that arise with alarming regularity, we are faced with major challenges in dealing with natural and technological hazards and global issues, such as climate change and terrorism.

What makes these risks all the more difficult to address is that the world has become more interdependent and interconnected; what occurs in one nation or geographical region is likely to have ripple effects across the globe. The information age is also more integrated, creating new forms of communication and greater risks that are not easy to evaluate. All of this implies that new approaches to risk management are required. These measures need to combine the latest scientific knowledge on risk assessment with a better appreciation of the importance of improving individual and collective decision-making processes.

While significant progress has been made in quantitatively assessing risks, there is also a growing recognition that we need to integrate psychological and behavioral elements into our risk management strategies. By recognizing the cognitive biases and simplified heuristics used by decision-makers, we should be better able to develop effective strategies for coping with them. Today, risk assessment and risk management are no longer the sole domain of scientists, engineers, and economists. The disciplines of finance, geography, history, insurance, marketing, political science, psychology, sociology, and the decision sciences now work together, challenge one another, and in the process, build new approaches.

In this edited volume we offer a view into the present and future of risk management. We invited leading thinkers in risk management and the behavioral sciences to address the question: What is the future of risk management based on what we have learned from our past research? While this book is not intended to provide a comprehensive analysis of the topic, it allows the reader to benefit from the experience and perspective of a number of respected scholars in the field as they look back at recent discoveries and at some of the important open questions we still face.

Over its 35-year history, the Wharton Risk Center has focused its research on how individuals, organizations, and government at all levels can deal with extreme events. While many decisions regarding low-probability, high-consequence events are based on intuitive thinking—with emotions, past experience, and cognitive biases playing a key role—more deliberative thinking such as the use of decision analysis and cost-benefit analysis can provide important insights for developing effective strategies.

Organization of the Book

The book is organized into five parts, each of which addresses avenues for practitioners and researchers to consider. We briefly summarize below the chapters in each of these parts.

Behavioral Factors Influencing Decision-Making
Under Risk and Uncertainty

Part I probes the behavioral and psychological factors that influence decision-making in risky situations. Why do some people invest in protective measures to prevent severe losses from the next disaster, while others do not? What catastrophes or personal hardships elicit widespread compassion that other less salient events do not? What factors influence people in their risk perceptions, risk-taking, and risk management? The chapters point to several new directions as this topic is quickly evolving and needs more attention in the future.

Paul Slovic and Daniel Västfjäll discuss three nonrational psychological mechanisms that confound the arithmetic of compassion: psychophysical numbing (insensitivity to large numbers of losses of human lives), pseudoinefficacy (being deterred from helping one person because one cannot help others), and the prominence effect (the disconnect between our stated values and the values revealed by our actions). Their chapter contrasts risk as feelings with risk as analysis and suggests that it is time to examine strategies that acknowledge the psychological challenges of intuitive thinking and encourage more systematic and reasoned deliberative thinking.

Elke U. Weber confirms that the concept of risk can be interpreted as a statistic via metrics like the variance of outcomes or as feelings driven by emotional responses. She shows how the DOmain-SPEcific Risk-Taking (DOSPERT) scale differentially predicts observed real-world risk taking in different domains by incorporating domain-specific perceptions of risk, and how the Columbia Card Task (CCT) captures risk-taking in dynamic environments. Weber concludes by showing how risk can be better managed by appreciating subjective perceptions of risk, including risk as feelings, so that one can reframe problems in ways that align observed behavior more closely to desirable behavior.

Baruch Fischhoff recognizes that assessing the quality of individuals' decision-making is technically demanding. He then raises the question as to how we can communicate the findings from our research on risk and choice to key decision-makers in ways that will make a difference in their behavior. He suggests that future risk research should focus on a longitudinal study of decision-making competence and methods for communicating the quality of risk research.

Craig E. Landry, Gregory Colson, and Mona Ahmadiani highlight the limitations of expected utility theory in explaining why individuals do not invest in protective decisions. They then suggest alternative models of choice that reflect the role that subjective probability and preference parameters play in the decision-making process. The authors recommend survey-based studies using panel data over time at the individual and household level for developing models that explain natural hazard risk management decisions.

Mark Pauly focuses on what we know about the mix of rationality and irrationality in consumers, focusing on health insurance purchasing in the United States as an illustrative example. He notes that a rational model of choice, such as expected utility maximization, is highly demanding in terms of time and data collection. He also points out that there are individuals who do not make the optimal decision of purchasing highly subsidized health insurance when they should know they are getting a good deal. Pauly concludes that there are fewer deviations from the rational model in health insurance than other insurance markets in part because health-related extreme events are less common and losses are rarely correlated across exposures.

Robert J. Meyer concludes Part I with a discussion as to why we often fail to learn as much as we should from disasters. He argues that much of the blame lies in how our brains are innately wired to learn; we repeat actions that give positive rewards and avoid those that produce negative returns. While these instincts work well in most circumstances, when applied to protective decisions for rare events, the reward structure sometimes is reversed. In the immediate wake of a disaster it is easy to see the benefits of protection, but as time passes, the positive returns from these investments become harder to see, eventually leading to their abandonment. As a result, disasters often are destined to repeat themselves.

Improving Risk Assessment

Part II explores how risk assessment provides the scientific ingredients for developing risk management strategies. What data should individuals, groups, businesses, and government take into account when evaluating risk and determining what strategies to consider and examine carefully? Given the uncertainty of extreme events, what tools can organizations consider when developing long-term strategies for undertaking protective measures and reducing future losses from potential disasters?

Robert Muir-Wood begins his chapter by noting that the March 2015 Sendai Declaration, signed by 187 countries, was concerned with achieving substantial reductions in disaster casualties by 2030. He then raises the question as to whether the benchmark years 2005–2015 employed in the Sendai process, for comparison with the future 2020–2030 period, provide a biased sample, capable of indicating spurious evidence of progress. Muir-Wood concludes that goals for casualty risk reduction should be directed at individual countries so they are owned by institutions with the power to alter future outcomes. However, the extreme volatility of mega-catastrophes means that catastrophe models, with their long-term synthetic histories, should be used for setting and measuring national targets for disaster casualty reduction based on "expected" fatalities.

Robin Dillon focuses on the importance of learning from near-misses and notes that people's own experience influences how they interpret these events. If they haven't had a disaster they may believe that the near-miss lowers their probability of a future disaster because they previously escaped unharmed. She summarizes recent experiments on false alarms that reveal that individuals exposed to two false alarms are likely not to heed future warnings. Dillon concludes by highlighting the importance of emergency managers understanding people's responses to near-misses to successfully communicate risk of hazardous situations to the public.

Paul J. H. Schoemaker contends that business leaders will increasingly have to prevent or mitigate industry-wide risks through better industry-level collaboration. He explains that American credit unions weathered the 2008–2009 financial crisis relatively well because industry leaders recognized the importance of focusing on strategic issues related to regulation, technology, and business models as early as 1997. He also discusses why other sectors in the financial services field did not fare as well. The leadership challenges at an industry level are to deploy strategies and capabilities that are flexible enough to deal with unanticipated black swan events as well as a rising tide of systemic risks.

Adam Rose focuses on questions associated with measuring economic resilience by proposing an operational metric and advocating the use of cost effectiveness and cost-benefit analysis to make prudent and careful resource management decisions. He highlights the direct and indirect benefits and co-benefits that emerge from undertaking risk reduction measures, and proposes the use of innovative financing instruments and insurance to incentivize these expenditures now rather than waiting until the next disaster occurs.

Developing Better Risk Communication Strategies

The chapters in Part III examine challenges in risk communication. How do we issue warnings so that people will pay attention to risks that matter? Why don't people pay attention to the lessons from past disasters when making decisions regarding investing in protective measures? The goal of such strategies is to engage stakeholders more effectively in the risk management process.

Robin Gregory and Nate Dieckmann highlight the importance of informed deliberation by stakeholders in evaluating the uncertainty associated with different proposed programs for managing future environmental risks. They propose several methods for eliciting stakeholder opinions to help overcome judgmental biases that often arise when dealing with the unfamiliar and novel choices associated with upstream technologies. Gregory and Dieckmann also note the importance of communicating uncertainty so that people understand why experts' predictions for a specific phenomenon may differ and that individuals presented with identical information may interpret the uncertainty differently as the result of varying beliefs, worldviews, or motivations.

Barbara A. Mellers, Philip E. Tetlock, Joshua D. Baker, Jeffrey A. Friedman, and Richard J. Zeckhauser discuss the factors that improved accuracy in a four-year geopolitical forecasting tournament and the characteristics of the best forecasters. Top performers tended to use many distinctions along the probability scale. The authors use the data from the forecasting tournament to investigate the number of categories necessary to maximize forecasting accuracy. The intelligence community in the United States currently recommends a seven-point rating scale for expressing uncertainty. A comparison of forecasters' original accuracy scores with the scores they would have obtained after rounding forecasts to seven bins shows that prediction errors grow if analysts are only allowed to convey seven degrees of doubt. Even worse, the accuracy of the best forecasters suffers the most when probability scales do not have sufficient shades of gray.

Lisa A. Robinson, W. Kip Viscusi, and Richard Zeckhauser argue that warnings, appropriately employed, are often superior to command and control regulation in limiting individuals' exposures to risks. Unfortunately, products imposing vastly different dangers are often required by regulations or standards to employ the same warning. California Proposition 65's indiscriminate labeling of 800+ substances as carcinogens or reproductive toxins is an exemplar. Individuals cannot be expected to distinguish among such risks when making consumption decisions. Other warnings, such as about mercury in some seafoods, simply confuse. Consumers, failing to identify those fish that are safe, may stop eating healthy seafood. Significant welfare losses can be expected. Warnings should be designed in a manner that leads consumers to, at the least, distinguish between serious and mild risks.

Role of Risk Mitigation, Risk-Sharing, and Insurance

The chapters in Part IV focus on the need to prepare for the financial impacts of adverse events. How can insurance encourage those at risk to undertake loss reduction measures before the next disaster? How does one deal with issues of affordability? What is the appropriate role of the public sector in dealing with the costs of catastrophic risk? Risk-sharing is a key principle in the management of disasters, and discussions about fairness and affordability in designing insurance programs are now getting more attention.

Carolyn Kousky discusses many converging trends that might make natural disasters increasingly harder to insure, such as dependent and systemic risks. In the face of such changes, a more thoughtful approach to risk management that stresses targeted mitigation and develops complementary roles for the public and private sectors—in both risk reduction and risk transfer arrangements—can improve insurability.

Howard Kunreuther proposes that insurers follow the example of the nineteenth-century factory mutual insurance companies who required those requesting insurance to invest in risk-reducing measures as a condition for coverage. Today, state regulators need to allow insurers to charge risk-based premiums so they can incentivize their clients to undertake loss reduction measures. There is also a need to use choice architecture to frame the problem in ways that those at risk will want to purchase insurance and invest in protective measures. The public sector can play an important role by addressing fairness and affordability issues, as well as providing protection against catastrophic losses that are currently uninsurable.

W. J. Wouter Botzen examines economists' contention that insurance and risk reduction measures are substitutes so that individuals who purchase insurance are less likely to invest in risk mitigation measures than those who are uninsured. Surveys in Germany and New York City reveal that those who purchase insurance also mitigate, implying that there is not always a moral hazard problem associated with the purchase of insurance as the theory of insurance has traditionally assumed. He suggest additional research on how one can utilize insurance to provide financial incentives to encourage individuals to better prepare for the next disaster before it is too late.

Jeffrey Czajkowski provides empirical evidence that windstorm losses due to stronger building codes have been reduced by 40 to 60% and are cost-effective with respect to new construction. At the same time he shows that many local communities do not enforce their building codes in part due to the lack of financial and technical resources. Surveys of Oklahoma homeowners' attitudes toward building codes reveal that most favor a law requiring new homes to be better designed to withstand high winds. Czajkowski concludes that future research should focus on what drives building code enforcement at the local level and the degree of consumer support for improved building codes when the actual costs are explicitly indicated.

Government and Risk Management

Part V examines important and growing questions about the role of government in dealing with extreme events. What is the right mix for the public and the private sectors to play in providing protection against risk? Should government intervention be more local or more federal? How does such intervention affect personal responsibility and the demand for protection? The degree of public-private partnerships will naturally vary for different risks.

Cary Coglianese notes that all risk management requires forming the right kind of partnership between the public and private sectors and illustrates this point by stressing the importance of creating effective relationships between private and public actors, such as when government regulation is coupled with private insurance (and vice versa). He says that, to facilitate a constructive partnership, decision-makers and organizers need to satisfy four core factors to solve a particular problem: *interface, incentives, information, institutions*—or what he calls the "four *i*'s." Coglianese concludes with a call for more behavioral research on the fit between public- and private-sector risk management interventions, as well as the important role of distributional politics in affecting the success of public-private partnerships.

Robert W. Klein contends that insurance regulation can enhance social welfare if it addresses market failures that it can remedy or ameliorate and seeks outcomes consistent with a competitive market. He also argues that regulation that promotes efficient insurance markets contributes to effective risk management. Using these basic principles as guidelines, he examines the performance of current regulatory policies with respect to the following insurance-related issues for hurricanes and other catastrophic risks: pricing and underwriting, adequacy of coverage, the management of residual market mechanisms, and the solvency of insurance companies, as well as the implications of these policies for catastrophe risk mitigation.

Erwann O. Michel-Kerjan concludes the book by analyzing how the federal government in the United States has played a more important role in intervening after disasters in recent years than it has done historically. This new reality may have created significant moral hazard: if they expect to be financially supported after a disaster, people, firms, and communities might invest less in pre-disaster preparedness than they would otherwise. He proposes a transparent national accounting system of how much is spent on disaster relief, where the money is coming from and where it is going; in other words, who pays for this spending and who benefits from it. These data should provide inputs to proposing better disaster preparedness policies based on measurable evidence, as well as providing greater incentives for states and other interested parties to invest in catastrophe risk management today.

As noted, this volume offers a snapshot of risk management today along with directions for future research. We look forward to deeper financial analysis, thoughtful policy discussions, and conversations among the wide array of stakeholders in the arena of risk management. Our hope is that 35 years from now, scholars, business people, civil servants, and the concerned public will have tools that provide even greater ability to make informed decisions to deal with extreme events.

PART I

Behavioral Factors Influencing
Decision-Making Under
Risk and Uncertainty

CHAPTER 1

The Arithmetic of Compassion and the Future of Risk Management

Paul Slovic and Daniel Västfjäll

The organizing principle for what we shall discuss is a concept, the arithmetic of compassion, taken from an insightful poem by Zbigniew Herbert titled "Mr. Cogito Reads the Newspaper" (1974). Mr. Cogito intently studies a front-page story of a murder of three people, but his eye slips indifferently over the report of a killing of 120 soldiers. So many of them, and so distant, they cannot "speak to the imagination"—the soldiers become an abstraction.

Early efforts to define and assess risk focused almost entirely on technical analyses of direct consequences of risk events and their likelihood of occurring. More recently, we are coming to understand the important psychological, economic, social, and political factors that also needed to be incorporated, side-by-side, with the quantitative risk calculations. Risk perception and risk communication have been recognized as essential elements of a complete and useful risk analysis.

In confronting the difficult management decisions posed by catastrophic threats, we will, in this chapter, briefly outline some new directions that we hope will make future risk management even more effective in addressing such high-stakes decisions. We shall present research demonstrating three nonrational psychological mechanisms that confound the arithmetic of compassion: psychic numbing, pseudoinefficacy, and the prominence effect. After documenting these obstacles to rational decision-making, we shall point toward ways to diminish them—a roadmap for future research and its application to risk management.

Risk as Feeling and Risk as Analysis in the Face of Catastrophic Losses

Risk management in the modern world relies upon two forms of thinking (Kahneman 2011). *Risk as feelings* refers to our instinctive and intuitive reactions to danger. *Risk as analysis* brings logic, reason, quantification, and deliberation to bear on hazard management. Compared to analysis, reliance on feelings tends to be a quicker, easier, and more efficient way to navigate in a complex, uncertain, and dangerous world. Hence, it is essential to rational behavior. Yet it sometimes misleads us. In such circumstances we need to ensure that reason and analysis also are employed.

Particularly problematic is the difficulty of comprehending the meaning of catastrophic losses of life when relying on feelings. Research reviewed below shows that disaster statistics, no matter how large the numbers, lack emotion or feeling. As a result, they fail to convey the true meaning of such calamities and they fail to motivate proper action to prevent them.

The psychological factors underlying insensitivity to large-scale loss of life apply to catastrophic harm resulting from human malevolence, natural disasters, and technological accidents. In particular, the psychological account described here can explain, in part, the failure to respond to the diffuse and seemingly distant threat posed by global warming or the presence of nuclear weaponry. Similar insensitivity may also underlie our failure to respond adequately to problems of violence, famine, poverty, and disease afflicting large numbers of people around the world.

Psychic Numbing and the Value of Human Lives

This brings us to a crucial question: How *should* we value the protection of human lives? An analytic answer would look to basic principles or fundamental values for guidance. For example, Article 1 of the Universal Declaration of Human Rights adopted by the United Nations (1948) asserts that "all human beings are born free and equal in dignity and rights." We might infer from this the conclusion that every human life is of equal value. If

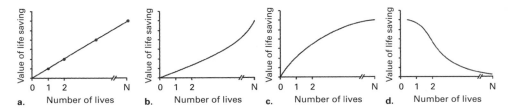

Figure 1.1. Normative models where (a) every life is of equal value and (b) large losses threaten group or societal survival; descriptive models of (c) psychophysical numbing and (d) compassion fade.

so, then—applying a rational calculation—the value of saving N lives is N times the value of saving one life, as represented by the linear function in Figure 1.1a.

An argument can also be made for judging large losses of life to be disproportionately more serious because they threaten the social fabric and viability of a group or community (see Figure 1.1b). Debate can be had at the margins over whether one should assign greater value to younger people versus the elderly, or whether governments have a duty to give more weight to the lives of their own people, and so on, but a perspective approximating the equality of human lives is rather uncontroversial.

How *do* we actually value human lives? Research provides evidence in support of two descriptive models linked to risk as feeling and intuitive thinking that reflect values for life saving profoundly different from those depicted in the normative (rational) models shown in Figures 1.1a and 1.1b. Both of these descriptive models demonstrate responses that are insensitive to large losses of human life, consistent with apathy toward large losses of life and the ruminations of Mr. Cogito in the poem described.

Psychiatrist Robert Jay Lifton coined the term *psychic numbing* to describe the loss of feeling that occurred in the aftermath of the devastation at Hiroshima and Nagasaki (Lifton and Mitchell 1995). Research suggests that *psychophysical numbing* might be a more apt term for the form of insensitivity depicted in the descriptive model in Figure 1.1c. There is considerable evidence that our affective responses and the resulting value we place on protecting human lives follow the same sort of "psychophysical function" that characterizes our diminished sensitivity to changes in a wide range of perceptual and cognitive entities—brightness, loudness, heaviness, and wealth—as their underlying magnitudes increase (Stevens 1975).

The model in Figure 1.1c represents a value structure in which the importance of saving one life is great when it is the first, or only, life saved but diminishes as the total number of lives at risk increases. Thus, psychologically, the importance of saving a life pales against the background of a larger threat: We may not "feel" much difference, nor value the difference, between saving 87 lives or saving 88. This is the first waypoint in our concern about the arithmetic of compassion.

Fetherstonhaugh et al. (1997) demonstrated psychophysical numbing in the context of evaluating people's willingness to fund various lifesaving interventions. In a study involving a hypothetical grant-funding agency, respondents were asked to indicate the number of lives a medical research institute would have to save to merit receipt of a $10 million grant. Nearly two-thirds of the respondents raised their minimum benefit requirements to warrant funding when there was a larger at-risk population, with a median value of 9,000 lives needing to be saved when 15,000 were at risk (implicitly valuing each life saved at $1,111), compared to a median of 100,000 lives needing to be saved out of 290,000 at risk (implicitly valuing each life saved at $100). Thus, respondents saw saving 9,000 lives in the smaller population as more valuable than saving more than 10 times as many lives in the larger population. The same study also found that people were less willing to send aid that would save 4,500 lives in a Rwandan refugee camp of 250,000 than in a camp of 11,000. Decreasing the at-risk population from 250,000 to 245,500 likely seemed less valuable than decreasing it from 11,000 to 6,500, demonstrating a sensitivity to proportion, rather than the actual number, that is consistent with a psychophysical model.

Research on psychophysical numbing is important because it demonstrates that feelings necessary for motivating lifesaving actions are not congruent with the normative and rational models in Figures 1.1a and 1.1b. The nonlinearity displayed in Figure 1.1c is consistent with the devaluing of increases in loss of life in the context of large-scale tragedy. It thus explains why we do not feel any different upon learning that the death toll in a genocide, such as happened in Darfur in western Sudan, is closer to 400,000 than to 200,000. What it does not fully explain, however, is apathy toward genocide, inasmuch as it implies that the response to initial loss of life will be strong and maintained, albeit with diminished sensitivity, as the losses increase. We next present evidence in support of a second descriptive model, termed *compassion fade*, that appears better suited to explain apathy and inaction in the face of large losses of lives (Figure 1.1d).

Compassion fade is hinted at in a question posed by the American writer Annie Dillard (1999) as she reads a newspaper headline: "Head Spinning Numbers Cause Mind to Go Slack." She writes of "compassion fatigue" and asks, "At what number do other individuals blur for me?"[1]

An answer to Dillard's question is beginning to emerge from recent behavioral research examining people's willingness to donate monetary aid to people whose lives are endangered. Studies by social psychologists find that a single individual, unlike a group, is viewed as a psychologically coherent unit. This leads to more extensive processing of information and stronger impressions about individuals than about groups. Consistent with this, a study in Israel found that people tend to feel more distress and compassion and to provide more aid when considering a single victim than when considering a group of eight victims (Kogut and Ritov 2005). A follow-up study in Sweden found that people felt less positive affect and donated less monetary aid toward a pair of starving children than to either individual alone (Västfjäll, Slovic, and Mayorga 2015). Perhaps the blurring that Annie Dillard asked about begins for groups as small as two people. A follow-up study done by the same researchers found that the downward trend of feelings and donations continued as the number of children in need increased from one to two to eight.

Whereas the psychophysical model implies that the value of protecting two lives is less than twice the value of protecting one life $(1 + 1 < 2)$, the model of compassion fade indicates that, in some situations, the value of two lives is less than the value of one life $(1 + 1 < 1)$!

Pseudoinefficacy

Decisions to protect others are strongly motivated by perceived efficacy (Cryder, Loewenstein, and Scheines 2013), therefore another way that reliance on feelings leads to nonoptimal reactions to catastrophic threats comes from factors that create an illusion of inefficacy that demotivates action, even among those who have the desire and the means to protect and improve lives. It is tragic, indeed, when efficacy goes unrecognized and vital aid that could be provided is withheld due to this illusion of ineffectiveness that we have named *pseudoinefficacy*.

Our interest in this topic came from revisiting the results from a study in which Small, Loewenstein and Slovic (2007) gave people who had just participated in a paid psychological experiment the opportunity to contribute up to $5 of their earnings to the charity Save the Children. In one condition, respondents were asked to donate money to feed an identified victim, a seven-year-old African girl named Rokia, of whom they were shown a picture. They contributed more than twice the amount given by a second group who were asked to donate to the same organization working to save millions of Africans (statistical lives) from hunger. Respondents in a third group were asked to donate to Rokia, but were also shown the larger statistical problem (millions in need) shown to the second group. Unfortunately, coupling the large-scale statistical realities with Rokia's story significantly *reduced* contributions to Rokia.

Why did this occur? Perhaps the presence of statistics reduced the attention to Rokia essential for establishing the emotional connection necessary to motivate donations. Alternatively, recognition of the millions who would not be helped by one's small donation may have produced negative feelings that inhibited donations. Note the similarity here to the reduced desire to help 4,500 people in the larger refugee camp in the study by Fetherstonhaugh et al. (1997) as described above.

The findings from these two studies may have broad implications in light of the insights of Andreoni (1990), who contended that we help others not only because they need our help but because we anticipate and experience the *warm glow* of good feeling associated with protecting others. Subsequent empirical studies have supported this contention (e.g., Dunn, Aknin, and Norton 2008). Västfjäll, Slovic, and Mayorga (2015) hypothesized that knowledge of those "out of reach" (more in the large refugee camp and millions of starving people in Africa) may have triggered negative feelings that countered the good feelings anticipated from giving aid, thus demotivating action. A related explanation is that, compared to the large numbers of persons out of reach, the prospective aid seemed only a "drop-in-the-bucket" (Bartels and Burnett 2011). Although the results from these studies by Fetherstonhaugh et al. (1997) and Small, Loewenstein, and Slovic (2007) may appear at first glance to reflect inefficacy, this is not really inefficacy, because the donor can actually help some people (from 1 to 4,500). Instead, it is a form of *pseudo-inefficacy* that is nonrational.

We certainly should not be deterred from helping one person, or 4,500, just because there are others we cannot help. In the studies described above, there were millions out of reach. But further studies conducted by Västfjäll, Slovic, and Mayorga (2015) varied the number of children who needed humanitarian aid and the number who could not be helped. They found that even one child not being helped demotivated people from providing aid to those who could be helped. Participants indicated that they didn't *feel* as good about helping when they were aware that there were one or more others they could not help.

The Prominence Effect

Psychophysical numbing and compassion fade can explain why the public and some government officials fail to appreciate and take appropriate actions to intervene in genocides and mass atrocities. But many in government are quite aware of the gravity of these situations, think carefully about them, care deeply about the suffering, and yet still fail to act. What might account for this?

Again we look to psychological research for an explanation, specifically theoretical models of judgment and choice, to explain what we hypothesize is a systematic bias in decision-making that works to inhibit actions protective of large numbers of human lives. The discussion that follows is framed in the context of genocide and mass atrocities but the psychological principles can be extrapolated to other catastrophic threats.

Decisions to protect civilian lives by intervening in foreign countries are some of the most difficult and controversial choices facing national decision-makers. Although each situation is unique, these decisions typically involve tradeoffs that pit the value of human lives against other important objectives. There is often a striking disconnect between the high value placed on saving human lives expressed by top government officials and the apparent low value revealed by government decisions not to intervene. Specifically, when multiple objectives are in play, highly regarded humanitarian values appear to collapse in relation to national security and economic security objectives.

Although each situation is unique, decisions involving tradeoffs that pit the value of human lives against other important objectives are quite common. For example, in 2011 the United States supported military action to protect the lives of civilians living in Libya and intervened aggressively to protect a threatened population of Yazidi people in Iraq in 2014. On the other hand, the United States has done little to intervene in the genocide in Darfur or the mass atrocities in Syria that have led to hundreds of thousands of deaths and millions of displaced persons.

One explanation for such inconsistency is that the threat to lives in Darfur or Syria has not been valued highly enough to compete against other political, economic, cultural, or military objectives. What we observe is a discrepancy between the high value placed on saving human lives expressed by top government officials and the apparent low value revealed by government inaction when millions are threatened.

When considering objectives that might influence life-protecting interventions, national security comes foremost to mind. Yet the rhetoric of two recent American presidents, George W. Bush and Barack Obama, leaves no doubt that, in terms of expressed values, national security and humanitarian lifesaving are *both* vital objectives.

In the few situations where the United States has intervened with the stated objective of saving lives, there were presumed security benefits as well. The United States justified the attack on Saddam Hussein in Iraq on the grounds that he possessed weapons of mass destruction. Only when that proved false was there a highlight on the atrocities he had perpetrated. Libyan leader Muammar Gaddafi had long been known as a "loose cannon," addicted to violence at home and elsewhere. His menacing visage had adorned the cover of *Time* magazine four times since 1986, when Ronald Reagan referred to him as "this mad dog of the Middle East." Security objectives were also important in the more recent Iraq example. In addition to protecting the Yazidis, the United States protected American military and diplomatic personnel stationed nearby in Erbil. Without that security objective, would the United States have aided the Yazidis?

In contrast, humanitarian intervention in Darfur may have been blocked by threats to security. The United States has long sought to obtain intelligence regarding terrorist operations from the Sudanese government (Albright 2004). Sudanese president Omar al-Bashir, who takes a back seat to no one as a murderer, has at times provided the American government with information about terrorist activities. These examples suggest a hypothesis that the United States only seems to launch humanitarian interventions when security interests are also served by such actions. The threat to human rights posed by security objectives is well recognized in the political world (e.g., OHCHR 2008).

Turning to theory, rational choice models typically assume that choices are consistent with expressed values. However, a great deal of empirical research has shown that the values indicated by these two modes of assessment often differ. One explanation for such inconsistency has centered on evidence for systematic discrepancies in weighting associated with expressed and re-vealed preferences.

A study by Slovic (1975) found that difficult choices were systematically decided in favor of the alternative that was superior on the most important attribute. Tversky, Sattath, and Slovic (1988) used this finding as a spring-board to a general theory of choice called the *contingent weighting model*. At the heart of this model was the *prominence effect*, which recognized that the values revealed through choices or decisions tend to differ systematically from directly expressed or stated values. Specifically, in certain contexts, the more prominent attributes are weighted more heavily in choices than in judgments reflecting expressed preferences or values. The presumed explanation for this effect is that, unlike expressed values, chosen actions need to be justi-fied, and decisions congruent with prominent attributes are inherently more defensible.

We argue that the prominence effect may underlie the apparent discrep-ancy between expressed and revealed values regarding whether or not to act to protect large numbers of civilian lives under attack in foreign coun-tries. Specifically, we hypothesize that national security is the prominent dimension in the context we are discussing here. As chosen actions need to be justified, deciding in favor of security likely makes a stronger argument than deciding in favor of protecting nameless, faceless foreign lives, no matter how many thousands or millions of lives are at stake.

But if the prominence effect is indeed infiltrating top-level policy deci-sions and causing decision-makers to systematically devalue humanitarian actions, we doubt that the decision-makers are consciously aware of this. The prominence mechanism we assume to be driving the decision-making pro-cess is not a consciously expressed devaluation of distant lives; this would be abhorrent to leaders who truly do value those lives. Rather, we believe that prominent objectives, in particular those offering enhanced security, draw attention away from less prominent goals. All eyes are on options that protect the homeland, and decision-makers fixated on security objectives likely fail to consider as seriously the numbers of people under siege and left to die. Therefore, compensatory weighing of costs and benefits associ-ated with seeking security and protecting distant lives is not carefully addressed.

Thus, meaningful action to prevent genocides and other mass atrocities faces two psychological obstacles. The prominence effect may lead to deci-sions that favor inaction, even when this contravenes deeply held values. And decision-makers can get away with this because the public is psychologically numbed. As Samantha Power (2003, xxi) observed: "No U.S. president has ever made genocide prevention a priority, and no U.S. president has ever suffered politically for his indifference to its occurrence. It is thus no coincidence that genocide rages on."

The three psychological obstacles to humanitarian interventions described in this chapter apply as well to other hazards. Consider, for example, global climate change. Statistical projections of diffuse, seemingly distant mass consequences may be diminished by psychic numbing. The assessment of what we can do as individuals may create pseudoinefficacy, causing us to think that our efforts are ineffectual. The prominence effect may lead to a disconnect between our stated values for protecting the planet (which increasingly align with the scientific evidence) and the values revealed by our actions, which likely will align with prominent objectives such as the near-term comfort, convenience, and efficiency of doing the wrong thing. Reports estimate that the carbon cost of 50,000 people traveling from across the globe to the Conference of the Parties (COP21) gathering in Paris in 2015 to address the climate dilemma and report on proposed solutions was some 300,000 tons of CO_2 (Slovic 2016).

Implications for Risk Management

You are—face it—a bunch of emotions, prejudices, twitches, and this is all very well as long as you know it. Successful speculators do not necessarily have a complete portrait of themselves, warts and all, in their own minds, but they do have the ability to stop abruptly when their own intuition and what is happening Out There are suddenly out of kilter.

If you don't know who you are, this is an expensive place to find out.

—Adam Smith, *The Money Game*

Whether managing an investment portfolio or foreign policy, "if you don't know who you are, this is an expensive place to find out." Our first aim in calling attention to the emotions, warts, and twitches that jeopardize modern risk management is simply to create awareness of these psychological foibles, an alert so to speak. Numbing, pseudoinefficacy, and prominence bias are not simple to overcome. And while the first two of these obstacles are immediately recognizable when we are reminded of them, we fail to appreciate the problems they create and thus may fail to develop defense mechanisms to mitigate their harm. Prominence is less recognizable and especially problematic as it directly affects our actions, often in ways that contravene our considered values. So, be warned!

With awareness come the challenges of coping. The basic message is that risk managers in both the public and private sectors need to make decisions and set policies in ways guided by an understanding of the sometimes strange and perverse computations of the arithmetic of compassion. We don't have the solutions to debiasing the three psychological mechanisms we have described here. But we do have some suggestions that may serve as first steps to the creation of improved management. Our coverage will be brief. More detail can be found in Slovic et al. (2013); Västfjäll, Slovic, and Mayorga (2015); and Gregory, Harstone, and Slovic (2018).

Combating Psychic Numbing

A natural response to the growing awareness of our insensitivity to problems of scale is to consider ways to educate our intuitive appreciation of numbers. But how can we modify our gut instincts to better understand and respond to problems large in scope? This is not an easy question to answer, but we can speculate about possible ways forward.

One way of infusing intuition with greater feeling is by changing the way we frame information. The affective system primarily deals with the here and now and with concrete images. We speculate that reframing a large-scale problem may be a way of increasing affect, attention, and action. For instance, "800,000 killed in the last 100 days" can be broken down and reframed as "One life lost every 11 seconds." Both the one life lost and the near-time horizon of "every 11 seconds" induce accessible images and thus are likely to create more affect and different information processing (Trope and Liberman 2003).

More generally, if statistics represent "human beings with the tears dried off," tears and feeling can be increased by highlighting the images that lie beneath the numbers. For example, organizers of a rally designed to get the

U.S. Congress to do something about 38,000 deaths a year from handguns piled 38,000 pairs of shoes in a mound in front of the Capitol (Associated Press 1994). Students at a middle school in Tennessee, struggling to comprehend the magnitude of the Holocaust, collected six million paper clips as a centerpiece for a memorial (Schroeder and Schroeder-Hildebrand 2004). In this light it is instructive to reflect on the characterization by Holocaust survivor Abel Hertzberg: "There were not six million Jews murdered: there was one murder, six million times."

When it comes to eliciting compassion, psychological experiments demonstrate that the identified individual victim, with a face and a name, has no peer, providing the face is not juxtaposed with the statistics of the larger need (Small, Loewenstein, and Slovic 2007). But we know this as well from personal experience and media coverage of heroic efforts to save individual lives. The world watched tensely as rescuers worked for several days to rescue 18-month-old Jessica McClure, who had fallen 22 feet into a narrow abandoned well shaft. Charities such as Save the Children have long recognized that it is better to endow a donor with a single, named child to support than to ask for contributions to the bigger cause. The world paid scant attention to the cumulative mortality between 2011 and 2015 in the Syrian civil war as it climbed steadily to more than 250,000 deaths, but the photo of a three-year-old refugee, Aylan Kurdi, lying face down on a Turkish beach brought unprecedented attention and concern to the victims of that conflict. At least for a while.

The face need not even be human to motivate powerful intervention. A dog stranded aboard a tanker adrift in the Pacific was the subject of one of the most costly animal rescue efforts ever (Vedantam 2010). Hearing this, columnist Nicholas Kristof (2007) recalled cynically that a single hawk, Pale Male, evicted from his nest in Manhattan, aroused more indignation than two million homeless Sudanese. He observed that what was needed to galvanize the American public and their leaders to respond to the genocide in Darfur was a suffering puppy with big eyes and floppy ears: "If President Bush and the global public alike are unmoved by the slaughter of hundreds of thousands of fellow humans, maybe our last, best hope is that we can be galvanized by a puppy in distress."

Further to this last point, Paul Farmer (2005) has written eloquently about the power of images, narratives, and first-person testimony to overcome our "failure of imagination" in contemplating the fate of distant, suffering people.

Such documentation can, he asserts, render abstract struggles personal and help make human rights violations "real" to those unlikely to suffer them. Who hasn't gained a deeper understanding of the Holocaust from reading Elie Wiesel's *Night* or *The Diary of Anne Frank*?

Similarly, the statistics of sea level rise do little to stimulate our imagination and concern regarding climate change. Translating the numbers into maps showing changes on a familiar coastline would do better. Far better yet, would be images of familiar and valued landmarks under water.

Combating Pseudoinefficacy

Given that pseudoinefficacy appears to be a robust phenomenon with significant implications, it is important to consider how it can be attenuated, eliminated, or reversed. Facing catastrophic threats, it is invariably the case that even our best efforts cannot protect everyone at risk. Thus, it would be unfortunate indeed if we let this "incompleteness" deter us from accomplishing what is within our grasp.

But countering pseudoinefficacy might not be easy. Much like visual illusions that persist even when we know them to be false, the illusion of pseudoinefficacy may be similarly hard to dispel. One strategy used to debias persistent and deadly visual illusions is to remove the deceptive cues. When pilots on a simulated visual approach to a landing strip were misled by the pattern of runway lights, causing them to land short of the runway, the pattern of flights was quickly and successfully changed (Palmisano and Gillam 2005). In light of pseudoinefficacy and drop-in-the-bucket thinking, we can delete or minimize reference to the larger scope of the problem one's efforts are trying to attenuate. The wrong approach is exemplified by the charity seeking donations that put the statistic "3 million in need" above the picture of a starving child, likely demotivating many donors.

Schwarz and Clore (1983) successfully blocked the intrusion of irrelevant feelings into a person's judgment of their well-being by merely reminding respondents about the true source of their feelings (the weather). In keeping with a related study by Schwarz et al. (2007), perhaps reminding people that the source of the discouraging feelings they experience when facing a daunting challenge is the part they *cannot* help, and not the part they can, would reduce or eliminate pseudoinefficacy.

Perhaps a lesson in efficacy might also combat pseudoinefficacy. Consider the famous starfish story by American author Loren Eiseley (1969):

> While wandering a deserted beach at dawn, stagnant in my work, I saw a man in the distance bending and throwing as he walked the endless stretch toward me. As he came near, I could see that he was throwing starfish, abandoned on the sand by the tide, back into the sea. When he was close enough I asked him why he was working so hard at this strange task. He said that the sun would dry the starfish and they would die. I said to him that I thought he was foolish. There were thousands of starfish on miles and miles of beach. One man alone could never make a difference. He smiled as he picked up the next starfish. Hurling it far into the sea he said, "It makes a difference for this one." I abandoned my writing and spent the morning throwing starfish.

Combating Prominence

If strategies to educate intuition and diminish numbing and pseudoinefficacy are successful they will create an upsurge of concern that will call for action by decision-makers. Prominence bias could undercut these efforts, leading decisions made in the service of defensibility to violate strongly held values for protecting lives and property. The finding that quantification of one's basic values prior to making a choice led choices to be consistent with those values suggests that structured decision-aiding techniques might effectively counter prominence bias. Gregory, Harstone, and Slovic (2018) show how decisions about whether the United States should intervene in another country to stop genocide could be aided by tools such as objectives hierarchies, performance measures, and consequence tables. A structured decision-aiding approach has the capability to examine carefully a vague doctrine, such as "protect the national interest" or "promote humanitarian interventions," and transform it into an organized framework that promotes both understanding and discussion. Of course, a decision-aiding framework cannot "make" the tough choices required of the U.S. government with respect to interventions intended to reduce genocide and mass atrocities. What it can do is to improve the quality and extent of intervention deliberations, laying the groundwork for a more comprehensive and nuanced understanding of the threats posed to American values and interests using a common language for analysis that facilitates input and involvement from all key parties.

Looking Ahead

It is time to examine strategies for managing catastrophic threats with an acknowledgment of the psychological challenges described in this chapter and a recognition of the possibilities held by decision analytic methods to encourage thoughtful deliberation. This is a remedy that is quite modest in that it requires only the acknowledgment of the potential for structured deliberations to help bridge feelings of risk with the discipline of a reasoned approach. With this new model as a guide, it may be possible to design legal and institutional mechanisms that will enable us to respond to threats of mass harm to humans and the environment with a degree of intensity that is commensurate with the high value we place on protecting individual lives.[2]

Notes

1. She struggles to think straight about the great losses that the world ignores: "More than two million children die a year from diarrhea and eight hundred thousand from measles. Do we blink? Stalin starved seven million Ukrainians in one year, Pol Pot killed two million Cambodians" (Dillard 1999, 130–131).

2. In the event that a structured decision-aiding process cannot be implemented, a colleague has suggested another mechanism to induce more balanced weighting of humanitarian concerns during the process of decision-making: ensure that a spokesperson for those concerns is at the table.

References

Albright, M. (2004, March 24). Full text: Madeleine Albright statement. National Commission on Terrorist Attacks upon the United States. Washington, DC.

Andreoni, J. (1990). Impure altruism and donations to public goods: A theory of warm-glow giving. *Economic Journal, 100*(401), 464–477.

Associated Press. (1994, September 21). 38,000 shoes stand for loss in lethal year. *The Register-Guard* (Eugene, OR), p. 6A.

Bartels, D. M., & Burnett, R. C. (2011). A group construal account of drop-in-the-bucket thinking in policy preference and moral judgment. *Journal of Experimental Social Psychology, 47*, 50–57.

Cryder, C. E., Loewenstein, G., & Scheines, R. (2013). The donor is in the details. *Organizational Behavior and Human Decision Processes, 120*(1), 15–23.

Dillard, A. (1999). *For the time being.* New York: Knopf.

Dunn, E. W., Aknin, L. B., & Norton, M. I. (2008). Spending money on others promotes happiness. *Science, 319*, 1687–1688.

Eiseley, L. (1969). The star thrower. In *The unexpected universe.* Orlando, FL: Harcourt Brace.

Farmer, P. (2005, March). *Never again? Reflections on human values and human rights.* Presented at the Tanner Lectures on Human Values, Salt Lake City, Utah. Retrieved from http://tannerlectures.utah.edu/lecture-library.php

Fetherstonhaugh, D., Slovic, P., Johnson, S. M., & Friedrich, J. (1997). Insensitivity to the value of human life: A study of psychophysical numbing. *Journal of Risk and Uncertainty, 14*(3), 283–300.

Gregory, R., Harstone, M., & Slovic, P. (2018). Improving intervention decisions to prevent genocide: Less muddle, more structure. *Genocide Studies and Prevention, 11*(3), 109–127.

Herbert, Z. (1974). Mr. Cogito reads the newspaper. In *Mr. Cogito* (J. Carpenter & B. Carpenter, Trans.). Hopewell, NJ: Ecco Press.

Kahneman, D. (2011). *Thinking, fast and slow.* New York: Farrar, Straus, & Giroux.

Kogut, T., & Ritov, I. (2005). The singularity effect of identified victims in separate and joint evaluations. *Organizational Behavior and Human Decision Processes, 97*(2), 106–116.

Kristof, N. (2007, May 10). Save the Darfur puppy. *New York Times.* Retrieved from https://www.nytimes.com/2007/05/10/opinion/10kristof.html

Lifton, R. J., & Mitchell, G. (1995, August/September). The age of numbing. *Technology Review,* 58–59.

OHCHR. (2008, July). *Human rights, terrorism, and counter-terrorism* (Fact Sheet No. 32). Office of the United Nations High Commissioner for Human Rights. Retrieved from http://www.ohchr.org/Documents/Publications/Factsheet32EN.pdf

Palmisano, S., & Gillam, B. (2005). Visual perception of touchdown point during simulated landing. *Journal of Experimental Psychology: Applied, 11*, 19–32. doi:10.1037/1076-898X.11.1.19

Power, S. (2003). *A problem from hell: America and the age of genocide.* New York: HarperCollins.

Schroeder, P. W., & Schroeder-Hildebrand, D. (2004). *Six million paper clips: The making of a children's holocaust memorial.* Minneapolis, MN: Kar-Ben.

Schwarz, N., & Clore, G. L. (1983). Mood, misattribution, and judgments of well-being: Informative and directive functions of affective states. *Journal of Personality and Social Psychology, 45*, 513–523.

Schwarz, N., Sanna, L. J., Skurnik, I., & Yoon, C. (2007). Metacognitive experiences and the intricacies of setting people straight: Implications for debiasing and public information campaigns. *Advances in Experimental Social Psychology, 39*, 127–161.

Slovic, P. (1975). Choice between equally valued alternatives. *Journal of Experimental Psychology: Human Perception and Performance, 1*, 280–287.

Slovic, P., Zionts, D., Woods, A. K., Goodman, R., & Jinks, D. (2013). Psychic numbing and mass atrocity. In E. Shafir (Ed.), *The behavioral foundations of public policy* (pp. 126–142). Princeton: Princeton University Press.

Slovic, S. (2016). COP21 and business as usual. *Environment: Science and Policy for Sustainable Development, 58*(4), 48–52.

Small, D. A., Loewenstein, G., & Slovic, P. (2007). Sympathy and callousness: The impact of deliberative thought on donations to identifiable and statistical victims. *Organizational Behavior and Human Decision Processes, 102,* 143–153.

Stevens, S. S. (1975). *Psychophysics.* New York: Wiley.

Trope, Y., & Liberman, N. (2003). Temporal construal. *Psychological Review, 110,* 403–421.

Tversky, A., Sattath, S., & Slovic, P. (1988). Contingent weighting in judgment and choice. *Psychological Review, 95,* 371–384.

United Nations (1948). Universal Declaration of Human Rights. Retrieved from http://www.un.org/en/universal-declaration-human-rights/

Västfjäll, D., Slovic, P., & Mayorga, M. (2015). Pseudoinefficacy: Negative feelings from children who cannot be helped reduce warm glow for children who can be helped. *Frontiers in Psychology, 6*(616). doi:10.3389/fpsyg.2015.00616

Vedantam, S. (2010). *The hidden brain: How our unconscious minds elect presidents, control markets, wage wars, and save lives.* New York: Spiegel & Grau.

CHAPTER 2

"Risk as Feelings" and "Perception Matters"

Psychological Contributions on Risk, Risk-Taking, and Risk Management

Elke U. Weber

In December 2015, twenty-five thousand of the world's top climate change experts and negotiators met in Paris. They were hard at work on the latest round of commitments to reduce the risks of climate change, a looming global crisis that already threatens the existence of low-lying island nations in the South Pacific and Inuit settlements in the Arctic. Global climate changes also have the potential to create economic hardship and social unrest for hundreds of millions of people now and in the near future and to make large parts of our planet uninhabitable within a few generations (IPCC 2014). There was some media coverage and public attention to this event. However, the vast majority of public, politician, and media attention—and associated concern, and call for action—went to the risk posed by Islamist extremism. Earlier that month, terrorist attacks on Paris had left 130 people dead and hundreds wounded (BBC 2015).

A growing number of American parents are no longer vaccinating their children to protect them against childhood disease risks like measles, mumps, and rubella, because they fear unsubstantiated or very low probability side-effects like autism or nervous system problems. At the same time, these parents may smoke in their home or drive in ways that expose their children to vastly greater health and safety risks, while also exposing them and vulnerable others (infants, the elderly, the immune-compromised) to adverse health effects by virtue of not being inoculated (Chen et al. 2011).

For the past several years I have been well aware that my pension and other savings are invested in ways that expose me to unnecessary risks and leave money on the table. Last year I went as far as paying for the services of an independent financial advisor to tell me how to precisely shift these investments, but I have still to follow through on the advice I received, at unknown but major costs to my financial well-being down the road. Instead, I spent considerable time this morning to make some contingency plans if a threatened Italian rail strike goes into effect tomorrow (I am writing this at the Bellagio Center of the Rockefeller Foundation), and spend a good deal of time on major purchases to make sure that I get the best value for my money.

These three examples show that the perception of risk and action in the face of risk can be very idiosyncratic and inconsistent, and not in line with those that technical experts or even, at times, our own better judgment would recommend. Standard economic tools used to assess and manage risk fail to capture this complexity. Over the past 50 years scholars have started to combine the descriptive theories and insights of psychology with the normative frameworks of economics (e.g., Kunreuther 1978; Johnson et al. 1993).

In this chapter, I will provide a brief summary of my contributions to the topic of risk, which have had the following goals: (a) building descriptive theory and models about human perceptions of risk and actions in the face of risk and uncertainty, that is, models of how real people—from citizens and consumers to policymakers and managers—*actually* make decisions under these circumstances, in contrast to the normative models of economics that tell us how we ought to make such decisions; (b) applying these psychological theories and insights to explain economic puzzles or so-called anomalies like the ones at the beginning of this chapter, that is, observed deviations in reported reactions or behavior from what normative economic models would predict; and (c) to (re)design the way risky choices are described and presented to people or organizations, such that the decision format and context utilizes the sources of human strengths identified in our investigations of actual decision processes and minimizes the impacts of human shortcomings also identified in our investigations. This in turn has been shown to help people achieve their long-term goals, in domains that range from suboptimal levels

and modes of pension savings (Weber 2004b) to eating disorders like buli-
mia or obesity (Steinglass et al. 2012), and to action in the face of climate
change risks (Weber and Stern 2011; Kunreuther et al. 2014; Kunreuther and
Weber 2014; Patt and Weber 2014).

What Is Risk?

Different communities interpret the concept of *risk* in different ways. For the
general public, risk often refers to likelihood of adverse consequences, worrying about the "risk of rain" for an outdoor wedding or the "risk of frost"
ruining a citrus crop. Economics, statistics, and engineering use the term to
refer to the unpredictability of outcomes, which is typically quantified as the
standard deviation or variance of possible outcomes of an event or action
around the expected value or expected utility. This makes risk a quantity that
can be assessed objectively and that is an unvarying attribute of the risky
choice option (Weber and Johnson 2009a). Psychology, in contrast, treats risk
as a psychological construct, that is, as a subjective experience or impression
that may differ between individuals, groups, cultures, and situations (Weber,
Blais, and Betz 2002; Figner and Weber 2011; Weber and Ancker 2011). It also
makes it a concept that can be influenced by factors other than probability
and outcomes levels (Weber and Milliman 1997). It may involve feelings of
dread, vulnerability, catastrophic potential, and uncontrollability (Slovic
et al. 2004; Bracha and Weber 2012), which can vary between individuals or
groups as a function of cultural beliefs or differences in past experience. In
this chapter I will review modifications that my research and that of others
have made to standard views of *risk as a statistic* and follow that with a summary of the evidence that I and others have provided for *risk as a (subjective)
feeling*.

Risk as a Statistic

Metrics like the variance or standard deviation of outcomes quantify the
degree to which the outcomes of an action are uncertain. These measures of
risk are widely used in economics, finance, and many engineering contexts.
An upside of these metrics is that they integrate information about both the
likelihood of different outcomes and their extremity, that is, the degree to

which they deviate from the expected value, and give us insight into the likelihood or likely role of extreme events. One downside of measuring unpredictability this way is the fact that variance and standard deviation weigh upside and downside variability the same in an expected value framework, and not so very differently in an expected utility framework with moderate levels of risk aversion. This does not coincide with people's perceptions of riskiness in many situations, where downside variability is seen as contributing to risk, but upside variability as not contributing or contributing significantly less, because upside increases in unpredictability also increase outcomes (Weber 1988). The conjoint expected risk measure by Luce and Weber (1986), derived from a set of desirable axioms about perceptions of risk, keeps the advantages of the variance metric, but decomposes variability into upside and downside components that can be differentially weighted. It also provides separate weights (model parameters) for the probability of positive or negative outcomes (i.e., outcomes above or below the expected value) in their own right (aside from their contribution to the positive or negative semivariance). This again reflects empirical observations in many contexts that show that people value the probability of "winning" and dislike the probability of "losing" in their own right, as there is an inherent pleasure in being a winner and an aversion to being a loser, aside from the actual values of wins or losses (Weber 1988).

Using variance or standard deviation as a metric of unpredictability does poorly in predicting observed judgments of risk in another important respect, namely by failing to capture the relative nature of people's perceptions of variability and risk (Weber 2004a). In the 2004 book chapter just cited, I tell the apocryphal story of a news conference on the occasion of a new book published by the Ohio humorist James Thurber, who also had recently gotten married. One of the journalists asked Thurber: "How do you like your new wife?" To which Thurber's reply was: "Compared to what?" This response makes us laugh because it makes the point that most, if not all of our judgments are relative and depend very much on the reference point we are using. This insight underlay prospect theory, formulated by Kahneman and Tversky in 1979 as a descriptively more accurate version of expected utility theory that evaluates outcomes as gains or losses relative to a reference point rather than on an absolute scale; work on this theory won Kahneman the Nobel Prize in Economic Sciences in 2002.

What is true for the perception of outcomes, as described by prospect theory, is also true for the perception of differences or deviations. Classical psychophysics, dating back almost two hundred years, showed that people perceive increases in intensity as proportional to the starting value. Thus I only need to turn up the volume of tone very little when the initial sound level is low, before a listener will tell me "noticeably louder." But when the initial volume is already high, I will need to crank it up quite a bit more before the listener will again give the "noticeably louder" signal, a regularity that was described in 1834 in a law by a different Weber (E. H. Weber 1978): $\Delta I\ /\ I = $ constant. More recently, insights about neuronal adaptation (e.g., Tobler and Weber 2013) show that we, as homo sapiens, are wired to be sensitive to changes in the environment, with neurons decreasing their firing rate in response to constant stimulation. Because of finite neural firing rates, sensitivity to changes in the environment needs to have the proportional characteristic described by E. H. Weber's (1978) law. Translating this into sensitivity to risk, it should not be a surprise that variability of outcomes is perceived proportionally to the expected value of a risky option (Weber 2010). As a simple demonstration, the risk of a 50:50 lottery (say, a coin toss) that results in either a win of $150 or a loss of $50 will seem large (+/− $100 from an expected value of $50). However, the same deviation of outcomes around an expected value of $1 million dollars (i.e., a 50:50 lottery between $999, 900 and $1,000,100) is obviously completely negligible.

This makes the coefficient of variation, which divides the standard deviation by the expected value and thus measures variability per unit of return, a far more descriptive metric of perceived riskiness, which is widely used in many applied areas like engineering or agricultural economics (Weber, Shafir, and Blais 2004; Weber 2010). Perceiving risk in proportion to expected value also provides a resolution to Rabin's (2000) calibration theorem puzzle. Rabin showed that expected utility theory predicts that a risk-averse expected-utility maximizing individual who, from any initial wealth level, turns down a gamble with a 50% chance of losing $100 and a 50% chance of gaining $110, should turn down 50:50 bets of losing $1,000 or gaining any sum of money, clearly not a very realistic prediction.

Risk as Feelings

Risk as feelings, a phrase coined by Hsee and Weber (1997) and popularized in a subsequent literature review under this title by Loewenstein et al. (2001), refers to the fact that perceptions of risk are driven by emotional responses just as much or more than by a rational accounting of the unpredictability of outcomes or likelihood and magnitude of loss. The predominant use of feelings, including feelings of being at risk, to make decisions ("if it feels good, approach; if it feels scary, back away") has been referred to as the affect heuristic (Finucane et al. 2000) or as emotion-based decision-making (Weber and Lindemann 2008).

Such feelings include the psychological risk dimensions first documented by Fischhoff and colleagues (1981), which include feelings of dread, vulnerability, catastrophic potential, and uncontrollability. Slovic and colleagues grouped these feelings into two dimensions that influence people's intuitive perceptions of health and safety risks in ways common across numerous studies in multiple countries and that explain differences between the risk perceptions of members of the general public versus those of technical experts (Slovic 1987; Slovic et al. 2004). The first dimension, *dread risk*, captures emotional reactions to hazards like nuclear reactor accidents, or nerve gas accidents. That is, things that make people anxious because of a perceived lack of control over exposure to these events and because their consequences may be catastrophic. The second dimension, *unknown risk*, refers to the degree to which a risk (e.g., DNA or genetic modification technology) is seen as new, with a perceived lack of control due to unforeseen or unforeseeable consequences. The risk of climate change scores high on the unknown dimension, but does not elicit feelings of dread (Weber 2006; Weber and Stern 2011), whereas terrorism recently replaced nuclear power as the posterchild of the hazard that scares people the most (Weber and Fox-Glassman 2016).

These feeling-based evaluations of risk provide an explanation for the moderating effect of familiarity on perceptions of the risk of a hazard or risky choice option, holding objective information about the probability distributions of possible outcomes constant (e.g., Weber, Siebenmorgen, and Weber 2005). Feeling that we know a product, an investment, a person, or an environment gives rise to the feeling of familiarity, which in turn not only "breeds liking," but also produces lower feelings of risk and increased feelings of control (Weber, Siebenmorgen, and Weber 2005). The association between familiarity and lower levels of risk can be legitimate, when greater personal experience with a risky option (e.g., 20 years of working in a nuclear power plant without any accidents) provides a more reliable database to assess existing danger, but it may also be spurious, as when the stock of a company simply has a familiar name or is of a local and familiar firm (Huberman 2001).

Since risk is in part a feeling, it turns out that people often make different decisions when they learn about the risks (especially small-probability risks) of choice options in two different ways: (a) by personally experiencing them (in trial and error learning, over time, the way animals other than humans need to learn about the contingencies and outcomes of risky decisions); or (b) by having them described to them numerically the way I earlier described gambles, or graphically, a benefit of the ability to symbolically represent and communicate information available to homo sapiens (Hertwig et al. 2004; Weber, Shafir, and Blais 2004). Decision-makers make different choices when they learn about the probabilities and outcomes of the choice options from experience (a), than from description (b), especially when small-probability events are involved. Decisions from description are well described by prospect theory (Kahneman and Tversky 1979), which is based on hundreds of studies of choices between described risky options, typically monetary lotteries (e.g., a lottery between winning $10,000 with probability 0.01 or losing $50 with probability 0.99 or $30 for sure). In such choices, decision-makers tend to overweight the impact of small-probability events, especially when such events have large positive or negative valence (e.g., a 0.001 chance of making $5,000, or a 0.005 chance of brain damage as the side effects of vaccinating against measles). Decisions from experience, on the other hand, are described by classical reinforcement learning models that iteratively update the decision-maker's impression of the quality of the choice option and thus give recent events more weight than distant events (Weber, Shafir, and Blais 2004).

It can be argued that such updating is adaptive in dynamic environments, where circumstances might change. Because rare events (e.g., large financial losses) have a smaller probability of having occurred recently, they have (on average) a *smaller* impact on the decision than their objective likelihood of occurrence would suggest. When they do occur, however, they have a much *larger* impact on the decision than suggested by their probability. This makes learning and decisions from experience more volatile across respondents and past outcome histories than learning and decisions from description (Yechiam, Barron, and Erev 2005).

These reinforcement learning models and their predicted more volatile responses to small-probability risks as the result of recent personal experiences with the outcome of risky choice options seem to describe the general public's dynamic and fluctuating reactions to small-probability risks far better than rational choice models or their psychological extensions like prospect theory. This includes changes in the perceptions and responses of postmenopausal women to hormone replacement therapy and its benefits and side-effect risks, changes in the responses of national governments like Germany to the benefits and risks of nuclear power generation before and after major reactor accidents, or changes in beliefs about the risks of subprime mortgages before and after the 2007/08 financial crisis (see Weber 2017 for more discussion of these examples). It also explains my lack of concern about the risks of my ill-invested pension savings (low probability, never yet experienced, well in the future) versus my disproportionate concern about a rail strike.

Some studies have explicitly examined the relationship between perceptions of riskiness in financial decisions based on a more analytic assessment of expected volatility versus those based on a less well-defined assessment of subjective feelings of risk (Klos, Weber, and Weber 2005; Weber, Siebenmorgen, Weber 2005; Weber, Weber, and Nosić 2013). The former analytic assessment asks people for their prediction of the median return of a risky investment option over, say, the next three-month period, as well as their estimates of the 10th and 90th percentile of the return distribution, from which three data points the predicted standard deviation of expected returns can be estimated. The latter intuitive and feelings-based assessment asks people to rate the riskiness of the investment option on a graphic rating scale that is labeled with "no risk at all" to "extremely high risk" at the end points. All three studies find that these two risk assessments are positively correlated, though not necessarily very highly. More importantly, it is the latter subjective and feelings-based assessment and not the former analytic one that predicts people's risky decisions. Furthermore, this is not just a phenomenon found among members of the public with poor financial education, but also found in the risk judgments and decisions of financial investment opportunities made by University of Chicago MBA students (Holtgrave and Weber 1993).

To Take Risks or to Manage Risks?

In some contexts, perceptions of risk are a variable of interest in their own right, resulting, for example, in anxiety or stress that may have negative health implications. In most contexts, however, they are simply an intermediate construct to explain behavior and decisions in environments of risk and uncertainty. When making risky decisions, one can do one of two things: (a) select among available action alternatives that differ in risk and returns as a function of one's appetite for risk (i.e., risk attitude, either embracing riskier options if "risk seeking" or avoiding them if "risk averse"), or (b) try and modify existing action alternatives and their levels of risk to adjust them to one's appetite for risk. Most studies of risky choice assume option (a), namely that decision-makers choose between existing and presented options, that is, that they take risks or refuse to take risks.

In contrast, two classic studies of risk-taking of high-level executives in Canadian and American firms (MacCrimmon and Wehrung 1986) and of American and Israeli executives (Shapira 1986) in the 1980s took a more open-ended and qualitative approach, interviewing managers about both their perceptions of risk and their behavior in the face of risk. This evidence supports the risk-as-feelings view as being more broadly endorsed than the risk-as-statistic view. A vice-president for finance reported in Shapira (1986) that "No one is interested in getting quantified measures"; and a senior vice-president observed, "You don't quantify the risk, but you have to be able to feel it" (March and Shapira 1987).

These two studies also found that executives resonate more to perspective (b) of "managing risks" rather than "taking" risks. Clearly the distinction between taking and managing risks hinges on the perceived degree of control available to decision-makers to modify the current or future consequences of available response options.

Of Shapira's (1986) respondents, 75% saw risk as controllable and modifiable, including by rejecting initial risk estimates and securing new information, partly by attacking the problem with different perspectives, thus "eliminating the unknowns" and "controlling the risk" (March and Shapira 1987). MacCrimmon and Wehrung (1986) found that executives managed risks in a simulated in-basket task by delaying decisions and delegating them to others.

To Take Risks

To explain why people take on different amounts of risk, economics as well as psychology have introduced the concept of risk attitude. Traditionally in economics, risk attitude is inferred as a model parameter directly from people's risky choices, under the assumption that the decision-maker maximizes expected utility and particular functional forms that map objective value to subjective utility (see, e.g., Weber and Johnson 2009a). In this expected utility framework, a concave utility function is indication of risk aversion, whereas a convex function describes risk seeking.

As an alternative, the risk-return framework of risk-taking in finance sees risk-taking as a compromise between the desire for returns and the minimization of risks, where differences in one's appetite for risk result in different tradeoffs. Weber and Milliman (1997) generalized this framework by allowing risks and returns to be subjective impressions, as discussed above, rather than the variance and expected value of the outcome distribution of the risky choice option. This opens multiple avenues for two decision-makers to differ in their degree of risk-taking. They could perceive either the risks or the returns of choice options to be different, while having the same attitude toward perceived risk (i.e., the same tradeoff coefficient between the two). Only when both decision-makers have the same perceptions of risks and returns can observed differences in risk be taken as an indication of differences in attitude toward (perceived) risk. This generalized risk-return framework also provides a mechanism to explain widely observed differences in risk-taking by the same decision-maker in different domains.

The DOmain-SPEcific Risk-Taking (DOSPERT) scale (Weber, Blais, and Betz 2002) grew out of the psychological risk-return framework and empirical support for its superior ability to describe risk-taking (Figner and Weber 2011). It describes risky behaviors in five or six different domains (financial, further subdivided into gambling vs. investment decisions; health/safety; recreational; ethical; and social), for which respondents rate the likelihood they would engage in the behavior, as well as their perceptions of the riskiness and expected returns of these activities. This allows the DOSPERT scale to assess not just risk-taking propensity, but also two important motivators of such behavior, namely perceived risks and benefits. Research using the DOSPERT scale has demonstrated that, in many cases, individual differences in risk-taking are less driven by differences in the appetite for risk itself (risk attitude, i.e., liking or disliking risk) than by individual differences in the *perception* of risks and returns. These differences in risk perception can be based either in objective differences in circumstances (Weber and Hsee 1998; e.g., Chinese decision-makers having larger social networks that effectively "cushion" them from catastrophic losses) or in psychological explanations that are less defensible. Observed gender differences in risk-taking across domains, for example—with women taking less risk in financial, recreational, and ethical decisions, but greater risk in social decisions—can be explained by their risk perceptions. Women, compared to men, perceive risks in financial, recreational, and ethical domains to be higher than males do, but perceive risks to be lower in the social domain. Risk perception, in turn, is influenced by gender-stereotypic differences in familiarity with risk-taking in these domains and with the available choice options.

Risk-taking measured by DOSPERT subscales differentially predicts observed real-world risk-taking in different domains. Hanoch, Johnson, and Wilke (2006), for example, recruited documented risk-takers in specific DOSPERT domains: skydivers, bungee jumpers, hang-gliding enthusiasts, and scuba divers for the recreational domain, gym members versus smokers for the health domain, casino gamblers for the gambling domain, and members of stock-trading clubs for the investment domain. Their data showed that individuals who exhibited high levels of risk-taking behavior in one content area also scored significantly higher than all other participants on this DOSPERT subscale (e.g., bungee jumpers on the recreational risks subscale), but had moderate levels of risk-taking in other risky domains (e.g., financial). Comparing a large number of risk-taking scales used in applied settings, Harrison et al. (2005) recommend the DOSPERT scale for its ability to assess risk-taking in different everyday domains and for its ability to separate perceptual and attitudinal reasons for taking risks. Li et al. (2015) showed that the DOSPERT financial risk-taking subscale predicted the credit-worthiness (FICO) scores of American respondents across a wide age-range very well and far better than the domain-independent method of inferring risk attitude from gambling choices by Holt and Laury (2002), an instrument widely used by economists.

The DOSPERT scale has been translated into German, Spanish, Dutch, French, Japanese, Mandarin, Hungarian, and Polish, and validated in these countries. A shorter (30-item) version also exists (Blais and Weber 2006).

The Columbia Card Task (CCT) (Figner et al. 2009) is a "gamefied" assessment tool that captures risk-taking in dynamic environments, where risk and return levels change over time. The CCT presents respondents with multiple rounds of a card game, in which cards can be turned over, with "good" cards resulting in gains, but the first "bad" card resulting in a large loss and the termination of the round. By varying the gain and loss amounts as well as the relative frequency of good and bad cards across rounds, people's risky decisions in the CCT can be decomposed into gain and loss sensitivity as well as attitude toward risk.

Use of the CCT has allowed for more incisive diagnoses of the sources of changes in risk-taking across the life span, from children to adolescents to adults (Figner et al. 2009; Van Duijvenvoorde et al. 2015). For example, whereas adolescents are known for taking great risks in many real-world domains (e.g., substance use, dangerous driving, unsafe sex), they do *not* show greater risk-taking than children or adults on many risk-taking tasks in the lab (Figner et al. 2009). To test the hypothesis that adolescents take greater risks only when affective processes are involved, but not under cold/deliberative task conditions, a hot and a cold version of the CCT was created. The hot CCT is designed to trigger affect by allowing participants to choose the cards they would like to turn over sequentially, with immediate outcome feedback provided after each card. The cold CCT is similar to the hot version but reduces involvement of affective processes by employing a single-time decision of how many cards the decision-maker would like to turn over and by delaying outcome feedback until all game rounds have been played. Self-reports and skin conductance, a physiological measure of emotional arousal (Figner and Murphy 2011), verify that the hot CCT triggers stronger affective processes than the cold CCT, which triggers more deliberative decision processes (Figner et al. 2009).

As predicted, adolescents take more risks than children and adults only in the hot CCT, but similar risks as children and adults in the cold CCT (Figner et al. 2009). Risk-taking in the hot (but not cold) CCT is accompanied by diminished information use. Participants who take greater risks neglect relevant information—that is, fail to appropriately adjust the number of cards they turn over—particularly in response to changes in the magnitude of the loss. Adolescents' risk-taking in the hot (but not cold) CCT is also related to a measure of cognitive control. Those better able to inhibit prepotent responses in a so-called Go/No-Go task take less risk in the hot CCT (Figner et al. 2009).

To Manage Risks

Managing risks, for example the societal risk of global climate change over the twenty-first century, involves the careful evaluation of a broad range of current and future decisions, made under high degrees of risk and uncertainty and with consequences over a long temporal and spatial range, from upfront and virtually certain costs in economic growth and physical comfort for developed countries to highly uncertain benefits to future generations in faraway countries that can be predicted only with great imprecision. The assessment of the risks and benefits or costs and benefits of different scenarios going into the future can, in turn, guide current decisions designed to avoid undesirable consequences in the future.

Recent efforts have been made to inform bodies like the United Nations Intergovernmental Panel on Climate Change (IPCC) and the policy users of their assessment reports about modes of human information processing and choice under risk and uncertainty that deviate from and complement the rational-economic model (Kunreuther et al. 2014). Broadening the range of human motivation and human cognition considered in existing models has important implications for public policy (Weber 2006, 2013). Consideration of bounded rationality and of the existence of a broadened human objective function (i.e., the fact that people have a much wider set of goals and objectives than those self-regarding material goals postulated by the model of homo economicus) has important implications for climate change risk management. Thus, Patt and Weber (2014) argue that existing models in this area (e.g., integrated assessment models) vastly underestimate the degree of uncertainty in predicted consequences of different action scenarios that are due to human perceptions and responses to technological innovation or economic (dis)incentives. Kunreuther and Weber (2014) provide examples of how a proper appreciation of the human reaction to risk, uncertainty, and longtime horizons can explain seemingly irrational behavior and, perhaps more important, suggest ways of reframing existing decisions in ways that align observed behavior more closely to desirable action.

Conclusions

Given finite attention and processing capacity and the resulting tendency to allocate scarce capacity to decisions and events close in time and space (Weber and Johnson 2009b), human society has developed a division of labor whereby individual or social problems that require longer time horizons or greater attention than typically available are assigned to professionals. Thus we put epidemiologists and medical researchers in charge of exploring and dealing with health risks, climatologists in charge of climate risks, and so on.

The relationship between public and technocratic perceptions of risk as well as responses to risks or to perceived changes in risk is complex. Weber and Stern (2011) describe some of the differences between scientists and non-scientists in risk assessment. Scientists use multiple methods to guard against error in their assessment of causal relationships and uncertainty, including observations and experiments, systematic observation and measurement, mathematical models that incorporate theories and observational data and are tested against new data, systems of checking measurements and peer-reviewing research studies to catch errors, and scientific debate and deliberation about the meaning of the evidence, with special attention given to new evidence that calls previous ideas into question. Scientific communities sometimes organize consensus processes such as those used by the Intergovernmental Panel on Climate Change to clarify which conclusions are robust and which remain in dispute. Although these methods do not prevent all error, the scientific methods identify unresolved issues and allow for continuing correction of error. Nonscientists' ways of perceiving risks and responding to risk and uncertainty, reviewed in this chapter, leave them more vulnerable to systematic misunderstanding. Personal experience can easily mislead (Weber 1997), judgment can be driven more by affect, values, and worldviews than by evidence (Slovic 1987), and attention and response can be very selective and incomplete (Weber and Johnson 2009b).

When expert and public perceptions of risk disagree, the way in which the two perceptions interact typically does not follow a normative model of influence. While one would expect that people would let their personal perception of risk be informed and influenced by the more comprehensive and systematic expert risk assessment, which they have at least indirectly commissioned, public and media attention and response to risk are typically more swayed by personal exposure and memorable events than by statistical summaries or theoretical arguments or models (Weber 2006; Zaval et al. 2014). At the same time, regulatory bodies often need to respond to public perceptions or changes in public perceptions of risk, even when domain experts disagree with these assessments, because public fear, even when unfounded, has negative consequences for public health and creates barriers to responses or nonresponses that might be advocated by technical experts.

A better understanding of where and why normative economic models of risk perception, risky choice, and risk management deviate from descriptive models of how such judgments and choices actually get made has tremendous payoffs in multiple ways. First, it allows for better predictions of the effect that change introduced by nature (e.g., in the form of extreme weather or earthquakes), the marketplace (e.g., in the form of technological innovation), or by policymakers (e.g., in the form of tax incentives or changes in regulation) will have on the perceptions of and responses to risk and uncertainty by members of the general public and other stakeholders. Second, it provides entry points for the design of decision environments (Johnson et al. 2012; "choice architecture," broadly defined) that help people overcome cognitive and emotional limitations and achieve the full range of their objectives (Weber 2013).

References

BBC (British Broadcasting Corporation). (2015, December 9). Paris attacks: What happened on the night. https://www.bbc.co.uk/news/world-europe-34818994

Blais, A.-R., & Weber, E. U. (2006). A domain-specific risk-taking (DOSPERT) scale for adult populations. *Judgment and Decision Making, 1*, 33–47.

Bracha, A., & Weber, E. U. (2012). *A psychological perspective of financial panic* (Public Policy Discussion Paper No. 12–7). Federal Reserve Bank of Boston.

Chen, S. Y., Anderson S., Kutty, P. K., Lugo, F., McDonald, M., Rota, P. A., . . . & Seward, J. F. (2011). Health care–associated measles outbreak in the United States after an importation: Challenges and economic impact. *Journal of Infectious Diseases, 203*, 1517–1525.

Figner, B., Mackinlay, R. J., Wilkening, F., & Weber, E. U. (2009). Affective and deliberative processes in risky choice: Age differences in risk taking in the Columbia Card Task. *Journal of Experimental Psychology: Learning, Memory, and Cognition, 35*, 709–730.

Figner, B., & Murphy, R. O. (2011). Using skin conductance in judgment and decision making research. In M. Schulte-Mecklenbeck, A. Kuehberger, & R. Ranyard (Eds.), *A handbook of process tracing methods for decision research* (pp. 163–184). New York: Psychology Press.

Figner, B., & Weber, E. U. (2011). Who takes risks, when, and why? Determinants of risk taking. *Current Directions in Psychological Science, 20*, 211–216.

Finucane, M. L., Alhakami, A., Slovic, P., & Johnson, S. M. (2000). The affect heuristic in judgment of risks and benefits. *Journal of Behavioral Decision Making, 13*, 1–17.

Fischhoff, B., Lichtenstein, S., Slovic, P., Derby, S. L., & Keeney, R. L. (1981). *Acceptable risk*. New York: Cambridge University Press.

Hanoch, Y., Johnson, J. G., & Wilke, A. (2006). Domain specificity in experimental measures and participant recruitment. *Psychological Science, 17*(4), 300–304.

Harrison J. D., Young, J. M., Butow, P., Salkeld, G., & Solomon, M. J. (2005). Is it worth the risk? A systematic review of instruments that measure risk propensity for use in the health setting. *Social Science & Medicine, 60*, 1385–1396.

Hertwig, R., Barron, G., Weber, E. U., & Erev, I. (2004). Decisions from experience and the effect of rare events. *Psychological Science, 15*, 534–539.

Holt, C. A., & Laury, S. K. (2002). Risk aversion and incentive effects. *American Economic Review, 92*(5), 1644–1655.

Holtgrave, D. & Weber, E. U. (1993). Dimensions of risk perception for financial and health risks. *Risk Analysis, 13*, 553–558.

Hsee, C. K., & Weber, E. U. (1997). A fundamental prediction error: Self–other discrepancies in risk preference. *Journal of Experimental Psychology: General, 126*, 45–53.

Huberman, G. (2001). Familiarity breeds investment. *Review of Financial Studies, 14*(3), 659–680.

IPCC (Intergovernmental Panel on Climate Change). (2014). Summary for policymakers. In *Climate Change 2014: Mitigation of Climate Change. Contribution of Working Group III to the Fifth Assessment Report of the Intergovernmental Panel on Climate Change.* Cambridge: Cambridge University Press.

Johnson, E. J., Hershey, J., Meszaros, J., & Kunreuther, H. (1993). Framing, probability distortions and insurance decisions. *Journal of Risk and Uncertainty, 7*, 35–51.

Johnson, E. J., Shu, S. B., Dellaert, B. G. C., Fox, C., Goldstein, D. G., Haeubl, G., . . . & Weber, E. U. (2012). Beyond nudges: Tools of a choice architecture. *Marketing Letters, 23*, 487–504.

Kahneman, D., & Tversky, A. (1979). Prospect theory: An analysis of decision under risk. *Econometrica 47*(2), 263–292.

Klos, A., Weber, E. U., & Weber, M. (2005). Risk perception and risk behavior in repeated gambles. *Management Science, 51*, 1777–1790.

Kunreuther, H. (1978). *Disaster insurance protection: Public policy lessons.* New York: John Wiley.

Kunreuther H., Gupta, S., Bosetti, V., Cooke, R., Dutt, V., Ha-Duong, M., & Weber, E. U. (2014). Integrated risk and uncertainty assessment of climate change response policies. In *Climate Change 2014: Mitigation of Climate Change. Contribution of Working Group III to the Fifth Assessment Report of the Intergovernmental Panel on Climate Change.* Cambridge: Cambridge University Press.

Kunreuther, H., & Weber, E. U. (2014). Aiding decision making to reduce the impacts of climate change. *Journal of Consumer Policy, 37*, 397–411.

Li, Y., Johnson, E. J., Weber, E. U., Enkavi, A. Z., Gao, J., & Zaval, L. (2015). Cognitive ability and knowledge predict real-world financial outcomes. *Proceedings of the National Academy of Sciences, 112*, 65–69.

Loewenstein, G. F., Weber, E. U., Hsee, C. K., & Welch, E. (2001). Risk as feelings. *Psychological Bulletin, 127*, 267–286.

Luce, R. D., & Weber, E. U. (1986). An axiomatic theory of conjoint, expected risk. *Journal of Mathematical Psychology, 30*, 188–205.

MacCrimmon, K. R., & Wehrung, D. A. (1986). *Taking risks: The management of uncertainty.* New York: Free Press.

March, J. G., & Shapira, Z. (1987). Managerial perspectives on risk and risk taking. *Management Science, 33*, 1404–1418.

Markiewicz, L., & Weber, E. U. (2013). DOSPERT's gambling risk-taking scale predicts excessive stock trading. *Journal of Behavioral Finance, 14*, 1–14.

Patt, A., & Weber, E. U. (2014). Perceptions and communication strategies for the many uncertainties relevant for climate policy. *Wiley Interdisciplinary Reviews: Climate Change, 5*, 219–232.

Rabin, M. (2000). Risk aversion and expected utility theory: A calibration theorem. *Econometrica, 68*, 1281–1292.

Shapira, Z. (1986). Risk in managerial decision making. Unpublished MS, Hebrew University.

Slovic, P. (1987). Perception of risk. *Science, 236*, 280–285.

Slovic P., Finucane, M. L., Peters, E., & MacGregor, D. G. (2004). Risk as analysis and risk as feelings: Some thoughts about affect, reason, risk, and rationality. *Risk Analysis, 24*, 311–322.

Steinglass, J., Figner, B., Berkowitz, S., Weber, E. U., & Walsh, T. (2012). Increased capacity to delay reward in anorexia nervosa. *Journal of International Neurological Society, 18*, 1–8.

Tobler, P., & Weber, E. U. (2013). Valuation for risky and uncertain choices. In P. Glimcher & E. Fehr (Eds.), *Neuroeconomics: Decision making and the brain* (2nd ed., pp. 149–172). New York: Elsevier.

Van Duijvenvoorde, A. C. K., Huizenga, H. M., Somerville, L. H., Delgado, M., Powers, A., Weeda, W. D., . . . & Figner, B. (2015). Neural correlates of expected risks and returns in risky choice across development. *Journal of Neuroscience, 35*, 1549–1560.

Weber, E. H. (1978). De subtilitate tactus. In H. E. Ross & D. J. Murray (Eds. and Trans.), *The sense of touch*. London: Academic Press. (Original work published 1834.)

Weber, E. U. (1988). A descriptive measure of risk. *Acta Psychologica, 69*, 185–203.

Weber, E. U. (1997). Perception and expectation of climate change: Precondition for economic and technological adaptation. In M. Bazerman, D. Messick, A. Tenbrunsel, & K. Wade-Benzoni (Eds.), *Psychological perspectives to environmental and ethical issues in management* (pp. 314–341). San Francisco: Jossey-Bass.

Weber, E. U. (2004a). Perception matters: Psychophysics for economists. In I. Brocas & J. Carrillo (Eds.), *The psychology of economic decisions* (Vol. 2, pp. 165–176). Oxford: Oxford University Press.

Weber, E. U. (2004b). The role of risk perception in risk management decisions: Who's afraid of a poor old-age? In O. S. Mitchell & S. P. Utkus (Eds.), *Pension design and structure: New lessons from behavioral finance. Part I: Research on decision-making under uncertainty* (pp. 53–66). Oxford: Oxford University Press.

Weber, E. U. (2006). Experience-based and description-based perceptions of long-term risk: Why global warming does not scare us (yet). *Climatic Change, 77*, 103–120. doi:10.1007/s10584-006-9060-3

Weber, E. U. (2010). On the coefficient of variation as a predictor of risk sensitivity: Behavioral and neural evidence for the relative encoding of outcome variability. *Journal of Mathematical Psychology, 54*, 395–399. doi:10.1016/j.jmp.2010.03.003

Weber, E. U. (2013). Doing the right thing willingly: Behavioral decision theory and environmental policy. In E. Shafir (Ed.), *The behavioral foundations of policy* (pp. 380–397). Princeton: Princeton University Press.

Weber, E. U. (2017). Understanding public risk perception and responses to changes in perceived risk. In E. J. Balleisen, L. S. Bennear, K. D. Krawlec, & J. B. Wiener (Eds.), *Policy Shock: Recalibrating Risk and Regulation after Oil Spills, Nuclear Accidents and Financial Crashes*. Cambridge: Cambridge University Press.

Weber, E. U., & Ancker, J. S. (2011). Cultural differences in risk taking and precaution: The relative roles of risk perception and risk attitude In J. B. Wiener, M. D. Rogers, P. H. Sand, & J. K. Hammitt (Eds.), *The reality of precaution: Comparing risk regulation in the United States and Europe* (pp. 480–491). Cambridge: Cambridge University Press.

Weber, E. U., Blais, A.-R., & Betz, N. (2002). A domain-specific risk-attitude scale: Measuring risk perceptions and risk behaviors. *Journal of Behavioral Decision Making, 15*, 263–290.

Weber, E. U., & Fox-Glassman, K. (2016). *Global warming does not scare us (yet): Climate risks and other natural hazards in the psychological risk dimension space*. Working paper, Center for Decision Sciences.

Weber, E. U., & Hsee, C. K. (1998). Cross-cultural differences in risk perception but cross-cultural similarities in attitudes towards perceived risk. *Management Science, 44,* 1205–1217.

Weber, E. U., & Johnson, E. J. (2009a). Decisions under uncertainty: Psychological, economic, and neuroeconomic explanations of risk preference. In P. Glimcher, C. Camerer, E. Fehr, & R. Poldrack (Eds.), *Neuroeconomics: Decision making and the brain* (pp. 127–144). New York: Elsevier.

Weber, E. U., & Johnson, E. J. (2009b). Mindful judgment and decision making. *Annual Review of Psychology, 60,* 53–86. doi:10.1146/annurev.psych.60.110707.163633

Weber, E. U., & Lindemann, P. G. (2008). From intuition to analysis: Making decisions with our head, our heart, or by the book. In H. Plessner, C. Betsch, & T. Betsch (Eds.), *Intuition in judgment and decision making* (pp. 191–208). Mahwah, NJ: Lawrence Erlbaum.

Weber, E. U., & Milliman, R. (1997). Perceived risk attitudes: Relating risk perception to risky choice. *Management Science, 43,* 122–143.

Weber, E. U., Shafir, S., & Blais, A.-R. (2004). Predicting risk-sensitivity in humans and lower animals: Risk as variance or coefficient of variation. *Psychological Review, 111,* 430–445.

Weber, E. U., Siebenmorgen, N., & Weber, M. (2005). Communicating asset risk: How name recognition and the format of historic volatility information affect risk perception and investment decisions. *Risk Analysis, 25,* 597–609.

Weber, E. U., & Stern, P. (2011). Public's understanding of climate change in the United States. *American Psychologist, 66,* 315–328. doi:10.1037/a0023253

Weber, M., Weber, E. U., & Nosić, A. (2013). Who takes risks when and why: Determinants of changes in investor risk taking. *Review of Finance, 17,* 847–883.

Yechiam, E., Barron, G., & Erev, I. (2005). The role of personal experience in contributing to different patterns of response to rare terrorist attacks. *Journal of Conflict Resolution, 49,* 430–439.

Zaval, L., Keenan, E. A., Johnson, E. J., & Weber, E. U. (2014). Understanding local warming: How warm days lead to increased belief in global warming. *Nature Climate Change, 4,* 143–147.

CHAPTER 3

Risk-Based Thinking

Baruch Fischhoff

For 15 years, I headed an undergraduate major in Decision Science. It has been successful enough that, in the College of Humanities and Social Sciences, it lags only economics and psychology in popularity among disciplinary majors. About one-fifth of entering students list it as a possible major—a startling percentage given that no high school teaches decision science. It also gets many "refugees" from other departments (e.g., physics, engineering, architecture), who find that Decision Science provides a better balance of quantitative and qualitative approaches to basic and applied problems. Some students find the major satisfying enough to stay in touch after graduation. One, when visiting campus during Spring Carnival, observed that "I can't turn it off." He went on to describe instances in which he saw the world differently due to his education.

It was a gratifying comment for an educator. Perhaps we, collectively, have been doing our part in meeting the demand attributed to H. G. Wells: "Statistical thinking will one day be as necessary for efficient citizenship as the ability to read and write."[1] However, it was also a sobering comment, raising the empirical question of how our curriculum had, in fact, affected our students' decision-making competence and confidence in those abilities.

The same question applies to our field overall. In 40-some years, it has grown dramatically from its origin as a handful of individuals committed to doing research that was both analytically and behaviorally informed, with the dual missions of contributing both to science and public welfare (Slovic, Kunreuther, and White 1974; Slovic, Fischhoff, and Lichtenstein 1976; Jungermann and DeZeeuw 1977; Kunreuther et al. 1978). "The List" maintained by

Sarah Lichtenstein had fewer than 100 members, including some behind the Iron Curtain whose work was restricted because they used terms like "subjective" and "utility." Today, the field is represented in societies, journals, meetings, agencies, consultancies, and regulations. It is disseminated through classes, texts, websites, TED talks, and trade books that include nonfiction bestsellers (Ariely 2008; Thaler and Sunstein 2008; Kahneman 2011). In thinking about the future of risk research, it is important to ask how well we have fulfilled our version of George Miller's (1969) admonition to "give psychology away," for the common good.

Ideally, encounters with our work will make people better decision-makers, by helping them to recognize decision points, devote proper resources to them, estimate risks and benefits, balance intuitive and reflective responses, assess uncertainties in their beliefs, resolve ambiguities in their preferences, and defend themselves from needless regret, knowing that they have done what they could to make the best choices possible in complex, uncertain, and sometimes unfriendly circumstances.

Less ideally, encounters with our work will leave people worse off, by undermining their intuitive ways of thinking, drowning them in bewildering arrays of potential biases, without providing useful alternatives ways to deal with the risk decisions in their lives. Members of our public might end up unduly humbled by a "gotcha brigade" of researchers dedicated to highlighting human failings. Or, they might end up overly confident, convinced that they are now immune to the follies illustrated in others' behavior.

At the professional level, progress in risk management research and practice is obvious—witness the celebration of the Wharton School's Risk Management and Decision Processes Center that prompted this book. But what about the spillover effects to everyday life? To what extent do people, as individuals and society, think more clearly about risks, due to our work? The answer to that question should set our agenda for creating and applying the needed science. Those applications might include providing people with better information, helping them to articulate their preferences, clarifying the positive and negative roles of emotion, and protecting them from deceptive advertising and unsafe products. When risk professionals manage to provide that support, they put themselves out of business, having allowed people to fend for themselves. They can then move on to address other, more difficult decisions.

The next two sections discuss the challenges of assessing how well people think about risks. The first focuses on the question of how well people make specific choices, the second on the question of how well they have mastered the skills needed for decision-making in general. The following section considers ways to enhance the transfer of knowledge from the professional world of risk research to the practical world in which people make risk decisions and live with their consequences. Each section leads to a proposal for a strategic research initiative. The concluding section asks how the field can organize itself to address these opportunities.

How Well Can People Think About Specific Risk Decisions?

The title of Dan Ariely's well-known *Predictably Irrational* (2008) captures one general pattern found in risk research: people are, to some extent, predictably irrational, in the sense that they make judgments and decisions contrary to normative accounts of how they should behave. The title of Daniel Kahneman's *Thinking, Fast and Slow* (2011) captures a fundamental distinction that can guide predictions of such irrationality: knowing whether people are thinking fast or slow. Fast thinking can produce more irrational decisions (in Ariely's sense) when people who stop to think have better heuristics in their cognitive repertoire than the ones that immediately come to mind. Slow responses can produce more irrational decisions when people have learned, or instinctively know, what to do, so that reflection wastes time or leads them astray. The better our science, the better we can predict the roles and outcomes of fast and slow thinking. The title of Paul Slovic's important collection *The Feeling of Risk* (2001) raises analogous questions about how the feeling of risk can direct and misdirect decisions.

Although clearly conditional, these accounts are often cited as making universal statements about how well people think about risk and uncertainty. That oversimplification changes "predictably" from a property of situations, some of which produce irrational responses, to a property of individuals, who bring irrationality wherever they go. Slow thinking is always better. Feeling is always problematic. Accentuating the negative in these ways reflects a figure-ground effect; problems (biases) are more salient than the processes that produce them (heuristics). Focusing on problems can serve the public if it directs researchers to places where help is needed. It can also serve researchers' egos, by making them the arbiters of others' limitations.

There are procedures for evaluating the optimality of any specific choice and, to a lesser extent, the rationality of the processes leading to it (von Winterfeldt and Edwards 1986; Fischhoff and Eggers 2012; von Winterfeldt 2013). These procedures ask to what extent people manage to choose options in their own best interest, despite any limits to their knowledge, cognitive abilities, and affective control. The preferred option is typically defined as some variant of that "having the greatest expected utility." Performing that calculation requires understanding how individuals formulate their choices; for example, it should capture cases where people are willing to bear the consequences of poor choices in return for the benefits of learning from experience (Einhorn 1986; Baron 1994). The best option could be one that violates the expected utility standard, if it enables decision-makers to defend a "sacred" (or "protected") value, of the sort that allows no tradeoffs (Baron and Spranca 1997; Atran and Axelrod 2008). It could also be one that reflects nonconsequentialist goals, such as wanting to choose independently (e.g., for adolescents or the elderly) or to be ruled by passion (e.g., for love or war).

Thus, although conceptually straightforward, assessing the quality of individuals' decision-making is technically demanding. It requires taking the broad view needed to identify the kinds of decisions that individuals want to make. There are many thoughtful reflections on "what makes a good decision" that could inform that assessment (Yates, Veinott, and Patalano 2003; Baron 2008). However, there is no systematic procedure for applying them, sensitive to the potential diversity in individuals' preferences for decision-making consequences and processes. In its absence, observers risk incomplete accounts. They may rush to judgment, wrongly concluding that decision-makers cannot understand risks, leading to policies that manipulate people who could manage their own affairs. Conversely, observers may be overly creative in justifying decision-makers' choices and competence, leading to policies that deny them needed protection in situations where they cannot fend for themselves.

Risk Research Need 1: Procedures for Evaluating How Well People Make Risk Decisions

Various authors have offered frameworks accounting for subsets of the factors potentially shaping risk decisions. For example, Grether and Plott (1979) proposed a taxonomy of potential artifacts in experimental choice tasks. Lerner and Tetlock (1999) provided one for factors determining how accountable people feel for their choices. Milkman, Chugh, and Bazerman (2009) have a related proposal for characterizing debiasing procedures. Lita Furby and I created a framework for specifying the prospects offered in stated preference studies (Fischhoff and Furby 1988; Fischhoff 2005). Florig et al. (2001) developed a procedure that characterizes diverse risks in common terms. When applied consistently, such schemes fulfill some of Gary Becker's (1976) call to ensure that preferences are stable across related decisions, an assumption underlying revealed preference analyses. Such frameworks reflect past research by focusing on factors that have been found to affect choices. They protect future research by circumscribing the set of potential explanations, thereby reducing the risk of ad hoc interpretations. By putting diverse studies on a common footing, such frameworks structure the kind of rolling meta-analyses that can provide the transparency advocated by the open science movement (Braver, Thoemmes, and Rosenthal 2014). Because risk management addresses real problems, the set of potentially relevant factors is naturally diverse. Having shared procedures for evaluating decisions would provide a foundation for orderly interventions and accumulation of knowledge.

How Can We Tell How Well People Think About Risk Decisions Generally?

Even were there authoritative accounts of how well people make specific risk decisions, that alone would not answer the question of how well people make risk decisions overall—and whether they are getting better over time. Such a general assessment could mean attempting to weight those specific decisions in terms of which matter most. Is it the repeated ones or the unique ones? The easy ones or the hard ones? Decisions involving heart and soul, or pocketbook? Researchers in healthcare services must make such cross-decision comparisons when allocating societal resources. Others need not.

An alternative question asks to what extent individuals have mastered the general skills needed to make risk decisions. If those skills have increased over time, then risk research might take some credit. The "Flynn effect" (Flynn 1987, 2009) provides reason for optimism regarding the skills defined by intelligence tests. Those scores appear to be going up over time. The vigorous debate over the meaning of these changes captures the challenges of such assessments. The internal validity of widely used IQ tests has been studied extensively. However, their external validity remains open to question. To what extent do they assess the skills that people need to succeed in life, rather than just test-taking abilities that are correlated with success? Do the tests create an illusion of validity, or self-fulfilling prophecy, by directing resources to people who score well, thereby helping them to succeed (Einhorn 1982)?

Tests of individual differences in decision-making competence are a long way from affecting college admissions, the way that IQ tests do. Indeed, until recently, they hardly existed at all. There have long been tests of individual differences in cognitive style. However, those had such limited predictive validity that George Huber (1983) once proposed abandoning the search, arguing that anything big enough to have practical value would have been found already, then followed his own advice by moving on to study organizational change.

One source of researchers' disinterest in individual differences was Walter Mischel's (1968) account of how situational factors often overwhelm personality factors. Psychologists codified the tendency to neglect situational factors when interpreting others' behavior as the "fundamental attribution error" (Ross 1977). Another source of researchers' disinterest was their focus on widely shared psychological processes, relevant to creating a general picture of how people think. A third source was experimentalists' need to vary tasks across studies, when probing the effects of situational factors, rather than standardizing their tasks, as required for individual difference measures. A fourth source was having different participants in most studies, which avoids learning effects, but forfeits the chance to observe behavior over time and tasks.

In our own research, an opportunity arose to add a battery of common decision-making tasks to a 20-year longitudinal project, the Center for Education and Drug Abuse Research, led by Ralph Tarter. We found that performance on these tasks was correlated, suggesting a common factor of decision-making competence (DMC). Moreover, DMC scores were correlated with measures of plausible antecedents and consequences, suggesting the external validity of our tasks. For example, participants with higher DMC scores were more likely to come from intact homes and less likely to exhibit oppositional defiance disorder and other risk behaviors. Moreover, those correlations remained after controlling for scores on tests of fluid and crystalized intelligence (Parker and Fischhoff 2005). These initial patterns have generally borne up in subsequent research (Bruine de Bruin, Parker, and Fischhoff 2007b; Parker, Bruine de Bruin, and Fischhoff 2007, 2015; Missier et al. 2015), including evidence of stability over an 11-year period (Parker et al.

2018). Similar patterns have also emerged in concurrent research into the skills demanded by reasoning tasks and imperfectly captured by intelligence tests (Stanovich and West 2000, 2008).

One sustained attempt to track the quality of lay thinking over time is the National Science Foundation's survey of "science literacy" (National Science Board 2014). Although motivated by the desire to make science more useful, these surveys have not attempted to assess decision-making abilities or scientific reasoning skills (Drummond and Fischhoff 2015). Rather, they have evaluated respondents' knowledge of facts that might be interpreted as markers of those abilities (e.g., "The center of the earth is hot"). As a result, they say relatively little about the extent to which the seeming rise in public skepticism about science reflects less ability to reason like scientists or less willingness to believe the factual premises underlying scientists' reasoning (Lewandowsky et al. 2012).

Research Need 2: A Shared Set of Validated Decision-Making Competence Measures

Assessing changes in decision-making skills over time requires standard instruments and places to deploy them. In creating our measure of DMC (Parker and Fischhoff 2005; Bruine de Bruin et al. 2007b), we included tasks that would interest researchers concerned with specific tasks (e.g., calibration, framing) and the overall skill set. Although we modeled our tasks on ones in the literature, no scientist should presume to prescribe others' measures. One institutional model for balancing scientific freedom and standardization is the NIH-sponsored PROMIS (Patient-Reported Outcomes Measurement Information System) consortium. Its website hosts any measure that meets its criteria for empirically demonstrated psychometric validity.[2] As a bonus, it offers users support in the form of applying item response theory to produce compact question sets. Researchers who use PROMIS measures produce results that are readily comparable to those from other studies. If risk researchers developed a PROMIS-like set of canonical DMC measures, they would be positioned for the kind of big science needed to study individual differences properly. That means having a data collection operation that is large enough to examine patterns in cross-sectional analyses and stable enough to capture developments in individuals and cohorts over time.

Although risk researchers have helped to refine such studies (Bruine de Bruin, Parker, and Fischhoff 2007a; Bruine de Bruin et al. 2011; Bruine de Bruin and Fischhoff 2017), they have rarely been central to their creation (Mellers et al. 2015).

How Can We Communicate Our Work Best?

If people are making better decisions and revealing greater decision-making competence, that could reflect the cumulative impact of our research, books, talks, and courses. More direct evidence is found in experimental tests of interventions intended to reduce judgmental biases. Such debiasing studies have had mixed results. Just hearing about biases has no apparent effect on performance. Some success has been found with training that involves prompt, unambiguous feedback, supplemented by explication of unintuitive processes (Milkman, Chugh, and Bazerman 2009; Morgan 2014; Mellers et al. 2015; Morewedge et al. 2015). Studies of how well and how long such training transfers to actual decision-making are limited—and difficult to conduct. Thus, we know little about how exposure to our research affects individuals' confidence in their abilities. To that end, our goal might be inspiring humility: speaking with enough pride to draw attention to our research, while creating realistic expectations for how much difference it makes, as befits the difficulty of the decisions that people face, the limits to our science, and the apprenticeship needed to master it.

The science of science communication has identified challenges common to conveying any science (Fischhoff and Scheufele 2013, 2014): audiences might not understand the methods of a specific science or of science itself. They might lack the substantive knowledge (Bruine de Bruin and Bostrom 2013) needed to make sense of new findings. They might not know how strong a field is overall or how far specific findings can be extrapolated. They might struggle to decipher scientists' disagreements and expressions of uncertainty, especially when the science is contested (e.g., vaccines, climate change). They might be so committed to their beliefs that they quickly explain away contrary results and embrace supporting ones (Lewandowsky et al. 2012; Corner, Whitmarsh, and Xenias 2012).

Outside of the classroom, scientists have few opportunities to educate their audiences about the basics of their science. Rather, they must take people as they are, with diverse, imperfect backgrounds, and provide enough context for recipients to interpret science appropriately. Complaints about scientists who seem to contradict one another or hype their work suggests that such context is often missing (e.g., Kolata 2016; McKay 2016). One way to provide it is with standard reporting formats that present information in a predictable format that gradually educates audiences in how scientists think about their work. The following exhibits offer four such approaches. As with all communications, their usefulness is an empirical question, answered more easily for immediate impacts (do users understand the content of the communication? can they use it to make sound inferences?) than for long-term ones (are they wiser decision-makers?).

General Disclosure

In *Risk: A Very Short Introduction* (Fischhoff and Kadvany 2011), we briefly reported results from many behavioral experiments, within a page limit that precluded elaborating on the strengths and weaknesses of each. Instead, the book offered general guidance, in the list that follows, on how the conditions of an experiment could affect the quality of the performance that it reveals. Each factor is common knowledge for scientists, but perhaps not to consumers of their work. Given the diverse studies that we reported, we made no attempt to assess the overall magnitude, or even sign, of these effects. However, researchers could do that for their own individual studies, providing readers with guidance on whether they observed particularly good or bad performance.

1. [Research tasks] are clearly described, so that researchers can see how people make them. That clarity can produce better decisions, if it removes the clutter of everyday life, or worse decisions, if that clutter provides vital context, such as what choices other people are making.
2. [Research tasks] have low stakes, reflecting researchers' limited budgets. That can produce better decisions, if it reduces stress, or worse decisions, if it reduces motivation.
3. [Research tasks] are approved by university ethics committees. That can produce better decisions, if it reduces participants' worry about being deceived, or worse decisions, if it induces artificiality.

4. [Research tasks] are focused on researchers' interests. That can produce worse decisions, if researchers are studying biases, or better decisions, if researchers are seeking decision-makers' secrets of success. (Fischhoff and Kadvany 2011, 110)

Methodological Audit

As part of a project investigating behavioral responses to smart grid electricity technology, Davis et al. (2013) reviewed 32 field trials of interventions (e.g., in-home displays of electricity usage). Using the CONSORT protocol for Cochrane Collaboration reviews, they characterized each study in terms of six methodological flaws found to affect medical clinical trials (Moher et al. 2010). For example, as seen in Figure 3.1, only four studies had low risk of volunteer selection bias, which can overestimate the impact of interventions—by studying people predisposed to change. The clinical trial literature has estimates of the size of the bias from some of these sources. Risk researchers could routinely characterize their research in such terms, winning points for their candor, while gradually educating their audiences about how science works. Fischhoff and Davis (2014) offer a detailed version of this audit, expanded to include the strength (or *pedigree*) of the underlying science (Funtowicz and Ravetz 1990).

Running Summary

No study stands alone. Its interpretation depends on knowledge of boundary conditions (list above) and methodological standards (Figure 3.1). When studies measure the same variable, meta-analysis can provide aggregate estimates of key variables (e.g., survival rates, sleep duration) (Braver, Thoemmes, and Rosenthal 2014). When studies measure related phenomena, funnel diagrams, like Figure 3.2, preserve the identity of the individual studies, while suggesting general patterns. In this example, the open triangles are from new studies. They reveal no overall effect of the experimental manipulation (x axis), and cluster closer to zero as the standard error decreases (y axis), as would be expected with orderly data. The gray cone shows the region for statistically nonsignificant results. The black circles are results

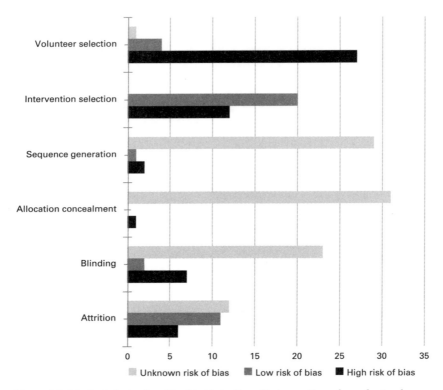

Figure 3.1. Methodological audit of field studies of interventions for reducing home electricity consumption. *Source:* Davis et al. (2013).

from 43 previous studies. They show an overall effect, but a disorderly one (outside the cone), leading the authors to question that research (Shanks et al. 2015). Although Figure 3.2 may be a daunting display at first glance, its elements are conceptually simple (e.g., how precise are the estimates, how anomalous is the pattern), meaning that it should possible to explain it, with some design work.

Integrative Decision Frame

When studies inform theories, the quality of the work is paramount (list above and Figure 3.2). When studies inform decisions, their practical relevance matters as well. Figure 3.3 is a tabular format recently adopted by the

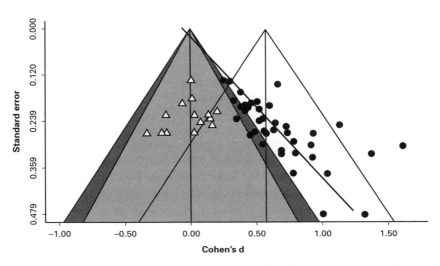

Figure 3.2. Funnel plots of related experimental studies. Cohen's d measures effect size for the difference between two groups (Cohen 1992). *Source:* Shanks et al. (2015).

Decision Factor	Evidence and Uncertainties	Conclusions and Reasons
Analysis of condition		
Current treatment options		
Benefit		
Risk		
Risk management		
Benefit-Risk Summary Assessment		

Figure 3.3. The U.S. Food and Drug Administration's benefit-risk framework. *Source:* FDA (2013).

U.S. Food and Drug Administration (FDA) to summarize its evaluations of pharmaceuticals submitted for approval (Fischhoff 2017). The rows show how FDA frames its decisions. Namely, its risk-benefit decisions depend on the (medical) condition, the current treatment options, the expected benefits, the attendant risks, and the opportunities for managing risks (post-approval). The columns show that FDA distinguishes questions of science (on the left) from their regulatory implications (on the right). The former explicitly recognize uncertainty (Institute of Medicine 2014). The latter depend on

FDA's legal framework and understanding of its public (see also Schwartz and Woloshin 2013).

Research Need Number 3: Methods for Communicating the Quality of Risk Research

Researchers have tacit knowledge of how to interpret their work that observers, even those trained in other scientific disciplines, lack. Unless they provide that context, researchers risk evoking too much or too little credence for their studies. Like many decision science formulations, the four exhibits represent ways of organizing information that might not occur to people spontaneously but should be comprehensible if executed well. Recognizing that context should be good for the science as well. For example, Figure 3.2 gives greater credence to studies with orderly patterns of results, relative to studies with novel findings of uncertain provenance. The list of boundary conditions suggests how to make the case for "orchids," results that appear under highly specific conditions, hence might reveal interesting processes, even if they do not support grand claims about the human condition. Thus, developing standard ways to place risk research in context could improve the research itself, along with its contribution to aiding specific decisions and improving general decision-making competence.

Conclusion

The ultimate payoff for society's investment in risk research is better risk decisions. That goal can be advanced by addressing three research needs: (a) developing better procedures for evaluating the quality of individual decisions; (b) understanding decision-making competence, as it varies across individuals and over time; and (c) placing the science in context, so that observers know how to use it in their decision-making. The three research programs outlined here would advance these goals, contributing to the science and the society that supports it.

Our goal when interacting with any public might be the mature enthusiasm that we seek with our students: excitement about the research, tempered by recognition of its limits; wariness about biases, balanced by respect for the power of heuristics; enthusiasm about the clear signals that experiments can offer, muted by the difficulty of generalizing their results; pride in the tension between simplicity and precision in theoretical accounts; the ability to think analytically, whatever one's level of technical mastery (National Research Council 2011).

People who can absorb, and live with, these tensions when consuming our work should come away with appropriate feelings of self-efficacy when making risk decisions. That perspective should afford them more satisfying lives, despite inevitable setbacks. It might give them an edge, in competition with over—or under—confident others. Another former student once returned a book with the comment, "I didn't realize that people thought that deeply." He was referring to a philosopher of science (Lakatos 1970). What if the consumers of our work thought the same about us?

To that end, the Wharton Risk Management and Decision Processes Center has seeded the world with people who speak the language of risk that it has helped to create. As the number of those people grows, they should increasingly find common cause, able to see and sustain solutions requiring their shared perspective. Over time, such thinking might become so natural that turning it off no longer is an option.

Notes

1. The less pithy actual quote was something like, "The time may not be very remote when it will be understood that for complete initiation as an efficient citizen of one of the new great complex world-wide states that are now developing, it is as necessary to be able to compute, to think in averages and maxima and minima, as it is now to be able to read and to write" (Wells 1911, 204; see also Tankard 1979).

2. See HealthMeasures, "PROMIS," www.healthmeasures.net/explore-measurement-systems/promis.

References

Ariely, D. (2008). *Predictably irrational: The hidden forces that shape our decisions.* New York: HarperCollins.

Atran, S., & Axelrod, R. (2008). Reframing sacred values. *Negotiation Journal, 24,* 221–246.

Baron, J. (1994). Nonconsequentialist decisions. *Behavioral and Brain Sciences, 17*(1), 1–10.

Baron, J. (2008). *Thinking and deciding.* New York: Cambridge University Press.

Baron, J., & Spranca, M. (1997). Protected values. *Organizational Behavior and Human Decision Processes, 70,* 1–16.

Becker, G. (1976). Introduction. In *The economic approach to human behavior* (pp. 3–14). Chicago: University of Chicago Press.

Braver, S., Thoemmes, F., & Rosenthal, R. (2014). Continuously cumulating meta-analysis and replicability. *Perspectives on Psychological Science, 9*(3), 333–342.

Bruine de Bruin, W., & Bostrom, A. (2013). Assessing what to address in science communication. *Proceedings of the National Academy of Sciences, 110* (Supplement 3), 14062–14068.

Bruine de Bruin, W., & Fischhoff, B. (2017). Eliciting probabilistic expectations: Collaborations between psychologists and economists. *Proceedings of the National Academy of Sciences, 114*(13), 3297–3304.

Bruine de Bruin, W., Manski, C. F., Topa, G. & van der Klaaw, W. (2011). Measuring consumer uncertainty about future inflation. *Journal of Applied Econometrics, 26*, 454–478.

Bruine de Bruin, W., Parker, A., & Fischhoff, B. (2007a). Can adolescents predict significant events in their lives? *Journal of Adolescent Health, 41*, 208–210.

Bruine de Bruin, W., Parker, A., & Fischhoff, B. (2007b). Individual differences in adult decision-making competence (A-DMC). *Journal of Personality and Social Psychology, 92*, 938–956.

Cohen, J. (1992). A power primer. *Psychological Bulletin, 112*, 155–159.

Corner, A., Whitmarsh, L., & Xenias, D. (2012). Uncertainty, scepticism, and attitudes towards climate change: Biased assimilation and attitude polarisation. *Climate Change, 114*, 463–478.

Davis, A. L., Krishnamurti, T., Fischhoff, B., & Bruine de Bruin, W. (2013). Setting a standard for electricity pilot studies. *Energy Policy, 62*, 401–409.

Drummond, C., & Fischhoff, B. (2015). Development and validation of the scientific reasoning scale. *Journal of Behavioral Decision Making, 30*(1), 26–38.

Einhorn, H. J. (1982). Learning from experience and suboptimal rules in decision making. In D. Kahneman, P. Slovic, & A. Tversky (Eds.), *Judgment under uncertainty: Heuristics and biases* (pp. 268–283). New York: Cambridge University Press.

Einhorn, H. J. (1986). Accepting error to make less error. *Journal of Personality Assessment, 50*(3), 387–95.

FDA. (2013). *Structured approach to benefit-risk assessment for drug regulatory decision making.* Draft PDUFA V implementation plan, FY2013–2017. Silver Spring, MD: U.S. Food and Drug Administration.

Fischhoff, B. (1992). Giving advice: Decision theory perspectives on sexual assault. *American Psychologist, 47*, 577–588.

Fischhoff, B. (2005). Cognitive processes in stated preference methods. In K.-G. Mäler & J. Vincent (Eds.), *Handbook of environmental economics* (pp. 937–968). Amsterdam: Elsevier.

Fischhoff, B. (2013). The sciences of science communication. *Proceedings of the National Academy of Sciences, 110* (Supplement 3), 14033–14039.

Fischhoff, B. (2017). Breaking ground for psychological science: The U.S. Food and Drug Administration. *American Psychologist, 72*(2), 118–125.

Fischhoff, B., & Davis, A. L. (2014). Communicating scientific uncertainty. *Proceedings of the National Academy of Sciences, 111* (Supplement 4), 13664–13671.

Fischhoff, B., & Eggers, S. (2012). Questions of competence: The duty to inform and the limits to choice. In E. Shafir (Ed.), *The behavioral foundations of policy* (pp. 217–230). Princeton: Princeton University Press.

Fischhoff, B., & Furby, L. (1988). Measuring values: A conceptual framework for interpreting transactions. *Journal of Risk and Uncertainty, 1*, 147–184.

Fischhoff, B., & Kadvany, J. (2011). *Risk: A very short introduction*. Oxford: Oxford University Press.

Fischhoff, B., & Scheufele, D. (Eds.). (2013). The science of science communication. *Proceedings of the National Academy of Sciences, 110* (Supplement 3).

Fischhoff, B., & Scheufele, D. (Eds.) (2014). The science of science communication II. *Proceedings of the National Academy of Sciences, 111* (Supplement 4).

Florig, H. K., Morgan, M. G., Morgan, K. M., Jenni, K. E., Fischhoff, B., Fischbeck, P. S., & DeKay, M. (2001). A deliberative method for ranking risks (1): Overview and test bed development. *Risk Analysis, 21*, 913–922.

Flynn, J. R. (1987). Massive IQ gains in 14 nations: What IQ tests really measure. *Psychological Bulletin, 101*, 171–191.

Flynn, J. R. (2009). *What is intelligence: Beyond the Flynn effect*. Cambridge: Cambridge University Press.

Funtowicz S. O., & Ravetz, J. (1990). *Uncertainty and quality in science for policy*. London: Kluwer.

Grether, D. M., & Plott, C. R. (1979). Economic theory of choice and the preference reversal phenomenon. *American Economic Review, 69*(4), 623–638.

Huber, G. P. (1983). Cognitive style as a basis for MIS and DSS designs: Much ado about nothing? *Management Science, 29*, 567–577.

Institute of Medicine. (2014). *Uncertainty in assessing pharmaceutical risks and benefits*. Washington, DC: National Academy Press.

Jungermann, H., & deZeeuw, G. (Eds.). (1977) *Decision making and change in human affairs*. Dordrecht: Reidel.

Kahneman, D. 2011. *Thinking, fast and slow*. New York: Farrar Straus & Giroux.

Kolata, G. (2016, August 11). We're so confused: The problems with food and exercise studies. *New York Times*. Retrieved from https://www.nytimes.com/2016/08/11/upshot/were-so-confused-the-problems-with-food-and-exercise-studies.html

Kunreuther, H., Ginsberg, R., Miller, L., Sagi, P., Slovic, P., Borkan, B., & Katz, N. (1978). *Disaster insurance protection: Public policy lessons*. New York: Wiley.

Lakatos, I. (1970). Falsification and the methodology of scientific research programmes. In I. Lakatos and A. Musgrave (Eds.), *Criticism and the growth of scientific knowledge* (pp. 91–196). Cambridge: Cambridge University Press.

Lerner, J. S., & Tetlock, P. E. (1999). Accounting for the effects of accountability. *Psychological Bulletin, 125*(2), 255–275.

Lewandowsky, S., Ecker, U. K., Seifert, C. M., Schwarz, N., & Cook, J. (2012). Misinformation and its correction: Continued influence and successful debiasing. *Psychological Science in the Public Interest, 13*, 106–131.

McKay, P. (2016, August 13). According to a recent study. . . . *Pittsburgh Post-Gazette*. Retrieved from http://www.post-gazette.com/life/2016/08/06/Peter-McKay-According-to-a-recent-study/stories/201608060020

Mellers, C., Stone, E., Murray, T., Minster, A., Rohrbaugh, N., Bishop, M., . . . & Tetlock, P. (2015). Identifying and cultivating superforecasters as a method of improving probabilistic predictions. *Perspectives on Psychological Science, 10*(3), 267–281.

Milkman, K. L., Chugh, D., & Bazerman, M. H. (2009). How can decision making be improved? *Perspectives on Psychological Science, 4*(4), 379–383.

Miller, G. (1969). Psychology as a means of promoting human welfare. *American Psychologist, 24*, 1063–1075.

Mischel, W. (1968). *Personality and assessment.* New York: Wiley.

Missier, F. D., Hansson, P., Parker, A. M., Bruin de Bruine, W., Nilsson, L.-G., & Mäntylä, T. (2015). Unraveling the aging skein: Disentangling sensory and cognitive predictors of age-related differences in decision making. *Journal of Behavioral Decision Making.* doi:10.1002/bdm.1926

Moher, D., Hopewell, S., Schulz, K. F., Montori, V., Gøtzsche, P. C., Devereaux, P. J., . . . & Altman, D. G. (2010). CONSORT 2010 explanation and elaboration: Updated guidelines for reporting parallel group randomised trials. *BMJ* 340:c869.

Morewedge, C. K., Yoon, H., Scopelliti, I., Symborski, C. W., Korris, J. H., & Kassam, K. S. (2015). Debiasing decisions: Improved decision making with a single training intervention. *Policy Insights from the Behavioral and Brain Sciences, 2*, 129–140.

Morgan, M. G. (2014). The use (and abuse) of expert elicitation in support of decision making for public policy. *Proceedings of the National Academy of Sciences, 111*, 7176–7184.

National Research Council. (2011). *Intelligence analysis for tomorrow.* Washington, DC: National Academy Press.

National Science Board. (2014). *Science and engineering indicators 2014* (NSB 14-01). Arlington, VA: National Science Foundation.

Parker, A. M., Bruine de Bruin, W., & Fischhoff, B. (2007). Maximizers vs. satisficers: Decision-making styles, competence and outcomes. *Judgment and Decision Making, 2*(6), 342–350.

Parker, A. M., Bruine de Bruin, W., & Fischhoff, B. (2015). Negative decision outcomes are more common among people with lower decision-making competence: An item-level analysis of the Decision Outcome Inventory (DOI). *Frontiers in Psychology, 6.* doi:10.3389/fpsyg.2015.00363

Parker, A. M., Bruine de Bruin, W., Fischhoff, B., & Weller, J. (2018). Robustness of decision-making competence: Evidence from two measures and an 11-year longitudinal study. *Journal of Behavioral Decision Making, 31*, 309–470.

Parker, A. M., & Fischhoff, B. (2005). Decision-making competence: External validity through an individual-differences approach. *Journal of Behavioral Decision Making, 18*, 1–27.

Ross, L. (1977). The intuitive psychologist and his shortcomings: Distortions in the attribution process. In L. Berkowitz (Ed.), *Advances in experimental social psychology, 10* (pp. 173–220). New York: Academic Press.

Schwartz, L., & Woloshin, S. (2013). The drug facts box: Improving the communication of prescription drug information. *Proceedings of the National Academy of Sciences, 110*, 14069–14074

Shanks, D. R., Vadillo, M. A., Riedel, B., Clymo, A., Govind, S., Hickin, N., . . . & Puhlmann, L. M. (2015). Romance, risk, and replication: Can consumer choices and risk-taking be primed by mating motives? *Journal of Experimental Psychology: General, 144*(6), 142–158.

Slovic, P. (Ed.). (2001). *The feeling of risk.* London: Earthscan.

Slovic, P., Fischhoff, B. & Lichtenstein, S. (1976). Cognitive processes and societal risk taking. In J. S. Carroll and J. W. Payne (Eds.), *Cognition and social behavior* (pp. 165–184). Potomac, MD: Erlbaum.

Slovic, P., Kunreuther, H., & White, G. (1974). Decision processes, rationality and adjustment to natural hazards. In G. F. White (Ed.), *Natural hazards: Local, national and global*. New York: Oxford University Press.

Stanovich, K. E., & West, R. F. (2000). Individual differences in reasoning: Implications for the rationality debate? *Behavioral and Brain Science, 23*, 645–726.

Stanovich, K. E., & West, R. F. (2008). On the relative independence of thinking biases and cognitive abilities. *Journal of Personality and Social Psychology, 94*, 672–695.

Tankard, J. W. (1979). The H.G. Wells quote on statistics: A question of accuracy. *Historia Mathematica, 6*, 30–33.

Thaler, R. H., & Sunstein, C. R. (2008). *Nudge: Improving decisions about health, wealth, and happiness*. New Haven, CT: Yale University Press.

von Winterfeldt, D. (2013). Bridging the gap between science and decision making. *Proceedings of the National Academy of Sciences, 110*, 14055–14061.

von Winterfeldt, D., & Edwards, W. (1986). *Decision analysis and behavioral research*. New York: Cambridge University Press.

Wells, H. G. (1911). *Mankind in the making*, 5th ed. London: Chapman and Hall.

Yates, J. F., Veinott, E. S., & Patalano, A. L. (2003). Hard decisions, bad decisions: On decision quality and decision aiding. In S. L. Schneider & J. C. Shanteau (Eds.), *Emerging perspectives on judgment and decision research* (pp. 13–63). New York: Cambridge University Press.

CHAPTER 4

Structured Empirical Analysis of Decisions Under Natural Hazard Risk

Craig E. Landry, Gregory Colson, and Mona Ahmadiani

Microeconometric models of insurance and mitigation choices most often apply reduced-form approaches (Smith and Baquet 1996; Talberth et al. 2006; Martin, Martin, and Kent 2009; Naoi, Seko, and Sumita 2010; Teisl and Roe 2010; Landry and Jahan-Parvar 2011; Botzen and Van Den Bergh 2012; Petrolia, Landry, and Coble 2013; Petrolia et al. 2015). Many applications that employ a choice-theoretic structure do so in simulations (e.g., Babcock 2015) and assume specific functional forms in application (e.g., Holt and Laury 2002; Cohen and Einav 2007) rather than letting the data determine what model fits. What would be preferred is a general structure that nests one or more models describing individual choice under uncertainty. This approach would provide a flexible, yet axiomatic, framework for empirical analysis and permit empirical results to provide feedback on appropriate theoretical structures in particular contexts. The complexity surrounding choice under risk and uncertainty, however, makes this a particularly challenging endeavor.

Theoretical models of choice under risk and uncertainty include von Neumann and Morgenstern's expected utility theory, the Savage axioms on risk and ambiguity, Tversky and Kahneman's prospect theory, and Loomes and Sugden's regret aversion, among others. From a practical standpoint, empirical analysis must contend with estimation of (typically subjective) probabilities, representation of wealth levels, and assessment of conditional losses or gains. Survey and experimental methods can be employed to assess risk and time preferences (Charness, Gneezy, and Imas 2013), but fundamental issues can cause major problems in isolating preferences and beliefs (Gilboa, Postlewaite, and Schmeidler 2008) or identification of the influence of covariate effects on probabilities, expected loss, or other preference parameters (Hallstrom and Smith 2005). In this chapter, we review some of the pitfalls encountered in previous work on natural hazard risks and explore empirical approaches that could be pursued to incorporate structural parameters or estimate structural models of choice under risk of natural hazard.

A General Framework for Risky Choices

Natural hazards are a form of catastrophe risk, implying low probabilities, high conditional losses, and spatial correlation in occurrence. Sophisticated computer models with copious weather, property, topography, and hydrological data can estimate "objective" loss probabilities for weather hazards (Czajkowski, Kunreuther, and Michel-Kerjan 2013), but individuals do not generally possess such estimates. Insurance rates (Krutilla 1966) and building restrictions can serve as information signals for individuals, but most empirical results suggest that individuals are not particularly well informed about the likelihood of natural hazards or their consequences (Meyer et al. 2014). As such, we focus on classes of models that employ subjective assessments of probability. In doing so, we eschew consideration of probability weighting functions (partly to simplify our exposition), as we consider these as primarily applied to objective probabilities (though they could be applied to subjective distributions, one would be hard-pressed to separately identify probabilities and weights in most cases).

Cartwright's text *Behavioral Economics* (2011) posits the following generalized framework for reference-dependent utility of a prospect x:

$$U(x) = \sum\nolimits_{i=1}^{n} p_i[\eta u(x_i) + h(x_i, r)], \tag{1}$$

where p_i is the probability of state i, $u(x_i)$ is an evaluation index for state i, η is a parameter to be estimated, and $h(\cdot)$ is some function that depends upon the outcome and a reference point (r). If $\eta = 1$ and $h(\cdot) = 0$, the decision model is expected utility. If p_i reflects the personal probability distribution of an individual based on Bayesian probability theory, $U(x)$ is subjective expected utility. In the above formula, $h(\cdot)$ represents the reference-dependent portion of an individual's utility under risk, and the combination of $h(\cdot) \neq 0$ and various specifications of p_i illustrate the formulation of disappointment, regret theory, rank-dependent utility function and original and cumulative prospect theory.

The disappointment model as provided by Bell (1985) and later enhanced by Loomes and Sugden (1986) takes the prior expectation of prospect x as the reference point (r); therefore, the reference-dependent portion of the structural model is represented by:

$$h(x_i, r) = D(u(x_i) - E[U(x_i)]), \qquad (2)$$

where D is an increasing reverse S-shaped function and $\eta = 1$. As it is demonstrated in the formula, the prior expectation can be context specific but a natural candidate is the expected utility of a prospect.

Regret aversion as proposed by Loomes and Sugden (1982) and Bell (1982) and axiomatized by Sugden (1993) and Quiggin (1994) defines regret as the disutility of not having chosen the ex-post optimal alternative. Modifying Cartwright's formulation, regret-theoretical expected utility (RTEU) of prospect x is obtained by assuming $\eta = 1$ and $h(\cdot)$ as the regret-rejoice function, where (1) r is the best possible outcome that the individual could have attained in the same state of nature, and (2) expectation is taken over the subjective probability distribution of future states of the world. The regret-theoretical expected utility modified based on Cartwright's formulation is denoted as:

$$h(x_i, r) = g(u(x_i) - u(y_i)), \qquad (3)$$

where y is the forgone outcome.

Application of the regret theory in individual's decision toward catastrophe risk compared to the base model of expected utility suggests that when expected utility theory predicts a high optimal level of insurance, the regret theory compensates for the fact that there will be some states of the world for which no insurance is optimal ex post. In other words, anticipation of regret should prevent an individual from making extreme decisions (Braun and Muermann 2004).

The rank-dependent utility function (RDU) initially introduced by Quiggin (1982) is the special case of cumulative prospect theory (Tversky and Kahneman 1992) when instead of p_i, the weighted probability of $w_i = \pi(p_i + p_2 + \cdots + p_n) - \pi(p_{i+1} + p_2 + \cdots + p_n)$ is used, where $\pi(p) = \dfrac{p^\gamma}{(p^\gamma + (1-p)^\gamma)^{1/\gamma}}$, $h(\cdot) = 0$

and $\eta = 1$. The weighting function in rank-dependent utility and cumulative prospect theory that is proposed to address the so-called certainty effect transforms objective cumulative probabilities into subjective cumulative probabilities. In contrast to prospect theory where the loss aversion parameter separates the expected value of loss and gain, in this model, losses and gains are considered equally important in individual's decision-making process.

Botzen and Van Den Bergh (2009) estimate risk premiums for flood insurance and report the expected utility function that results in the same risk premium as rank-dependent and prospect theory. They argue that indication of the degree of risk aversion that corresponds to rank-dependent and prospect theory can aid in determining what range of risk premium is most suitable for policy analysis.

Generally speaking, the descriptive failure of expected utility in explaining different aspects of bounded rationality, and the sufficiency of the above models in delivering the full spectrum of what is required for decision under risk and uncertainty, reveal the reason behind growing empirical studies in this area.

If the empirical problem can be cast in discrete outcome space and subjective probabilities and outcomes can be estimated or assessed, parameter restriction tests and information criteria could, in principle, be used to test competing models of risky choice in the context of natural hazards. The chief challenge is identification of all relevant parameters from empirical data, though panel data could be very helpful in this regard.

Tanaka, Camerer, and Nguyen (2010) formulate a similar model in application to development economics. They devise a theoretical model to evaluate prospects within the context of a stylized set of lottery comparisons defined over both gains and losses. They combine their theoretical model with an experimental instrument that is designed to elicit information on individual risk tolerance, permitting estimation of bounds on risk aversion parameters over gain and loss domains (and a probability weighting parameter). Their results indicate that subjects' choices in the experiment are not consistent with expected utility but are consistent with prospect theory (asymmetric S-shaped evaluation function around a reference point).

Liu (2013) applies the model in an empirical context of agriculture technology adoption in China. She derives risk aversion, loss aversion, and probability weighting parameters following Tanaka, Camerer, and Nguyen and develops a simple description of possible states under a dichotomous choice of technology adoption that captures much of the inherent risk of pest infestation and the relative costs and benefits. Applying this framework in the context of a proportional hazard model, she finds evidence consistent with theory—respondents with lower levels of risk aversion, those that overweight low probability events (like pest infestation), and those that exhibit less loss aversion are more likely to adopt the new technology.

Natural Hazard Applications

Subjective Probabilities

Models of individual decision-making in risky situations are typically formulated with probabilities describing the likelihood of various states; this is a natural extension of probability theory, but it is not at all clear that people process information about risk in such a manner. This problem is particularly acute for catastrophe risk, as the opportunity to form accurate priors is extremely limited. As such, probabilities in this context are best treated as subjective, or perhaps ambiguous. Aside from applications of weighting functions in cumulative prospect theory, subjectively derived probability estimates have played a fairly limited role in empirical analysis, particularly in the area of natural hazards (where objective probabilities are difficult to come by).

Direct elicitation and indirect assessment are available for estimating an individual's subjective risk perceptions (Hampton et al. 1973; Norris and Kramer 1990). Direct elicitation involves asking subjects to assign likelihood to an individual outcome or range of outcomes, from which point estimates or probability distributions can be derived. Indirect assessments are made through inference based on individual choices in gambles, naming odds, response to visual manipulatives, or rankings; indirect modes are often simpler for subjects to evaluate. These methods have seen application in agriculture, where growers are asked to evaluate probability distributions for yield (Smith and Mandac 1995), price (Schnitkey et al. 2003; Shaik et al. 2008), and crop losses due to adverse weather events (Menapace, Colson, and Raffaelli 2013, 2015). Exploration of the determinants of risk perception indicates significant effects by family background, education, social position, prior experience, and geographical location (Kogan and Wallach 1964; Harrison et al. 2007).

Some of our current work (Ahmadiani and Landry 2017) employs subjective risk estimates in empirical analysis of preferences in the context of natural hazards. Using detailed field and survey data from a 1998 Federal Emergency Management Agency study of the National Flood Insurance Program, we estimate a bivariate probit model that examines purchase of flood insurance (revealed preference data) and willingness to purchase additional coverage for shoreline erosion (stated preference data). The flood insurance data have been studied previously (Kriesel and Landry 2004; Landry and Jahan-Parvar 2011), but not in conjunction with erosion protection data. Their combination permits an analysis of multi-peril coverage for coastal hazards. Insurance price information is derived from detailed structural data (for flood) or randomly assigned (for erosion).

Our risk perception data are nominal; likelihood of flood loss is measured as a binary response to a question regarding concern over floods, while the likelihood of erosion loss is measured by categorical response to a question regarding the likelihood of losing a home due to shoreline erosion in the next 30 years. A first-stage regression converts the nominal survey responses into fitted probabilities that are used in the second stage. Unbiased standard errors are estimated via bootstrapping (Efron and Tibshirani 1986). While not a structural model, utilizing survey data to proxy for subjective risk perceptions improves the model and incorporates structural parameters in estimation. Using survey data in this way presents a useful alternative when objective risk estimates are difficult to come by or highly ambiguous in the eyes of subjects.

Preference Parameters

Critical decision parameters in analysis of individual choice in the presence of natural hazards include risk tolerance, time preference, intertemporal substitution, reference points, and loss aversion. Identifying this plethora of parameters with empirical microdata can prove especially challenging. Standard income, labor, and consumption data are often inadequate, so many researchers have turned to primary survey data with context-specific questions to gauge risk tolerance and other aspects of preference (e.g., Barsky et al. 1997). Dohmen et al. (2011) find evidence to support the validity of the survey-based personal assessment approach when compared to binding decisions with salient incentives in an experimental context.

Experimental methods assessing risk tolerance include the multiple price list (MPL) approach of Holt and Laury (2002) and the simplified MPL of Eckel and Grossman (2008). Using carefully crafted experimental designs with salient and tangible incentives introduces finely gradated exogenous variation in uncertain outcomes that permits assessment of risk tolerance. There is evidence, however, that subjects often misunderstand these complex instruments, thus providing responses that are inconsistent with theory (e.g., multiple switching in the MPL). Moreover, the domain of experimental risk is often different from the context of empirical analysis (Menapace, Colson, and Raffaelli 2016). Some of our previous work (Petrolia, Landry, and Coble 2013; Petrolia et al. 2015) applied MPL data to natural hazard insurance (flood and wind) and mitigation, though due to inconsistent response, we could only use counts of the number of safe choices from MPL. Results do suggest, however, that risk aversion over the loss domain is a significant predictor of insurance purchase and mitigation behavior, whereas risk aversion over gains is not.

While methods other than experiments are available for assessing risk aversion (Charness, Gneezy, and Imas 2013), they typically require collection of primary data. Experimental methods, further, can only be used in data collection modes that permit secure interactions among researchers and subjects. There are plenty of empirical analyses that attempt to measure risk aversion in the context of insurance (Outreville 2014), but most do not attempt to apply structural models or discern between competing formulations of choice under risk and uncertainty.

Another area where surveys could be usefully employed is gauging reference points. Reference points in risk and uncertainty are likely to be context specific and exhibit substantial individual heterogeneity. Knowledge of reference points permits the researcher to specify gain and loss domains in exploration of asymmetric risk preferences and loss aversion. Whereas risk tolerance, loss aversion, and subjective beliefs can be difficult to econometrically identify in cross-sectional survey data, reference points may be more straightforward, and are critical in an assessment of prospect theory.

Discussion and Conclusions

Presuming that most empirical analysis of decision-making in the context of natural hazards will be survey based, future research should seek to employ panel methods. A targeted analysis of natural hazards and human dynamics employing multiple cross-sectional clusters tracked over time would provide

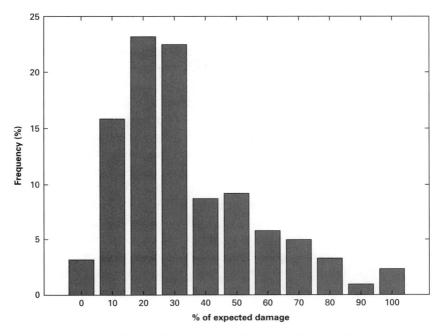

Figure 4.1. Expected damage from Category 3 hurricane (expressed as percentage of structure value).

variability in information sets that would facilitate econometric identification of multiple preference parameters that would likely be otherwise endogenous (due to common omitted variables). Moreover, the use of quasi-experimental designs could assist in identifying key probability or preference parameters. For example, Hallstrom and Smith (2005) and Bin and Landry (2013) use the occurrence of hurricanes to assess how beliefs about likelihood of damage evolve over time (though only indirectly through analysis of housing values). While survey-based panel data are expensive and difficult to collect, the potential gains in identification are very appealing.

We plan to explore other critical aspects of risk perception and preference in recently collected data. Information on flood and wind insurance and mitigation collected from the U.S. Gulf Coast (Petrolia, Landry, and Coble 2013; Petrolia et al. 2015) includes data on subjective expectation of loss. We measured this as the percentage of structure value that subjects expect to lose conditional on a Category 3 storm (wind speeds of 111–130 m.p.h.) directly striking their community at high tide. Figure 4.1 depicts the results in the form of a histogram. The mean response is 33.8%, and expected damage is increasing in higher risk flood zones and proximity to the coastline. With information on assessed building value or replacement cost we can thus derive an estimate of conditional expected loss.

Another survey recently conducted along the Gulf Coast (with Stephen Scyphers at Northeastern University) sought to measure similar expectations and likelihood of loss, but includes two storm levels and will permit a within comparison of responses due to changing storm magnitude and also a between comparison of sequencing effects. Some subjects received Category 2 and 3 storms in the survey, whereas other subjects received Category 3 and 4. This survey also included a choice experiment to assess preferences for rebuilding in the wake of a complete loss of structure. Subjects were asked to choose among rebuilding as is (with some out-of-pocket cost net of insurance settlement or disaster assistance), rebuilding better (lowering probability of future loss, but at higher cost), accepting a buyout from a nature group that would ensure the property is not built upon again, or accepting a buyout from a redeveloper. While these analyses should prove informative, the data probably will not permit a complete structural assessment of competing models of risky decision-making in the context of natural hazards (as in equation (1) or following the work of Tanaka, Camerer, and Nyugen). This, however, remains a primary goal or our research agenda.

References

Ahmadiani, M., & Landry, C. E. (2017). Economic value of multi-peril coastal hazard insurance. *SSRN Electronic Journal.* doi:10.2139/ssrn.2907033

Babcock, B. A. (2015). Using cumulative prospect theory to explain anomalous crop insurance coverage choice. *American Journal of Agricultural Economics, 97*(5), 1371–1384.

Barsky, R. B., Juster, T. F., Kimball, M. S., & Shapiro, M. D. (1997). Preference parameters and individual heterogeneity: An experimental approach in the health and retirement study. *Quarterly Journal of Economics, 112*(2), 537–579.

Bell, D. E. (1982). Regret in decision making under uncertainty. *Operations Research, 30*(5), 961–981.

Bell, D. E. (1985). Disappointment in decision making under uncertainty. *Operations Research, 33*(1), 1–27.

Bin, O., & Landry, C. E. (2013). Changes in implicit flood risk premiums: Empirical evidence from the housing market. *Journal of Environmental Economics and Management, 65*(3), 361–376.

Botzen, W. J. W., & Van Den Bergh, J. C. (2009). Bounded rationality, climate risks, and insurance: Is there a market for natural disasters? *Land Economics, 85*(2), 265–278.

Botzen, W. J. W., & Van Den Bergh, J. C. (2012). Monetary valuation of insurance against flood risk under climate change. *International Economic Review, 53*(3), 1005–1026.

Braun, M., & Muermann, A. (2004). The impact of regret on the demand for insurance. *Journal of Risk and Insurance, 71*(4), 737–767.

Cartwright, E. (2011). *Behavioral economics.* New York: Routledge.

Charness, G., Gneezy, U., & Imas, A. (2013). Experimental methods: Eliciting risk preferences. *Journal of Economic Behavior & Organization, 87,* 43–51.

Cohen, A., & Einav, L. (2007). Estimating risk preferences from deductible choice. *American Economic Review, 97*(3), 745–788.

Czajkowski, J., Kunreuther, H., & Michel-Kerjan, E. (2013). Quantifying riverine and storm-surge flood risk by single-family residence: Application to Texas. *Risk Analysis, 33*(12), 2092–2110.

Dohmen, T., Falk, A., Huffman, D., Sunde, U., Schupp, J., & Wagner, G. G. (2011). Individual risk attitudes: Measurement, determinants, and behavioral consequences. *Journal of the European Economic Association, 9*(3), 522–550.

Eckel, C. C., & Grossman, P. J. (2008). Forecasting risk attitudes: An experimental study using actual and forecast gamble choices. *Journal of Economic Behavior & Organization, 68*(1), 1–17.

Efron, B., & Tibshirani, R. (1986). Bootstrap methods for standard errors, confidence intervals, and other measures of statistical accuracy. *Statistical Science, 1,* 54–75.

Gilboa, I., Postlewaite, A. W., & Schmeidler, D. (2008). Probability and uncertainty in economic modeling. *Journal of Economic Perspectives, 22*(3), 173–188.

Hallstrom, D. G., & Smith, V. K. (2005). Market responses to hurricanes. *Journal of Environmental Economics and Management, 50*(3), 541–561.

Hampton, J. M., Moore, P. G., & Thomas, H. (1973). Subjective probability and its measurement. *Journal of the Royal Statistical Society. Series A (General), 136*(1), 21–42.

Harrison, G. W., Lau, M. I., & Rutström, E. E. (2007). Estimating risk attitudes in Denmark: A field experiment. *Scandinavian Journal of Economics, 109*(2), 341–368.

Holt, C. A., & Laury, S. K. (2002). Risk aversion and incentive effects. *American Economic Review, 92*(5), 1644–1655.

Kogan, N., & Wallach, M. A. (1964). *Risk taking: A study in cognition and personality.* Oxford: Holt, Rinehart & Winston.

Kriesel, W., & Landry, C. (2004). Participation in the National Flood Insurance Program: An empirical analysis for coastal properties. *Journal of Risk and Insurance, 71*(3), 405–420.

Krutilla, J. V. (1966). An economic approach to coping with flood damage. *Water Resources Research, 2*(2), 183–190.

Landry, C. E., & Jahan-Parvar, M. R. (2011). Flood insurance coverage in the coastal zone. *Journal of Risk and Insurance, 78*(2), 361–388.

Liu, E. M. (2013). Time to change what to sow: Risk preferences and technology adoption decisions of cotton farmers in China. *Review of Economics and Statistics, 95*(4), 1386–1403.

Loomes, G., & Sugden, R. (1982). Regret theory: An alternative theory of rational choice under uncertainty. *Economic Journal, 92*(368), 805–824.

Loomes, G., & Sugden, R. (1986). Disappointment and dynamic consistency in choice under uncertainty. *Review of Economic Studies, 53*(2), 271–282.

Martin, W. E., Martin, I. M., & Kent, B. (2009). The role of risk perceptions in the risk mitigation process: The case of wildfire in high risk communities. *Journal of Environmental Management, 91*(2), 489–498.

Menapace, L., Colson, G., & Raffaelli, R. (2013). Risk aversion, subjective beliefs, and farmer risk management strategies. *American Journal of Agricultural Economics, 95*(2), 384–389.

Menapace, L., Colson, G., & Raffaelli, R. (2015). Climate change beliefs and perceptions of agricultural risks: An application of the exchangeability method. *Global Environmental Change, 35*, 70–81.

Menapace, L., Colson, G., & Raffaelli, R. (2016). A comparison of hypothetical risk attitude elicitation instruments for explaining farmer crop insurance purchases. *European Review of Agricultural Economics, 43*(1), 113–135.

Meyer, R. J., Baker, J., Broad, K., Czajkowski, J., & Orlove, B. (2014). The dynamics of hurricane risk perception: Real-time evidence from the 2012 Atlantic hurricane season. *Bulletin of the American Meteorological Society, 95*(9), 1389–1404.

Naoi, M., Seko, M., & Sumita, K. (2010). Community rating, cross subsidies and underinsurance: Why so many households in Japan do not purchase earthquake insurance. *Journal of Real Estate Finance and Economics, 40*(4), 544–561.

Norris, P. E., & Kramer, R. A. (1990). The elicitation of subjective probabilities with applications in agricultural economics. *Review of Marketing and Agricultural Economics, 58*(2–3), 127–147.

Outreville, J. F. (2014). Risk aversion, risk behavior, and demand for insurance: A survey. *Journal of Insurance Issues, 37*(2), 158–186.

Petrolia, D. R., Hwang, J., Landry, C. E., & Coble, K. H. (2015). Wind insurance and mitigation in the coastal zone. *Land Economics, 91*(2), 272–295.

Petrolia, D. R., Landry, C. E., & Coble, K. H. (2013). Risk preferences, risk perceptions, and flood insurance. *Land Economics, 89*(2), 227–245.

Quiggin, J. (1982). A theory of anticipated utility. *Journal of Economic Behavior & Organization, 3*(4), 323–343.

Quiggin, J. (1994). Regret theory with general choice sets. *Journal of Risk and Uncertainty, 8*(2), 153–165.

Schnitkey, G. D., Sherrick, B. J., & Irwin, S. H. (2003). Evaluation of risk reductions associated with multi-peril crop insurance products. *Agricultural Finance Review, 63*(1), 1–21.

Shaik, S., Coble, K. H., Knight, T. O., Baquet, A. E., & Patrick, G. F. (2008). Crop revenue and yield insurance demand: A subjective probability approach. *Journal of Agricultural and Applied Economics, 40*(3), 757–766.

Smith, J., & Mandac, A. M. (1995). Subjective versus objective yield distributions as measure of production risk. *American Journal of Agricultural Economics, 77*(1), 152–161.

Smith, V. H., & Baquet, A. E. (1996). The demand for multiple peril crop insurance: Evidence from Montana wheat farms. *American Journal of Agricultural Economics, 78*(1), 189–201.

Sugden, R. (1993). An axiomatic foundation for regret theory. *Journal of Economic Theory, 60*(1), 159–180.

Talberth, J., Berrens, R. P., McKee, M., & Jones, M. (2006). Averting and insurance decisions in the wildland–urban interface: Implications of survey and experimental data for wildfire risk reduction policy. *Contemporary Economic Policy, 24*(2), 203–223.

Tanaka, T., Camerer, C. F., & Nguyen, Q. (2010). Risk and time preferences: Linking experimental and household survey data from Vietnam. *American Economic Review, 100*(1), 557–571.

Teisl, M. F., & Roe, B. E. (2010). Consumer willingness-to-pay to reduce the probability of retail foodborne pathogen contamination. *Food Policy, 35*(6), 521–530.

Tversky, A., & Kahneman, D. (1992). Advances in prospect theory: Cumulative representation of uncertainty. *Journal of Risk and Uncertainty, 5*(4), 297–323.

CHAPTER 5

Mixing Rationality and Irrationality in Insurance Demand and Supply

Mark Pauly

Introduction

Insurance deals with circumstances people do not like to think about. Death, financial loss, illness, and natural catastrophes must be put out of mind if a person is to get out of bed in the morning and get on with their life. You get a letter from the water company telling you that if the line from your house to the main at the street fails you will be responsible for the cost of digging it up and replacing it, but for $50 the company will do it—but in years of home ownership you have never had such a failure and you have no idea how likely it is to happen. You are choosing between a health plan with a $5,000 deductible and another that pays 60% starting at $3,500 but requires you to cover the difference up to a bill of $10,000—and costs $100 a month more. It is far from obvious what choice you should make. No surprise then that people often make mistakes (to be discussed at length further) in how they deal with protecting themselves against the consequences of adverse financial events. Some have gone so far as to suggest that insurance purchasing in general is irrational (Rabin 2000; Rabin and Thaler 2001)—and there are stories under which this is true in some respects—but the most plausible conclusion is that things are mixed with behavior of both types, rational and irrational, being exhibited (Kunreuther, Pauly, and McMorrow 2013).

In this chapter I want to discuss what we know (or at least speculate to be true) about the mix of such behaviors in health insurance purchasing in the

United States. By "rationality," I will mean behavior consistent with expected utility maximization, given insurance prices and the circumstances of the buyer and the health risks being faced. There are other models of behavior under risk and, as far as I know, no other model has been universally anointed as rational. So, I define any behavior other than expected utility maximization as irrational. Thus, in this chapter I will take the narrow perspective of a true believer in economics as a description both of how individuals do and should behave; that is limiting, because there is only one way to be rational but many ways to be irrational, all of which have their adherents, I will reconsider this single-minded view in the conclusion.

Of course, the American health insurance market has never been unregulated or unfettered. Beginning with its origin with Blue Cross hospital insurance plans chartered under special state legislation in the 1930s, there has always been a mix of regulations and subsidies that affect what is bought. Some of this regulation is intended (and may actually work) to correct irrationality, but some of it may foster inefficient if not irrational behavior. So we will have to take that into account and may not always be able to separate out the causes of either irrational or inefficient behavior. The list of what we do not know is much larger than the list of what we know, but laying out both may be of value.

Nor have scholars agreed that behavior was rational. Over decades the primary focus by far has been on those who are uninsured (Somers and Somers 1967), but the primary explanation by far has not been irrationality but lack of "affordability" (Bundorf and Pauly 2006; Gruber 2008). Status quo bias and other faults have sometimes been mentioned (Liebman and Zeckhauser 2008), but the drive to persuade taxpayers to support and pay has been the main thrust to offset unaffordability. This was the focus of Medicare because, when it was passed in 1965, being old was virtually synonymous with being poor and high risk. Medicaid was passed at the same time to cover the "deserving" poor (mothers, those with disabilities), but it was only with the passage of the Affordable Care Act (ACA) in 2010 that coverage for able-bodied poor adults was included, and some states have resisted.

In this sense "irrationality" (however defined) has been less central to the debate about reforms of this kind of insurance than of other kinds. But it has been important, though it has also been inevitably tangled with the debate over affordability. In this chapter I will try to pull out the discussion of irrationality per se. I will conclude that it is present, and that after health reform it may become more salient, but that there are political limits in a democracy to the extent to which government can force citizens to be "rational" by its technical definition rather than based on their own preferences.

The Margins of Behavior

We first note that there are several different dimensions of health insurance market behavior that are of interest. The most obvious one is at the level of the person: some buyers may be behaving rationally while others are not. Often analyses make much of finding that there appears to be a nontrivial number of buyers in the latter category, while ignoring the number in the former, even if it is larger. For example, if we think that the 18% of the population that was uninsured at one point in time was irrational, we might need to acknowledge that 82% were rational. Of course, market equilibrium can be affected and disrupted even if only some buyers behave in a particular way, because their behavior may affect both prices and products offered. However, policy judgments depend crucially on what fraction of the population does what. In a country as large as the United States one can always find some irrationality; the question is whether it rises to the level of public concern, which begs the further question of how high the level needs to be before there is public concern. Perhaps there is some level at which taxpayers will decide that diminishing returns have set in and will permit a small fraction of the population to remain uninsured.

Another margin is whether the consumer buys insurance at all when there exists an offer in the market for a policy at a premium at which the consumer would have higher expected utility than remaining uninsured. The wholly uninsured have been a major focus in U.S. public policy, culminating in the passage of the Affordable Care Act which attempts to use a combination of subsidies and penalties to induce all people to purchase coverage that meets certain minimum standards. The issue here is that, in the face of the availability of charity care and insurance that is, correctly or incorrectly, regarded as overpriced by low risks, some may rationally choose to remain uninsured.

Finally, a third margin asks whether, given that some coverage is purchased, the policy the buyer chooses is the one (among policy-premium combinations available) that maximizes expected utility. Here there is enormous scope for variation and redesign, and the actual variety of plan options is dizzying. It would not be surprising if some buyers get it wrong.

Behavior Away from the Known Optimum

Judging empirically that people make insurance choices that maximize their expected utility is impossibly demanding of data. In addition to knowing the premiums they face, one needs to know the risks they face and, most challengingly, their degree of risk aversion. Rather than try to score perfection, most analyses do one of two things: (1) look for patterns of behavior inconsistent with expected utility maximization regardless of these empirical value, or (2) imagine some plausible values of risk and risk aversion and then judge whether behavior is consistent with such plausible values. In both cases, we seek not to show that things are perfect but that they are or are not "reasonably close" (whatever that may mean) to rational behavior, allowing for small deviations with small consequences.

Finally, there is another approach which tries to affirm that at least some behavior is rational. Rather than looking for subtle instances of irrationality, it looks for evidence that basic economic postulates about consumer behavior are satisfied. At the most extreme, can we rule out the hypothesis that insurance purchases are random? Even if people buy the wrong coverage, do they respond to higher premiums by buying less of it? Do people change behavior when nothing changes, or persist in behavior when important things (like premiums and risks) change? We will look at some examples of this.

The Broad Issues in Health Insurance

With the passage of the Affordable Care Act, there have been changes in the numbers of people with insurance and the kind of insurance they have. That Act took the form of subsidizing insurance in a means tested fashion, and minimum coverage also declined as income rose. There is a mandate requiring coverage for all regardless of income, government sponsored "exchanges" where consumers can buy individual coverage, and heavy regulation of coverage and premium rating in all markets.

We will initially concentrate on the period before the ACA's mix of sub-sidies and regulation affected the market to look for insights into individual purchasing behavior—since to some extent the ACA had a goal of correct-ing "irrationalities"—and then examine the evidence we have to date on its effects.

Let us begin with the headcount of the number and proportion of the pop-ulation who had no insurance, public or private. While data are not very reliable, it appears that about half of the population lacked health insurance (all private) just before World War II, but that proportion fell dramatically during and after the war to a low point of about 12–14% of the population in the late 1970s. In addition to the government financed Medicare program that covered nearly all elderly and the federal-state Medicaid program that covered about half of poor people, there was a substantial expansion in employment-based coverage stimulated by favorable tax treatment for com-pensation received in this fashion (relative to taxable money wages). From that low point, the percentage uninsured grew slowly to hit a maximum of about 18% (or more than 50 million people) in the recession, but implemen-tation of the ACA along with recovery from the recession has reduced the fraction by about a third, to about 10% of the population, a twenty-first century low though much different from the Congressional Budget Office and other projections of a 60% reduction.

How can this fluctuation be explained, and how much of it was due to rational responses to changed incentives (larger subsidies, high incomes, and higher threat of large medical bills) and how much to irrationality in the sense of undervaluing insurance on the market relative to what would be chosen under an expected utility (EU) benchmark? We do not have a definitive de-composition; my judgment is that irrationality played a relatively minor role in either the growth or the shrinkage of the uninsured population. Even the individual mandate, initially a part of the ACA and now repealed, seems to have made little difference.

Here is some of the circumstantial evidence. The best case for irrational-ity is with the numbers of people who failed to obtain heavily subsidized coverage. The Medicare population pays a modest premium for part of the coverage but the subsidy rate is 90%; only about 2% of those eligible turn it down. In group insurance, the average explicit employee contribution is about 25% (though there is some variation), and only about 4–6% of eligible work-ers take no coverage from any source. The highest rejection rate is among Medicaid beneficiaries, where about a quarter of those eligible do not enroll, deterred by bureaucratic complexity and by the fact that they can obtain after-the-fact coverage should they use covered medical services. The largest proportion of uninsured is among those not eligible for either group or government cover, where (depending on income) a third to a half remain uninsured rather than purchase unsubsidized individual coverage.

For the most part, remaining uninsured among this group appeared rational. The administrative loading on individual insurance was and still is relatively high so it is not sufficiently valuable to modestly risk-averse people. The uninsured have available to them bad debt and charity care, and are frugal in their level of spending, so their financial risk is amazingly small relative to the premiums for individual insurance without subsidies (Pauly, Leive, and Harrington 2015). Additionally, there may be a modest amount of adverse selection especially in states which limited risk rating (more on adverse selection and rationality later). So, at most, a relatively tiny fraction of people failed to take actuarially favorable insurance (in group and Medicaid coverage); while conventional wisdom has it that young men irrationally think themselves immortal and lack coverage, there were (and still are) plenty of good reasons to turn down overpriced coverage if you are a healthy young man.

The next set of issues concerns the nature of coverage. We first describe the features of rational behavior. One reason not to buy coverage for a medical expense for a risk-averse person maximizing expected utility is that the administrative expense or "loading" attached to that coverage is so large as to offset the risk premium the person attached to reducing risk. This is the standard explanation for deductibles: processing claims that are small relative to wealth adds more cost than the value of the threat to wealth. It is also a reason to exempt from coverage services purchased with certainty, like annual physicals and other forms of preventive care: if they are sure to be bought and used by virtually all beneficiaries, they add more to premiums than they would cost out of pocket. Some preventive services, however, may suffer from inefficiency (not irrationality) if they avoid future risky medical expenses and those expenses are already covered. Then the incremental premium for preventive care should reflect such cost offsets—though this is really only needed if the use of the service responds to the presence of coverage (Pauly and Held 1990).

The same behavioral phenomenon points in a different direction for rational coverage of services that respond to both the uncertain incidence of illness and the size of cost sharing. With indemnity coverage impractical, there can be moral hazard. The rule of thumb here is that, other things equal, cost sharing should be higher the more responsive the service is to cost sharing, that is, the more responsive is demand.

If consumers can become fully informed about the marginal benefit from various rates of use of medical care, the patterns of deductibles and coinsurance that would emerge in competitive markets would usually be second-best optimal. Of course, if there are some supply-side tools that can discourage physicians from furnishing care of low benefit relative to its cost, coverage can be more generous, but in general the resulting pattern would be optimal.

Before we discuss reasons why this optimistic forecast may not always make sense, it is useful to note that the broad pattern of private insurance coverage in the United States even before regulation is consistent with rational consumers buying in rational markets. The most heavily insured kind of care was inpatient care, which generally represents losses large relative to wealth and use unresponsive to cost sharing. Physician services are intermediate, and their cost-sharing levels hover around 15%. Finally, prescription drugs and dental care appear to have lower average losses (though there are exceptions), more discretion as to use, and so display a cost-sharing percentage of about 30%. The overall pattern is not irrational.

The only exception is nursing home care, but the crowding out by Medicaid and the intrinsic low value of nursing home insurance if the marginal utility of income is lower for frail people are sufficient to explain this behavior as broadly rational. That is, most people should expect that if they have a long stay in a nursing home their private income and wealth will be consumed and then Medicaid will pay. It would not be rational to buy insurance privately if it only replaced what Medicaid might eventually spend, unless one wanted access to nursing homes with higher amenities, or felt stigma on being on Medicaid (which itself is probably not counted as rational).

However, within this overall reasonable pattern researchers have identified anomalies. The most discussed have been services of high marginal benefit that seem nevertheless underused under conventional levels of cost sharing (Choudhry et al. 2011). "Underuse" here means both high clinical value services relative to their cost and low clinical value services with even lower cost, but the advocates for value-based cost sharing have strongly emphasized the first strategy (Chernew, Rosen, and Fendrick 2007). There is one easy case here which was emphasized in the early discussion of value-based cost sharing. If for some reason the sequelae of a preventive treatment were generously covered and if changes in the use of that preventive service were both responsive to cost sharing and generated cost offsets, coverage of the preventive service should be reduced by the amount of the cost offset, potentially to zero. Such "money saving" examples represent flaws in insurance design, not irrational behavior by patients. But what if patients systematically underestimate—or overestimate—the marginal benefit from some service? The poster child for the former is the use of statins after a heart attack. It is very difficult to tell what causes the underuse—is it present-period bias with hyperbolic discounting and all that, or is it that physicians have put too little effort into convincing patients of the value of the treatment?

In either case, the result is "ex post" nonoptimal and irrational. Moreover, rather than spend real resources on convincing patients of value, it may be cheaper to lower cost sharing (while raising the premium) to get them to do what they should.

This literature gives much more emphasis to reducing patient cost sharing for undervalued services than to increasing it for overvalued services, though Viagra and other lifestyle products are often cited as candidates for increases, along with more costly treatments with almost no evidence for additional value but definitely higher cost, like robotic surgery for prostate cancer.

There is research to suggest other patterns of insurance purchasing which are irrational, generally involving choosing a policy from a menu of policies which, given the patient's risk (e.g., the drugs they take), is dominated by another plan in the set (Abaluck and Gruber 2011). This seems especially true of seniors' choice of Medicare drug coverage, though it may also apply to Medigap. There is evidence that choices improve over time, and regulation ensures that none of the choices will leave patients with serious disincentives for use of effective care—but several hundred dollars could be saved. We will discuss challenges in coming up with remedies in these cases later.

Finally, some of the literature links the broad concept of value to cost effectiveness measures, but does not describe how cost effectiveness and cost sharing should rationally be related. Presumably all services whose effectiveness relative to their cost is too small to meet benchmark standards for good value should not be covered at all. Partial coverage instead is rationalized by heterogeneity in the benefits from a service that cannot be directly observed by the insurer, so instead cost sharing discourages low value use—even if the perception of value is biased (Pauly 2015).

To sum up, there is some suggestion that consumers may irrationally discount the future and thus undervalue preventive care. A tiny minority of citizens just do not get the idea that they need health insurance. That is about it. For overall coverage, there is not massive evidence that most people fail to buy care or that they choose broad patterns that put generous coverage in places where the EU model says you should not.

Our judgment is that there is a modest amount of systematic irrationality connected with insurance design, but confusion over the facts on clinical effectiveness may be a much stronger motive for inefficient behavior. There is considerable scope for insurance redesign, and finally considerable innovation both on policy design (increasing coverage for care that people underconsume) and new organizations like accountable care organizations which are supposed to reorganize the supply side (though there is as yet no good evidence that they do).

The last broad category of potential irrationality concerns issues of market dynamics and consistency of various subgroups in terms of the overall policy design features they do or do not choose. One example that offers evidence for rationality (though not efficiency) is adverse selection. The ACA regulated premiums by prohibiting or limiting the extent to which premiums could vary with risk known to insurers and patients, like age and the presence of chronic conditions. The ACA exchanges have operated in fear that this would cause healthy people to stay away from the coverage they offer. That will only happen if potential buyers correctly understand their loss probabilities and conclude that, because insurance for them is overpriced relative to its benefits, buying it will lower their expected utility. This is rational if antisocial behavior. The evidence is not yet in; it does not appear that there has been enough adverse selection to trigger a death spiral (which is limited in any case by large subsidies to low-income low risks), but some insurers have run into problems with the removal of subsidies for high risks. Hence there is enough rationality to cause trouble. Adverse selection, undesirable as it is, is a tribute to rational buyer behavior.

Less explainable is the behavior of nontrivial numbers of low-income people choosing bronze plans in the ACA exchanges. Bronze plans have lower premiums but less generous coverage than silver plans. But for people with incomes below 250% of the poverty line, there are additional generous "cost-sharing" subsidies to silver plans only—meaning that the incremental benefits from paying a little more for a silver plan are much greater than the incremental premium. And indeed most people in this income range gravitate toward silver plans. But not all. Analysis speculates that these potential buyers who think little of the value of insurance but do want to avoid the mandate penalty view buying a bronze plan as a cheaper way of "punching your ticket"—to spend as little as possible and still be in compliance with the law.

Another phenomenon is at the other end of the income distribution—the uninsured with incomes so high they are not eligible for subsidies. Amazingly, about 30% of those who would need to use the individual market have incomes this high, and yet remain uninsured. Those with similar incomes who do buy individual insurance rarely use exchanges; the great bulk of them buy coverage privately through brokers or directly from individual insurers not offering on the exchange. Some of these policies are "grandfathered" in and need not meet all the exchange rules, but that is a shrinking minority. The data are not very precise but it appears that this set of "non-poor uninsured" had a slightly smaller proportional reduction from the ACA than did the uninsured who are subsidized. The most obvious conclusion is that the mandate penalty is insufficient to motivate coverage and, indeed, even though the penalty is rising it is still usually only a fraction of the premium for the cheapest eligible plan. Are these people irrational (or at least as irrational as they were when they remained uninsured before the ACA)? One is tempted to say yes, but the expected out-of-pocket payment on average for this group is low, both because of low use of care and bad debt reductions, so they may simply be the end of the distribution of people willing to take a chance that they will not have sizable medical bills.

What to Do?

The overall pattern for health insurance purchasing is not wildly inconsistent with rational behavior, but there are enough examples of irrationality to give support to behavioral theories and to raise policy concerns about the outcomes. The pattern of directed subsidies and regulations in the ACA so far seems much more directed at redistribution to help people afford coverage or to cushion the blow of complying with the mandate than with explicit correction of irrationalities in purchasing behavior. However, the movement toward value-based insurance points much more in that direction and is

obtaining growing congressional support. However, congressional (or political) support cuts both ways. The bias among members of Congress (and
some public health advocates) that preventive care has to be a good thing,
despite fairly weak evidence, is also baked into the law in a number of places.

Indeed, the bias toward legislating coverage of preventive care even when
it is not cost effective is another kind of irrationality, but this time it is one
that affects political choice, not consumer choice. For example, the ACA
requires insurance to cover in full all recommendations for vaccines from
a government-appointed physician-dominated advisory board, the Advisory
Committee on Immunization Practices, even though that board has no expertise in economics or insurance design and has recommended vaccines that
are not cost effective by the usual standards (Pauly, Sloan, and Sullivan 2014).
Likewise, the law requires Medicare to cover physical checkups even though
the evidence suggests that these are at best a waste of time and money. The
clear implication is that an appeal to "the government" to correct consumer
irrationalities may not always itself be rational.

Whatever the reasons why policymakers think consumers should rationally be incentivized toward particular medical services by lower cost sharing, there is a potential conflict in prospect: lowering cost sharing raises
premiums. Consumers get that money back in benefits, but the essential feature of value-based cost sharing is that consumers do not think the benefits
are worth the extra money (or they would already have bought them). While
there are ways to nudge rather than compel, and while offsetting higher premiums with higher subsidies will work if the government has the money,
it does not seem that there will be clear sailing ahead (Pauly 2014). Politics
in the short run are so unpredictable, and everything about the ACA is so
political, that technical issues of irrationality—whether it is present and whether
and how it might be corrected—will obscure this debate for a while. At
some point, however, there will need to be more analysis in order to generate a
resolution.

Finally, there has been some recent research on the irrational pattern of
posted prices for medical services, where list prices can vary by four or five
times across different hospitals for the same service in the same town. A number of groups have reacted to this observation by advocating legislation designed to improve price transparency so that consumers can choose to move
to lower cost sellers from high cost sellers. While such more rational shop-
ping behavior by consumers might help to lower spending, there is skepticism as to both the magnitude of the reduction and whether consumers will

react to price differences once they know about them. On the first point, it is only a small sliver of total medical spending that consumers pay out of pocket, even for the one-third with high deductible health plans (Pauly and Burns 2015). Most spending is fully covered by insurance, and even spending in a deductible where the consumer knows that total spending will cover the deductible (so the marginal out-of-pocket payment is zero) should not motivate search.

Recent research by Brot-Goldberg, Chandra, Handel, and Kolstad (2017) finds little evidence that a population of workers compelled to take high deductible coverage gravitated toward lower priced sellers. Buyers may be unfamiliar with price searching, they may judge quality by price, or their incentive to search may be attenuated by the tax subsidy to the health savings account that covers the deductible. Even more puzzling, there appears to be no rational explanation for why sellers charge the different prices. "Greed" is usually offered as the explanation for the high-priced sellers, but why are there low-priced sellers apparently resistant to greed? And even more puzzlingly, when they charge low prices why do they fail to publicize and advertise those low prices to attract more customers? The easiest short-run explanation is that the current pattern of list prices is a confused artifact from recent times in which almost no customers paid list prices, but that it provides no guidance as to what will happen next and what pattern of prices would emerge if transparency were taken seriously. More recently, narrow network plans have been driving consumers to low-priced sellers where the insurer negotiated the low price, leaving little scope to buyer search behavior, rational or otherwise.

The Individual Mandate

One of the alleged key pieces of the ACA, and certainly key in the Supreme Court case that found the program constitutional, is the individual mandate—a tax or penalty on those who fail to obtain a qualified health insurance policy, whether from the exchange, the employer, or Medicaid. Many believe that the mandate that low risks buy coverage through the exchange is key to preventing a death spiral in the exchange because otherwise the average premium will rise if higher risks participate. This is probably incorrect, because virtually all exchange participants receive substantial subsidies, so even low risks are not paying premiums into the exchange that are more than their expected benefits, which is what is needed to cross-subsidize high risks and prevent adverse selection. Instead, the premium and cost-sharing subsidies pick up almost all of the cost regardless of the average premium. This means that even if, by chance, low risks stopped joining exchanges, the average premium would rise but subsidies per person would rise to keep it affordable for the remaining participants; hence they would not drop out to start a death spiral (in fact, it would cost the government less in total if the low-risk dropouts did not receive subsidies).

Whatever the case for adverse selection—which, though inefficient, is highly rational behavior—the individual mandate does affect those who might irrationally choose to be uninsured. Theoretical estimates suggest that such schemes should make a difference in behavior (Gruber 2008). How well does the ACA version function? On the surface, the penalty for not obtaining insurance in 2016 seems somewhat formidable, the larger of $695 per adult or 2.5% of adjusted family income. The latter penalty, for example, would amount to $2,500 for a household with income in excess of $100,000, though it does not apply to undocumented immigrants. Within the set of those at risk for the fine, only 7.5 million people actually paid the fine; about twice as many were judged eligible for exemption from the obligation to pay based on some kind of hardship—being homeless, changing jobs, uninsured property loss, or, in the final version, whatever the individual can document as a hardship. Moreover, the fine itself usually is only a small fraction of the premium for coverage—the $2,500 fine mentioned above would compare with a family premium in excess of $10,000. Finally, the logic of the penalty is somewhat questionable—why is the fine larger for higher income families who presumably have less need to be stimulated to buy a policy they can afford.

The answer, of course, is that the design was in part political, one that attempted to be nonconfiscatory and not drive people into bankruptcy. The tradeoff appears to have had limited impact on insurance purchasing, compared to other schemes that proposed fines at or close to the premium for a qualified plan. Therefore the failure to buy insurance is thought to be irrational, but its correction is politically weak. Perhaps not surprisingly in a democracy, politicians have been unwilling to be heavy-handed in overriding such decisions. The recent elimination of the mandate by the Trump administration is consistent with this political motivation. They presumably judged that citizens in general are willing to accept an uninsured percentage in the 8–9% range as "approximate universal coverage." The alternative solution, "single-payer" schemes which make insurance free but higher taxes compulsory, may end up being a different choice, though the massive economic distortion (according to most economists) from increasing taxes by $1.6 trillion to cover the half of medical spending now paid privately may deter this approach.

Conclusion

There are certainly cases where health insurance purchasing and design do not fit the conventional EU maximizing economic model of choice under uncertainty. Nevertheless, while there is no precise way to quantify such matters, it is my impression that deviations from that model are less common in health insurance than in many other insurance markets. In part that is because low-probability high-consequence events are less common in health insurance, and losses are rarely correlated across exposures (except for epidemics), so consumers in a rough-and-ready way have figured out what is most sensible to cover well and where to find the lowest cost way of financing insurance—for example, by taking advantage of the tax subsidy for employment-based insurance. There is still a tendency to undervalue catastrophic coverage (largely corrected by the ACA) and confusion in picking out the best policy for one's own circumstances from a set of fairly similar policies. Errors at worst cost people money, not access to lifesaving care. There is still a serious problem in generating supply-side markets for medical care that are rationally organized and within which consumers can shop efficiently—the combination of moral hazard and noncompetitive traditions in pricing and bargaining hang over this market. And the most serious question of all—how to ration lifesaving but very expensive new technology is a topic no one will confront except with the irrational assertion that all health is priceless.

Particularly with some of the improvements from the ACA, I think this market now is in less need of guidance from (often confused) government or from behavioral economics as applied to insurance than many other insurance markets. For once, threats to health may be pushed aside by floods, earthquakes, and tornadoes as the highest priority objects of insurance coverage. A strong shift in the political winds to the left could bring in single payer coverage, but I suspect we will make do with the ACA framework for decades to come. Not that there will not be many opportunities for hand-wringing over both irrationality and inefficiency, but that there will be no better solution to doing the best we can.

References

Abaluck, J., & Gruber, J. (2011). Choice inconsistencies among the elderly: Evidence from plan choice in the Medicare Part D program. *American Economic Review, 101*(4), 1180–1210.

Brot-Goldberg, J. S., Chandra, A., Handel, B. R., & Kolstad, J. T. (2017). What does a deductible do? The impact of cost sharing on health care prices, quantities, and spending dynamics. *Quarterly Journal of Economics, 132*(3), 1261–1318.

Bundorf, M. K., & Pauly, M. V. (2006). Is health insurance affordable for the uninsured? *Journal of Health Economics, 25*(4), 650–673.

Chernew, M. E., Rosen, A. B., & Fendrick, A. M. (2007). Value-based insurance design. *Health Affairs, 26*(2), w195–w203.

Choudhry, N. K., Avorn, J., Glynn, R. J., Antman, E. M., Schneeweiss, S., Toscano, M., . . . & Levin, R. (2011). Full coverage for preventive medications after myocardial infarction. *New England Journal of Medicine, 365*(22), 2088–2097.

Gruber, J. (2008). Covering the uninsured in the United States. *Journal of Economic Literature, 46*(3), 571–606.

Kunreuther, H. C., Pauly, M. V., & McMorrow, S. (2013). *Insurance and behavioral economics: Improving decisions in the most misunderstood industry.* Cambridge: Cambridge University Press.

Liebman, J., & Zeckhauser, R. (2008). *Simple humans, complex insurance, subtle subsidies* (No. w14330). Cambridge, MA: National Bureau of Economic Research.

Pauly, M. V. (2014). Demand for insurance that nudges demand. In A. J. Culyer (Gen. Ed.), *Encyclopedia of health economics* (pp. 167–174). Amsterdam: Elsevier Science.

Pauly, M. (2015). Cost-effectiveness analysis and insurance coverage: Solving a puzzle. *Health Economics, 24*(5), 506–515.

Pauly, M. V., & Burns, L. R. (2015). *When is medical care price transparency a good thing (and when isn't it)?* Wharton School of the University of Pennsylvania.

Pauly, M. V., & Held, P. J. (1990). Benign moral hazard and the cost-effectiveness analysis of insurance coverage. *Journal of Health Economics, 9*(4), 447–461.

Pauly, M., Leive, A., & Harrington, S. (2015). *The price of responsibility: The impact of health reform on non-poor uninsureds* (No. w21565). Cambridge, MA: National Bureau of Economic Research.

Pauly, M. V., Sloan, F. A., & Sullivan, S. D. (2014). An economic framework for preventive care advice. *Health Affairs, 33*(11), 2034–2040.

Rabin, M. (2000). Diminishing marginal utility of wealth cannot explain risk aversion. In D. Kahneman & A. Tversky (Eds.), *Choices, values, and frames* (pp. 202–208). Cambridge: Cambridge University Press.

Rabin, M., & Thaler, R. H. (2001). Anomalies: Risk aversion. *Journal of Economic Perspectives, 15*(1), 219–232.

Somers, H. M., & Somers, A. R. (1967). *Medicare and the hospitals: Issues and prospects.* Washington, DC: Brookings Institution.

CHAPTER 6

The Disaster Cycle

What We Do Not Learn from Experience

Robert J. Meyer

Introduction

The city of Miyako lies on the northeast coast of Japan, about a four-hour train ride on the Shinkansen from Tokyo. It is a small city (the 2014 population was slightly more than 56,000) that for many years was primarily known as a fishing center and jumping-off spot for visiting some of Japan's most spectacular points of natural beauty, such as the unique rock formations of Jodogahama beach. On March 11, 2011, however, Miyako became known for something far more tragic. At 2:46 p.m. the city was shaken by one of the strongest seismic events ever recorded, the great Tohoku earthquake. The quake was centered in the Pacific about 200 miles southeast of Miyako, and registered 9.0 on the Richter Scale—63 times stronger than the earthquake that destroyed San Francisco in 1906.

At first, the city seemed to withstand the blow. Japan sees numerous earthquakes, and as a result has some of the world's most stringent building codes. While there was some initial damage, this was precisely the kind of event the city was designed to survive. However, it was not built to survive what followed. Shortly after 3 p.m. a tremendous Tsunami—later estimated to be almost 130 feet high—came funneling up Miyako's bay, destroying everything in its path. When the water subsided, over 4,000 structures lay in ruin, along with the virtual entirety of the city's 960-boat fishing fleet.

Most tragically, while many were able seek safety as the tsunami rolled in, 420 residents lost their lives.

In the days that followed, Miyako was descended on by news reporters anxious to document the destruction. While much could be seen from the ground, better perspectives could be achieved from the hills just above the city. It was in the course of walking the wooded trails above the city that reporters came upon an intriguing site: a series of widely spaced 6-foot monuments, each inscribed in old kanji. What drew them to the monuments was not their presence, but rather the irony of the message they carried: "High dwellings are the peace and harmony of our descendants. Remember the calamity of the great tsunamis. Do not build any homes below this point." The monuments, it turned out, were erected shortly after an earthquake and tsunami of similar magnitude destroyed the city in 1933, an event that killed some 22,000. At the time, nothing could be done to bring back those who had lost their lives, but the hope was that a warning could be given to those who would resettle in the area. Surely no one would forget such a horrific event. Surely, future residents would learn from past mistakes. But in time, of course, people did forget. As the years passed and other tragedies took the greater share of minds, the same port valley was gradually settled, only to have the tragic cycle repeat a century later.

In this chapter, I will explore the reasons behind one of the most challenging barriers that risk manager's face when trying to persuade people and organizations to undertake protective action: Why, in the immediate wake of a disaster, we see a sudden surge of concern for the risk, only to watch it quickly fade with the passage of time. Why disasters, it seems, are invariably destined to repeat themselves.

The Dark Side of Trial-and-Error Learning

I first began thinking about why disaster cycles occur about a decade ago while writing an essay on the failings of preparedness in advance of Hurricane Katrina (Meyer 2006). Katrina, it seemed, was a poster child for poor learning. Many of the thousands of structures that were destroyed along coastal Mississippi during the storm were reconstructions of the same buildings that had been wiped out in the same location by Hurricane Camille 36 years earlier. Likewise, the city of New Orleans seemed to learn little from its near-miss with Hurricane Ivan just the year before—an event that exposed numerous flaws in its ability to house tens of thousands who lacked the ability to comply with evacuation orders. To me, these events were perplexing; how could people and communities fail to learn when the stakes are life or death?

One could imagine, of course, a range of explanations. One, for example, might be that disaster cycles are more an illusion than real; perhaps people and communities *do* learn after losses, but learning just takes time. Each disaster exposes something new about how better to prepare, and it just takes several waves of losses to finally get it right. No one would suggest that significant advances have not been made in our ability to protect against natural hazards over the years. The problem with this, however, is that there are just too many counterexamples for this to be the complete story. Losses from natural disasters worldwide have increased—not decreased—over the years as more and more property has been put at risk, and it is easy to conjure examples of apparent overt forgetting, such as repeating rebuilding in locations prone to recurrent flooding (Kunreuther, Meyer, and Michel-Kerjan 2012).

To reconcile this, I suggest that the culprit at least partially lies in the fundamental psychology of how we learn. The argument goes like this. One of the most remarkable of all human skills is our ability to learn to perform complex tasks through simple trial and error. Think of learning to play tennis. When we miss a serve we instinctively try to recall the body movement that preceded the error and make a mental note to try something different next time. If the next serve is good we again recall what we just did and try to repeat it. In time, this primitive instinctive cycle of repeating actions that yield good outcomes while avoiding those that do not allows skills to build—while perhaps not enough to allow us to turn pro, at least enough to play a credible game. It is how we first learn to walk, develop tastes in foods and music, and, indeed, acquire most of the preferences and habits that govern day-to-day life.

But as beneficial as trial-and-error may be as a mechanism for learning in most aspects of our lives, it also has a dark side—when applied to learning about the value of protection, one can easily see how it can lead to behaviors that are not simply undesirable, but ultimately deadly. The reason is that in these contexts reward structures become flipped, such that it is the actions that are the best for us in the long run that go unrewarded, while those that are bad for us in the long run get reinforced. It is this reversal that explains, for example, why many of us are prone to put on weight, why some become addicted to drugs and alcohol, and why it is hard to reverse these habits once they become entrenched. Abstinence carries no immediate rewards, while indulgence carries many. And, of most relevance here, this provides a natural explanation for why we sometimes make poor protective choices when faced with known risks, choosing courses of action that lead us into, rather than away from, harm's way. Not unlike the hapless dieter who cannot avoid desserts, the task of taking protective action requires one to repeatedly invest in actions whose benefits are rarely immediately seen, but whose costs always are.

To illustrate, consider the case of decisions to put up storm shutters in advance of hurricanes. For the last several years our research group has been conducting "real time" surveys of coastal residents in the United States in an effort to study how people make decisions to prepare for hurricanes. One of the major findings has been a consistent—and disturbing—paradox in protective decisions. On one hand, when we have asked people to estimate the probability that their homes will be affected by hurricane-force winds (of 75 m.p.h. or more), people are consistently pessimistic in their judgments. In Hurricane Sandy in 2012, for example, the average probability residents in coastal New Jersey gave for experiencing hurricane-force winds was over 80%, when the objective probability computed by the National Hurricane Center's computers was never more than 30% in any location (Meyer et al. 2014). This estimation bias is not, by itself, surprising, as presumably it is fueled both by the intense media coverage storms receive and the fact that the National Hurricane Center deliberately overwarns; a larger area of the coastline is warned to prepare for hurricane winds than is actually likely to experience them.

But here is the problem: when we ask people what they are doing to prepare for the threat they believe they are facing, most tend to underprepare, with a dramatic example being storm shutters. Shutters are costly to initially acquire, and have, essentially, one purpose: to protect the windows of a home from breaking in the face of hurricane-force winds. Yet, a consistent finding in our studies is that only half of all residents who reported owning removable shutters indicated that they either had or intended to put them up. The finding has proven remarkably robust. We found similar results among coastal residents in North Carolina facing hurricanes that proved to be near-misses and that actually made landfall (Earl in 2010 and Irene in 2011), people living in Louisiana and Mississippi with a long history of experience with hurricanes (Isaac in 2012), and people living in the northeast (Irene in 2011 and Sandy in 2012).

This reluctance to put up shutters that were purchased for the very purpose of protection illustrates how the powerful instinct to repeat actions that reward and avoid those that punish can lead us astray, producing behaviors that are contrary to those that our conscious belief systems might otherwise prescribe. Storm shutters, for all their benefits, are not easy to put up, nor are they easy to take down. There is a tangible penalty for putting up the shutters unnecessarily. Of course, there is a far *larger* penalty for not putting them when they *are* necessary, but that's a benefit that residents will rarely see. Because of overwarning, the odds heavily favor that if one goes through the effort of putting shutters up, one will end up discovering that, in hindsight, they were not actually needed. The prudent homeowner who put up shutters for a storm that fizzles gets to spend a day taking them down, while watching the imprudent neighbor who did not put them up enjoy a relaxing day at the beach. Worse, even if one puts up shutters and the storm *does* hit, the benefits will likely go unseen. While one can certainly draw comfort from imagining what damage might have occurred had the shutters *not* been installed, this reward is subtle, and offset by imagining the equally plausible event that nothing would happened.

When faced with the decision whether to put up storm shutters (or take most protective actions), a mental battle thus wages between two psychological forces: the instinct *not* to put them up born of years of trial-and-error experience, and the conscious knowledge that one probably *should* in light of one's beliefs that hurricane winds are likely. Unfortunately, in many of these battles it is instinct, not reason, that emerges the winner.

Trial-and-error learning also helps to explain why the protective behaviors that people *do* engage in are sometimes the wrong ones, or actually do little to reduce the risk of harm from rare events. In the 1770s, for example, the guilds of Toulouse in France annually convened local monks to conduct a ritualistic blessing of the Garonne River, believing that the ceremony prevented the river from flooding (Pfister 2009). Much more recently, a 2012 survey of beliefs about preparedness conducted by the Federal Emergency Management Administration (FEMA) revealed widespread misbeliefs about the actions that should be taken to avoid harm from natural disasters (FEMA 2013). It found, for example, that 72% of respondents mistakenly believed that if one is in a car and a tornado is approaching, one should seek shelter under a highway overpass (that's the *last* place one would want to be), and 32 percent believed that one can protect homes from a tornado by opening windows (doing so will either have no effect or increase damage). The reason for the persistence of these beliefs, of course, is that the rarity of the hazards means that they will be repeatedly—and mistakenly—reinforced. Floods on the Garonne are infrequent, and hence the blessing would have worked far more often than not. Tornados are rare and affect very small locations—hence someone who opens their windows every time a tornado warning is issued will find themselves in an intact home far more often than a destroyed one.

What We Are Actually Forgetting

As compelling as trial-and-error learning might be at first blush as an explanation for disaster cycles, it has trouble when confronted with one bit of data about risk perception: the fact that people tend to have pretty clear (and in some cases exaggerated) memories of past disasters. The stone memorials to the 1933 tsunami above Miyako, for example, were regularly viewed by local residents in the years leading up to 2011, and there is a large literature in psychology showing that when people are asked to judge the probability that they will experience a low-probability adverse event (such as a terrorist attack), the numbers they tend to give are typically far larger than those reality would dictate (e.g., Slovic 1987). Even when people personally did not experience a disaster, memories are artificially kept alive through textbooks, monuments, and legends, such as the flood myths that dominate almost all early religions (Harris 2006). In short, if a forgetting story is to be told about disaster cycles, it can't require people to actually forget disasters.

In an attempt to solve this puzzle, in 2012 I undertook an experiment to see if disaster cycles could be reproduced in a controlled laboratory setting where subjects had a monetary incentive to remember losses from past adverse events (Meyer 2012). In the experiment, subjects played a "hurricane preparedness" game in which they took up residence in a hypothetical home in an imaginary coastal area that was prone to periodic hits by hurricanes. Periodically hurricanes would approach the coast (displayed by an animated map), sometimes scoring a direct hit, sometimes a glancing blow, but most often turning away without threatening harm. If subjects believed their homes were going to be hit, they had the opportunity to purchase protection. At the end of the game they were paid an amount that was tied to the starting value of the home minus losses from storms and investments in protection. In principle, with just a little bit of experience subjects should have been able to learn that the best way to make money was to wait until the storm was just about to hit, then buy as much protection as possible.

What I observed, however, was that subjects did not consistently do this. Investments in protection oscillated over time consistent with disaster cycles: experienced losses from a hurricane would make subjects *over*invest in protection when the next one was coming, but then *under*invest after several periods with no losses. What was puzzling about this behavior was that the time gap between these successive events was seconds; it was thus unlikely that subjects had literally forgotten the previous losses. Yet, the disaster cycles were observed.

Two bits of evidence suggested a likely explanation for this behavior. First, it turned out that not experiencing a loss in one period reduced subjects' inclinations to invest in protection in the next regardless of *why* there had not been a prior loss. It mattered little whether the lack of a loss was due to the absence of a storm threat or investments in protection that *precluded* losses: both served to diminish subsequent investments. This behavior was clearly puzzling; as noted, the game was for them to have literally forgotten the benefits of an investment in protection that occurred just a few minutes earlier. Given this, whatever mechanism was driving this "forgetting" effect must have been operating under subjects' cognitive radar screens. This hypothesis was confirmed by a second bit of evidence. After each storm each subject was asked to rate how worried they were in advance of the storm and whether they felt that their level of investment was appropriate. If the effect was a conscious one, the carry-over effect should have been manifested in these measures; that is, not experiencing a loss from one storm would make them overtly believe that there was less of a need for protection given the next. But this is not what was observed; a lack of prior losses diminished subsequent investments in protection, but, paradoxically, did not diminish their stated need for protection.

The most likely mechanism, therefore, was that what was being quickly forgotten after each non-loss event were memories for the *emotion* that accompanied each loss, which was a critical subconscious driver of decisions to invest. As each storm approached, subjects were fully aware of the risk, but as time passed without an experienced loss, what gradually faded were memories for how losses *felt* at the time they were being experienced. The presence of this subconscious emotion seemed to be a necessary catalyst for motivating investments.

This mechanism thus provides a natural means of reconciling why there are disaster cycles in the face of clear memories of past disasters. The warning tablets above Miyako were certainly effective in keeping conscious memories alive of the 1933 disaster, but what they could not keep alive were the emotional memories of the event; what it felt like to witness widespread destruction, to experience the loss of loved ones. Without this memory it became too easy to return and rebuild, to expose new residents to the risk of a repeat event.

The Reality (and Mechanics) of False Alarms

At this point it would seem that I have reached a rather dismal view of the ability of people to learn to see the value of protection from raw experience. If it is indeed the case that a vivid emotional memory for an actual loss is needed to prompt the sense of mental urgency needed to invest in protection, the task of emergency managers may be beyond reach; actual losses from disasters are, by definition, quite rare. Of course, there are close calls and near-misses aplenty, but trial-and-error learning suggests that such encounters may do far more harm than good when it comes to teaching the value of protective investments.

The idea that taking protective actions that ultimately prove unneeded makes it less likely to comply the next time is, of course, an idea familiar to all children who have been cautioned by their parents not to cry wolf—referencing Aesop's fable of the shepherd boy who repeatedly fooled villagers into believing that a wolf is attacking his flock, only to be unable to recruit aid once the real threat materialized. In real life, however, the situation is far from black and white. While trial-and-error instincts not to repeat protective actions that have proved unneeded (or that lacked clear benefits) are indeed real, they do not necessarily always win the battle with deliberative considerations of how one should prudently react to a potential risk.

Attempts to understand why cry wolf (or false alarm) effects occur has been a major focus of work in psychology and human factors for almost 50 years. Indeed, in many contexts the effect is quite real. Most of us, for example, have learned to ignore car alarms when they go off (other than to wish they would get turned off), and fire alarms are frequently ignored in homes and buildings when they are known to be defective. Perhaps the best-known experimental work on false alarms was done in the 1980s by the psychologist

Shlomo Breznitz, who studied physiological responses to repeated false alarms in labs (e.g., Breznitz 1984). In the standard experiment a subject is warned that they may experience a shock—but the shocks do not always materialize. The emotional response to these warnings turns out to resemble a roller-coaster. When a subject first hears a warning, there is a startle response or a reflexive surge of anxiety. As the seconds pass after the warning, this initial anxiety wanes as respondents adapt to the oncoming threat, only to have it build again in the moments leading up to the expected onset of the event. While repeated false alarms do not change the shape of this anxiety curve, they do decrease its amplitude; unreliable warnings trigger lower levels of anxiety than reliable ones.

On the other hand, attempts to see if false alarms have similar dulling effects in the field for warnings that have life-or-death consequences have proven equivocal. Consider the case of air-traffic controllers. In the 1990s the Federal Aviation Administration installed computerized systems designed to warn air-traffic controllers of impending midair collisions. Computer systems track plane altitudes and trajectories, and if two (or more) planes look to be headed to the same general location an audible alarm goes off, giving the controller one minute to reroute the aircraft. These alarms, however, are prone to false-positive warnings: almost half the time when an alert sounds there is no need to take any action. In 2009, Christopher Wickens and colleagues did a study of responses of air-traffic controllers to 495 conflict alerts, and, fortunately for fliers, found little evidence of cry wolf effects: repeated exposure to false alarms did little to degrade the speed with which air-traffic controllers responded to these alerts.

Likewise, researchers have also had difficulty finding evidence for cry wolf effects in hurricane evacuation decisions. For example, in the summer of 1996 residents of North Carolina were subject to two hurricane landfalls in quick succession, both of which triggered evacuation orders: Bertha in late July and Fran in mid-September. Whereas Bertha proved to be something of a false alarm, Fran was a more serious threat. In a post-storm survey of coastal residents, Kirstin Dow and Susan Cutter found that the false alarm of Bertha did little to impede evacuation rates for Fran (which were much higher), and only 2% of respondents indicated that they would be less inclined to evacuate in the future because the actual impact of the storms proved less than feared (Dow and Cutter 1998).

It is important to note, however, that cry wolf effects can be quite real in some settings. They can, for example, be quite real for discrete hazards such as shocks and fires, where warnings are unreliable forecasts of an oncoming event. Apartment residents learn to ignore fire alarms that have a reputation for being faulty, and the U.S. Geological Survey would be ill-advised to implement earthquake warnings given the current state of seismic forecasting. Because pre-event signals would have a high rate of false positives, community sirens that warn of an imminent earthquake that does not then materialize would, in time, be less effective in triggering protective responses.

It is also the case that cry wolf effects can manifest themselves in more subtle ways than a direct misbelief in the diagnostic value of an alarm. A good example is the 1964 tsunami that killed 21 residents of Crescent City, California (Yutzy 1964). Crescent City was a small town where the task of issuing evacuation orders lay with the head police sheriff. In the previous year he responded to a tsunami alert by ordering businesses along the coast immediately to close and evacuate. It turned out to be a false alarm, and he received widespread criticism among the local shop owners for making the wrong call. Hence, when he received a similar alert late at night in the spring of 1964 he hesitated about issuing a warning; this time, better to wait and see if the threat was real. When the first of a series of waves hit the coast, he finally issued the warning, but by then it was too late.

On the other hand, cry wolf effects are less salient for warnings that are issued *after* a hazard has actually been observed and the false alarm lies simply in the misprediction of the severity of its impact. This helps explain why cry wolf effects have been hard to find for hurricane evacuations; unlike broken fire alarms, they are rare, and are issued only after a storm has been observed and is tangibly moving toward the coast. In that sense, there has been no false alarm. While those who evacuate may return to find that the water did not rise as far as feared, residents are just as likely to feel relief that their homes were spared by a very real threat than annoyance that they left unnecessarily. Moreover, the rarity of storm evacuations implies that when the next one arises, past inconveniences are likely to be distant memories that pale next to the immediate—and very real—threat posed by an approaching storm.

To Warn or Not?

This discussion begs an obvious question: given the ambiguous evidence of false alarm effects, what should emergency managers do when receiving information about an uncertain hazard? Just such a dilemma was faced by Florida's Rick Scott in 2014 when deciding whether to order an evacuation of the state's coastal areas in advance of a developing tropical storm, Erika. The storm was approaching the Leeward Islands, and the National Hurricane Center's most reliable forecast models were predicting that in three days it could be bearing down on the highly populated southeast coast of the state as a fully blown hurricane. It had been a decade since Florida had experienced a direct hit by such a storm, and Scott, as much as anyone, was keenly aware that a direct hit on an unprepared state could prove disastrous.

But just what action, if any, should be taken, was unclear. In its forecast discussions, the National Hurricane Center cautioned that it was much less certain about the three-day forecast than usual. The reason was that this year's El Niño was producing unusually strong high-level westerly winds that had the potential to weaken the fledgling storm well before it might affect the state.

Scott was thus on the horns of a dilemma, not unlike that faced by the sheriff of Crescent City in 1964 when news of a possible tsunami reached him. If he ordered a state of emergency and Erika weakened, many would surely accuse him of having needlessly cried wolf, something that could cause people to ignore later warnings when storm threats were real. On the other hand, if he did not give the order and the hurricane indeed materialized, the state might not have the time needed to fully prepare for the impact—an outcome that would, at the very least, doom his governorship.

The next day—with impact now two days away—the governor made his decision: he would declare the state of emergency. The Florida National Guard was called up and directed to potential impact areas. News media interrupted normal broadcasts to carry the governor's message and to disseminate the latest on the storm. Supermarket shelves were rapidly depleted of supplies as residents raced to prepare for the coming storm. Florida would be ready for Erika.

But Erika, of course, never arrived. As forecasters had suspected, the winds of El Niño weakened the storm and deflected it south to Hispaniola, and within 12 hours it was nothing more than a mass of comparatively harmless thunderstorms. Rather than bringing disaster, Erika turned out to be something of a positive by bringing welcome rain to a state that had been in the midst of a drought. Erika, in short was a big to-do about nothing.

Whether Rick Scott made the right call, of course, could be argued both ways. There certainly would be ample reason to worry that his actions might ultimately prove to have done more harm than good. When the next storm starts to threaten the state, he may be more reluctant to pull the trigger in ordering emergency preparations, recalling the resources that were wasted in preparing for Erika. Residents, for their part, may come to treat states of emergency with greater casualness, believing that the governor issues them indiscriminately whenever the hint of a threat arises.

But I would argue that his call was indeed the right one. While alarm desensitization *is* a very real phenomenon, it tends *not* to operate when three conditions hold: (1) the warning events are infrequent; (2) the phenomenon that is the source of the threat is observable in advance; and (3) the consequences of a maximum adverse impact are large.

As illustrated earlier in the case of North Carolina's experience with Hurricane Bertha, the interval between warning events needed for false alarm memories to fade can be surprisingly short. And people's memories for weather events are notoriously poor; when autumn passes into winter and worries turn from heat waves to freezes, few recall the meteorological details of hurricanes that were near-misses. Meteorologists, in essence, get a mulligan for past bad forecasts. People are more than willing to believe that the next forecast of the "big one" will, this time, be on target.

But even in cases where warnings that turn out to be false alarms are in close temporal proximity, desensitization is unlikely as long as there is a tangible attribution as to *why* the event did not materialize. As noted, people tend not to encode as false alarms storms whose impacts were not as great as warned—they did, after all, occur. This effect is amplified when the event has significant impacts in other places, and becomes the focus of salient news coverage. As an example, when Hurricane Andrew ravaged southern Miami-Dade County in 1992, neighboring Broward County experienced only limited effects. But few in Fort Lauderdale are likely to recall Andrew as a false alarm. The more likely emotion was thankfulness for having averted catastrophe.

Conclusions: The Challenge of Managing What People Learn from Disasters

In 2000, officials in the city of Galveston, Texas, voted to erect a monument atop the city's seawall. It was a statue of a woman half submerged in the sea, one arm desperately stretching for the sky, the other holding a small child. It was erected to remind residents and visitors why the seawall was there in the first place: the great hurricane of 1900 that took the lives of some 8,000. The seawall was—and remains—one of America's best examples of successful hazard adaption; in the years that followed it served its intended purpose, allowing the city to escape largely unharmed from multiple encounters with such storms. A great example of learning from experience.

Unfortunately, the lessons taught by the Galveston seawall were not absorbed by many. While few who gazed on the statue would deny that it was a moving symbol, it did little to discourage many from viewing the seawall with a certain measure of scorn. To some, the seawall was an ugly barrier that deprived the community of a nice beach that might attract tourists, and it dissuaded wealthy Houstonians looking to build beach homes. For the latter, the best property lay on the unprotected coasts away from the city, such as the Bolivar Peninsula to the north. Ample space to build, unobstructed views of the turquoise Gulf waters.

Of course, you can anticipate the next part of the story. In 2008 Hurricane Ike swept through the area, leaving Galveston intact but wiping out virtually all of the newer homes that had been built on the Bolivar Peninsula. For the majority of residents these were unrecoverable losses, as only 39% carried flood insurance. Not only had most failed to learn about the value of safe locations, but they also had failed to learn the value of minimal risk protection (FEMA 2008).

So how might risk managers solve this problem? One intuitive approach is to look for novel ways to flip the natural reward structure in protection, such that protective investments are the behavior that gets most frequently rewarded, not laxness. An example of one such initiative is the Institute for Home Building and Safety's Fortified for Safer Living (FSL) program, in which homeowners who invest in a battery of protective measures are awarded FSL certification—akin to a Good Housekeeping seal of approval. The hope, of course, is that the reward value of FSL certification will grow in time as homeowners see it translate into higher home valuations and greater social approval. Greater objective safety ends up as a nice by-product.

In the same vein, one might also explore methods that focus on the cost side—ways of making *failing* to invest in protection the more effortful action. For example, a coastal community might automatically distribute hurricane preparation packages to all homeowners, with the program being paid for by property taxes. A resident who feels that they do not need the protection in a given year could elect to file paperwork to opt out, receiving a small refund. In time, of course, residents would hopefully find that the burdensomeness of the refund process was not worth the small savings, the result by default being a better-prepared community.

I would suggest, however, that the benefits of such persuasive programs will at best be incremental; no matter how much a homeowner might be attracted to the notion of receiving an FSL stamp of approval, this will be a hard sell in areas that have not seen a strong hurricane in many years. As noted earlier, the only sure-fire catalyst that exists to promote protection is an experienced loss—and at that only in the immediate aftermath of the event. Convincing those who lack emotional experience of the value of protective investments is an uphill battle.

Would it be possible to create *virtual* memories for losses? Unfortunately, the evidence for this is also not encouraging—but not for the lack of trying. As an example, one of FEMA's tactics for encouraging homeowners to buy flood insurance is to expose them to ads that vividly display the consequences of flood, and then encourage them to mentally simulate what it would feel like to suffer such an event without insurance coverage. Likewise, in the early 2000s the Red Cross attempted to heighten awareness of earthquake risks in California by setting up large visuals in prominent tourist locations in San Francisco showing what the area would look like given a large quake. Not surprisingly, neither effort has been effective in boosting protective investments, for a simple reason: everything we know about emotional reactions to disasters says that the experience of a loss has to be real—it is not something that can be manufactured by brief exposures to a compelling visual, a moving monument, or a warning sign.

Given this, the best strategy for overcoming disaster cycles may be to accept the fact that they are unavoidable—but then make the most of them in the brief interval that exists before the emotional memories fade. The famous advice attributed to Winston Churchill never to let a good crisis go to waste could not be more relevant than for disasters. As such, we may have to accept that learning *will* occur, but it will be a two steps forward, one step back process. But this advice comes with a word of caution: planners must realize that the window for action after disasters is likely to be far shorter than they might assume or need. It would be a mistake to assume that as long as objective memories for past disasters are kept alive, people can be convinced to see value in large protective investments, or that persuasion can be achieved by an appeal to rational logic about long-run expected returns. Decisions about protection are ultimately fueled by emotions, and the best chance for acting lies in the preciously short time when they are still heightened after a catastrophe strikes.

References

Breznitz, S. (1984). *The psychology of false alarms*. Hillsdale, NJ: Lawrence Erlbaum.

Dow, K., & Cutter, S. L. (1998). Crying wolf: Repeat responses to hurricane evacuation orders. *Coastal Management, 26*, 237–252.

FEMA. (2008). *Hurricane Ike impact report*. Retrieved from Federal Emergency Management Administration website: https://www.fema.gov/pdf/hazard/hurricane/2008/ike/impact_report.pdf

FEMA. (2013). *Personal preparedness in America: Findings from the 2012 FEMA National Survey*. Retrieved from the Federal Emergency Management Administration website: https://www.fema.gov/media-library-data/1409146548070-7c8016a9a41b65b2c584ffacdbe4f920/2012_FEMA_National_Survey_Report_FINAL_508_v11.pdf

Harris, A. K. (2006). *Flood risks in the religions of the ancient world* (working paper). American Military University (APUS). Retrieved from https://www.academia.edu/1427821/Flood_Myths_in_the_Religions_of_the_Ancient_World

Kunreuther, H., Meyer, R. J., & Michel-Kerjan, E. (2012). Overcoming decision biases to reduce losses from natural catastrophes. In E. Shafir (Ed.), *The behavioral foundations of public policy* (pp. 398–413). Princeton, NJ: Princeton University Press.

Meyer, R. J. (2006). Why we under-prepare for hazards. In R. J. Daniels, D. F. Kettl, and H. Kunreuther (Eds.), *On risk and disaster: Lessons from Hurricane Katrina* (pp. 153–174). Philadelphia: University of Pennsylvania Press.

Meyer, R. J. (2012). Failing to learn from experience about catastrophes: The case of hurricane preparedness. *Journal of Risk and Uncertainty, 45*(1), 25–50.

Meyer, R. J., Baker, J., Broad, K., Czajkowski, J., & Orlove, B. (2014). The dynamics of hurricane risk perception: Real-time evidence from the 2012 Atlantic hurricane season. *Bulletin of the American Meteorological Society, 95*(9), 1389–1404.

Pfister, C. (2009). Learning from nature-induced disasters: Theoretical considerations and case studies from Western Europe. In C. Mauch & C. Pfister (Eds.), *Natural disasters, cultural responses: Case studies toward a global environmental history* (pp. 17–40). Lanham, MD: Lexington Books.

Slovic, P. (1987). Perception of risk. *Science, 236*(4799), 280–285.

Wickens, C. D., Rice, S., Keller, D., Hutchins, S., Hughes, J., & Clayton, K. (2009). False alerts in air traffic control conflict alerting system: Is there a "cry wolf" effect? *Human Factors, 51*(4), 446–462.

Yutzy, D. (1964). *Aesop 1964: Contingencies affecting the issuing of public disaster warnings at Crescent City, California* (Research Note 4). Disaster Research Center, Ohio State University, Columbus.

PART II

Improving Risk Assessment

CHAPTER 7

Using Models to Set a Baseline and Measure Progress in Reducing Disaster Casualties

Robert Muir-Wood

Introduction

In March 2015, the Sendai Framework for Disaster Risk Reduction 2015–2030 was signed by representatives from 187 countries in Sendai, Japan (UNISDR 2015). The framework built on two previous United Nations (UN) global initiatives: the International Decade for Natural Disaster Risk Reduction that ran from 1990 to 1999, and the Hyogo Framework for Action: Building the Resilience of Communities to Disasters that ran from 2005 to 2015.

Neither of the two previous UN decades of disaster reduction had set targets to assess whether the program of work was succeeding in reducing the casualties and economic impacts of disasters. Without such measurement it would be difficult to prove that achievements in founding new national disaster agencies, for example, had actually restrained disaster impacts. In particular, since 1990, rapid economic development and population growth were believed to have placed many more buildings and people in harm's way. Worldwide catastrophe casualties were significantly higher in the decade starting in 2000 than during the 1990s. Without targets or consistent measurements, it was impossible to know whether the new national disaster agencies changed what was built, how people were educated around disasters, and how warnings were delivered.

In the buildup to the Sendai Framework many papers were written and discussions held around how progress on disaster risk reduction should be measured (see, for example, reports undertaken for the Department for International Development in the United Kingdom, by Muir-Wood 2012, Michel-Kerjan et al. 2013, and Mitchell et al. 2014). Based on the experience of the 2005 Millennium Development Goals, the simplest and most powerful goals are specific in their measurable outcomes: for example, by 2015, a reduction in annual maternal mortality in childbirth by three-quarters, and a reduction in deaths among children under five years old by two-thirds. Such simplicity is possible because progress can be monitored from annual mortality statistics, collected by each country.

By their nature, however, disasters are infrequent extremes for which it is not possible to identify the true national average behavior from a single year, or even a single decade. Take the Haitian example. From 1900 to 2009 fewer than 10 people were killed by earthquakes in Haiti. Then in one afternoon in January 2010 more than 200,000 died. For the 1900–2009 period the annual average casualties were less than 0.1. For the period 1900–2010 the annual average casualties were at least 2,000. Finding an average from such statistics is clearly highly sensitive to how the baseline is set. Attention to these statistics could impede disaster risk management, rather than aid it.

For Haiti, any decadal sample through the twentieth century would have significantly understated the potential for casualties, just as a decade including the year 2010 would dramatically overstate the averages. We are dealing with a highly skewed or "fat-tailed" distribution in which the mean (the true long-term average) is multiples higher than the mode (the number for which half the decadal observations lie above and half below). Most decades will underestimate the average, while occasionally a decade will arrive containing a mega-catastrophe and the statistics for that decade will then be biased very high.

The situation in Haiti is by no means an outlier. There are many other countries for which it is impossible to determine from history what constitutes the average level of disaster fatalities. This includes situations when, as in Haiti or Myanmar, a high casualty catastrophe has recently happened, but also in countries such as Barbados, or Jamaica, on the front line of plate boundaries and in the path of intense hurricanes, where there has been no mass casualty disaster for more than a century. While we have robust statistics for the annual loss of life from lightning strikes or snake bites, even in California or Seattle, our annual statistics on earthquake fatalities, for example, await the occurrence of some rare catastrophe which will then come to dominate the statistics.

This difficulty in measuring disaster outcomes could mean that resilience goals are weakened to focus on actions alone. A goal might be set to retrofit the greatest number of schools to reduce their potential to collapse in strong earthquake shaking. However, it would be better to achieve a measurable reduction in earthquake fatalities among children. In pursuit of goals focused on actions, schools might end up being retrofitted in areas where there is very little prospect of earthquakes. Also the focus on schools might miss the point that children only spend one-sixth of their time at school and are therefore more at risk from the collapse of their homes.

Even going into the final negotiations at the Sendai meeting, there were still multiple versions of how casualty disaster targets should be framed. In some alternatives there were quantitative targets, such as a 50% reduction in disaster fatalities. Then there was the question of how any target should be measured. Eventually the first Sendai goal was defined as the intention to "substantially reduce global disaster mortality by 2030, aiming to lower average per 100,000 global mortality rate in the decade 2020–2030 compared to the period 2005–2015" (UNISDR 2015).

This language was arguably the weakest of the various alternatives that had been proposed, employing the term "substantially reduce" rather than any proportional target. The goal would henceforth rely on the comparison of two time periods of data. But this leads to significant questions. Is the period from 2005 to 2015 a good representation of the true average level of worldwide disaster casualties in 2015? How can we test the data to discover whether there is likely to be some bias in the statistics? It would not be appropriate that a goal determined by the comparison between two sets of decadal disaster data should be achieved, or fail, simply because the original baseline data misrepresent the true averages.

This leads onto the first of the themes of this chapter: whether the disaster statistics from 2005 to 2015 are representative of the true average level of disaster fatalities in 2015 and hence provide a robust baseline from which to measure genuine improvements in reducing disaster risk? How could one make an improved measure of the 2015 baseline?

Another set of questions emerge around what organization commands the resources to achieve this global goal. The UN's own agency for disaster risk reduction (the UNISDR) only employs a handful of personnel. The goal is the product of the accumulated outcomes across many different countries. Realistically there is no preexisting global agency that could own this goal. It is only at country level that a goal on disaster casualty reduction can be owned and enabled through national policies and actions. In which case, why was the goal for disaster casualty reduction not targeted at the national level? Then, at the end of the period of comparison, it would be possible to see which countries had, or had not, achieved their targets.

At the same time, in attempting to set a uniform national target, such as a 50% reduction in disaster casualties, one can also imagine the disputes that would break out between countries that had already achieved substantial reductions in disaster mortality, and those developing countries in which disaster reduction policies had yet to be fully implemented. One can readily imagine how the agenda at Sendai might have shifted to creating a global target on disaster casualties: so as to avoid the political disputes that would be inevitable in setting consistent national targets. There would be no political disputes around setting a global target precisely because the target was not owned by anyone.

As to what would have constituted an appropriate national target, we have the example of Japan, a country beset by natural hazards, which instituted systems after 1950 to collect detailed local community information on the impacts of disasters, a decade before the country embarked on a massive program of investment in disaster risk reduction. Hence we have baseline statistics that make it possible to measure what was achieved through arguably the most effective national campaign ever instituted of targeted investments in improved resilience.

This is the second major theme for this chapter: what other countries can learn from Japan around how to apply the most effective investments in reducing disaster impacts.

Having identified both that a global target remains unowned, and that, for at least some perils, national targets cannot be effectively monitored based on empirical data alone, how can we measure progress in disaster risk reduction?

The challenge of catastrophic extremes is that the recent historical record provides an incomplete picture of potential future events. Faced with the problem of identifying how to calculate expected catastrophe risk, through the 1980s a probabilistic simulation approach was developed, which is now universally employed for the business of catastrophe insurance. Losses are modeled from each of the simulated events and preserved in an "event loss table." The key output of a model is then the annual loss exceedance probability distribution (displaying the annual probability of obtaining a certain size of loss), whether for a single property or for a large number of properties and locations. Catastrophe models are predominately designed to output financial loss. This could be the direct loss resulting from property damage, or the loss caused by the interruption of business income, or the additional expenses required to house a family or business while their property is repaired.

Earthquake catastrophe models have also been designed to output expected loss of life and injuries (see, for example, So and Spence 2013). For this purpose, the location of the population is distributed within the buildings according to at least two "typical" but "antipodal" times of day (such as early afternoon and nighttime).

For perils for which there is the prospect of a forecast, the modeling of casualties requires first establishing who is likely to be situated in the path of the peril, and then what proportion of those people can be expected to safely evacuate.

The third and final theme of this chapter is to acknowledge that catastrophe models can provide a solution to the conundrum around how to set measurable national targets for disaster casualty reduction. While work is ongoing to design and calibrate models that output the appropriate metrics, we already have examples of cities and governments employing models to set and measure progress on disaster risk reduction. Together, these three themes offer ways forward in accomplishing what the Sendai Framework for Disaster Risk Reduction hopes to achieve: measurable improvements in disaster preparation and outcomes.

The Volatility of the Global Record on Disasters

How can we test the degree to which the period from 2005–2015 provides a true average of current worldwide disaster casualties? The record of disaster mortality data is generally considered complete (at least for the larger events) back to 1970. The data used here were collated from a single source: the Emergency Events Database (EM-DAT) maintained by the Centre for Research on the Epidemiology of Disaster (CRED 2015). For cyclones, EM-DAT does

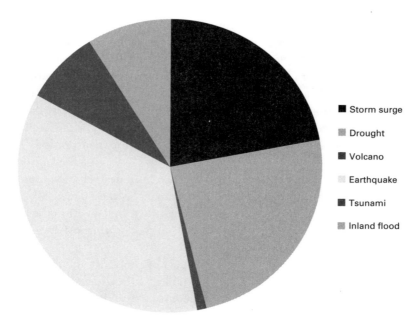

■ Storm surge

▨ Drought

■ Volcano

▨ Earthquake

■ Tsunami

▨ Inland flood

Figure 7.1. Proportion of disaster deaths by hazard type, 1970–2014.

not separate surge from wind impacts so this data was supplemented with the SURGEDAT database.[1]

Figure 7.1 displays the contribution to the annual mortality data 1970–2014 from the six principal perils (drought, volcanic eruption, earthquake, tsunami, inland flood, and storm surge). As seen in Figure 7.2, plotting the annual disaster mortality back to 1970, there is significant year-on-year variability. The two highest mortality years are dominated by single catastrophes: the Bangladesh storm surge of 1970 and the Ethiopian drought and famine of 1984. The period from 1985 to 2003 showed relatively few mega-catastrophes. The 2005–2014 decade had two years with exceptional mortality: 2008 (dominated by the Wenchuan, China earthquake as well as Cyclone Nargis in Myanmar) and 2010 (with the Port au Prince, Haiti, earthquake).

In considering the breakdown of disaster deaths by hazard type, earthquake contributes a little more than one-third of the total. Next comes drought, very dominated by events in Africa in the 1970s and 1980s. While there is the potential to forecast all the wet perils, storm surge, tsunami, and inland flood, the main contributors to the global mortality totals are from

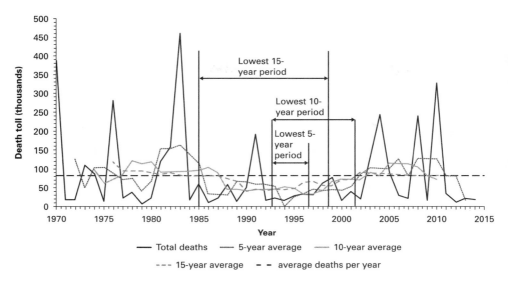

Figure 7.2. The annual death toll from all natural perils, 1970–2015, with moving 5-year, 10-year, and 15-year averages displayed alongside average deaths per year.

events where evacuation destinations had not previously been identified, where people were unaware that they were at risk, and where forecasts were not delivered, most notably in Bangladesh in 1970 and in Myanmar in 2008.

In reviewing how disaster casualties have varied through time, we can see there is significant volatility, with a small number of extreme catastrophe loss years dominating the picture. Meanwhile about half the years have low levels of casualties, with their annual total being only around a quarter of the overall mean. These data display a fat-tailed distribution, in which the size and frequency of extreme mortality years are much higher than would be expected in a simple normal distribution. In a high casualty year, we can see that a large proportion of the fatalities have been contributed by a single large disaster, or in a couple of years by two large disasters. We can also see from applying 5-year, 10-year, and 15-year filters to the data that the averages have moved quite significantly through time. In particular the 1990s prove to have been a quiet decade for the highest casualty disasters.

By dividing the annual numbers of fatalities by the interpolated global population for that year, the number of casualties has been normalized into a casualty rate: the annual global casualties per 100,000 population (Figure 7.3). In plotting this annual casualty rate by year, this has the effect

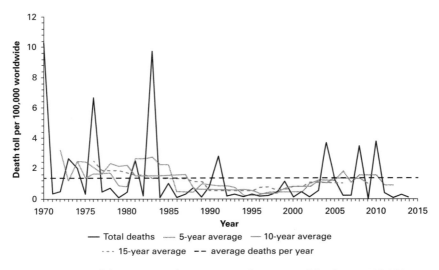

Figure 7.3. Annual disaster casualties, measured in terms of deaths per 100,000 worldwide.

of raising the contribution of earlier catastrophes relative to more recent events, as global population has continued to grow. Instead of the highest peaks in casualties at both the beginning and end of the record, the 2005–2014 period now becomes closer to the long-term average. However, within this normalized data set the low number of casualties between 1985 and 2004 becomes even more striking.

Given the focus within the Sendai Framework of wanting to compare the rate of casualties across two decades of observation, it is instructive to observe how the 10-year average has varied over the record. Through the 1990s, the decadal averages were consistently less than half the long-term average. This highlights the difficulty in assuming that a 10-year period will give a representative sample of the long term. To see the degree to which a small number of the highest mortality events dominate the statistics, we can rank each disaster (normalized per 100,000 of global population at the date of the event) and show in Figure 7.4 the degree to which the cumulative total above some threshold (defined as "casualties per 100,000") contributes to the overall total fatalities (the "proportion of data captured").

As can be seen, the largest catastrophes dominate the statistics, with almost 90% of the mortality generated by the top 16 catastrophes and 50% by the top five. Hence decadal averages from this data are themselves likely to

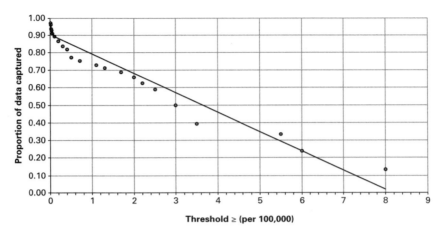

Figure 7.4. The proportion of disaster mortality data captured at each individual event threshold value (per 100,000) from 1970 to 2015.

be quite volatile as they are determined by whether one or more high-casualty catastrophes occurred in that time window. For the Sendai Framework to be effective in driving improvements, the baseline needs to best represent the mean catastrophe mortality for the year 2015.

Simulating the Occurrence of High Mortality Catastrophes

Given the degree to which the statistics on disaster mortality are dominated by the larger events, how does their random occurrence affect the decadal averages? We can explore this by simulating multiple decades of random event occurrence (Pears-Piggott and Muir-Wood 2016).

In the simulation process, the threshold for the definition of "large mortality events" was selected to be 0.1 per 100,000, capturing 95.6% of the mortality. All those disaster events that fall below this threshold were considered to comprise a background level of mortality that was added back in for the decade after the large event simulation had been completed. Resampling the large event mortality data was undertaken using 50,000 iterations and the assumption of Poisson event independence to determine the number of large events in a particular decade based on the mean recurrence interval. We find in this analysis that, assuming that the mortality rates of catastrophes (i.e., the proportion of global population exposed and their levels of protection)

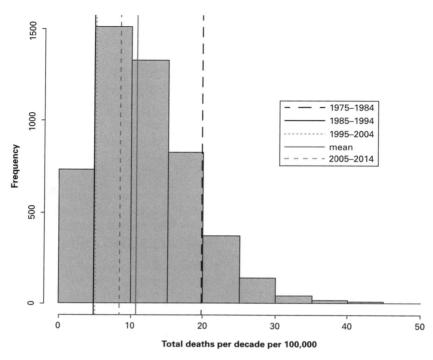

Figure 7.5. Decadal disaster mortality rates (per 100,000) superimposed on the resimulation of decadal casualties, based on the assumption that the casualty rates for each significant disaster have not changed since 1970.

have remained completely unchanged, the decade from 2005 to 2014 falls on the 35th percentile of the overall distribution of decadal mortalities (see Figure 7.5). Hence if nothing had changed since 1970 around the proportion of the worldwide population killed in each disaster, then there is a 65% chance that the level of mortality experienced over a 10-year period would be higher than that actually obtained in the 2005–2014 period.

The Impact of Disaster Risk Reduction on the Current Level of Casualties

Clearly it is not realistic to assume that nothing has changed to alter catastrophe casualty rates since 1970. For example, since the first mega-catastrophe

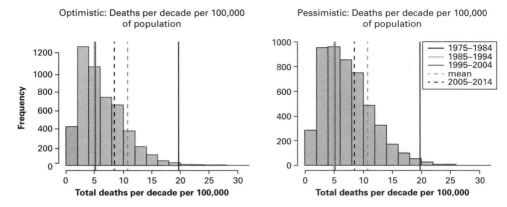

Figure 7.6. Decadal disaster mortality rates (per 100,000 population) superimposed on 50,000 resampled distributions of decadal mortalities based on assuming "optimistic" and "pessimistic" improvements in peril-specific mortalities.

in the record, the 1970 Bangladesh cyclone, there has been massive investment in improved warnings of storm surge and the provision of more than 3,000 storm surge evacuation shelters. As demonstrated by the largest storm surge since 2000, Cyclone Sidr, which hit the coast of Bangladesh in 2007, the casualties were only around 1–2% of those experienced in 1970 when there were few warnings and no evacuation destinations.

Better forecasting and early intervention has dramatically reduced the mortality from African droughts since the 1980s. Also, the extraordinary resource of videos and publicity from the 2004 Indian Ocean and 2011 Japan tsunami has educated populations in low-lying coastal locations about other coastlines at risk and triggered investment in tsunami warning systems and evacuation drills.

Yet not every peril has shown such improvements and it is important to consider what has changed one peril at a time. In setting a fair baseline (appropriate for 2015) for measuring casualty reduction, we should take into consideration the best understanding of how casualties for different classes of hazard have altered over time. There is no simple way of quantifying these changes. We have reviewed the evidence for improvements around casualty reduction by disaster category and where appropriate by geography and then made some simple judgments around what impact they have had overall for that class of hazard (see Pears-Piggott and Muir-Wood 2016 for more details). Given the significant uncertainty in this assessment, we have developed a range of perspectives and labeled these assumptions "optimistic" and "pessimistic," according to what magnitude of improvement we believe should be applied.

Based on these optimistic and pessimistic modifications of the casualty history, the population of larger events has been resampled in 50,000 random simulations each representing the occurrence of disasters across a decade. After the simulation, the background mortality from events below the "large event threshold" has then been added back in. The actual 2005–2014 casualties are then overlaid on this distribution to discover what percentile they represent (see Figure 7.6). For the pessimistic set of assumptions, the 2005–2014 decade is found to lie at the 66th percentile, while with the optimistic set of assumptions the 2005–2014 decade is at the 83rd percentile. In effect, if nothing else changed, and if the occurrence rate of catastrophes remains consistent with that experienced since 1970, we would expect over the next decade there is between a two-thirds to five-sixths chance that casualties will be lower than those experienced from 2005 to 2014.

One of the challenges of using empirical data on disasters concerns the degree to which disaster occurrence tends to be the principal driver of actions taken to reduce the levels of risk. A territory without a recent major catastrophe is likely to exhibit higher vulnerability than an equally hazardous territory that has suffered such a catastrophe—even though the experience from historical data of catastrophe loss in the two regions suggests the reverse. On a national level, the higher the loss of life or economic loss over some period (for example, Japan in the 1950s), the more one might expect a reduction in these metrics in a subsequent period when lessons are learned and actions have been taken. If several years go past without a major catastrophe, without any incentive for investment in disaster risk reduction, the vulnerability to future catastrophes may tend to increase.

It typically takes 3–6 years for the lessons from a severe catastrophe to be identified and implemented. As the proportion of buildings built to the new code expands year by year, the mean vulnerability of the building stock is reduced. Within six years of 2005 Hurricane Katrina, the flood defenses around the city of New Orleans had been significantly improved. Following the 1970 storm surge in Bangladesh, in which some 300,000 people died, actions have included a program to build cyclone shelters as well as prepare the population for future cyclone warnings. As a result, there has been a very significant reduction in loss of life from cyclones.

What Constitutes Best Practice in Disaster Risk Reduction: The Japanese Experience

Which country can demonstrate best practice in taking actions to reduce the impact of disasters? We need a nation with scrupulous record-keeping, as well as a class of hazard that is not too volatile and infrequent so that empirical data can be used to demonstrate progress. Some hazard types (in particular earthquakes) have low rates of activity but high severity, which, as we have seen for Haiti, makes it impossible to determine mean casualty rates from a few decades of data. For many countries, available information on fatalities or disaster impacts is simply not complete before 1980.

Japanese floods (inland and coastal) provide one of the best examples of proven reductions in disaster impacts. A national campaign of disaster risk reduction was instituted in 1960 after catastrophic storm surge floods in 1959 caused more than 5,000 deaths. Most importantly, detailed monitoring had preceded the introduction of the campaign so there is unusually good baseline data on fatalities and properties flooded from before the new measures were introduced. The Disaster Countermeasures Basic Act, implemented in 1961, legislated a change from a reactive to a proactive approach to disasters in the country (Mitchell et al. 2014). Regional disaster prevention plans were enforced, including forecasting systems, flood defenses, warning criteria, rescue systems, and emergency communications. There was large-scale construction of multipurpose dams for both flood control and water supply, allied with programs for river channel expansion, increased retention capacity, and the production of flood hazard maps.

Data sources from Japan (the Fire and Disaster Management Agency (FDMA), the Japan Meteorological Agency (JMA), Japanese official Chronological Scientific Tables, and the General Insurance Association of Japan) provide detailed data on disaster losses back to 1945.

Several typhoons in the 1940s and 1950s caused more than a thousand deaths, including the storm surge from Typhoon Vera in 1959, which resulted in more than 5,000 deaths around Nagoya. However, since 1960 there has not been a single typhoon that has caused more than 320 deaths (see Figure 7.7).

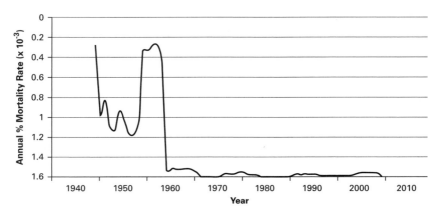

Figure 7.7. Five-year running mean of the annual typhoon mortality rate (relative to total population) in Japan, 1941–2009. *Sources*: JMA and FDMA data.

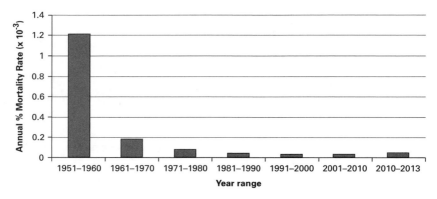

Figure 7.8. Annual mortality rates per decade from typhoons in Japan, 1951–2013.

For typhoons, the change in the average annual mortality rate was rapid, from 1.1 per 100,000 people in the 1950s to 0.08 per 100,000 people in the 1970s (see Figure 7.8). The 1950s was a period of intense and damaging typhoon activity, which reduced during the 1960s and 1970s, so this reduction is not all linked with the implementation of disaster risk reduction policies in 1961. However, the persistence of low mortalities even when typhoon activity picked up again after 1990 highlights that this reduction does reflect the results of active intervention.

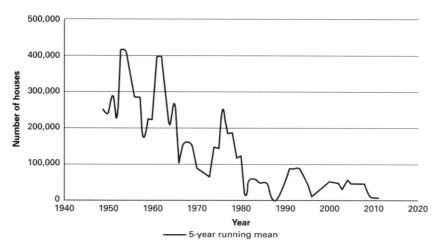

Figure 7.9. Number of houses inundated by typhoons or precipitation floods in Japan, 1945–2011. *Sources:* JMA and FDMA data.

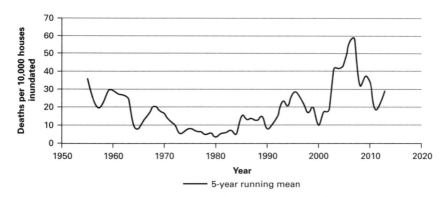

Figure 7.10. Number of deaths (per 10,000 houses inundated) in Japan by typhoons, 1951–2013. *Sources:* JMA and FDMA data.

Structural flood control measures also led to a significant decrease in the number of houses inundated (see Figure 7.9). However, in comparing statistics on properties flooded and people killed, after the 1960s and 1970s the policy around evacuations appears to have weakened. From 1951 until the 1980s, there was a general decrease in the number of deaths per 10,000 houses inundated by typhoons, but the number of deaths per 10,000 houses flooded has risen by a factor close to three since the early 1980s (see Figure 7.10). It appears that the initial focus was on saving lives, principally through evacuations. Since the 1980s, trusting in the ubiquitous flood defenses, people have become less observant of the need to evacuate when they are warned of an oncoming disaster.

Japanese examples suggest that, where there has not previously been a focus on saving lives in disasters, significant improvements can be made over a period of one or two decades. When comparing the 1950s with the 1990s, Japan achieved a compound reduction in fatalities of more than 50% per decade.

Using Catastrophe Models to Measure Improvements in Disaster Casualties

While it proved possible to demonstrate the success of flood disaster management in Japan, for other disaster categories such as earthquakes and tsunamis, even in Japan the catastrophes are too rare and their impacts too diverse to be able to easily demonstrate the success of strategies around disaster risk reduction.

Ultimately all attempts to measure improvements in catastrophe mortality empirically will be undermined by the strong volatility in catastrophe occurrence. Furthermore, exposure to extreme events is continually changing as a result of new construction, urbanization, and population increases, especially in high-growth countries. Therefore, attempting to compensate for the volatility of occurrence by extending the duration of a sample inevitably introduces inconsistent information.

These problems in measuring average disaster casualties are comparable to those faced by insurers in measuring catastrophe risk costs. Recent history cannot be expected to reveal the true averages or what can be expected around the infrequent extremes. For these reasons, since 1990 the insurance industry has embraced the use of probabilistic catastrophe modeling. A catastrophe loss model contains a synthetic catalog of at least 10,000 and more often 100,000 years of extreme events for a particular hazard and region. The process of generating the synthetic catalog is based on the scientific understanding of what determines the structure, severity, and geography of the hazard. Wherever possible, the synthetic catalog and hazard outputs are calibrated against history.

For each simulated event, the hazard will be defined as one or more interrelated footprints, which, for an earthquake, could comprise a map of the level of ground shaking, another to capture the ground deformation of liquefaction and land sliding, another for the water depths (and potentially velocities) of the tsunami, and even another for the extent of subsequent urban fires. For a tropical cyclone, beyond the wind footprint, there could also be a storm surge flood footprint and another for inland flooding. These secondary peril footprints can be particularly important for large offshore earthquakes as well as intense tropical cyclones when it is the tsunami (as in 2011 in Japan) or the storm surge (as in the Philippines in 2013) which becomes the principal cause of casualties.

For an insurer, details of the insured properties, including their relevant parameters such as value, location, and construction type, are entered into the model. For each simulated event at that location, precompiled vulnerability functions relate the severity of the hazard to the loss expected for that individual property. The loss cost is calculated for each of the simulated events with respect to "the exposure." Then, by multiplying the expected loss from each of the events with the event's annual probability of occurrence, and summing across all the events, it becomes possible to generate the average annualized loss to the individual property or the portfolio of properties. This then becomes the basis for setting insurance premiums.

Beyond sharing the same probabilistic treatment of the hazard, the disaster casualty catastrophe model diverges from the model designed only to calculate insurance losses. For estimating disaster casualties, we have two alternate situations. The first situation is where there is no warning. Most casualties occur in buildings that undergo total or partial collapse. Therefore we need to know the probability of the building collapsing from the shaking, and also how many people are expected to have been in the building at the time.

In the second situation, there is the potential for a warning ahead of a storm surge or tsunami, or even a post-earthquake fire. We first need to know how many people are located in situations where they would die if they did not evacuate. Then the question is: what proportion of those in the path of the hazard will have successfully evacuated and escaped? For this we will want to know how well these people are informed about the peril, the degree to which a specific warning has been communicated to them, the ability of people to evacuate in the available time, their reaction to the evacuation alert, and whether their intended destinations are themselves beyond the extent of the tsunami or flood (in a number of coastal towns in the 2011 Japan tsunami, the evacuation destinations were themselves overwhelmed).

In both these situations, we will need to develop a new class of exposure data around the locations of people. People shift location through the day, from where they work to where they live. We need to capture these relocations by selecting representative times of day, for example the middle of the workday and the middle of the night (and perhaps another representative time to capture traveling between these locations). To balance the probabilities of being situated at one or other location, these exposure distributions are weighted for what proportion of the week they represent (for example, at home: 65%, at work: 25%, traveling and other locations: 10%).

We might use a series of proxies for developing the human exposure—for example, knowing the population in each neighborhood and the distribution of housing units, or the number of workers in different industry sectors and the locations of public, commercial, and industrial premises. Based on situating the population at two or more times of day, for each scenario we can model the collapse rate of these buildings and hence the expected casualties. The output of such probabilistic casualty models includes the annualized number of expected fatalities as well as the total number of fatalities that can be expected at key "annual probabilities," for example the "1-in-50-year" or "1-in-100-year" disaster.

For those perils like tsunamis and storm surges, where there is the potential to evacuate to safety, we can estimate what proportion of the people at risk do not evacuate and therefore are likely to become casualties. These predicted proportions can be checked against the level of evacuation achieved in recent storm surge and tsunami catastrophes. The extraordinary publicity that followed the 2004 Indian Ocean and 2011 Japan tsunamis as well as the 2012 Haiyan storm surge in Tacloban, Philippines, has significantly raised the global consciousness around warnings of imminent coastal inundation.

The catastrophe modeling paradigm has principally been used to help insurance entities quantify financial risk, and hence the large majority of catastrophe models have been developed for high- and upper-middle-income countries with an active insurance industry. However, there are a number of current programs to expand the development of catastrophe models into all countries (as in those produced by the Global Earthquake Model foundation),[2] providing the opportunity to extend these models so they can be used to output information on casualties.

Conclusion: Beyond Sendai

Of all the goals developed for the 2015 Sendai Framework for Disaster Risk Reduction, arguably the most important was the first goal related to saving lives in disasters. Unfortunately, the UN process, with its requirement to gain the endorsement of all countries, is not well suited to creating mechanisms that require national institutions to sign up to deliver on outcomes. As the targets on global casualty levels are not owned by any agency, they will not directly drive actions that can reduce the most lives.

Sendai was a missed opportunity. We can only reflect on how this goal could have been structured to have a greater impact. There are four components to an optimal goal.

- First the goal should have been directed to individual countries so that it could be owned by their national disaster risk reduction agencies and backed by the relevant ministries.
- Second, the goal should have been stated in terms of "expected lives lost," encouraging the use of consistent catastrophe loss models, or an appropriate blending of models (to capture the rare extremes) and empirical observations.
- Third, the targets for the reduction in "expected lives lost" should have been designed to be both challenging and achievable. This could have involved a uniform 50% reduction applied across all countries, or it could have been based on an exercise to band countries into a few different target categories based on what were their principal perils and what progress they had already made in disaster risk reduction.
- Finally progress on the targets should have been monitored by an independent risk auditor, so that the metrics for each country were trusted and progress could be confidently assessed.

The models that would be required for monitoring progress would not all be available at the start of the 2015–2030 period, but could have been developed at least by the middle of the period, when national progress could have been modeled retrospectively.

If the idea of relying on catastrophe models might be considered too futuristic, the Japanese government was optimistic that something more radical and model-based would come out of the Sendai negotiations. Soon after the Sendai conference was concluded, at the end of March 2015, the Tokyo city government announced that over the next decade it planned to halve the expected casualties from a repeat of a Magnitude 7.3 earthquake directly beneath the city (equivalent to the earthquake actually experienced in 1855) (Japan Economic Newswire 2015). Measurement of performance against this target would be accomplished by modeling the expected casualties both from the earthquake shaking and from the fires that were expected to follow.

The previous year, the Japanese government had announced a plan to reduce the casualties from a great Nankai trough subduction zone earthquake to the south of Honshu by 80% over the next decade, again testing progress using catastrophe models (*Japan Times* 2014).

As with a number of previous actions around disaster risk management, Japan has set out to be the pioneer in this new area: to employ catastrophe loss modeling techniques to set and measure progress in disaster risk reduction. It is expected that other cities and regions will want to follow Japan's leadership in the catastrophe loss modeling of casualties. There is an urgent need to apply models to identify those actions that can most reduce casualties ahead of the next disaster. If the United Nations and other bodies wish to increase the probability of success in preparing for and responding to disasters, these models, their applications, and the data obtained from them are indispensable now and will be in the years to come.

Notes

1. SURGEDAT: The World's Storm Surge Data Center, at http://surge.srcc.lsu.edu/.
2. See https://www.globalquakemodel.org/.

References

CRED. (2015). *The human cost of natural disasters: A global perspective.* Brussels: Centre for Research on the Epidemiology of Disasters.

Japan Economic Newswire. (2015, March 31). Gov't sets goal to halve victims in possible major quake in Tokyo.

Japan Times. (2014, April 1). Reducing disaster related deaths (Editorial). Retrieved from https://www.japantimes.co.jp/opinion/2014/04/01/editorials/reducing-disaster-related -deaths-2/#.W2wAM_lKipo

Michel-Kerjan, E., Hochrainer-Stigler, S., Kunreuther, H., Linnerooth-Bayer, J., Mechler, R., Muir-Wood, R., . . . & Young, M. (2013). Catastrophe risk models for evaluating disaster risk reduction investments in developing countries. *Risk Analysis, 33*(6), 984–999.

Mitchell, T., Guha-Sapir, D., Hall, J., Lovell, E., Muir-Wood, R., Norris, A., . . . & Wallemacq, P. (2014). *Setting, measuring and monitoring targets for reducing disaster risk: Recommendations for post-2015 international policy frameworks.* London: Overseas Development Institute.

Muir-Wood, R. (2012). *The use of catastrophe loss modelling methodologies to design and monitor disaster resilience goals and indicators in a post-MDG framework.* Washington, DC: RMS.

Pears-Piggott, M. I. B., & Muir-Wood, R. (2016). What constitutes a global baseline for worldwide casualties from catastrophes? *International Journal of Disaster Risk Reduction, 17,* 123–127.

So, E., & Spence, R. (2013). Estimating shaking-induced casualties and building damage for global earthquake events: A proposed modelling approach. *Bulletin of Earthquake Engineering, 11*(1), 347–363.

UNISDR (2015). Sendai framework for disaster risk reduction. United Nations Office for Disaster Risk Reduction. Retrieved from https://www.unisdr.org/we/coordinate/sendai -framework

CHAPTER 8

Learning from All Types of Near-Misses

Robin Dillon

Introduction

Would you be inclined to purchase flood insurance after a flood demolishes your house? What if the flood did not impact you, but demolished a neighboring town? After an earthquake, would you be more or less likely to invest in preventive mitigation measures? Would it depend on how much damage your house received in the earthquake? Howard Kunreuther and colleagues have spent more than three decades interviewing and surveying people in disaster-prone areas. Their research has led to the conclusion that most individuals make insurance purchase decisions based on their *perceptions of their risk* (Kunreuther 1996; Palm 1998), and a significant factor in the perception of their risk is their past personal experience, specifically negative outcomes from past events. For example, Kunreuther and Pauly (2004) found that people who had recently personally suffered flood damage would often purchase flood insurance, and Siegrist and Gutscher (2006, 2008) found that the perceptions of future risk are strongly influenced by people's past experience with flooding. Palm (1998) found similar effects for earthquakes, that is, experiencing damage made people believe their own home was at risk for future damage, and thus they were more likely to purchase earthquake insurance than others whose homes escaped damage. Similar research results have been found for why people evacuate for hurricanes. For example, Mileti and Sorensen (1990) found that people who feel safe staying at home will not evacuate, and those who do not feel safe will evacuate, and this feeling of safety is influenced by past experiences.

The problem with this risk heuristic is that most people's prior experience with a hazard is that they do not experience severe damage and may interpret their experience as evidence of their own resiliency. For example, most "hurricane-experienced" people are actually on the fringe of the storm (Weinstein 1989), and they experience few to no negative outcomes. How people interpret these near-miss events when no negative outcome is realized critically impacts their future decisions regarding preparedness actions. When Hurricane Wilma in 2005 required an evacuation notice for the Florida Keys, the local newspaper reported that less than 10% of the 78,000 residents evacuated (Royse 2005). Wilma was Florida's eighth hurricane since August 2004 and the fourth evacuation in 2005 for the Florida Keys. The Monroe County sheriff Richard Roth is quoted in the article as saying, "I'm disappointed [that people do not heed the evacuation warning], but I understand it. . . . They're tired of leaving because of the limited damage they sustained during the last three hurricanes" (Royse 2005).

Similarly, Baker (1979) found that as the length of residency of households living in hurricane-prone areas increased, the likelihood of evacuating from hurricanes decreased. For example, Carter (1980) in a 3-year study on response to hazard warnings discovered that people without hurricane experience will evacuate earlier than those who have experienced a hurricane; and Cross (1980) found that risk perception associated with hurricane threats decreased as length of residency increased in vulnerable coastal communities. As these examples illustrate, because many exposed individuals have not experienced severe or even moderate past damage, they are learning from these past events that complacency is an acceptable approach to future hazard warnings, but too often their outcome was not the result of a good plan but rather of good luck. What these residents are overlooking are the random differences that can make the next hurricane different from the last hurricane (e.g., wind speed, direction, etc.) and perhaps the next one will be more dangerous.

This challenge of interpreting prior experience is true in most situations involving risk. For example, March, Sproull, and Tamuz (1991) considered near-collisions in aviation and realized that these events can be interpreted two different ways—as evidence of the threat of the hazard and as evidence of the system resiliency: "Every time a pilot avoids a collision, the event provides evidence both for the threat [of a collision] and for its irrelevance. It is not clear whether the . . . organization came [close] to a disaster . . . or that the disaster was avoided" (10).

To identify near-misses requires a subjective interpretation of events that in many cases has no obviously bad outcome (at least to the observer). People think of the events in terms of what happened (which may be mentally coded as a "1" for event happened) and what did not happen (which may be mentally coded as a "0" for event did not happen). But how should near-misses be appropriately coded? Near-misses actually exist on the spectrum from 0 to 1 where some may be a 0.1 (almost a 0), others may be a 0.9 (almost a 1), and still others may be anywhere in between (0.2, 0.4, 0.5, 0.8, etc.). If people code anything that is not a 1 as a 0, then it will be impossible to expect them to learn the appropriate lessons from these events. The challenges of recognizing near-misses, appropriately coding these events, and then learning from these prior near-miss experiences are the focus of this chapter.

Recent Near-Miss Research Findings

Recent research (Dillon and Tinsley 2008; Dillon, Tinsley, and Cronin 2011; Tinsley, Dillon, and Cronin 2012) studied different types of "near-misses," and focused on near-miss events where a negative outcome could have happened because of hazardous conditions but did not because of chance (Dillon and Tinsley 2008). Tinsley, Dillon, and Cronin (2012) demonstrate that some of these near-misses have cues that highlight resilience (i.e., a disaster was successfully avoided), while others highlight vulnerability (i.e., a disaster nearly occurred). They show in a series of studies that when near-misses have clearly salient information about danger, the events will prompt people to scrutinize near-misses more critically, whereas for events without this clear danger cue, people will confidently view these near-miss events as successes, fail to learn from the event, and thus fail to prepare for the next potential hazard.

For example, one study that reanalyzed evacuation survey data from Lindell, Lu, and Prater (2005) collected six months after Hurricane Lili (the deadliest and costliest hurricane of the 2002 Atlantic hurricane season) showed that prior near-miss experiences in the sense of having evacuated for a prior hurricane which was later deemed unnecessary led to less protective action in the form of evacuation for Hurricane Lili. Subsequent lab studies (Dillon, Tinsley, and Cronin 2011; Tinsley, Dillon, and Cronin 2012) demonstrate that participants supplied with resilient near-miss information (i.e., near-misses without salient cues of significant problems) chose to evacuate significantly less than those with no near-miss information, but participants given near-miss information that highlighted vulnerabilities with salient cues chose to evacuate more. Their explanation for this behavior was that participants stated both lower perceived risks and lower concern about potential consequences when placed in situations describing resilient near-misses versus participants in situations with vulnerable near-misses.

When examining the causes of lower perceived risk, these studies (Dillon, Tinsley, and Cronin 2011; Tinsley, Dillon, and Cronin 2012) consistently show that individuals were not updating (i.e., lowering) their beliefs about the probabilities of negative outcomes. These studies found no evidence that participants tried to calculate new probabilities. Instead, their evidence showed that participants simply *felt differently* about the initial probabilities that they were given and in the case of resilient near-misses felt that, for example, a 20% probability was not as bad as participants in other conditions perceived a likelihood of 20% to be. Interestingly, their results show that statistical risk is a relative, not absolute, piece of information. The same numerical percentage can have a different "feeling" or "flavor" depending on the prior experience with near-misses. In one particular study (Dillon, Tinsley, and Cronin 2011), the researchers were primarily concerned with manipulating the probability of a hurricane storm (from 10% to 70%) and found no indication that the given chance of being hit (10–70%) influences how much more or less often people with near-miss information took protective action. If participants were normatively using near-miss information to recalculate the probability of getting hit, the results should have shown different levels of probability revisions for different levels of starting probability values, but instead across various levels of given storm probabilities, people showed evidence that near-miss information was still consistently affecting their behavior, making them less likely to mitigate a statistically given risk.

This research is a good demonstration of how people's own experiences influence how they interpret any given statistically generated risk in order to try to understand what the risk means for them personally. Statistically estimated risk levels (as given by an external source, such as weather specialists or the government) should exert some influence on protective behavior. Yet, this statistical risk is always interpreted through an individual's own experiences and thus those experiences will modify (either amplify or attenuate) protective behavior. Prior "hits" (as studied by Kunreuther and colleagues) make people more likely to take protective action (for the same given statistical risk). Prior near-misses with no cues to highlight vulnerability can make people less likely to take protective action (for the same given statistical risk).

Thus the conclusion from this research area is that near-miss information seems to be changing people's frames of reference. A certain probability of hit that might have felt risky before, feels less risky if the impacted individuals escaped unharmed in the past. Thus one could argue that people are behaving "rationally," but they are only rational within their own frame of reference. This presents a challenge to emergency managers who need to warn people of the risks of future hazards where each person has learned different lessons regarding the risk perception of the hazard from their own prior experiences.

The Impact of Repeated False Alarms

To further explore the role of repeated near-miss events, we looked at one particular type of near-miss, the false alarm, and developed a lab experiment to examine general responses to being repeatedly warned in what later turns out to be a false alarm. False alarms represent a specific type of near-miss, because the person of interest is warned of a potentially hazardous event and when the hazardous event does not impact the individual, there are no signals that a bad event almost occurred. A high false alarm ratio (or repeated overwarnings) is considered by many emergency managers and researchers to be problematic because of the perceived complacency among the population that will occur when the public is continuously warned but not impacted by an event (Simmons and Sutter 2009). In the case of tornadoes, roughly three out of four tornado warnings issued by the National Weather Service are false alarms (Erdman 2014). This is primarily a result of the fact that tornado warnings are issued for large areas so the tornado being warned for might be 20 or more miles from a particular person's location (Simmons and Sutter 2009). Also, the probability that a tornado will strike any one home in a warned area is low, and so warning response is a nontrivial decision.

To test the impact of repeated false alarms on individual perceptions of risk, we created an online exercise where 157 undergraduate students participated for class credit. The design was a 2×2 where participants were presented with scenarios over three simulated time periods. In each time period, participants encountered either a large or small tornado event and after rating their risk and their personal decision about mitigating actions to take, they are told they have been convinced to either (1) cancel plans and seek shelter, or (2) continue with plans.

Specifically, in the first time period, half the participants were presented with a tornado warning for either a large or small event:

Version 1 (small, time 1):

You are visiting relatives in Norman, Oklahoma for two weeks over the summer when the following warning is broadcast on the television:

"Doppler radar is detecting severe weather conditions likely to produce a small tornado. Winds of 50–85 m.p.h. are possible within the warned area. Seek shelter in a bathroom or basement away from windows."

Version 2 (large, time 1):

You are visiting relatives in Norman, Oklahoma for two weeks over the summer when the following warning is broadcast on the television:

"Doppler radar is detecting severe weather conditions likely to produce a DANGEROUS tornado. Winds exceeding 85 m.p.h. and producing major damage are possible within the warned area. Seek shelter in a bathroom or basement away from windows."

All participants were then asked: "What do you believe the risk is to your personal safety from this reported severe weather event?" (0 = not at all risky, 10 = very risky). Then each participant is told what his or her response was to the forecasted storm for time period 1: cancel plans and seek shelter or continue with plans based on the random assignment to one of the two conditions. The cancel plans and seek shelter condition read:

(Response 1): Your aunt who has spent her whole life in Oklahoma is inclined to ignore the warning and continue watching the television. Your other relatives convince everyone to seek shelter for about two hours in the unfinished basement until the weather alert is removed. Upon further research, you learn that no tornadoes were spotted in the warning area during the alert and that 70% of all tornado warnings are false alarms.

The continue-with-plans condition read:

> (Response 2): Your aunt who has spent her whole life in Oklahoma is inclined to ignore the warning and continue watching the television. She persuades the rest of your relatives to continue with plans and to not seek shelter from the tornado. After the alert is removed, upon further research, you learn that no tornadoes were spotted in the warning area during the alert and that 70% of all tornado warnings are false alarms.

If participants read about a small tornado in time period 1, they also read about a small tornado forecast in time period 2 (and the same for the large storm condition).

Version 1 (small, time 2):

Three days later, you are still visiting your relatives in Norman, Oklahoma when the same warning is broadcast on the television:
    "Doppler radar is detecting severe weather conditions likely to produce a small tornado. Winds of 50–85 m.p.h. are possible within the warned area. Seek shelter in a bathroom or basement away from windows."

Version 2 (large, time 2):

Three days later, you are still visiting your relatives in Norman, Oklahoma when the same warning is broadcast on the television:
    "Doppler radar is detecting severe weather conditions likely to produce a DANGEROUS tornado. Winds exceeding 85 m.p.h. and producing major damage are possible within the warned area. Seek shelter in a bathroom or basement away from windows."

All participants were then again asked: "What do you believe the risk is to your personal safety from this reported severe weather event?" (0 = not at all risky, 10 = very risky). In time period 2, unlike in time period 1, before participants were told their response, all participants are asked:

> You already have plans to go to the birthday party of your cousin at a local restaurant. You and your cousin have celebrated each other's

birthday together since you were five years old. You call ahead to the restaurant and the party has not been canceled.

Would you continue with your plans as scheduled or postpone them? (1 = continue with plans as scheduled, 2 = postpone plans).

Then based on the participant's randomly assigned condition from time period 1 (cancel plans and seek shelter, or continue with plans), participants are told the same information in time 2, either that their relatives reinforce their plan or override their plan. Then the "cancel plans and seek shelter" condition read:

Your relatives convince you that it is not safe to go to the birthday party, and instead seek shelter for about two hours in the unfinished basement until the weather alert is removed. Later you again learn that no tornadoes were spotted in the warning area during the alert.

The "continue plans" condition read:

Your relatives convince you to go to the birthday party, and not seek shelter from the tornado. After the weather alert is removed, you again learn that no tornadoes were spotted in the warning area during the alert.

Time period 3 is similar to time period 2. Those participants in the small tornado condition read:

Seven days later, you are still visiting your relatives in Norman, Oklahoma when the same warning is broadcast on the television:

"Doppler radar is detecting severe weather conditions likely to produce a small tornado. Winds of 50–85 mph are possible within the warned area. Seek shelter in a bathroom or basement away from windows."

Participants in the large tornado condition read:

Seven days later, you are still visiting your relatives in Norman, Oklahoma, when the same warning is broadcast on the television:

"Doppler radar is detecting severe weather conditions likely to produce a DANGEROUS tornado. Winds exceeding 85 m.p.h. and producing major damage are possible within the warned area. Seek shelter in a bathroom or basement away from windows."

All participants were again asked: "What do you believe the risk is to your personal safety from this reported severe weather event?" (0 = not at all risky, 10 = very risky). And then finally, all participants read and were asked regarding the time period 3 forecasted storm:

You have plans for a very important meeting that is related to some research that you are doing for school. You are leaving tomorrow so the meeting will not be able to be rescheduled. You have called ahead and the meeting has not been canceled.

Would you continue with your plans as scheduled or postpone them? (1 = continue with plans as scheduled, 2 = postpone plans).

When asked about the risk to personal safety, in all three time periods, those who saw the large forecasted storm thought the storm was a higher risk, but over time, everyone's perception of the risk declined with the repeated false alarms. The perception of risk by storm condition is shown in Figure 8.1.

As the graph in Figure 8.1 demonstrates, while perception of the risks of the large storm is greater than the small storm, in both cases, perception of the risks is decreasing over time. Additionally, the gap between large and small storm is also decreasing.[1] This study replicates the actual experience of the Florida Keys in 2004–2005 with the four evacuations in two years. With each subsequent evacuation, fewer people left. This effect has been referred to as "normalization of deviance," and has been documented in many different situations. Over time, an event that was originally a cause for concern no longer raises alarms and the deviance becomes normalized (Vaughan 1996, 1998). The term was first used to describe the decision-making culture at the National Aeronautics and Space Administration just prior to the Challenger space shuttle disaster but has also been used to describe the decision-making culture at NASA again prior to the Columbia space shuttle disaster, and the decision-making environment on the Deepwater Horizon oil rig prior to BP's Macondo blowout. The influence of repeated near-misses explains, in part, how people may become complacent to statistical risk and thus why they fail to explore steps to mitigate that risk when they regularly take chances

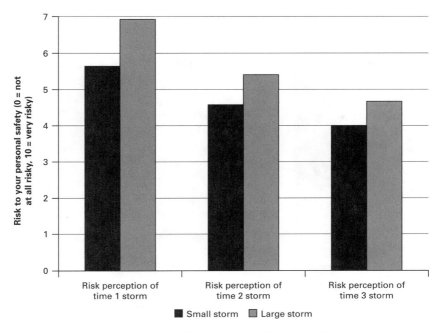

Figure 8.1. Risk perception of possible storm over three storm forecasts.

and experience the good (albeit lucky) outcome. The acceptance of additional risks becomes normalized over time.

Consider the impact in the experiment of informing the participant of their response action (either cancel plans and seek shelter, or continue with plans) in the first time period. Again, remember this was an assigned condition as participants were told the response to the first storm forecast after the assessment of risk in time period 1 and were told the response to the second forecast after the assessment of risk and after they said what they would do in time period 2. In examining the responses, there was no effect on perception of risk based on the participant's assigned condition. In other words, the assigned response condition (their being told that they were convinced to either cancel plans and seek shelter or continue with plans) did not have an influence on the participant's perceived risk of the situation.[2]

We then examined participants' individual response as to whether their reaction had been to cancel plans and seek shelter or continue with plans in time periods 2 and 3. Figure 8.2 shows the percentage of respondents by

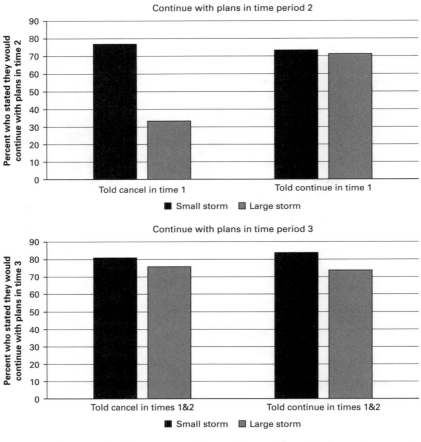

Figure 8.2. Percentage of participants who would continue with plans after tornado warnings in time periods 2 and 3.

condition who stated they would continue with their plans in time period 2 and time period 3. The only group to cancel plans and seek shelter in a significant percentage were those in the second storm time period in the condition where the storm was large and the participants had been told that they had been convinced to cancel plans and seek shelter in time period 1. In that condition, 33% of participants would continue with plans, compared to 76% in the small storm condition and 71–84% in all the other conditions. Yet, by the third storm time period (after two false alarms), the majority of participants in all conditions continue with their plans with no significant difference between conditions. In other words, even when participants are told that they had been convinced to seek shelter (at times 1 and 2) and that the storm is large, after two false alarms, people no longer seek shelter.

While this was a lab experiment and undergraduate participants faced no actual danger and did not have to incur any costs of actions, the results are still interesting and generalizable. The results suggest that people can be nudged to seek shelter by cues that suggest this is appropriate behavior. When participants were told that their family had convinced them to seek shelter at time 1, they were more inclined to seek shelter for the same hazard at time 2 (than those who had been told their family had convinced them to continue with their plans). However, this window of opportunity to influence people's reaction seems to be open for only a limited time. After two false alarms, the vast majority of participants ignored the tornado warning—regardless of whether or not they had been nudged to heed this warning in the past. Additionally (and unfortunately), the size of impending storm did not matter—after two false alarms even those facing a large storm warning were not likely to cancel their plans. A possible influencing factor is that storm size did not change across participants' warnings. Perhaps if people encountered a small storm false alarm followed by a large storm warning they might be more inclined to heed this warning than those who first encountered a large storm false alarm followed by a second storm warning.

Recommendations and Future Challenges

Our natural environment produces many examples of near-misses: a random tree pattern saves one's house from a mud slide, shifting weather conditions saves one's home from a wildfire, or an impending hurricane fails to produce the winds predicted or the track turns at the last moment missing a major metropolitan area along the coast. Because a near-miss is an instance when a potential hazard could have caused damage but by chance did not, what may be particularly salient is the positive outcome in the face of this hazard (e.g., "I was fine last time" or "the system worked").

Those who educate the public about natural disasters need to realize that the same objective facts about the costs and statistically calculated risk of an impending hazard will be interpreted differently by people based on their own prior experience. Prior near-miss information will influence what becomes salient and thus how people respond to a warning and this prior experience with near-misses and false alarms will be compounded over time. Thus, it is not enough to just outline facts such as estimated costs and probabilities. The narrative or story that accompanies these facts is important, as is the salience of prior good versus bad outcomes. Since this near-miss influence seems to operate automatically, people may need explicitly to be taught to counteract their gut feelings even if they have been lucky on more than one occasion.

Possible actions to mitigate the influence of near-misses include: (1) inducing counterfactual thinking, and (2) heightening awareness of how perceptions of risk can change. Prior research has shown that people with counterfactual mindsets can be motivated to learn from past events (McMullen 1997; Markman and Tetlock 2000; Morris and Moore 2000), where a counterfactual mindset is a concept in psychology that prompts people to consider possible alternative outcomes that could have happened. If, for example, people consciously note that they were quite close to a failure outcome and that they personally could have acted to avoid it (i.e., not blame circumstances), people may learn to alter future behaviors. However, all near-misses do not necessarily evoke counterfactual thoughts (Kahneman and Miller 1986), and not all counterfactual thoughts yield effect learning. Research has shown that people can be primed with counterfactuals to think more critically of near-miss events (similar to Roese 1994; Galinsky, Moskowitz, and Skurnik 2000; Kray and Galinsky 2003; Kray, Galinsky, and Wong 2006) and that counterfactual priming should promote more risk-averse decisions. In the context of near-misses, managers might engage in counterfactual thinking about near-misses by asking questions such as: Was this event a complete success or really an event somewhere on the continuum between success (0) and failure (1)? What factors, if changed, would have resulted in a failure, and how robust are these factors to change?

NASA's Goddard Space Flight Center instituted a process that attempts to create an environment for such reflection called "Pause and Learn" (Rogers and Milam 2005) following the criticism of NASA's culture in the report of the Columbia Accident Investigation Board in 2003. In a Pause and Learn workshop, teams or groups can gather and discuss among themselves what they learned from some recent event, usually a project milestone. These are not exclusively dictated by accidents, close calls or mishaps, but can closely examine "perceived" successes also. This enables the individuals to learn from each other and raises the expectation that what happens is for them to learn from. This also provides an opportunity for a group to think closely about the events and to consider alternative possible outcomes, and to consider whether successes could have been failures if not for certain fortunate chance events. These events continue throughout the development lifecycle so that as the project progresses, people remain vigilant in their identification of problems. Emergency managers could adopt a similar approach to reflect on evacuation orders and shelter-in-place warnings independent of the storm's outcome and associated damage, so that the evaluation of the decision-making process is not biased by the outcome (which often has a significant luck component).

Other efforts might emphasize how people's perceptions of risk often change over time. People could be counseled to compare current choices to past ones to detect changing risk beliefs. Other activities to attenuate "risk creep" might focus attention on the merits of caution. For example, emergency managers reminding stakeholders that three out of every four tornado warnings issued by the National Weather Service are false alarms does not mean people should just ignore them. Understanding that the National Weather Service errs on the side of caution because it would rather overwarn than miss warning for a serious tornado should not cause people to ignore tornado warnings. As shown in the student experiment, people are naturally inclined to become accustomed to risks and over time to develop complacency, so emergency managers need to provide education that emphasizes vigilance to risk, not complacency.

Public Policy Implications

A better understanding of how observers view near-miss events can have important implications in public policy situations. Consider, for example, the decisions surrounding the Three Mile Island nuclear reactors in Middletown, Pennsylvania in the 1980s. At the time of the accident at Unit 2 (March 29, 1979), the first unit happened to be shut down for routine maintenance and refueling. Because of the close proximity and nearly identical design, the Nuclear Regulatory Commission ordered the undamaged first reactor to remain shut down pending further review and investigation. A decision had to be made at some point to restart the undamaged first reactor. It was ultimately restarted more than six years later (October 8, 1985), but not until after substantial political and public debate. The biggest disagreement between groups supporting restart and those opposing restart was how close the event at Unit 2 came to being a major catastrophe. Pro-restart groups felt that the accident was blown out of proportion and that the media sensationalized everything, effectively characterizing the event as a resilient near-miss: the system worked and no one was hurt. The anti-restart groups felt that a major catastrophe was narrowly averted (i.e., a vulnerable near-miss) and that restarting the other identical reactor was just giving bad luck another chance. Understanding how different events can be interpreted differently and how this interpretation can compound over time is important for managing risk communications regarding future hazardous events a priori and post hoc.

Conclusions

A better understanding of people's responses to prior near-miss events is critically important if emergency managers are going to successfully communicate risks of hazardous situations to the public. This is because in most hazardous areas, people are repeatedly exposed to similar hazards year after year (e.g., hurricanes in the southeastern United States, tornados in the midwestern United States, etc.). In reality, many people's prior experience with a particular hazard is that they did not experience severe damage. Although this might be fortunate in the short term (they escaped damage), this research suggests that in the longer term this will lead to more complacency and less protective action. Thus, emergency managers need to continue to highlight the vulnerability of the hazard in a risk message, but acknowledge that not all individuals will be impacted by every event. For example, risk messages could emphasize how the event was almost a bad event for those who did not experience damage. This should prompt more risk-averse behaviors and more mitigating actions. Of course, this strategy is not without some risk. Future work is still needed to explore the sustainability of this type of warning over multiple events.

Notes

1. These differences are statistically significant. Using 2 (storm size) × 3 (time period) mixed model ANOVA, the perception of risk has a significant main effect for the severity of the storm (small storm mean = 4.75, s.d. = 1.9; large storm mean = 5.68, s.d. = 1.9; $F_{(1,155)} = 9.4$, p = 0.003) and for time (risk time 1 mean = 6.22, s.d. = 2.2; risk time 2 mean = 4.97, s.d. = 2.1;

risk time 3 mean = 4.32, s.d. = 2.3; $F_{(2,310)}$ = 113.9, p < 0.001). Additionally, there is a significant interaction effect, $F_{(2,319)}$ = 2.96, p = 0.05.

2. Using 2 (response condition) × 3 (time period) mixed model ANOVA, the perception of risk still has a significant main effect for time ($F_{(2,310)}$ = 109.6, p < 0.001), but does not have a main effect for what response was performed ($F_{(1,155)}$ = 1.65, p = 0.2).

References

Baker, E. J. (1979). Predicting response to hurricane warnings: A reanalysis of data from four studies. *Mass Emergencies, 4*, 9–24.

Carter, T. M. (1980). *Community warning systems: The relationship between the broadcast media, emergency service agencies, and the National Weather Service.* In *Disasters and the mass media: Proceedings of the Committee on Disasters and the Mass Media Workshop* (pp. 214–228). Washington, DC: National Academy of Sciences/National Research Council.

Cross, J. A. (1980). Residents' concerns about hurricane hazard within the lower Florida Keys. In J. E. Baker (Ed.), *Hurricanes and coastal storms* (pp. 61–66). Tallahassee: Florida State University.

Dillon, R. L., & Tinsley, C. H. (2008). How near-misses influence decision making under risk: A missed opportunity for learning. *Management Science, 54*(8), 1425–1440.

Dillon, R. L., Tinsley, C. H., & Cronin, M. (2011). Why near-miss events can decrease an individual's protective response to hurricanes. *Risk Analysis, 31*(3), 440–449.

Erdman, J. (2014, April 22). Tornado warning false alarms: National Weather Service upgrades to impact-based warning system. Retrieved from the Weather Channel website: https://weather.com/safety/tornado/news/tornado-warning-false-alarms-impact-based-warnings-20140418

Galinsky, A. D., Moskowitz, G. B., & Skurnik, I. (2000). Counterfactuals as self-generated primes: The effect of prior counterfactual activation on person perception judgments. *Social Cognition, 18*(3), 252–280.

Kahneman, D., & Miller, D. T. (1986). Norm theory: Comparing reality to its alternatives. *Psychological Review, 93*(2), 136.

Kray, L. J., & Galinsky, A. D. (2003). The debiasing effect of counterfactual mind-sets: Increasing the search for disconfirmatory information in group decisions. *Organizational Behavior and Human Decision Processes, 91*(1), 69–81.

Kray, L. J., Galinsky, A. D., & Wong, E. M. (2006). Thinking within the box: The relational processing style elicited by counterfactual mind-sets. *Journal of Personality and Social Psychology, 91*(1), 33.

Kunreuther, H. (1996). Mitigating disaster losses through insurance. *Journal of Risk and Uncertainty, 12*(2–3), 171–187.

Kunreuther, H., & Pauly, M. (2004). Neglecting disaster: Why don't people insure against large losses? *Journal of Risk and Uncertainty, 28*(1), 5–21.

Lindell, M. K., Lu, J. C., & Prater, C. S. (2005). Household decision making and evacuation in response to Hurricane Lili. *Natural Hazards Review, 6*(4), 171–179.

March, J. G., Sproull, L. S., & Tamuz, M. (1991). Learning from samples of one or fewer. *Organization Science, 2*(1), 1–13.

Markman, K. D., & Tetlock, P. E. (2000). "I couldn't have known": Accountability, foreseeability and counterfactual denials of responsibility. *British Journal of Social Psychology, 39*(3), 313–325.

McMullen, M. N. (1997). Affective contrast and assimilation in counterfactual thinking. *Journal of Experimental Social Psychology, 33*(1), 77–100.

Mileti, D. S., & Sorensen, J. H. (1990). *Communication of emergency public warnings: A social science perspective and state-of-the-art assessment* (No. ORNL-6609). Tennessee: Oak Ridge National Laboratory.

Morris, M. W., & Moore, P. C. (2000). The lessons we (don't) learn: Counterfactual thinking and organizational accountability after a close call. *Administrative Science Quarterly, 45*(4), 737–765.

Palm, R. (1998). Demand for disaster insurance: Residential coverage. In H. Kunreuther & R. J. Roth (Eds.), *Paying the price: The status and role of insurance against natural disasters in the United States* (pp. 51ff.). Washington, DC: Joseph Henry Press.

Roese, N. J. (1994). The functional basis of counterfactual thinking. *Journal of Personality and Social Psychology, 66*(5), 805.

Rogers, E. W., & Milam, J. (2005, March). Pausing for learning: Applying the after action review process at the NASA Goddard Space Flight Center. In *Aerospace Conference, 2005 IEEE* (pp. 4383–4388). New York: Institute of Electrical and Electronics Engineers.

Royse, D. (2005, October 24). Wilma hurtles toward Florida. *Eugene Register-Guard*, p. A11.

Siegrist, M., & Gutscher, H. (2006). Flooding risks: A comparison of lay people's perceptions and expert's assessments in Switzerland. *Risk Analysis, 26*(4), 971–979.

Siegrist, M., & Gutscher, H. (2008). Natural hazards and motivation for mitigation behavior: People cannot predict the affect evoked by a severe flood. *Risk Analysis, 28*(3), 771–778.

Simmons, K. M., & Sutter, D. (2009). False alarms, tornado warnings, and tornado casualties. *Weather, Climate, and Society, 1*(1), 38–53.

Tinsley, C. H., Dillon, R. L., & Cronin, M. A. (2012). How near-miss events amplify or attenuate risky decision making. *Management Science, 58*(9), 1596–1613.

Vaughan, D. (1996). *The Challenger launch decision: Risky technology, culture, and deviance at NASA*. Chicago: University of Chicago Press.

Vaughan, D. (1998). Rational choice, situated action, and the social control of organizations. *Law and Society Review, 32*(1), 23–61.

Weinstein, N. D. (1989). Effects of personal experience on self-protective behavior. *Psychological Bulletin, 105*(1), 31–50.

CHAPTER 9

Managing Systemic Industry Risk

The Need for Collective Leadership

Paul J. H. Schoemaker

The world is more volatile, uncertain, complex, and ambiguous than ever. On the bright side, business leaders can take steps to prevent or mitigate industry-wide systemic risks through better industry-level collaboration. Importantly, we must distinguish between *systematic* and *systemic* risk. In finance, *systematic* or *beta risk* refers to the volatility of a traded stock price that cannot be reduced via portfolio diversification the way some idiosyncratic firm risk can. A stock's beta reflects the component of a firm's total risk that is correlated with the market portfolio. *Systemic risk*, in contrast, is an unwelcome event arising in one part of the industry (such as a bank failure) that then spreads to other parts of the industry through contagion. Beta risk may manifest itself as systemic risk if the prices of many stocks are impacted in unison, as in a housing crisis, but beta risk can also arise from causes that are not based on contagion. For example, the terrorist attacks like those of September 11, 2001, or the passing of unexpected new regulations following an election, may lift or lower all stocks in an industry in near unison. However, this correlated response is not due to contagion but to the simultaneous impacts of a single event on many stock prices.

This chapter examines risks that originate in a few firms and then "explode," creating adverse consequences for an entire industry through secondary effects. Notable cases of such systemic risk include Volkswagen's rigging of pollution tests in cars; manipulations by banks of the Libor benchmark lending rate; phone hacking by British tabloid newspapers; dangerous offshore drilling in the Gulf of Mexico; mega pharmaceutical fines and loss of trust; and the subprime mortgage mess that triggered the financial crisis of 2008.

Many of these risks started small but, over time, resulted in broad consequences for many players because of underlying interdependencies. In essence, small perturbations snowballed into disasters, causing havoc across the entire ecosystem. Such risks are too formidable to be controlled by any single firm and can even cause damage far beyond the industry itself. The process of *contagion*—whereby risks spread under the radar—is especially challenging to manage proactively. It could, for instance, start with bank employees approving substandard mortgage loans inside of a single department, which eventually spreads to become a widely accepted practice. Such metastases require leadership approaches that transcend the individual firm.

Understanding Systemic Risk

The problem of a few rotten apples within a single company—a rogue trader, a sinister engineer, or a corrupt manager—may at first not seem to constitute a systemic risk. But, if undetected, such rotten apples invariably impact healthy ones and may unleash contagion dynamics that are hard to spot at first—or to stop later. The surfacing of "ticking time bombs" such as fraud, unethical behavior, or dangerous practices that can spread should become an industry-wide responsibility in order to mitigate risks collectively. The chemical industry embraced this approach, for example, through its Responsible Care Partner Award, which is given to companies working together to reduce work-related fatalities. In addition, individual leaders should take steps to dampen such risks within their own companies—as behavior science director Wil van Haaren has done at Dow by using cognitive science insights and tools (Heumann 2016).

In an earlier article, Tom Donaldson and I laid out six risk factors that make industries especially prone to self-inflicted wounds and annexed a survey to score sectors or industry segments in terms of their potential systemic risk (Donaldson and Schoemaker 2013). The six risk factors we focused on were as follows:

Innovation is rapid. When industry participants race to embrace a radically new design or technology, contagion can easily flourish in the system as lagging firms rush to join the bandwagon. Examples of innovations that

catalyzed unintended consequences include new tax shelters sold by accounting firms; untested methods for bundling and selling mortgages; and high-
risk deep water drilling techniques. In each case, innovations by a few players
prompted others to copy or join the seemingly profitable bandwagon without fully understanding the risks posed by these innovations.

"Hush" dynamics prevail. For decades, the so-called tobacco hush prevented open discussions of cancer and addiction in the cigarette industry.
Similar problems occurred when Johns Manville "hushed" the evidence it had
gathered in-house about the dangers of asbestos. Hush dynamics were also
likely present in Volkswagen's tinkering with pollution controls and Takata's
hiding of the explosion risks of its airbags, although the full stories are
still being uncovered. Secrecy pressures, issued by corporate attorneys or
spurred by public relations concerns, often stifle open dialogue and data collection in a number of industries, including pharmaceuticals and medical
technology.

Experts are few. When an industry relies on a handful of highly specialized
experts to interpret, design, or produce new tools, high-risk circumstances are
created. Complex technical designs—whether they involve elaborate credit
default swap mechanisms or exotic adhesives—often involve significant information asymmetry between creators and those who manage implementation. Deep water drilling is one recent example where many relied on the
expertise of a few, to the collective detriment of many. The Deepwater Horizon explosion on April 20, 2010 on a BP drilling rig in the Gulf of Mexico
killed 11 workers, injured 115 crew, and gushed oil for months into the sea,
while regulators stood by hapless. The regulatory agencies involved were
highly dependent on BP and its subcontractors to contain this catastrophe,
lacking the requisite know-how, skills, or resources to step in themselves or
even credibly oversee the effort. By the time the well was sealed nearly three
months later, about five million barrels of oil had polluted the Gulf of Mexico.

Regulators are weak. It can be very dangerous for an industry to rely on
passive or weak regulators who lack the expertise, motivation, or integrity
to protect the common good. For example, in the Gulf of Mexico oil spill,
the industry's relationship with the U.S. Interior Department's Minerals
Management Service was far too cozy (Ebinger 2016). And in the case of the
subprime bubble, rating agencies failed to score risks properly, assigning
triple-A ratings to junk bonds. Indeed, there is evidence that independent
experts are sometimes co-opted through consulting fees and privileged access
to create a false sense of security, whether in financial markets or concerning

the safety of medical drugs through funded research and articles (Angell 2009). Also, regulatory agencies (such as the U.S. Environmental Protection Agency or the U.S. Securities and Exchange Commission) may simply not have enough qualified staff to inspect or enforce regulations.

Too much is hidden. Sometimes, an industry develops widespread practices outside of the public eye that would be difficult to justify to the public. Examples of industries that have operated too much in the shadows (to their own detriment) include the loan-approval practices that fueled the mortgage crisis; sales practices meant to bias prescribing physicians in the pharmaceutical industry; and investment advisors overpromising returns to clients. When a sales rep meets a doctor at a gas station or in a supermarket aisle to chat about their drugs and then pays the doctor's gas or food bill, they are clearly crossing an ethical line (*The Economist* 2013). Whenever practices that are well known and widely accepted *inside* of an industry look odd or improper to those outside of it, alarm bells should ring loud.

Critics are ignored. It is imperative that those who raise warning flags about the playing field being tilted be listened to. For example, how are pharmaceutical or medical device companies dealing with people who critique their unhealthy liaisons with doctors? Why has the medical devices industry fought against a public registry of all devices that are placed inside patients' bodies so that a recall can be conducted quickly, if need be? The central question here is the extent to which industry leaders close ranks when criticized versus listening to those raising legitimate concerns. The chemical industry, for example, clearly closed ranks after the disastrous leaks at Bhopal, in India, and in the car industry it will be telling to see how other car makers respond to the public criticism of the ignition problems at General Motors or the Volkswagen emissions scandal. One strong gauge is how the industry has dealt with whistleblowers in the past; another is how the industry responds to media critics. Relatedly, how does the industry deal with grass-roots organizations that raise concerns about their practices or products, such as MADD (Mothers Against Drunk Driving) or the group Ralph Nader founded, Public Citizen?

These six risk factors can help leaders and regulators assess the extent to which an entire industry is at risk of major collateral damage. Once this descriptive phase has been completed, there may well be an urgent need for joint actions to stem systemic risks from spreading. The remainder of this chapter addresses what these actions could or should be. They include better sharing of best practices, investing in leadership education, jointly developing industry scenarios, collectively designing early warning systems, tackling festering industry problems early on, adopting a collaborative approach in dealing with regulators, safeguarding the health of the industry's shared ecosystem, avoiding overly hostile responses to industry critics, concerned stakeholders or the media, and viewing competition as a means to an end, and not the end itself.

The Role of Industry Leaders

There are some encouraging examples of industries voluntarily enacting guidelines and restrictions as a form of self-policing, but sadly, this usually occurs after a significant incident has occurred (Haufler 2013; Sethi 2016). The chemical industry, for example, worked with regulators to prevent hazardous accidents after the release of poisonous gases following a train derailment in 1979 in Mississauga, Ontario, Canada (King and Lenox 2000). Although no one died, fears about a spreading cloud of chlorine gas resulted in the evacuation of over 200,000 people, leaving a deserted town in its wake.

One of the most catastrophic accidents to awaken an entire industry occurred in 1986, when Union Carbide's chemical plants leaked methyl isocyanate and other toxic chemicals in Bhopal, India (Shrivastava 1987). This mega-tragedy, estimated to have killed over 12,000 people with more than 200,000 injured, prompted much greater self-regulation as well as more external oversight (Bowman and Kunreuther 1988). More recently, the advertising industry has voluntarily enacted rules and guidelines to reduce the negative impact of various kinds of advertising on children. Although closing the barn door after the horse has bolted may seem futile, this is mostly how voluntary industry policing has occurred in the past. However, for systemic risks such as cybersecurity, nuclear warfare, terrorism, and global warming, the reactive approach may be too costly.

As shown in Figure 9.1, industry leaders must assess two sides of the risk coin: (1) how exposed their industry is to systemic risks that could damage the business for many players; and (2) how effective company leaders are in collectively reducing or managing those risks ahead of time. Juxtaposing these two questions and assuming binary responses to each, results in four distinct industry cases, as shown in the figure.

Being positioned in Cell I should not raise great alarm but does demand vigilant monitoring of the industry as a whole. An example would be U.S.

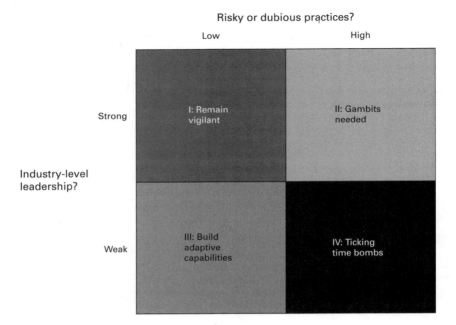

Figure 9.1. Two sides of the systemic risk coin.

credit unions, which weathered the recent financial crisis relatively well, as discussed later in the chapter. Cell II will require collective leadership to rein in "rotten apples," possibly using clever gambits that result in voluntary co-operation. Examples include the self-regulations mentioned above in the chemical industry as well as voluntary restrictions on advertising to children. Cell III calls for investments in collective leadership, which may be especially hard in countries such as the United States, where industry collaboration can be viewed as illegal collusion. The most disconcerting area is Cell IV, in which systemic risk is high while collective industry leadership is very weak, as we shall discuss later.

Considering that my earlier article with Tom Donaldson focused on assessing industry risk factors (i.e., the horizontal axis), I shall focus here on assessing the vertical axis of the chart, which is about improving collective leadership. Such leadership can be weak even if an industry has strong leaders for its individual companies. The best way to improve weak collective industry leadership is to start by assessing the current state of affairs and then think about remedies to bridge the gap between the current reality and what is needed. The questions in the list following offer a simple way to assess how well industry leaders are working together, at present, to identify, assess, improve, and monitor industry-wide risk. These broad descriptive questions can be further refined to better fit a specific industry. For example, they can be linked more directly to an industry's structure, technology, competitive dynamics, common practices, and institutional arrangements with the help of knowledgeable insiders.

To What Extent Does Your Industry Have . . . ?

1. Leaders whose business interests transcend those of their organization, with an eye to enhancing the well-being of the industry as a whole? Example: John Bogle founded Vanguard as a nonprofit organization to help individual investors adopt *passive* rather than *active* money management. He pioneered index funds in order to reduce fees from excessive portfolio churn typical in actively managed funds.

2. Examples of industry leaders gathering to identify and propose voluntary measures to reduce a looming industry risk? Example: the chemical industry did so following major chemical spills and advertising agencies voluntarily restricted advertising on children's shows following criticism of their (hidden) messages.

3. Notable instances where a majority of firms have agreed voluntarily to self-regulate risky activities to avoid damaging the collective interest of all players? Example: the academic research community involved in cloning experiments voluntarily agreed to a ban on human cloning for ethical reasons.

4. Neutral venues where industry leaders can meet, without fear of antitrust or litigation threats, to discuss important common risks? Example: the Wharton Risk Management and Decision Processes Center at the University of Pennsylvania has frequently hosted meetings among regulators, insurers, academics, and other stakeholders to discuss sector-wide challenges, concerns, and solutions.

5. A track record of collaborating with regulators and interest groups to establish reasonable standards and safeguards that protect the public or the environment? Example: the chemical industry's response following the Bhopal disaster.

6. A history of handling serious reputational damage in the public eye in a proactive rather than defensive manner? Example: the automobile industry meeting pollution standards as well as miles per gallon regulations.

7. Systemic risk scenarios in place to surface warning signals early, share best practices across a wide group of industry members, and jointly reduce collateral risk? Example: the Mack Institute for Innovation Management at the Wharton School convened multiple workshops with leaders from the life sciences sector (pharma, biotech, diagnostics, and devices) to develop scenarios about the intersection of information technologies and life science (Schoemaker and Schoemaker 2009).

To anchor these questions in the realities of doing business today, I will first address a challenging situation encountered in an insurance market entailing long-tail risks. Next, I will conclude with an example of how to systematically develop industry-wide adaptive capabilities. As I will show, a multipronged strategy has helped U.S. credit unions withstand the gale winds of change that have swept through their industry.

Strategy at the Industry Level

Speaking in confidence, the CEO of a large insurance company recently shared with me his view that various developments put his industry at far greater risk than the public or regulators realize (see the following list). So, what can far-sighted leaders practically do to mitigate the clouds that they see gathering over their industry (Kleindorfer and Wind 2009)? Public trust is crucial for companies that cover long-tail risks, such as long-term healthcare, life insurance, product liability, medical malpractice, and reinsurance. But smaller players—that often have fewer competitive advantages—may inadvertently resort to unduly aggressive marketing and pricing to survive, which was part of this CEO's problem.

Issues of Increasing Concern to a Far-Sighted CEO

1. The industry is locked into an old business model and innovation is limited to financial engineering; it is hard to point to genuine breakthroughs.

2. The industry is largely regulated at the state level, and due to competition among states for business, oversight may be too lax.
3. Regulators at the state level, and especially at the federal level, are often not sufficiently aware of systemic risks and capital needs.
4. The long-tail nature of the contingent claims sold creates short-term temptations to cut premiums and underfund reserves.
5. If some companies fail, the entire industry may end up paying for it via a fund equivalent to the Federal Deposit Insurance Corporation, which operates under a "pay as you go" regime.
6. There are no convenient executive venues for far-sighted industry leaders to meet and discuss systemic risks confidentially.
7. Some inept or dubious operators instill a collective short-term myopia and complacency that may lead to ruin in the long run.
8. Various bad apples are dropping seeds at present that may lead to another deep financial crisis later due to lean capital and overreliance on capital markets or government.
9. The industry was saved from greater calamity following the 2008–2009 crisis thanks to a roaring stock market rebound, but this was mostly luck.
10. It is dangerous to assume that the same will happen during the next crisis—as Japan sadly experienced during various decades of deflation.

To use a skating metaphor, strong insurers usually compete on "thick ice" and may push smaller rivals to the edges, where the ice is thinner. Thus far, no U.S. insurers have fallen through the ice (although the American International Group, Inc. (AIG) came close in 2008), but weather conditions may be turning against them in some markets. Also, many firms take false comfort from their collective fortune thus far. One CEO used the well-known analogy of frogs being very slowly boiled: At first they are happy they can manage the warmer water reasonably well, and even after some die, the stronger ones may view their ability to survive the tougher conditions as a competitive advantage. In addition, the surviving frogs tell each other reassuringly that the bad times can't last forever. And most disconcerting, the slowly worsening conditions surrounding them may never seem alarming enough, when viewed month to month, to justify bold action.

Cognitive psychologists use the term "just-noticeable difference" to describe people's limited sensitivity to small changes. For example, parents will not notice week to week that their children gradually get taller or heavier, but grandparents—who don't see them every day—may quickly spot this when they visit a few months later. In addition to this, many "frogs" may believe that bad things can indeed happen to other frogs, but not to them. They may hope, as another form of wishful thinking, that rescue will be on the way when things really get bad. However, as the lost decades in Japan clearly demonstrate, all of this may be illusory. The long sustained deflationary environment there essentially decimated the insurance industry, with very few survivors, even after the government tried to help.

Whether the firms skating on thin ice are actually foolish or quasi-rational given their limited options is a complex question. Joining a skating party when the ice is known to be melting is generally unwise, but once you are in, it might make sense to keep skating if exit is costly or impossible. It may even be rational to skate along the thin edges of the ice if there is no other room left and movement is necessary to survive. After all, no one knows when and where the ice will break first, and who will get pulled under. Some may survive on a floating ice block (such as a special product segment, customer group, or region), whereas others—who happen to be close to suddenly emerging cracks—will likely perish.

Perhaps the best that industry leaders can do in this case is to encourage government agencies to set tighter standards for the thickness of the ice and also to issue warnings that the industry is operating from a false sense of security. For their own companies and boards, these leaders can also develop scenarios to stress-test the adequacy of their reserves as well as build contingency plans in case things really sour. But this may not be enough if a Japan-like scenario materializes with negative interest rates, as this would deplete reserves for all players and slowly bleed the industry to death. Concerned industry leaders should embark on an open discussion about systemic risks, invite regulators and media to assure transparency, and develop industry scenarios that depict realistically what the risks are under favorable as well as highly adverse economic conditions. With that in hand, dashboards displaying various risk monitors can be developed and shared more broadly with the public, regulators, and other firms, so that everyone skates only on safe ice.

A positive example of how the U.S. insurance industry came together strategically is terrorism insurance. The 2002 passage of the Terrorism Risk Insurance Act and its subsequent renewals illustrate both collective as well as far-sighted industry leadership. Although I have focused here on problems within some insurance segments, it is premature to predict the demise of one of the largest industries in the world. Insurance companies have proven to be quite resilient over many decades, building on a long history tracing back to insuring ships of the Dutch East Indies Company in the sixteenth century, and even earlier in Genoa, Italy in the fourteenth century. With this comforting Bayesian thought in mind, let's now turn to a more recent example of collaborative leadership to stave off systemic risk in the near term.

Case Study: How Industry Leaders Strengthened American Credit Unions

The perseverance of credit unions during the deep recession of 2008 and 2009 is a welcome example of far-sighted collective leadership. Decades ago, several industry visionaries recognized that credit unions would encounter profound changes in regulation, technologies, and business models, and that most were ill-prepared. Various respected leaders joined forces and designed a multistage forum in which executives could meet and explore challenges, many of which dealt with systemic risk to their industry. One of the industry's leading associations, the Credit Union Executives Society (CUES)—whose primary mission is executive education—was well positioned to launch tailored leadership development programs for senior managers across the industry.[1]

Under the visionary leadership of Fred Johnson and its board, CUES launched its first program in 1997 at the Haas School of Business at the University of California at Berkeley. About 40 participants were invited to spend one week focusing on strategic issues facing their industry, using an outside-in perspective. In 1999, this same group of executives met for a full week at Cornell University's Johnson School of Business to focus on improving operations and negotiations. And in 2000, this senior executive cohort met for a third time at the University of Virginia's Darden School of Business to focus on personal leadership development. The Wharton School at the University of Pennsylvania joined in the initiative as well. This multiyear executive development program culminated in the awarding of a certificate that became the gold standard in the industry.

Since 15 such cohorts have completed the three-year training cycle by now, most credit unions have leaders in their executive teams, including presidents or CEOs, who are CUES alumni. At first, participation was limited to managers and executives from within the industry who showed leadership potential. Each cohort consisted of a broad representation of different types of American credit unions, as well as some from Canada and Australia. Each program was specifically tailored to address challenges facing credit unions, including the issue of systemic risk to the industry and what could be done collectively (such as sharing best practices, launching task forces, or sharing early warning signals).

Industry experts feel certain that credit unions weathered the deep financial crisis of 2008–2010 much better than banks thanks to greater strategic preparedness within the leadership ranks across the field (Smith and Woodbury 2010). Indeed, some credit unions actually *thrived* during the Great Recession, such as community development unions (Rosenthal 2012). Some of the hands-on learning programs were complemented with tailored scenario reports looking five years into the future of the industry. CUES distributed several of these scenario reports to a broad cross-section of industry participants, with the first issued in 2005, followed by one in 2010 and another in 2015 (CUES 2018). These sequential five-year looks into the future have had significant impact, prompting boards to ask how well their credit union was prepared for the various scenarios depicted. The typical answer was "insufficiently," which, over time, led to far more robust strategies. As collective awareness about systemic industry risks rose at senior levels across the industry, CUES continued its multilayered, long-term strategy of bringing executives together, while also expanding stakeholder involvement.

By 2016, about a thousand executives had elevated their leadership game, mastered new tools, and developed a trusted industry-wide network that could serve as an early warning system (Schoemaker, Day, and Snyder 2013). In addition, the credit unions' leading research think tank, the Filene Research Institute based in Madison, Wisconsin, got involved by issuing periodic strategy reports to help industry leaders stay abreast of important changes.[2] In addition to improving the collective strategic acumen of credit unions, CUES launched various board-level programs in partnership with leading business schools. An Advanced Leadership Institute was co-created with Harvard Business School from 2004 to 2008, bringing executives and their volunteer board members together in Boston. Similarly, a Directors Leadership Institute was offered at London Business School during 2002–2006, as well as one at IESE Business School in Barcelona from 2007 to 2009. Also, a Governance Leadership Institute was launched at the Rotman School of Management at the University of Toronto. Each of these programs was custom designed to foster strategic thinking, improved governance, and collaborative leadership across the industry.

Although many other industries have launched training programs, the CUES effort stands out for being especially prescient, considering how much the credit union industry changed over the past 20 years. One key to success was its carefully architected programs using cohorts spread out over three-year learning cycles across three different campuses. Also, its multilayered approach to inviting participants was key, starting with C-suite executives and then reaching deeper into the management ranks. Furthermore, expanding the program to include members of boards proved timely as well as innovative. Credit union boards, by charter, cannot pay their directors, so many are volunteers from the local business community or the credit union's own member base. Given this diversity, boards have tended to be the Achilles heel of credit unions, since many directors have lacked sufficient governance experience, leadership sophistication, or truly strategic mindsets to navigate the winds of change rocking the industry. By focusing less on operational details and more on the big picture, many of these boards rose to the occasion and started to support the change efforts proposed by their management teams. This transformation entailed a significant shift in mindset for many board members, who were often still wedded to the outdated leadership model of command-control that dominated in years past.

How to Handle Institutionalized Corruption

Thus far we have discussed two cases, both from the financial services sector, where systemic risks were rising and proactive steps were taken to address them. To my knowledge, neither case contained any criminal intent or malfeasance among the main players. But in many cases involving systemic risk, the problem is exacerbated by a growing subset of rotten apples who knowingly violate legal or ethical norms designed to protect the common good. Recent examples, still unfolding, include the Volkswagen scandal concerning rigged inspection tests via embedded software, as well as Wells Fargo creating phantom accounts *en masse* to meet sales targets. The problem of rotten apples spoiling it for others in an industry usually requires rather special remedies, including a heavy regulatory hammer and criminal penalties. But there are still some similarities with noncriminal cases as well in terms of early warning signals having been ignored by other industry leaders, regulators, or the media at large.

Let us briefly examine another financial services sector example where criminal behavior was indeed the main driving factor. The poster child for worst practices in this regard is the widely reported Libor scandal. "Libor"— an acronym for the London Interbank Offered Rate—reflects the rate at which the biggest banks borrow money from each other overnight. Established in the 1980s, it was supposed to accurately report overnight interbank rates. Soon, however, it became a benchmark for other interest rates, such as those used in short-term business loans, money market funds, and short-term bond funds. Because Libor drove so many other common rates in use, it started to be manipulated by some banks internally. The outcry was very loud when, in 2012, the Barclays Bank in the United Kingdom was charged with rigging the Libor rate for its own trading benefits. Unfortunately, these coordinated manipulations among a stealth network of traders had major consequences, since they meant many other derivative rates had been falsely set—amounting to trillions of dollars of transactions annually. Indeed, the very efficiency of financial markets depends on participants being able to observe the true level of those benchmark rates.

Following these shocking revelations, the chairman of Barclays, as well as its CEO, Bob Diamond, left their positions. Damning internal emails from Barclays traders revealed the depth of the fraud. One derivative trader, for example, had blatantly stated "we need a really low fix." Later, other banks besides Barclays were implicated in the Libor rigging scandal. As a result, yet another CEO, Piet Moerland of Rabobank in the Netherlands, stepped down as well. By 2014, UK authorities had reached settlements with five banking institutions, even though many claims continued against other companies as well as key individuals, adding greatly to the overall damage. The real cost of this self-inflicted industry wound far exceeds monetary fines and legal damages, involving the loss of reputation, evaporated trust, stricter regulations, and poor morale as well as lost talent. Several of the perpetrators were criminally convicted and are serving time in prison. The interesting question for our purposes is why so many industry leaders failed to act when evidence first surfaced of wrongdoing at lower levels.

The question is especially interesting because several of the industry risk factors described at the start of this chapter were present. For example, a widespread "hush" prevailed in the banking industry about rumors of rigging (see the second risk factor). We now know that hundreds of traders and bank executives either participated in or were aware of the rate-rigging going on. Even former Barclays traders working at other banks received information from old pals at Barclays and secretly traded on this illegal information. Silence was the pervasive industry norm as no one wanted to stick out their neck or be viewed as a snitch. As some point, perpetrators are in too deep to blow the whistle on others since they don't want to implicate themselves. Also, regulators were weak (the fourth risk factor). The Federal Reserve Bank of New York did issue a critical report in May of 2008, and shortly thereafter its president, Timothy Geithner, emailed Mervyn King, governor of the Bank of England, with suggestions on how to improve the accuracy of Libor. Yet nothing was done in response and critics were systematically ignored (see the sixth risk factor). When Libor rate manipulations were reported to the compliance department at Barclays on several occasions in 2007 and 2008, for example, the department failed to act. This example and others mentioned earlier suggest that human failings lower down in an organization—driven by ambition, misaligned incentives, hubris, and rationalization—can fester for a long time.

The leadership challenge at hand is to recognize such ticking time bombs early and then act decisively to stop the "cancer" from spreading. Traditional ethics programs in companies tend to focus on compliance, ethics training, and operational risk assessment. But rather than addressing "tone at the middle" of the organization, they should focus instead on the tone at the top. The aim is to foster a culture where people can discuss dubious behaviors openly and ensure that reward systems aren't creating conflicts between business objectives and integrity norms. Some of the practical steps leaders can take include better peripheral vision to detect anomalies sooner; looking for signs that unacceptable risks have been normalized ("everyone does it"); and encouraging whistleblowers instead of shunning or punishing them (Donaldson and Schoemaker 2013). Also, a central database about individual employees could be developed, as the accounting giant KPMG has done, to better assess staffing risks when making new assignments or promotions. The key point is not to treat ethics as something for just Legal and Human Resources to worry about. After all, most companies with scandals surging in the news *did* have top lawyers and maintained complex compliance programs. What matters even more is a broad tone of integrity at the top as well as open lines of communication that prevent untoward behavior from festering. All of this requires better leadership that operates from different premises, especially when it comes to industry-wide systemic risks. We will turn to this formidable challenge next.

Rethinking Industry Leadership

As widely practiced in the credit union industry and beyond, traditional models of leadership tend to emphasize strong top-down command. Although well-suited to manufacturing and mass production, these classic models are far less effective in a knowledge-based economy where human capital, business networks, empowerment, and bottom-up innovation play key roles (Uhl-Bien, Marion, and McKelvey 2007). They may also be ineffective in the realm of risk management, where issues are less routine, more complex, and often unknowable—as in the cases of climate change, cyberterrorism or human trafficking, for example.

Current academic thinking is focused on a leadership paradigm that can support highly adaptive and agile organizations (Obolensky 2010). Leadership experts today emphasize the limits of technical expertise and recognize that technocrats can seldom solve today's most demanding management problems—and in particular, the growing menace of systemic risk. Technical expertise resides in the head, whereas meeting risk challenges often involves the gut and the heart (Heifetz and Linsky 2004; Heifetz, Grashow, and Linsky 2009). Today's most effective leaders manage downward, upward, sideways, *and* through the middle (Useem 2001, 2011). The future of industry risk management may need to emphasize the collective role of leaders far more than today, both in preventing systemic risk as well as mitigating it.

Consider what it would have taken for an industry leader to stop the Libor collusion or the erosion of lending standards in the subprime market. Who is going to take the punch bowl away at the height of the party—especially if it ends up lowering everyone's bonus? As then-CEO of Citigroup, Chuck Prince put it succinctly, "When the music plays, you got dance." If Prince had stopped dancing, the firm would have quickly found another CEO; there is no shortage of happy feet. Many firms and leaders fell victim to willful blindness, turning a blind eye to what they (deep down) must have known was wrong (Heffernan 2011).

The problem is further exacerbated in the United States by tort law. Few general counsels of large firms would recommend that concerned CEOs meet with leaders from rival companies in order to tackle a common problem of systemic concern. The optics look bad, with charges of collusion or cartel behavior quickly likely to fly. The kind of risk management encouraged in this chapter—where leaders rise above firm-level concerns to safeguard their broader ecosystems—may require changes in the legal and regulatory regimes under which CEOs and boards function.

The challenge at an industry level is to blend strategy and leadership in nonlinear ways. As we shift the lens from business units to firms to industries to countries and finally to the global system, less will be under any individual leader's control. Leadership efforts bereft of strategic insight or acumen are bound to fail in the long run at any level. Based on research conducted on strategic leadership under uncertainty, using surveys with over 20,000 executives (Krupp and Schoemaker 2014), Figure 9.2 depicts a conceptual model of strategic leadership that entails traits and situational elements as well as transformational and adaptive ones.

As indicated, rather than react to events, effective strategic leaders shape and even create their own future. The commonly held view that leaders must adapt to an exogenous environment beyond their control is far too passive. As the late Wharton professor Russell Ackoff emphasized, most managers and leaders significantly underestimate how much influence they can have on their environment. Instead of planning *for* the future, Ackoff counseled, leaders should *plan the future* (Ackoff 1999). He termed this process "interactive planning" or "idealized thinking beyond current constraints." Ackoff used this approach to great effect in improving various complex social systems, from AT&T to global cities like Paris, as well as pressing social problems such as inner-city poverty or road traffic congestion (Ackoff 1978).

The challenge at the industry level is to deploy strategies flexible enough to accommodate a wide variety of situations—some anticipated, but many not. It is often unanticipated events like black swans and butterfly effects that offer the best opportunities for learning and improvement, but only if the leadership team has the right mindset to begin with. Surprises—especially deep crises—give leaders implicit permission to break rules, challenge the culture, reimagine their organizations, and create new routines. Conditions of instability and turmoil hide within them new possibilities and provide implicit organizational legitimacy to seize the moment (Habermas 1975). Unpacking strategic leadership into six basic elements, as shown in Figure 9.2, while drawing on an array of general tools and methods, can help industry leaders co-create effective means to control systemic risk.

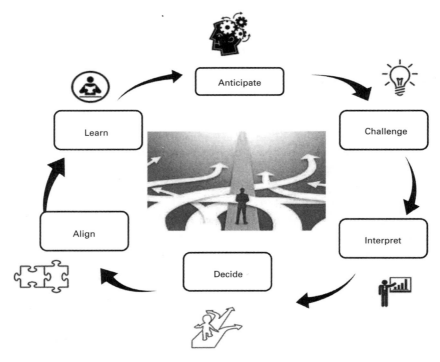

Figure 9.2. Six crucial capabilities of strategic leaders. *Source:* Krupp and Schoemaker (2014).

Conclusion

It is unfortunate that industries and societies often learn the hard way about systemic risks, perhaps because each risk seems different or even unique. Significant reforms seldom happen until a major crisis occurs, and this reactive approach too often results in only incremental improvements. Did we really make offshore drilling much safer following BP's massive oil spill in the Gulf of Mexico? Were key lessons truly learned—considering that this mega environmental disaster occurred after the Exxon Valdez caused an enormous oil spill in very pristine Alaskan waters decades earlier? Although Exxon is likely a much safer company now than before the spill, do the lessons apply industry wide?

The issue of concern is our limited collective learning and wisdom across circumstances and time. For example, the global financial crisis had many relevant precedents, from the Great Depression to the Savings and Loans crises a few decades back. It is not clear whether the root problem stems from (1) the deeper lessons being opaque or hard to generalize, (2) the scarcity of good remedies for better risk management, (3) people forgetting past accidents and remaining naively optimistic, or (4) the risks being viewed as societally acceptable, given the tradeoffs. It is clear, however, that the future will present us with risks that are simply too big to gamble on, since some may seriously damage the habitability of our planet—and possibly even wipe out large swaths of the human race.

For truly calamitous risks, the mounting evidence is clear: We need proactive measures, not reactive ones, and they must be developed collectively. In science, we see welcome precedents of expert communities trying to prevent mega disasters. Nuclear physicists, for example, have voluntarily agreed not to conduct elementary particle experiments in their giant accelerators if they do not already occur naturally in the universe. The aim is to protect humankind from falling victim to a weird singularity that puts us in a parallel universe or makes us vanish entirely. In biology, voluntary restrictions have been adopted about human cloning to prevent Frankenstein creations and eugenics. In the realm of artificial intelligence, we still need more protocols and safeguards to prevent the scenarios often depicted in science fiction, where computers take over the world (such as Hal refusing to listen to his master in the movie *2001: A Space Odyssey*). Likewise, we need to tackle climate change, cybercrime, nuclear power, biological warfare, and much more. All of these "wicked problems" require new risk management approaches that foster collective leadership behaviors involving government, society, *and* business.[3]

When adopting an industry- or sector-level view about systemic risk, several deeper issues surface about the competitive nature of capitalism as practiced in various forms around the world. Some may consider cut-throat rivalry a defining characteristic of free markets, aimed at securing lower prices for consumers, better service or quality, and continued innovation. But the Darwinian struggle for economic survival can only serve the greater good if conducted within a set of social contracts that at their roots are collaborative (Donaldson and Dunfee 1999). It hardly serves society if profit-maximizing firms fuel systemic risks that damage producers and consumers alike, if poorly priced negative externalities ruin our common earthly habitat, or if the myopic pursuit of self-interest leads to widespread distrust, resentment, and destabilizing inequality.

The broader phenomenon of "business,"—the activity that capitalism so deftly animates—is at bottom a cooperative endeavor involving production, distribution, and exchange for the purpose of achieving collective value (Donaldson and Walsh 2015). We often forget that even competitive markets are institutions that demand significant human cooperation for their design and maintenance. Leaders play a special role in fostering industry-wide collaboration, especially when facing systemic risks that are poorly understood, hard to control, and difficult to recover from. As indicated herein, this is precisely what our interdependent future will require in the area of risk management.

Acknowledgments

I very much thank Tom Donaldson from Wharton for his contributions to earlier drafts based on our joint research. I am also grateful to Howard Kunreuther and Erwann Michel-Kerjan for their detailed feedback, as well as Karen Christensen and Ann Bone for their fine independent editing.

Notes

1. The author served as academic director for the CUES CEO program at Berkeley and Wharton from 1998 to 2012.

2. See, for example, Aksoy (2013) (strategy focused); Goth, McKillop, and Wilson (2012) (governance focused); Gall, Groeneveld, and Soman (2012) (international cooperative banking focused); Haggart (2012) (policy focused); Dopico and Wilcox (2011) (long-term trends focused).

3. A compelling call for collective action ahead of time are the growing risks of climate change, as well as the daunting challenges these pose internationally to assure timely, coordinated responses that matter; see Hawken (2017).

References

Ackoff, R. L. (1978). *Redesigning the future.* New York: Wiley.

Ackoff, R. L. (1999). *Re-creating the corporation: A design of organizations for the 21st century.* New York: Oxford University Press.

Aksoy, L. (2013, February 25). *Linking member satisfaction to share of deposits: Applying the Wallet Allocation Rule in CUs.* Retrieved from https://filene.org/assets/pdf-reports/290 _Share_Deposits.pdf

Angell, M. (2009, January 15). Drug companies & doctors: A story of corruption. *New York Review of Books*. Retrieved from http://www.nybooks.com/articles/2009/01/15/drug-companies-doctorsa-story-of-corruption/

Bowman, E., & Kunreuther, H. (1988). Post-Bhopal behaviour at a chemical company. *Journal of Management Studies, 25*(4), 387–400.

CUES. (2018). Credit Union Management archive, Credit Union Executives Society. Retrieved from https://www.cues.org/marchive

Donaldson, T., & Dunfee, T. W. (1999). *Ties that bind: A social contracts approach to business ethics.* Cambridge, MA: Harvard Business Review Press.

Donaldson, T., & Schoemaker, P. J. (2013). Self-inflicted industry wounds: Early warning signals and Pelican Gambits. *California Management Review, 55*(2), 24–45.

Donaldson, T., & Walsh, J. P. (2015). Toward a theory of business. *Research in Organizational Behavior, 35*, 181–207.

Dopico, L., & Wilcox, J. (2011, February 10). *Impacts of mergers on credit union costs: 1984–2009.* Retrieved from https://filene.org/assets/pdf-reports/227_Dopico_Wilcox_Mergers.pdf

Ebinger, C. (2016, April 20). 6 years from the BP Deepwater Horizon oil spill: What we've learned and what we shouldn't misunderstand. Retrieved from Brookings website: https://www.brookings.edu/blog/planetpolicy/2016/04/20/6-years-from-the-bp-deepwater-horizon-oil-spill-what-weve-learned-and-what-we-shouldnt-misunderstand/

The Economist. (2013, March 2). Let the sunshine in. Retrieved from https://www.economist.com/business/2013/03/02/let-the-sunshine-in

Gall, A., Groeneveld, H., & Soman, D. (2012, May 25). International cooperative governance and market trends. Retrieved from https://filene.org/research/report/Market_Trends

Goth, P., McKillop, D., & Wilson, J. (2012, July 13). Corporate governance in Canadian and US credit unions. Retrieved from https://filene.org/research/report/Corp_Governance

Habermas, J. (1975). *Legitimation Crisis.* Boston: Beacon Press.

Haggart, B. (2012, February 21). *Keeping an eye on the ball: Credit unions, the level playing field, and competitive balance.* Retrieved from https://filene.org/assets/pdf-reports/260_Competitive_Balance.pdf

Haufler, V. (2013). *A public role for the private sector: Industry self-regulation in a global economy.* Washington, DC: Carnegie Endowment for International Peace.

Hawken, P. (Ed.). (2017). *Drawdown: The most comprehensive plan ever proposed to roll back global warming.* New York: Penguin.

Heffernan, M. (2011). *Willful blindness: Why we ignore the obvious.* New York: Simon & Schuster.

Heifetz, R., Grashow, A., & Linsky, M. (2009). Leadership in a (permanent) crisis. *Harvard Business Review, 87*(7/8), 62–69.

Heifetz, R. A., & Linsky, M. (2004). When leadership spells danger. *Educational Leadership, 61*(7), 33–37.

Heumann, J. (2016). Chemical industry leaders recognized for outstanding environment, health, safety initiatives. Retrieved from https://www.americanchemistry.com/Media/PressReleasesTranscripts/ACC-news-releases/Chemical-Industry-Leaders-Recognized-for-Outstanding-Environment-Health-Safety-Initiatives.html

King, A. A., & Lenox, M. J. (2000). Industry self-regulation without sanctions: The chemical industry's responsible care program. *Academy of Management Journal, 43*(4), 698–716.

Kleindorfer, P. R., & Wind, Y. (2009). *The network challenge: Strategy, profit, and risk in an interlinked world.* Upper Saddle River, NJ: Prentice Hall.

Krupp, S., & Schoemaker, P. J. (2014). *Winning the long game: How strategic leaders shape the future.* New York: PublicAffairs.

Obolensky, N. (2010). *Complex adaptive leadership. Embracing paradox and leadership.* Burlington, VT: Gower.

Rosenthal, C. (2012, February). *Credit unions, community development finance, and the Great Recession* (Working Paper 2012-01). Federal Reserve Bank of San Francisco. Retrieved from https://www.frbsf.org/community-development/files/wp2012-011.pdf

Schoemaker, P. (2013, June 10). How to defuse an ethical time-bomb in your company. Retrieved from https://www.inc.com/paul-schoemaker/how-to-defuse-an-ethical-time-bomb-in-your-company.html

Schoemaker, P. J., Day, G. S., & Snyder, S. A. (2013). Integrating organizational networks, weak signals, strategic radars and scenario planning. *Technological Forecasting and Social Change, 80*(4), 815–824.

Schoemaker, P. J., & Schoemaker, J. A. (2009). *Chips, clones, and living beyond 100: How far will the biosciences take us?* Upper Saddle River, NJ: FT Press Science.

Sethi, S. P. (Ed.). (2016). *Globalization and self-regulation: The crucial role that corporate codes of conduct play in global business.* New York: Palgrave Macmillan.

Shrivastava, P. (1987). *Bhopal: Anatomy of a crisis.* Cambridge, MA: Ballinger.

Smith, D. M., and Woodbury, S. A. (2010). *Withstanding a financial firestorm: Credit unions vs. banks.* Retrieved from https://filene.org/assets/pdf-reports/214_Smith_Firestorm.pdf

Uhl-Bien, M., Marion, R., & McKelvey, B. (2007). Complexity leadership theory: Shifting leadership from the industrial age to the knowledge era. *Leadership Quarterly, 18*(4), 298–318.

Useem, M. (2001). *Leading up: Managing your boss so you both win.* New York: Crown Business.

Useem, M. (2011). *The leader's checklist, expanded edition: 15 mission-critical principles.* Philadelphia: Wharton Digital Press.

CHAPTER 10

Measuring Economic Resilience

Recent Advances and Future Priorities

Adam Rose

The use of the term *resilience* in the context of natural disasters and terrorism has increased exponentially over the last 20 years. The term is in such widespread use today, and has been applied so broadly, that it is in danger of merely becoming a popular buzzword, which is undercutting its substance and usefulness. It is important to establish a precise definition and an operational metric to gauge its past effectiveness and future potential.

The essence of economic resilience, as defined in this chapter, as well as most resilience definitions in general, pertains to actions that maintain functionality of an entity or system and help it recover more rapidly. With regard to the economic dimension, resilience is applicable to individual businesses and households, individual sectors and markets, and the economy as a whole, including interactions between its various components (Rose 2017).

A poignant example relates to actions taken following the September 11, 2001 terrorist attacks on the World Trade Center. The rapid relocation of its business and government agency tenants, primarily to vacant office space in Midtown Manhattan and northeastern New Jersey, substantially reduced the potential losses in economic activity in the New York metropolitan area and the United States as a whole. For the latter, these relocation decisions averted 72% of potential losses in gross domestic product (GDP) (Rose et al. 2009).

Over the past 10 years, researchers at the Center for Risk and Economic Analysis of Terrorism Events (CREATE) have answered the following important questions (see, e.g., Rose, Oladosu, and Liao 2007; Rose 2009; Rose and Krausmann 2013):

- Is resilience a meaningful concept? Yes it is, especially from an economic perspective.
- Can resilience be rigorously defined? Yes, though it is complex and has multiple dimensions.
- Can resilience be empirically measured? Yes, and an operational metric has been established and successfully applied in several contexts.
- How effective has resilience been today? It has been very effective, and moreover has been relatively low-cost and hence cost-effective.
- Can a meaningful resilience index be established? Yes, if it has solid conceptual grounding, is based on actionable variables, and appropriate weights for individual indicators can be specified.

These questions have been answered in many case studies using a variety of economic models, including microeconomic, macroeconometric, input-output, and computable general equilibrium. They include actual events such as the World Trade Center attacks and the earthquakes in Northridge, California in 1994 and Wenchuan, China in 2008. They also include simulation studies of an anthrax attack, influenza epidemic, "dirty bomb" attack, airport attack, seaport disruption, a catastrophic earthquake, severe winter storm, tsunami, and targeted attacks on electric power and water systems.

This chapter briefly explains how the aforementioned critical questions surrounding economic resilience have been answered, modeled, and applied over the past decade. First, economic resilience is defined, including some of its major subtleties. Next an operational metric of resilience is presented, with a summary of the application of the metric by CREATE researchers and others in measuring resilience in case studies of simulated and actual events. The chapter then turns to the discussion of the cost-effectiveness and cost-benefit analysis of resilience. It concludes with a discussion of priorities for future research.

Defining Economic Resilience

Following Rose (2004, 2009), we begin with basic definitions and their relation to more general concepts of resilience and definitions in related fields.

These comparisons indicate that there are more commonalities than differences across various fields, especially with regard to the essence of the definitions.

In general, static resilience refers to the ability of the system to maintain a high level of functioning when shocked (see, e.g., Holling 1973). *Static economic resilience* is the efficient use of remaining resources at a given point in time. It refers to the core economic concept of coping with resource scarcity, which is exacerbated under disaster conditions. In general, dynamic resilience refers to the ability and speed of the system to recover (see, e.g., Pimm 1984). *Dynamic economic resilience* is the efficient use of resources over time for investment in repair and reconstruction. Investment is a time-related phenomenon—the act of setting aside resources that could potentially be used for current consumption in order to reestablish productivity in the future. Static economic resilience does not restore damaged capacity and is thus not likely to lead to full recovery.

Note that the definitions are couched in terms of functionality, typically measured in economics as the *flow* of goods and services, such as changes in GDP or broader measures of human well-being, as opposed to property damage. It is not the property (capital *stock*) that directly contributes to economic welfare but rather the flows that emanate from these stocks. Two things should be kept in mind. First, while property damage takes place at a point in time, the reduced flow, often referred to on the production side as business interruption, begins at the time of the disaster but continues until the system has recovered or attained a "new normal." Second, the recovery process, and hence the application of resilience, depends heavily on the behavior of economic decision-makers and on public policy. Of course, recovery is a multifaceted activity. It is not as simple as, for example, just automatically rebuilding a school destroyed by an earthquake, hurricane, or armed attack.[1]

Another important distinction is between *inherent* and *adaptive* resilience. The former refers to aspects of resilience already built into the system, such as the availability of inventories, excess capacity, substitutability between inputs, and contingent contractual arrangements accessing suppliers of goods from outside the affected area (imports). Resilience capacity can be built up through these means and is then accessed after the disaster. Adaptive resilience arises out of improvisation under stress, such as draconian conservation not otherwise thought possible (e.g., working many weeks without heat or air conditioning), changes in the way goods and services are produced, and new contracting arrangements that match customers who have lost their suppliers with suppliers who have lost their customers.

Economic resilience takes place at three levels:

- microeconomic (individual business, household, or government)
- mesoeconomic (individual industry or market)
- macroeconomic (combination of all economic entities, including their interactions)

At the microeconomic level, on the business supplier side, static economic resilience includes redundant systems, improved delivery logistics, and planning exercises. Several options also exist on the business customer side. Rose (2009, 2016) has developed a framework for analysis that connects customer-side resilience to decisions captured by the economic production function with respect to input choices. Examples include conserving inputs, using excess inputs (capacity and inventories), substituting among them locally, importing them, and altering the locations and timing of their use. For example, all inputs (capital, labor, infrastructure services, and materials) can be conserved to some extent. The major obstacle is the necessity of the input in the production process. The major obstacles to importing needed goods are logistics and transport costs. Broadening the supply chain (see, e.g., Sheffi 2005) by expanding the range of suppliers in place or on a contingency basis is an increasingly popular option. In essence, however, the micro level does not operate in isolation, but must also be evaluated in terms of its broader business ecology (Martin and Sunley 2015), at the meso and macro levels discussed below.[2]

Tierney (2007) makes the point that many of the features that make businesses inherently resilient are related to those that make them less vulnerable to disaster in the first place. Vulnerability is related to such features as business size, ownership characteristics, and type (e.g., a small business with an owner from a minority group, located in an "Old Town" building and selling a product with many substitutes, is more vulnerable and hence less inherently resilient than others). Businesses with some of these characteristics are also likely to have a lower capacity for adaptation (Center for Organizational Studies 2001).

At the mesoeconomic level, resilience can bolster an industry or market and include, for instance, industry pooling of resources and information and innovative pricing mechanisms. What is often less appreciated is the inherent resilience of market prices that act as the "invisible hand" to guide resources to their best allocation in the aftermath of a disaster (see, e.g., Horwich 2000). Some pricing mechanisms have been established expressly to deal with such a situation, as in the case of non-interruptible service premia that enable customers to estimate the value of a continuous supply of electricity and to pay in advance for receiving priority service during an outage. The price mechanism is a relatively costless guide to redirecting goods and services. Price increases, to the extent that they do not reflect "gouging," serve the purpose of reflecting highest value use, even in the broader social setting. Moreover, if the reallocation violates principles of equity, the outcomes can be adjusted by income or material transfers to the needy.

Industry competitiveness also has an effect on inherent resilience and the ability of both the firm and the industry to recover. Product characteristics and production technology have a major effect on the ability to adapt.

At the macroeconomic level, resilience is very much influenced by interdependencies between sectors. Consequently, macroeconomic resilience is not only a function of resilience measures implemented by single businesses but is also determined by the actions taken by all individual companies and markets, including their interaction. Examples of resilience options at the macro level would be economic diversity to buffer impacts on individual sectors and geographic proximity to economies not affected by disaster to facilitate access to goods or aid. Others include fiscal (e.g., infrastructure spending to boost the affected economy) and monetary policy (e.g., keeping interest rates low to stimulate private sector reinvestment). The macro level overlaps with the popular focus on "community resilience" and represents a more holistic picture (Norris et al. 2008).

Similar to Tierney, Martin and Sunley (2015) note that resilience is related to critical features of the regional economy. Other factors affecting resilience at the macro level include the extent to which the disaster affects customers and the demand for product. Locational and proximity aspects come into play ("hazardousness of place"), as does the size and level of economic development of the region. Agglomeration economies refer to the advantages of large city size in reducing costs of production that can remain intact and keep the city competitive after as disaster (see, e.g., Chernick 2005). However, the close proximity of businesses can make them more vulnerable in the first place. Martin and Sunley (2015) state that "the key contribution of the idea of resilience, in our view, is that it directs attention precisely to the impact shocks and their role in shaping the trajectories of regional growth and development" (11).

The previous examples relate primarily to *static economic resilience*. *Dynamic economic resilience* is applicable at all three levels as well, in this case in terms of expediting the recovery process and enhancing its outcome. At the micro level, this can be promoted through rapid processing of insurance claims and arranging financing so as to facilitate repair and reconstruction. At the meso and macro levels, it includes hastening and improving the economic effectiveness of the recovery process by improving logistics and coordinating recovery across sectors. Cross-cutting all three levels is adapting to changing conditions by promoting flexibility and translating short-run practices into sustainable ones through a continuous learning process (see, e.g., Chang and Rose 2012; Zolli and Healy 2012; Rose 2014).[3]

An Operational Metric

Following Rose (2004, 2009), we provide an admittedly crude but operational metric of resilience. *Direct* static economic resilience (DSER) refers to the level of the individual firm or industry (micro and meso levels) and corresponds to what economists refer to as "partial equilibrium" analysis, or the operation of a business or household entity itself. *Total* static economic resilience (TSER) refers to the economy as a whole (macro level) and would ideally incorporate what is referred to as "general equilibrium" effects, which include all of the price and quantity interactions in the economy, macro-aggregate considerations, and the ramifications of fiscal, monetary, and security policies related to the disaster.

An operational measure of DSER is the extent to which the estimated direct output reduction deviates from the likely maximum potential reduction given an external shock, such as the curtailment of some or all of a critical input. In essence, DSER is the percentage avoidance of the maximum economic disruption that a particular shock could bring about.

We illustrate the application of the definition with the following case study by Rose et al. (2009), who estimated the national and regional economic impact of the September 11, 2001 terrorist attack on the World Trade Center. The researchers refined available data indicating that more than 95% of the businesses and government offices operating in the World Trade Center area survived by relocating, primarily to Midtown Manhattan or across the river in northeastern New Jersey. Had all of these firms gone out of business, the potential direct economic loss in terms of GDP would have been $43 billion. However, relocation was not immediate, taking anywhere from a few days to as long as eight months for the vast majority of firms. Rose et al. (2009) calculated this loss in GDP at $11 billion. They were then able to apply the resilience definition provided in this section to estimate that the effectiveness of relocation as a resilience tactic in the aftermath of the 9/11 attacks was 72% ($43 minus $12, divided by $43).

Several studies have examined economic resilience in actual disasters or with the use of simulation studies. The major pioneer is Tierney (1997), who surveyed businesses in the aftermath of the Midwest floods in 1993 and the Northridge earthquake in 1994. Rose and Lim (2002) translated Tierney's findings into specific measures of resilience of the Los Angeles electricity system. They identified such factors as time-of-day use, electricity "importance" (dependence), and production recapture as key to understanding why businesses that averaged an X% reduction of electricity were able to continue operation at much less than an X% reduction in their production of goods and services. In fact, they found that these micro-level tactics resulted in a reduction of business interruption losses by more than 90% of baseline estimates, a level consistent with Tierney's survey responses.

Several other simulation studies have been undertaken to estimate the effects of resilience on losses from disasters, using the metric presented in the previous section. Kajitani and Tatano (2009) used a survey to estimate the resilience of Japanese industries to various types of lifeline disruptions from disasters. Their findings are the most definitive to date on a broad spectrum of resilience tactics. Rose, Oladosu, and Liao (2007) estimated the resilience of the Los Angeles water and power systems to a two-week outage due to a terrorist attack. They found that resilience could be as high as 90%, primarily due to production recapture. Rose and Wei (2013) examined such resilience tactics as excess capacity, inventories, and export diversion to reduce potential losses from a 90-day shutdown of a major U.S. seaport complex in a regional economy dominated by petrochemical production. They also examined the effectiveness of major government policies such as accessing the Strategic Petroleum Reserve but found it likely to be of limited help at the cost of considerable political capital. Overall, they found that the implementation of these resilience tactics could reduce GDP losses by more than 70%.[4]

Cost-Effectiveness and Cost-Benefit Analysis of Resilience

To make prudent resource management decisions, one must consider the cost of each resilience tactic as well as its effectiveness. One tactic might be capable of reducing more than twice the business interruption losses of another, but if it costs 10 times as much to implement, the former is not the better option.

We begin with a general overview of cost considerations. Most adaptive conservation more than pays for itself when it represents a productivity improvement, such as an increase in energy efficiency (producing the same amount but with less energy). A more general definition of conservation (reducing the amount of an input irrespective of its effect on output) can incur net positive costs. Input substitution requires a small penalty for using a less optimal input combination. Import substitution involves an increase in costs from utilizing higher-cost sources and/or increasing transportation distances. Relocation can be somewhat expensive if it involves a physical move; however, increasing the role of telecommunications, and the prospects for working in cyberspace and telecommuting, have significantly decreased this cost. Emergency planning exercises take little time and incur relatively low costs. Production rescheduling involves the payment of overtime wages.

Some resilience tactics are primarily inherent and simply await their utilization once the disaster strikes. The cost of inventories is just the carrying charge and not the value of the inventories themselves, which just replace resources that would have been paid for otherwise. Excess capacity involves a similar cost, though some excess capacity is often planned in order to enhance business flexibility or to accommodate downtime for maintenance; these aspects should not be charged to disaster resilience.

Once the cost per unit of effectiveness, expressed in percentage terms or in terms of dollars of net revenue from business interruption loss prevention, is determined, the options should be ranked from lowest cost to highest, and would likely yield the standard increasing marginal cost curve. Note, however, that since most conservation more than pays for itself, the function begins in the negative cost range.

Resilience can be couched in a benefit-cost analysis framework by considering its rewards as well. At the micro level, the benefits are the net revenue of business interruption losses avoided. At first this might best be represented by a horizontal marginal benefit curve, reflecting equal additional increments of benefits for each percentage increase in resilience. The optimal level of resilience would be at the point at which the marginal cost and marginal benefit curves intersect. Even without a precise numerical example, this enables us to draw some insights. All cost-saving resilience options would be taken, because they yield guaranteed net benefits. Also, given the relatively low cost of many of the tactics, at least in some of their initial applications, it is likely that a fairly high level of resilience would be chosen. Of course, this would best be juxtaposed to mitigation opportunities as well.

Co-benefits and the Resilience Triple Dividend

Background

Many analysts and practitioners believe that there is a significant underinvestment in disaster risk management (DRM), broadly defined to include both pre-disaster mitigation and post-disaster resilience. One way to strengthen the case for DRM is to examine its spillover effects. The broader framework for analysis is referred to as the resilience triple dividend (Surminski and Tanner 2016), which consists of the following three aspects: avoided disaster losses, economic potential unlocked through reduced risk, and development gains generated from "joint products."

The first category is simply the direct benefits of risk reduction through mitigation and resilience. The second represents various externalities stemming from resilience. The third relates to intended ancillary benefits. We refer to the broader benefits of DRM in the last two dividends as *co-benefits* (Hallegatte 2016; Rose 2016).

For example, when a business installs a sprinkler system to protect against fire spreading on its premises, it also helps protect adjacent buildings and an entire community (Kunreuther and Heal 2003). This is also the case for instituting better water drainage around its facilities that reduces flooding potential for the community and hence makes the operation of other businesses less risky. More broadly, actions by any one business can contribute to overall community well-being in terms of improving the quality of life and promoting economic stability. These co-benefits are not captured by the firm making the investments, and this leads to shortfalls in DRM. The third dividend results in underinvestment when all joint product opportunities are not taken into account. Overall, all three dividends can be enhanced by raising awareness of their potential; even the direct private sector benefits of DRM are not fully taken into account because of bounded rationality problems (Gigerenzer and Selten 2002).

Incentivizing Policies

Paying for DRM is a critical consideration. Many businesses, especially those in developing countries, do not have the necessary internal resources at their disposal. Several means of private financing for DRM have been developed and have been shown to be effective, though they are not without their limitations. Still, "disaster financing" often refers to risk spreading and government or philanthropic transfer payments rather than outright risk reduction, though the risk reduction can be incorporated into the former with innovative policy design.

Innovative financing instruments include land leases, land exchanges, "bonusing" incentives, and value capture. These are in addition to standard private sources such as grants, insurance/reinsurance, securitization, performance contracts, custom debt instruments, equity, guarantees, and loans (Brugmann 2012). These instruments apply primarily to pre-disaster mitigation, but are also applicable to post-disaster resilience in the recovery process, as well as to climate change adaptation (Linnerooth-Bayer and Hochrainer-Stigler 2015).

Credit is one alternative, but it is not unusual to only find it available from private sources at higher than market interest rates, especially given the desperation of borrowers in post-disaster situations. Moreover, unless appropriately devised, this instrument can lead to moral hazard, thereby exacerbating losses. Clearly, there is a role for government provision or regulation of credit in these situations. For example, where microcredit falls short, some Latin American countries have developed public-private partnerships for what is called an emergency liquidity facility.

Securitization is an approach where a stable and predictable revenue stream exists. It essentially represents a claim on these future earnings and can be sold to obtain capital at the beginning of the earnings stream. This is a popular private sector instrument, and the revenue stream could be diverted for DRM, or the instrument used more explicitly to fund DRM investments.

Another major approach is insurance. In the business sphere this is a valuable contributor because the outright absorption of catastrophic losses would lead to the demise of all but the largest and strongest enterprises. The disaster insurance business itself is in an especially precarious position given the magnitude and geographic concentration of claims, and typically requires a safety net of its own in the form of reinsurance or government backing. Covered losses are still only a fraction of total property and casualty losses from disasters—nearly 50% on average in a country like the United States, but a very low percentage in developing countries. One attribute of insurance that can be of immense help is the actuarial information that it provides in assessing risk. In this sense, insurance agents can serve as effective risk messengers.

Another type of insurance can also play an important role, though its prevalence today has been confined primarily to industrialized countries. This is ordinary business interruption insurance, which covers lost profits when a business cannot operate due to damage to its own facility, or contingent business interruption insurance, where the business is unable to operate because one of its suppliers (including utility lifelines) or employee access are disrupted (Rose and Huyck 2016). This form of insurance provides the working capital needed to purchase inventory for resale or inputs for production, over and above the standard property and casualty insurance policies, which cover repair and reconstruction.

A related instrument, sometimes referred to as "quasi-insurance," is the catastrophe (CAT) bond. This is used to spread extreme risks, whereby investors receive a premium in exchange for the bonds but forfeit the principal if a disaster strikes. Bond revenues represent a source of private capital that can be used for mitigation or building resilience capacity instead of after-the-fact recovery and reconstruction. Obviously, the upfront use of funds has a great deal of merit but has been underutilized. CAT bonds are increasingly being used by local government authorities but could also be adopted by the private sector (Michel-Kerjan and Kunreuther 2011).

Various other refinements of insurance products, as well as successful real world examples, are discussed in Swiss Re (2011). Also, insurance, through rate-reduction incentives, represents one of the most successful ways of promoting mitigation. Still, there is a long history of underadoption of insurance (Kunreuther et al. 1978), although lessons learned and research innovations are helping to improve design (Kunreuther, Michel-Kerjan, and

Pauly 2013). For example, Kunreuther and Michel-Kerjan (2010) have proposed combining multiyear property insurance with loans to promote mitigation that can reduce premiums.

The investment industry is likely to find various co-benefits of DRM appealing if they can be quantified. This includes bond-rating companies which seek to reflect asset risk in relation to the ability of bond issuers to make payments. It also includes investment companies, and mutual, hedge, and pension funds and others that have a long-term fiduciary responsibility to protect investments (Multihazard Mitigation Council 2015).

The presence of co-benefits helps to justify various types of expenditures on DRM at several levels. Those co-benefits internal to the firm can be counted as part of a broader set of returns on investment. Those external to the firm can be addressed in several ways. One is collective action by parties that are benefited. Governments can play a role here in coordinating efforts and subsidizing some part of the DRM for the common good. Even areas of risk finance, specifically with respect to governments or private donors providing assistance, can be rationalized by the existence of co-benefits. What is often considered bailing out individual businesses is justified in part because of the broader contributions to such objectives as economic stability, growth, and sustainability.

Co-benefits of DRM offer several attractive rewards to businesses. Some of these co-benefits are more certain, tangible, and immediate than the intended direct benefits of mitigation, which may never materialize if the disaster does not take place. Some of the co-benefits are consistent with a no-regrets strategy in that they yield cost savings irrespective of whether or not a disaster strikes. Some DRM investments provide protection against several hazards in addition to those that are the main focus. Others contribute to shared growth of the economy and to broader social benefits. Some represent payments for unpriced services, such as the environment; these payments enhance the reputation of businesses and can thus serve to increase long-run profits.

Future Research

We offer the following topics as priorities for future research:

Measuring static and dynamic economic resilience in practice. Very few studies have actually measured resilience in the aftermath of a disaster, and instead, analysts and policymakers have been overly dependent on simulation analysis. The author, in conjunction with colleague Noah Dormady, is engaged in two major studies to help rectify this issue. We are being supported by the new Critical Infrastructure Resilience Institute of the Department of Homeland Security to develop a conceptual framework and conduct survey research on static economic resilience in the aftermath of Superstorm Sandy, the landfall remnants of the Atlantic hurricane that occurred in 2012. This study will be based on many of the concepts presented in this chapter. We are also being supported by the National Science Foundation, along with colleagues Kathleen Tierney, Liesel Ritchie, and Charles Huyck, to undertake a study of dynamic resilience in the aftermath of Sandy. In this case, we are examining the potential and speed of recovery. This project revolves around the key questions: (1) Will the business invest in repair and reconstruction? (2) If so, in what location? (3) Will the new investment include major productivity enhancements? (4) Will the investment result in reducing vulnerability to future disasters? Again, a survey will be administered to collect the major portion of the data.

Identifying obstacles to resilience. The simulation studies referred to above are biased toward estimating resilience at its maximum effectiveness. This outcome is unlikely due to the disarray accompanying most disasters, administrative obstacles, and personal failings. Moreover, Rose (2009) has analyzed the erosion of resilience during large disasters as inventories are depleted, extreme conservation becomes onerous, and opportunities for recapturing production decline as customers abandon their traditional suppliers when they are unable to deliver within a time threshold. Research is needed on the extent of these obstacles and identifying ways to overcome them.

Evaluating inherent resilience potential. It is important to identify resilience that is inherent in the survival mechanisms of businesses and households from those that require government policy assistance. Likewise, more research is needed on the ability of markets to provide adequate price signals for resource allocation in a crisis. Much research exists on the role of sectoral diversification in cushioning a region from ordinary shocks, but not necessarily for idiosyncrasies of various types of disasters. This way, future recovery efforts can better capitalize on existing capabilities and minimize duplication of government services. The focus of government can then be on facilitating this inherent resilience by removing obstacles to private enterprise, reducing wait times for assistance, and more effectively targeting its role.

Costs of resilience. To make prudent resource management decisions, one must consider the cost of each resilience tactic as well as its effectiveness.

There is a need to go beyond anecdotal evidence on resilience and perform analyses of all the direct and indirect costs (including any negative side effects) of individual resilience tactics. Some of the more challenging areas relate to transportation systems, where rerouting and modal substitution, as well as cost savings through trip reduction via such options as telecommuting, should be explored. Once costs are specified, it is possible to juxtapose them to the benefits reflected in resilience effectiveness to perform solid risk management valuations. Ultimately, post-disaster resilience strategy should be compared to pre-disaster mitigation strategies in a benefit-cost framework to strike a better balance than currently exists.

Compiling resilience indices based on actionable variables. Recently, interest has shifted to identifying individual resilience indicators that can be aggregated into an overall index. This has emanated in part from the successful compilations of vulnerability indices. Several well-intentioned examples of resilience indices include Cutter, Burton, and Emrich (2010), Sherrieb, Norris, and Galea (2010), and Arup (2014) (see also the review by Cutter 2016), but many of their components are background conditions and many are not in fact important to the resilience of individual businesses or the economy as a whole during the crucial early stages of the recovery process. Specifically, resilience is not just the flip-side of vulnerability. A resilience index is not only useful for studying the recovery process, but also for improving it. This speaks to the importance of actionable variables. More research is needed to identify indicators that really matter to business decisions in the short run.

Climate change. Although there is skepticism about climate change in the popular press and political circles, scientists are nearly unanimous in their concern over its realities, even current ones, and the likelihood that potential damages will increase without major steps to mitigate and sequester its greenhouse gas (GHG) drivers (IPCC 2014). Moreover, given the centuries-long residence time of GHGs in the atmosphere, even major mitigation efforts will not reduce the threat that currently exists and will remain as at least a baseline in the foreseeable future. Climate change is already manifesting itself in sea level rise due to an increase in global temperatures, which have increased flooding and droughts, respectively. Many scientists are becoming convinced that climate change is already increasing the frequency and magnitude of tornadoes, hurricanes, and other severe storms. Resilience is a way of coping with this short-run climate variability. Moreover, lessons learned from it can carry over to improving long-run climate adaptation.

Cyber threats. In an increasingly interconnected society, we are becoming more vulnerable to terrorist attacks, natural disasters, and technological failures related to cyber systems. Of course, these ripple outward to more than just person-to-person and business-to-business interactions, but also to interactions across these individual units and with respect to critical infrastructure and the rest of the region. As with other threats, we cannot eliminate all cyber risk and need to utilize remaining resources more efficiently and recover more quickly when events occur. Unique opportunities exist here with respect to cloud and satellite technology in general (Rose 2015). The cyber area is also a major source of resilience capacity in relation to other threats as well and thus bears further exploration. For example, cyber storage of data (with backups) is less expensive and less vulnerable than most other options. Cyber capabilities are also better able to reduce losses through activities such as telecommuting.

Incentives to promote resilience. A major issue is how to increase resilience capacity and improve the effectiveness of its implementation. Businesses increase resilience capacity for the sake of their own profits, but resilience often yields spillover benefits in the form of positive externalities and public goods that benefit others in the region. However, the standard market failure outcomes, primarily underprovision of resilience, are likely to take place under these conditions. Related to this is the fact that not all businesses are aware of the benefits to their own operations either. Efforts to promote greater awareness within the private sector of resilience potential are just beginning, with one major theme being the co-benefits of disaster risk management (see, e.g., Surminski and Tanner 2016; Rose 2016). More research is needed on how to induce decision-makers to address resilience from the broader perspective of society. This would relate to research on innovative risk financing and on policy instruments, including traditional ones such as taxes, subsidies, regulation, and information campaigns, as well as innovative approaches.

Equity aspects and environmental justice. Disasters typically have disproportionate impacts across socioeconomic groups, as well as economic sectors and regions. Disasters typically hurt the poor and otherwise disadvantaged the most, because they are more vulnerable in the first place (see, e.g., Mileti 1999). But these groups have not been analyzed in terms of the effect that disaster resilience might have on them. It would be worthwhile to examine the impacts of resilience on lessening the burden on the weakest/poorest. These elements of society have fewer resources to build resilience capacity, but, at the same time, resilience is relatively less expensive than other tactics to reduce losses, so this may have a profound effect in narrowing the disparities of disaster impacts. Also, disadvantaged groups are likely to benefit differentially from the co-benefits of resilience.

Conclusion

Economic resilience is an effective way to reduce the costs of disasters. As defined in this chapter, it is geared to averting losses in economic activity (business interruption), such as GDP and employment, rather than property damage. This is important because recent major catastrophes have demonstrated that the former types of disaster-related costs can be much larger than the latter. While resilience is a process, often involving both preparedness and execution, we focus on post-disaster implementation. Many relatively inexpensive resilience tactics exist at the micro-, meso-, and macroeconomic levels. Moreover, many have an advantage of needing only to be reactive to an actual disaster, as opposed to pre-disaster mitigation, whose benefits need to be adjusted downward by the probability that the disaster will in fact occur. Of course, optimal risk management requires a balancing of pre-disaster and post-disaster strategies.

As terrorism and climate change impacts continue to climb, both in short-run variability and long-term trends, resilience will become increasingly important. It represents a valuable short-run response to extreme events that challenge the sustainability of societies. One major challenge is to learn from improvisations arising out of crises and to incorporate them into longer run adaptation and sustainability. Several other challenges have been identified in this chapter to broaden the concept of economic resilience, extend its applications, improve the measurement of its costs and benefits, incentivize it, and ensure it will be applied equitably.

Notes

1. Research on resilience is split into two camps. About half of the researchers view resilience as any action that can reduce losses from disaster, ranging from pre-disaster mitigation to post-disaster recovery. Not surprisingly, this group is dominated by engineers, whose work is primarily in the area of mitigation (see, e.g., Bruneau et al. 2003; Haimes 2006). The

other camp focuses on resilience as actions following a disaster. Steps can be taken to enhance resilience, acknowledging that it is very much a process, but such measures are usually not implemented until afterward (e.g., stockpiling of critical materials, development of emergency plans). Events, such as the World Trade Center attacks and Hurricane Katrina indicate that business interruption can be as large as or larger than property damage following a disaster. We focus on the second approach, noting that much of our analysis is applicable to mitigation as well.

2. Most of the resilience tactics associated with businesses are applicable to government and household operations as well, with some modification (see Rose 2009).

3. Resilience is sometimes conflated or confused with related terms such as vulnerability and sustainability. The reader is referred to Rose (2009, 2017) for a more detailed discussion.

4. The context in which the disaster strikes and resilience is implemented also has an influence on effectiveness. Relevant factors include the disaster type, magnitude, and recovery duration, as well as background conditions relating to the economy, such as its economic health at the time of the disaster and its geographic location. For example, inventories are finite and more likely to run out in disasters for which the duration of recovery is long. Production recapture also erodes over time, as customers begin to seek other suppliers. Excess capacity is dependent on the business cycle (e.g., one reason that relocation was so effective after the World Trade Center attacks was because New York City was in the throes of a recession, which then provided a great deal of vacant office and some manufacturing space).

References

Arup (2014). *City resilience framework*. London: Ove Arup & Partners International. Retrieved from https://assets.rockefellerfoundation.org/app/uploads/20150530121930/City-Resilience -Framework1.pdf

Brugmann, J. (2012). Financing the resilient city. *Environment and Urbanization, 24*(1), 215–232.

Bruneau, M., Chang, S. E., Eguchi, R. T., Lee, G. C., O'Rourke, T. D., Reinhorn, A. M., . . . & Von Winterfeldt, D. (2003). A framework to quantitatively assess and enhance the seismic resilience of communities. *Earthquake Spectra, 19*(4), 733–752.

Center for Organizational Studies. (2001). *Organizations at risk: What happens when small businesses and not-for-profits encounter natural disasters.* University of Wisconsin–Green Bay Center for Organizational Studies report. Retrieved from http://www.ecocalltoaction .com/images/Organizations_at_Risk.pdf

Chang, S. E., & Rose, A. Z. (2012). Towards a theory of economic recovery from disasters. *International Journal of Mass Emergencies and Disasters, 32*(2), 171–181.

Chernick, H. (Ed.). (2005). *Resilient city: The economic impact of 9/11.* New York: Russell Sage Foundation.

Cutter, S. L. (2016). The landscape of disaster resilience indicators in the USA. *Natural Hazards, 80*(2), 741–758.

Cutter, S. L., Burton, C. G., & Emrich, C. T. (2010). Disaster resilience indicators for benchmarking baseline conditions. *Journal of Homeland Security and Emergency Management, 7*(1).

Gigerenzer, G., & Selten, R. (Eds.). (2002). *Bounded rationality: The adaptive toolbox.* Cambridge, MA: MIT Press.

Haimes, Y. Y. (2006). On the definition of vulnerabilities in measuring risks to infrastructures. *Risk Analysis, 26*(2), 293–296.

Hallegatte, S. (2016). *Higher losses and slower development in the absence of disaster risk management investments* (Policy research working paper 7632). Development Economics, Climate Change Cross-Cutting Solutions Area, World Bank Group.

Holling, C. S. (1973). Resilience and stability of ecological systems. *Annual Review of Ecology and Systematics, 4*(1), 1–23.

Horwich, G. (2000). Economic lessons of the Kobe earthquake. *Economic Development and Cultural Change, 48*(3), 521–542.

IPCC (Intergovernmental Panel on Climate Change). (2014). *Working Group III contribution to the Fifth Assessment Report of the Intergovernmental Panel on Climate Change.* New York: Cambridge University Press.

Kajitani, Y., & Tatano, H. (2009). Estimation of lifeline resilience factors based on surveys of Japanese industries. *Earthquake Spectra, 25*(4), 755–776.

Kunreuther, H., Ginsberg, R., Miller, L., Sagi, P., & Slovic, P. (1978). *Disaster insurance protection, public policy lessons.* Cambridge: MIT Press.

Kunreuther, H. & Heal, G. (2003). Interdependent security. *Journal of Risk and Uncertainty, 26*(2/3), 231–249.

Kunreuther, H. C., & Michel-Kerjan, E. (2010). Market and government failure in insuring and mitigating natural catastrophes: How long-term contracts can help. In W. Kern (Ed.), *The economics of natural and unnatural disasters* (pp. 9–38). Kalamazoo, MI: W. E. Upjohn Institute for Employment Research.

Kunreuther, H., Michel-Kerjan, E., & Pauly, M. (2013). Making America more resilient toward natural disasters: A call for action. *Environment: Science and Policy for Sustainable Development, 55*(4), 15–23.

Linnerooth-Bayer, J., & Hochrainer-Stigler, S. (2015). Financial instruments for disaster risk management and climate change adaptation. *Climatic Change, 133*(1), 85–100.

Martin, R., & Sunley, P. (2015). On the notion of regional economic resilience: Conceptualization and explanation. *Journal of Economic Geography, 15*(1), 1–42.

Michel-Kerjan, E., and Kunreuther, H. (2011). Redesigning flood insurance. *Science, 333*(6041), 408–409.

Mileti, D. (1999). *Disasters by design: A reassessment of natural hazards in the United States.* Washington, DC: Joseph Henry Press.

Multihazard Mitigation Council. (2015). *Multihazard Mitigation Council approach to resilience incentives.* Washington, DC: National Institute of Building Sciences.

Norris, F. H., Stevens, S. P., Pfefferbaum, B., Wyche, K. F., & Pfefferbaum, R. L. (2008). Community resilience as a metaphor, theory, set of capacities, and strategy for disaster readiness. *American Journal of Community Psychology, 41*(1–2), 127–150.

Pimm, S. L. (1984). The complexity and stability of ecosystems. *Nature, 307*(5949), 321.

Rose, A. (2004). Defining and measuring economic resilience to disasters. *Disaster Prevention and Management: An International Journal, 13*(4), 307–314.

Rose, A. (2009). *Economic resilience to disasters* (CARRI Research Report 8). Washington, DC: Community and Regional Resilience Institute.

Rose, A. (2014). Economic resilience and the sustainability of cities in the face of climate change: An ecological economics framework. In D. A. Mazmanian & H. Blanco (Eds.), *Elgar companion to sustainable cities: Strategies, method and outlook* (pp. 336–353). Cheltenham: Edward Elgar.

Rose, A. (2015). *Measurement of cyber resilience.* Los Angeles: Center for Risk and Economic Analysis of Terrorism Events (CREATE), University of Southern California.

Rose, A. (2016). Capturing the co-benefits of disaster risk management in the private sector. In S. Surminski & T. Tanner (Eds.), *Realising the 'triple dividend of resilience': A new business case for disaster risk management* (pp. 105–127). Heidelberg: Springer.

Rose, A. (2017). Benefit-cost analysis of economic resilience actions. In S. Cutter (Ed.), *Oxford research encyclopedia of natural hazard science.* New York: Oxford University Press.

Rose, A., & Huyck, C. K. (2016). Improving catastrophe modeling for business interruption insurance needs. *Risk analysis, 36*(10), 1896–1915.

Rose, A., & Krausmann, E. (2013). An economic framework for the development of a resilience index for business recovery. *International Journal of Disaster Risk Reduction, 5,* 73–83.

Rose, A., & Lim, D. (2002). Business interruption losses from natural hazards: Conceptual and methodological issues in the case of the Northridge earthquake. *Global Environmental Change Part B: Environmental Hazards, 4*(1), 1–14.

Rose, A. Z., Oladosu, G., Lee, B., & Asay, G. B. (2009). The economic impacts of the September 11 terrorist attacks: A computable general equilibrium analysis. *Peace Economics, Peace Science and Public Policy, 15*(2).

Rose, A., Oladosu, G., & Liao, S. Y. (2007). Business interruption impacts of a terrorist attack on the electric power system of Los Angeles: Customer resilience to a total blackout. *Risk Analysis, 27*(3), 513–531.

Rose, A., & Wei, D. (2013). Estimating the economic consequences of a port shutdown: The special role of resilience. *Economic Systems Research, 25*(2), 212–232.

Sheffi, Y. (2005). *The resilient enterprise.* Cambridge, MA: MIT Press.

Sherrieb, K., Norris, F. H., & Galea, S. (2010). Measuring capacities for community resilience. *Social Indicators Research, 99*(2), 227–247.

Surminski, S., & Tanner, T. (Eds.). (2016). *Realising the 'triple dividend of resilience': A new business case for disaster risk management.* Heidelberg: Springer.

Swiss Re. (2011). *Closing the financial gap: New partnerships between the public and private sectors to finance disaster risks.* Zurich: Swiss Reinsurance.

Tierney, K. (1997). Impacts of recent disasters on businesses: The 1993 Midwest floods and the 1994 Northridge Earthquake. In B. Jones (Ed.), *Economic consequences of earthquakes: Preparing for the unexpected.* Buffalo: National Center for Earthquake Engineering Research.

Tierney, K. J. (2007). Businesses and disasters: Vulnerability, impacts, and recovery. In H. Rodriguez, E. Quarantelli, & R. Dynes (Eds.), *Handbook of disaster research* (pp. 275–296). New York: Springer.

Zolli, A., & Healy, A. M. (2012). *Resilience: Why things bounce back.* New York: Simon & Schuster.

PART III

Developing Better Risk
Communication Strategies

CHAPTER 11

Improving Stakeholder Engagement for Upstream Risks

Robin Gregory and Nate Dieckmann

Introduction

Although the U.S. Endangered Species Act (ESA) of 1973 is seen primarily as science-based legislation, engagement with stakeholders plays an important role in the development and implementation of actions to protect at-risk species and their habitat. One of the more visible species under consideration for ESA listing is the Pacific walrus (*Odobenus rosmarus divergens*), an iconic symbol of Arctic ecosystems but also an important food source for Native subsistence hunters. Walrus populations, currently stable, are predicted to decline over coming decades due to changes in sea ice and other factors linked to the upstream risks of climate change over the rest of this century (Jay, Marcot, and Douglas 2011).

As part of an ongoing process to determine whether listing of Pacific walrus is warranted, the U.S. Fish and Wildlife Service (FWS) is funding scientific studies paired with extensive stakeholder consultation. Scientists, who rely on both field observations and model results, face significant challenges due to multiple sources of uncertainty: predictions of the quantity or quality of sea ice 50 years from now are highly uncertain, and little is known about the future behavior and adaptability of walrus populations. Risk managers need to consider the results of scientific studies along with information from other sources, including both Native and non-Native resource users. In summer 2016, for example, the FWS hosted a facilitated workshop in Anchorage with 20 subsistence hunters who were asked to provide information based on their centuries-long traditions of walrus observation and hunting experience. The two days of discussion led to some remarkable exchanges between very different worlds, provided additional values-based and factual information useful to all parties, and helped everyone to appreciate the many challenges encountered when engaging with multiple stakeholders to manage upstream impacts of unknown magnitude, timing, and scope.

In this chapter we examine some of the recent advances in stakeholder engagement—a term we use to include members of the general public, Native Americans, and interest groups (e.g., nongovernmental organizations) as well as technical experts—that have been implemented by government agencies and a variety of both public and private organizations to help develop defensible strategies for predicting, valuing, and managing future risks. Our focus is on organized processes that rely on input from a broad spectrum of citizens to inform decision-makers (i.e., elected officials or government risk managers) about the pros and cons of various policy options aimed at addressing potentially significant upstream environmental risks.

The Deliberative Promise

Stakeholder engagement processes are popular because they establish an implied contract: you talk and we listen, or you write and we read. Much of the time, however, experience suggests that this contract is not honored—what's said or what's written is in an inappropriate language or addresses issues that are not considered relevant. As a result, little is communicated, understood, or remembered. The result is frustration and mistrust for citizens, lengthy delays and uncertainty for regulators and businesses, higher costs and a loss of efficiency for governments (Gregory 2017). To the extent that the initiatives under consideration are relied on to result in net gains to society and are expected to result in improvements to current practices, then society as a whole suffers a loss.

Much recent work has focused on one of the more challenging areas for engaging stakeholders: encouraging informed stakeholder participation in decisions about the management of risks associated with novel "upstream" technologies that remain in the design or experimentation phase and whose impacts are subject to significant uncertainty (Rogers-Hayden and Pidgeon 2007). Examples include geoengineering for climate change, nanotechnologies for monitoring human health, and assisted species migrations to avoid extinction. In each of these cases, actions are being discussed in light of what many experts perceive to be an urgent need for the implementation of novel ideas, paired with the apparent failure of current strategies. Of necessity this leads to the consideration of new alternatives, which may involve extensions of current activities or technologies (e.g., further reductions in auto fleet fuel requirements to reduce emissions, stronger sea walls to address higher wave levels) or the advancement of entirely new options (e.g., hydrogen-powered vehicles, relocation of threatened species).

Stakeholders range from technical experts, working in government or industry or academia, to members of interest groups or nongovernmental organizations and the lay public; not surprisingly, a wide range of values, beliefs, training, and levels of interest are displayed. The goal of the deliberative process is to help participants become better informed, while encouraging decision-makers to listen carefully to their expressed concerns. This requires individuals to trust the process enough to tell the truth and to remain open to learning, about both values (what matters to others?) and facts (what are the likely consequences of actions?). These two sides of risk communication interrelate: as people learn more about the nature of the upstream risks, and learn more about what is and what is not within their own control (e.g., through lifestyle choices) or the control of risk managers (e.g., through new regulations), their perspective on the nature and implications of the risk is likely to change. The deliberative process also requires decision-makers to keep an open mind and to listen carefully to the views and opinions of the participants. And it requires someone—referred to in this chapter as the analyst—who has both the technical and people skills to lead the deliberative process and to serve as a translator between the worlds of the potentially affected stakeholders or other participants and the needs of the decision-maker.

Values elicitation and information collection, as part of any risk or impact evaluation, are always dynamic. However, the shifting nature of risk perceptions is particularly important for upstream initiatives such as nanotechnologies or potential geoengineering responses to climate change. The associated technologies and actions are typically complex and the consequences of implementation are both highly uncertain, which leads to a variety of different interpretations, and difficult to imagine or make tangible, because they are removed from everyday life—few of us are asked to make choices on a regular basis that hold consequences for millions of people, potentially cost billions of dollars, or could result in irreversible effects.

Why does stakeholder engagement in decisions about upstream technologies matter—why not simply leave the tough policy questions to politicians and experts? A first reason is philosophical: a democracy requires that its citizens are informed and have meaningful input to consequential public policy choices (Stehr 2015). Although this is well accepted in the abstract, in several important policy contexts—researchers concerned that citizens are not listening to their warnings about the dangerous consequences of human-induced climate change, or agricultural experts concerned that misunderstandings about the benefits of new genetically modified crops will limit worldwide crop yields and result in widespread famine—leading scientists are warning that democracy is serving as a barrier to the introduction of innovative new technologies and "increasingly point to democracy as a reason for failure" (Stehr 2015, 450). In light of what are perceived to be failures of governance and a lack of leadership from elected politicians, some are now arguing that some more authoritarian forms of governance may become both justifiable and necessary (Beeson 2010). Finding ways to encourage and engage a better-informed citizenry could help to reduce the gap between the perspective of these experts/academics and the engagement objectives of public citizens.

A second reason is political: without meaningful stakeholder input, decisions are less likely to include key elements of the benefits, costs, and risks that matter most to citizens. These objectives—the considerations that matter to people in the context of a policy choice—form the key determinants underlying their support for, or opposition to, different technologies and actions. To the extent that selected alternatives speak to and enhance these objectives (e.g., provide additional jobs, reduce environmental pollution, improve community health), then they will be supported. To the extent that alternatives fail to address or negatively impact these concerns, then the proposed initiatives will be ignored or opposed and other mechanisms, including litigation in the courts or protests in the streets, are more likely to be employed. In her book on climate change, for example, Naomi Klein (2014) documents the rise of veto powers among communities and groups who feel that policies ignore their objectives and exclude them from relevant discussions; individual initiatives are then blocked by stakeholder protests, thereby challenging the testing or refinement of new ideas and encouraging retention of an unsatisfactory status quo.

This concern stems in part from the long-standing reliance as part of stakeholder engagement processes on benefit-cost analysis and economic metrics to summarize the estimated risks and impacts of proposed activities. As a result, discussions held with stakeholders tend to emphasize the more tangible benefits of an action such as changes in jobs, revenues, or environmental indicators like air or water quality. However, other related impacts concerned with a range of health and psychological effects such as stress and worry, or cultural effects such as impacts on the ability of a Native community to engage in its traditional hunting or gathering practices, are often not included because they are considered to be more difficult to measure in commensurate terms. To a large degree this is true: jobs or revenues may easily be denominated in dollars whereas cultural or psychological impacts are not. Yet rather than provide an excuse for omitting important concerns, this challenge should provide decision-makers and analysts with an impetus to identify appropriate, nonmonetary measures of the full range of anticipated consequences of alternatives (Gregory et al. 2012). In the context of a commitment to engage stakeholders effectively in deliberations about upstream technologies, there is no better way to push individuals away and create mistrust and anger than to set up rules of expression or engagement that needlessly limit the range of concerns under consideration.

A final reason why it matters to engage stakeholders effectively about upstream technologies is practical, in that the costs are far higher for processes that fail to incorporate stakeholder input in a meaningful and effective manner. In most cases it is the citizen taxpayer who funds these efforts, so if the processes are flawed or the results fail to provide helpful information, then scarce resources and time have been lost for no apparent gain. Despite their questionable logic, the high cost of many public participation processes—often involving millions or even tens of millions of dollars—is often used as a measure of their success: because large numbers of people appear before a decision-making panel or because large sums are spent by organizers, there is an assumption that some degree of evaluative comprehensiveness was achieved. However, involving a thousand people as compared to a hundred does not guarantee that there will be an improved understanding of citizens' perspectives; breadth is not a substitute for depth of understanding, and in many cases "less can be more" in that overly lengthy testimonials or multiple volume reports only discourage understanding and thoughtful responses on the part of decision-makers (Gregory et al. 2012).

The Deliberative Challenge

Whenever people's knowledge is limited, there is also an increased potential that, as they learn, their perspectives and opinions will be especially susceptible to the cues contained in new information. In such cases, decision heuristics such as availability or anchoring can play an important role in shaping and revising expressed opinions (Kahneman 2011). In other ways, however, people's lack of knowledge may encourage them to seek and interpret information about upstream technologies in ways that are consistent with their existing beliefs and worldviews (Kuhn 2001). Such motivated evaluations have many sources, ranging from perspectives related to personal gain and social desirability to broad, cultural worldviews that often operate at an automatic and largely unconscious level. Two dimensions are often used to summarize cultural worldviews: an individualist versus communitarian dimension, which represents the degree to which people tend to seek interaction and cooperation with others, and an egalitarian versus hierarchical dimension, which captures whether people feel that individuals should be treated the same or whether considerations such as family lineage, age, or intelligence should provide a guide for society's allocation of resources and status (Kahan, Jenkins-Smith, and Braman 2011). How an individual scores on cultural worldview scales is often closely related to their political views (e.g., on a liberal versus conservative scale) and, taken together, the two dimensions can help to predict and understand disagreements concerning risk perceptions and desired risk management strategies across a range of controversial technology and outcome domains (Whitmarsh 2011).

Recent findings also underscore that when confronted with a novel decision context or with information that is imprecise (for example, due to uncertainty or due to the conflicting predictions of experts), people will actively seek to make sense of it using whatever cues are (intentionally or unintentionally) provided to them. For example, studies suggest that motivated reasoning may be amplified when the information presented for evaluation involves more imprecise uncertainty ranges (Dieckmann et al. 2017); this emphasizes that the sense-making associated with information about controversial upstream technologies may be particularly susceptible to the influence of people's preconceptions and worldviews.

These characteristics raise challenges for the design of an effective engagement process, because people may be unwilling to allow risk managers or facilitators to assist them in either (a) learning more about what experts say regarding the facts behind the technology, or (b) learning more about their own views, in the specific context of the technology choices under consideration. In an earlier paper (Lichtenstein, Gregory, and Irwin 2007), we examined how people make tradeoffs when confronted with morally or ethically difficult issues and concluded that too often "What's bad is easy"—many of what might seem to be the toughest policy choices (on terrorism, gun control, abortion, climate change) are in fact not tough at all because (despite being largely uninformed) people know what they think should be done.

In the context of large-scale climate mitigation and adaptation actions, all leading policy alternatives pose value and ethical tradeoffs across different geographic and temporal scales. Climate mitigation options that include global-scale geoengineering technologies—currently much discussed in light of recent findings of the Intergovernmental Panel on Climate Change regarding the surprisingly swift rate of climate change (Berwyn 2017)—have been said to represent an "unprecedented human intervention into nature" (Corner et al. 2013). In such situations, informed choices call for a careful weighing of information and a profound degree of soul-searching. However, our worry is that most stakeholder participation approaches—including conventional surveys, benefit-cost ranking exercises, and many current large-scale public engagement processes—encourage quick responses that ignore key factual information and overly reflect the automatic choices and political ideologies characteristic of fast thinking, in contrast to the slower and more deliberative thinking that is needed to address such unfamiliar, multidimensional tradeoffs (Kahneman 2011).

In this sense, many upstream conditions contravene the usual assumptions for public participation: that people understand the questions asked of them and have thought sufficiently about the topic to express clear, considered, and relatively stable responses (Fischhoff 2005). Instead, it is likely that individuals' responses to novel technologies will reflect psychological biases such as the prominence effect (Tversky, Sattath, and Slovic 1988), by which people deal with unfamiliar choices by giving undue weight to one dimension of a choice and largely ignore other concerns. The psychologist Jonathan Baron has emphasized that, when people are faced with decisions that are ethically difficult, a common response is to actively seek to avoid these choices (Baron and Spranca 1997), characterizing them as involving protected values and thus "taboo" to the degree that they are not in a class of decisions that follow normal rules (e.g., less of a bad thing is preferred). For many people, as a result, the decisions that are most difficult—and therefore, one might argue, most in need of insight from judgmental aids—are not thought to merit careful attention because there is nothing difficult about them: think of Nancy Reagan and her "just say no" approach to drugs.

The challenge is how to (respectfully) open up these closed doors and encourage people to inhabit areas of their thinking and feeling where they are distinctly uncomfortable. Otherwise, many of the most important public policy issues of our day will continue to go forward without substantive and meaningful input from citizens.

Looking back on the past decade of research and practice, how well is the deliberative challenge raised by upstream technologies being met? For many important public policy issues, the unfortunate answer is: very poorly. For several decades, consultation processes have too often ended up looking more like educational initiatives, with well-intentioned scientists or government risk managers hoping to "spread the word" about the benefits of a new technology, than the transparent, two-way dialogues that were promoted in the abstract. As a result, the consultation forum has often seemed far more like a battlefield (Slovic 1997), with the different public and expert parties disagreeing about everything from what should be on the table (Should the fate of nuclear wastes be included as part of electricity generation talks? Should climate change be included as part of pipeline routing discussions?) to how information about impacts should best be expressed (e.g., should averages, best guesses, or ranges be used to summarize information in those frequent cases where expert disagreements lead to significant variations in their predictions of impacts).

Despite the many criticisms heaped on such partial and often misleading deliberations (NRC 1996), decision-makers continue to favor large-scale public participation efforts that place quantity over quality and fail to provide either the time or the cognitive support required to help people construct and express informed opinions. We share with many others the perspective that this dumbing down of the public dialogue is not benign: by setting the bar very low in terms of both quality and relevance, it simultaneously becomes less attractive for stakeholders to participate in public debates and easier for politicians or scientists to claim that public input is vague or irrelevant and thus can be ignored (Gregory 2017). We also share with other researchers the opinion that "a clear conclusion to be drawn from experience with deliberative science communication to date is that members of a varied cross-section of publics are perfectly capable of debating quite complex issues of environmental science, technology and policy with which they have little day-to-day familiarity given the right tools and sufficient opportunity to do so" (Pidgeon et al. 2014).

Advances in Deliberative Theory and Practice

Recent research in North America and Europe has focused on the development of several insightful methods for eliciting stakeholder opinions, including survey and deliberative polling approaches along with interactive processes emphasizing dialogue linked to learning. Surveys of stakeholders' opinions have become a common tool for learning about the views of citizens concerning upstream technologies and have had an important effect on policies undertaken at both the state and federal level. For example, Leiserowitz (2006) conducted surveys that examined perceptions of the risks of climate change and their basis in positive and negative associations with iconic imagery (e.g., melting glaciers). McCright and Dunlap (2011) examined the links between people's attitudes toward climate change and their political views (e.g., liberal versus conservative). Others have sought to combine conventional polling with small-group discussions, online participation, or the introduction of social media (Fishkin and Luskin 2005). Such "deliberative polling" approaches allow individuals to answer questions, participate in discussions via actual or virtual forums, and then return to the questions originally asked of them; researchers can track whether their stated positions or preferred actions have changed and evolved over time.

Another line of research, centered in the United Kingdom and in Canada, has focused on engagement strategies that combine interviews and small groups with telephone or web-based surveys, thus permitting researchers to calibrate results from multiple elicitation techniques (Rogers-Hayden and Pidgeon 2007). Nick Pidgeon and his UK colleagues describe these methods and examine their success in meeting four aspects of the engagement challenge: presenting well-articulated scenarios that anticipate questions of scale; communicating information and policy framings in a balanced manner; maintaining open deliberations that permit and encourage learning; and articulating the broader beliefs and worldview logics within which such decisions are embedded (Pidgeon et al. 2014).

There also has been a move toward more closely linking the insights from technical and public stakeholders rather than retaining the more traditional expert-public separation. As demonstrated by deliberative processes focused on resource management (McDaniels, Gregory, and Fields 1999) and climate change (Satterfield et al. 2012), this linking of insights can be done using formats such as small groups, multistakeholder advisory committees, or structured surveys. The intent in each case is to increase the likelihood that one shared set of recommendations could be passed on to decision-makers, under the assumption that the power and influence of the stakeholders' recommendations will be increased to the extent that there is agreement among different leading parties.

A related (and still experimental) option involves the use of decision-pathway surveys, which seek to mimic the depth of small-group deliberations by including competing civic priorities and factual tutorials to help examine individuals' reasoning and choice strategies (Gregory et al. 1997; Gregory, Satterfield, and Hasell 2016). The goal is to follow the logic and style of everyday conversation by using results from pre-survey interviews to start with a clear description of the decision context and key objectives (i.e., what matters in this situation), then proceed to a description of leading policy alternatives and their consequences (including critical uncertainties) before asking participants to rate or rank their preferred options. This familiar structure helps to set people's choices within a more realistic context—including the proposed scale of the policy initiative and its negative as well as positive aspects when compared to other actions—and provides a window into people's reasoning in the face of difficult tradeoffs across competing benefits, costs, and risks.

Underlying these new deliberative approaches is a radical conceptual foundation provided by the behavioral decision perspective known as "constructed preferences" (Lichtenstein and Slovic 2006), which maintains that when the evaluation task involves unfamiliar elements—as is the case with novel, upstream technologies—people's preferences will not be fully formed. Instead, both their values and their choices will be constructed in relation to existing mental models and worldviews, their interpretation of what an interviewer or survey is asking of them, and the various cues that are (intentionally or unintentionally) provided. In the context of a survey, for example, the constructed preferences approach suggests that although people's tendency may be to respond using an automatic, affective-rich mode of thinking, it is the responsibility of the survey designers to also engage the more deliberative, cognitive side of people's thinking in a manner that mirrors reasoning strategies recognized as underlying thoughtful or defensible choices. For example, survey designers can incorporate tutorials as part of the survey or set up a series of questions in which participants are first asked to identify the primary objectives that matter in the selected circumstances and then face up to the tradeoffs that exist with respect to these objectives—that each of the alternatives under consideration will result in better levels for some objectives but worse levels for others (Keeney 1992; Gregory, Satterfield, and Hasell 2016).

Several of the newer deliberative approaches also seek to shift the normal rules of the game so participants can move out of their normal comfort zone and consider new views. One example is to ask people to justify their choice: to express a set of reasons and a rationale that would prove convincing to others. Justification immediately places the individual in relation to others and, as such, has the potential to bring in a new set of considerations (anecdotally, President Obama was said to often ask his top advisors to articulate how they would justify a strategy choice, presumably as a way to help him later do the same). Other examples include the formation of a science court, whereby leading technical experts are asked to argue the merits of competing positions or hypotheses in front of their peers, and an ethics court, whereby participants are asked to articulate the principles or morals that underlie (or undermine) a selected action or strategy.

Incorporating Uncertainty

Any approach that seeks to encourage an informed dialogue about upstream technologies also will need to effectively deal with and communicate uncertainty. Yet there remains a reluctance to incorporate uncertainty when evaluating alternative management strategies for upstream technologies. This reluctance can take several forms, from attempts to ignore uncertainty entirely (following the false logic that uncertainty is "too complicated" for many stakeholders to understand) to presenting single-point best estimates and averages. At the opposite end of the spectrum is the inclusion of complex, highly technical uncertainty displays that are likely to overwhelm most nonexpert stakeholders. The result is a lack of clarity regarding the uncertainty surrounding anticipated outcomes and a loss of transparency in the evaluations used to guide stakeholders' comparisons among alternatives. The preferred uncertainty presentation should be matched to the decision context, in the sense of making salient what a decision-maker would need to know to make an informed value-based decision, as well as to the technical skills of the audience (Fischhoff 2012).

As analysts, we are seeking presentations that fall in the "goldilocks zone," in that they are not too simple (i.e., successfully communicate important aspects of uncertainty) but not too complicated (i.e., avoid overwhelming with irrelevant detail). However, assumptions always will be made by individuals about how they should interpret an uncertainty presentation, even in the case of the familiar and widely recommended two-point or three-point range (e.g., see Budescu, Broomell, and Por 2009; Durbach and Stewart 2011; Joslyn and LeClerc 2012). Consider increased temperatures due to climate change: stakeholders reviewing proposed mitigation policies may be asked to evaluate a range of different actions in light of information showing a likely temperature rise of at least 1 degree Celsius and as much as 4 degrees, with a best estimate of 2 degrees over the period under consideration. One important element that is not always explicitly described is the relative likelihood of each of the values in the range. Recent studies have shown that perceptions of the relative likelihood of values in the range (or underlying probability distribution) vary widely among lay people. Some individuals will view a range from 1 to 4 degrees as a flat distribution, so that all temperatures in the range are equally likely. Others will view the range as symmetric, with values closer to the middle of the range as more likely. Still others will view the distribution as skewed in one direction or another (Dieckmann, Peters, and Gregory 2015). Perceptions and interpretations of upstream risks also can be affected by unintentional cues in the display (e.g., whether the central point is described as a "best" estimate), the numerical abilities of the end user, and an individual's motivations and worldviews (Dieckmann et al. 2017).

Encouragingly, these effects appear to be attenuated when proper attention is paid to describing to stakeholders, in precise but understandable terms, what the uncertainty range means and how it should be interpreted. However, the implication of this research is that two individuals provided with identical information about the consequences of an action can reach very different conclusions about what it means (Wildavsky and Dake 1990; Morgan et al. 2002). Consider the example of sea-level rise. Suppose information is provided that the storm surge accompanying next week's expected hurricane-level winds may be as low as 1.5 meters or as high as 4.5 meters. Some individuals, particularly those who tend to be more optimistic, may interpret this as likely to result in a storm surge of 2 meters or less; others may interpret this same information as suggesting that a surge of at least 4 meters is likely.

In the same way, some individuals may assume that this range means that all storm-surge heights between 1.5 and 4.5 meters are equally likely (e.g., a flat distribution); others may interpret this range as meaning that something around 3 meters is most likely (e.g., a normal distribution); and others may interpret this presentation as suggesting that one or both of the endpoints is likely to happen (e.g., "1.5 meter rise if we're lucky, 4.5 meter rise if we're not").

Variations among groups will (to a limited extent) be predictable, including some differences between experts and laypersons, but within each group typically there will be wide variations depending on the context and elicitation approach. And in the case of upstream technologies, much of the uncertainty is irreducible in the short term—not to be resolved through new studies or well-targeted questions—which often brings in issues relating to the competence of the scientists conducting the studies and the timeliness of the upstream public policy debate itself (as one recent participant in a geoengineering survey asked: "why ask these questions now, before anyone knows what is really going on?"). Those in charge of the decision-making process need to be aware of these differences and not assume that everyone will interpret the information they present in an identical manner.

Another implication of the psychology underlying decisions characterized by uncertainty is that it is not enough to consider only the uncertainty about facts as part of a deliberative process. This is because different people legitimately will hold a variety of views about the risk consequences under consideration. For some individuals, a very low probability that the seawall in their neighborhood will collapse (e.g., as part of a 1-in-500-year event) is less important than making sure that the associated costs to taxpayers are kept quite low. Other individuals would be willing to pay substantially larger sums in order to increase their confidence that the same seawall will maintain its integrity. These differences in people's risk tolerances are to be expected and can play an important role in the reception given to a proposed risk management alternative.

Discussion

There are several exciting and timely new avenues of research concerned with improving the engagement of citizens as part of policy decisions that involve upstream technologies. This push for better engagement approaches is coming from decision-makers, who often are frustrated by the opposition they meet when attempting to put forth new policy options, as well as public stakeholders, who often feel that they are not meaningfully involved as part of public decision-making processes.

Unfortunately, little consensus exists on the best way forward. If nothing else, the word is out that traditional survey and benefit-cost approaches often miss important parts of the picture and, as a result, new methods are urgently needed to create a more informative dialogue between expert and public stakeholders and to help bring the many disenchanted and marginalized stakeholders back into discussions. As this concern makes clear, new criteria are also needed to aid in the selection and design of engagement processes: they need to be rigorous and pass the usual tests of peer review, but they also need to be accessible and provide a forum that simultaneously helps to bring people to the table to discuss the issues that truly concern them the most yet also encourages people to come with an open mind and be informed by the views of others. These goals are particularly important in the context of the consequential decisions now being faced by policymakers with respect to the development and governance of a variety of upstream technologies.

To achieve this mix of goals, the new set of successful engagement processes will need to understand, and carefully incorporate, the mix of fast and slow thinking responses that underlie how people typically construct the logic of their decisions. For stakeholders, this acceptance of decision-making reality creates the possibility that they can meaningfully be engaged as part of important policy decisions about emerging technologies. For analysts, it creates the need to design deliberative processes that meet the needs of decision-makers but are both emotionally and cognitively tractable. And for decision-makers and elected officials engaged in making tough decisions that involve weighing the benefits and risks of upstream technologies, it requires recognition of the need to make improvements to the current mix of less than successful engagement approaches. Although much about upstream technologies remains controversial, it is clear that both the stakes and the scrutiny have never been higher.

Acknowledgments

We thank the U.S. National Science Foundation, Decision Risk & Management Science program for funding support to Decision Research from SES Awards 1231231 and 1728807. All views expressed in this chapter are those of the authors.

References

Baron, J., & Spranca, M. (1997). Protected values. *Organizational Behavior and Human Decision Processes, 70*(1), 1–16.

Beeson, M. (2010). The coming of environmental authoritarianism. *Environmental Politics, 19*(2), 276–294.

Berwyn, B. (2017, December 26). Climate change is happening faster than expected, and it's more extreme. *Inside Climate News.* https://insideclimatenews.org/news/26122017/climate-change-science-2017-year-review-evidence-impact-faster-more-extreme

Budescu, D. V., Broomell, S., & Por, H. H. (2009). Improving communication of uncertainty in the reports of the Intergovernmental Panel on Climate Change. *Psychological Science, 20*(3), 299–308.

Corner, A., Parkhill, K., Pidgeon, N., & Vaughan, N. E. (2013). Messing with nature? Exploring public perceptions of geoengineering in the UK. *Global Environmental Change, 23*(5), 938–947.

Dieckmann, N. F., Gregory, R., Peters, E., & Hartman, R. (2017). Seeing what you want to see: How imprecise uncertainty ranges enhance motivated reasoning. *Risk Analysis, 37*(3), 471–486.

Dieckmann, N. F., Peters, E., & Gregory, R. (2015). At home on the range? Lay interpretations of numerical uncertainty ranges. *Risk Analysis, 35*(7), 1281–1295.

Durbach, I. N., & Stewart, T. J. (2011). An experimental study of the effect of uncertainty representation on decision making. *European Journal of Operational Research, 214*(2), 380–392.

Fischhoff, B. (2005). Cognitive processes in stated preference methods. In K.-G. Mäler & J. Vincent (Eds.), *Handbook of environmental economics* (Vol. 2, pp. 937–968). Amsterdam: North-Holland.

Fischhoff, B. (2012). Communicating uncertainty: Fulfilling the duty to inform. *Issues in Science and Technology, 28*(4), 63–70.

Fishkin, J. S., & Luskin, R. C. (2005). Experimenting with a democratic ideal: Deliberative polling and public opinion. *Acta Politica, 40*(3), 284–298.

Gregory, R. S. (2017). The troubling logic of inclusivity in environmental consultations. *Science, Technology, & Human Values, 42*(1), 144–165.

Gregory, R., Failing, L., Harstone, M., Long, G., McDaniels, T., & Ohlson, D. (2012). *Structured decision making: A practical guide to environmental management choices.* Hoboken, NJ: John Wiley & Sons.

Gregory, R., Flynn, J., Johnson, S. M., Satterfield, T. A., Slovic, P., & Wagner, R. (1997). Decision-pathway surveys: A tool for resource managers. *Land Economics, 73*(2), 240–254.

Gregory, R., Satterfield, T., & Hasell, A. (2016). Using decision pathway surveys to inform climate engineering policy choices. *Proceedings of the National Academy of Sciences, 113*(3), 560–565.

Jay, C. V., Marcot, B. G., & Douglas, D. C. (2011). Projected status of the Pacific walrus (Odobenus rosmarus divergens) in the twenty-first century. *Polar Biology, 34*(7), 1065–1084.

Joslyn, S. L., & LeClerc, J. E. (2012). Uncertainty forecasts improve weather-related decisions and attenuate the effects of forecast error. *Journal of Experimental Psychology: Applied, 18*(1), 126.

Kahan, D. M., Jenkins-Smith, H., & Braman, D. (2011). Cultural cognition of scientific consensus. *Journal of Risk Research, 14*(2), 147–174.

Kahneman, D. (2011). *Thinking, fast and slow.* New York: Farrar, Straus, & Giroux.

Keeney, R. L. (1992). *Value-focused thinking: A path to creative decisionmaking.* Cambridge, MA: Harvard University Press.

Klein, N. (2014). *This changes everything: Capitalism vs. the climate.* New York: Simon & Schuster.

Kuhn, D. (2001). How do people know? *Psychological Science, 12*, 1–8.

Leiserowitz, A. (2006). Climate change risk perception and policy preferences: The role of affect, imagery, and values. *Climatic Change, 77*(1–2), 45–72.

Lichtenstein, S., Gregory, R., & Irwin, J. (2007). What's bad is easy: Taboo values, affect, and cognition. *Judgment and Decision Making, 2*(3), 169–188.

Lichtenstein, S., & Slovic, P. (Eds.). (2006). *The construction of preference.* New York: Cambridge University Press.

McCright, A. M., & Dunlap, R. E. (2011). The politicization of climate change and polarization in the American public's views of global warming, 2001–2010. *Sociological Quarterly, 52*(2), 155–194.

McDaniels, T. L., Gregory, R. S., & Fields, D. (1999). Democratizing risk management: Successful public involvement in local water management decisions. *Risk Analysis, 19*(3), 497–510.

Morgan, G., Fischhoff, B., Bostrom, A., & Atman, C. (2002). *Risk communication: The mental models approach.* Cambridge: Cambridge University Press.

National Research Council (NRC). (1996). *Understanding risk: Informing decisions in a democratic society.* Washington, DC: National Academies Press.

Pidgeon, N., Demski, C., Butler, C., Parkhill, K., & Spence, A. (2014). Creating a national citizen engagement process for energy policy. *Proceedings of the National Academy of Sciences, 111*(Supplement 4), 13606–13613.

Rogers-Hayden, T., & Pidgeon, N. (2007). Moving engagement "upstream"? Nanotechnologies and the Royal Society and Royal Academy of Engineering's inquiry. *Public Understanding of Science, 16*(3), 345–364.

Satterfield, T., Conti, J., Harthorn, B. H., Pidgeon, N., & Pitts, A. (2012). Understanding shifting perceptions of nanotechnologies and their implications for policy dialogues about emerging technologies. *Science and Public Policy, 40*(2), 247–260.

Slovic, P. (1997). Trust, emotion, sex, politics, and science: Surveying the risk-assessment battlefield. In M. H. Bazerman, D. M. Messick, A. E. Tenbrunsel, & K. A. Wade-Benzoni (Eds.), *Environment, ethics, and behavior* (pp. 277–313). San Francisco: New Lexington, 1997.

Stehr, N. (2015). Climate policy: Democracy is not an inconvenience. *Nature, 525*(7570).

Tversky, A., Sattath, S., & Slovic, P. (1988). Contingent weighting in judgment and choice. *Psychological Review, 95*(3), 371–384.

Whitmarsh, L. (2011). Scepticism and uncertainty about climate change: Dimensions, determinants and change over time. *Global Environmental Change, 21*(2), 690–700.

Wildavsky, A., & Dake, K. (1990). Theories of risk perception: Who fears what and why? *Daedalus, 119*(4), 41–60.

CHAPTER 12

Improving the Accuracy of Geopolitical Risk Assessments

Barbara A. Mellers, Philip E. Tetlock, Joshua D. Baker,
Jeffrey A. Friedman, and Richard Zeckhauser

The chances of life-threatening events, such as terrorist attacks, hurricanes, floods, or earthquakes, are the lifeblood of risk analysis. Those in the business of measuring risks use a wide array of methods to quantify them. Perhaps the most common approach is statistical: risk is the relative frequency of a bad outcome in a well-defined set of outcomes. For instance, the annual risk of death in the United States due to terrorist attacks, floods, and earthquakes is 1 in 3.5 million (between 1970 and 2007), 1 in 8 million, and 1 in 9 million, respectively.

The Risk of Unique Events

In many cases, risks that matter are unique; they have no reference classes, perhaps because they have never occurred. What is the chance of war breaking out with North Korea or a cyberattack that leaves the United States completely defenseless? When reference classes do not exist, Bayesian methods allow decision-makers to express their beliefs about the chance of an outcome, given the available evidence (e.g., Gill 2015). Bayesian techniques allow people to report their beliefs about Trump being impeached, Greece exiting the Eurozone, or Iran complying with the 2015 nuclear agreement. Such beliefs provide the foundations of policy decisions, such as raising the federal minimum wage, reducing domestic nuclear stockpiles, or brokering a trade deal with China.

The meaning of probability is a controversial topic. Many people are skeptical that probabilities can ever be assigned to unique events (e.g., Mill 1882; Keynes 1937). Others argue that all events are, in some way, unique; it depends on how one defines the reference class (Berry 1993). This chapter demonstrates how we can improve the accuracy of forecasts about unique geopolitical events using better forecasters, improved psychological interventions, enhanced statistical algorithms, and response scales with a greater number of uncertainty distinctions.

In the U.S. intelligence community, clear communication of risk and uncertainty is essential. Yet quite often, analysts eschew numerical estimates as expressions of their beliefs. They prefer to express their hunches with phrases, such as "liable to happen," "distinct possibility," or "hard to tell." Psychological research on verbal uncertainty phrases shows that such vague verbiage is easily misconstrued. For instance, Wallsten et al. (1986) asked participants to assign numerical values to their interpretations of probability phrases. The resulting numbers differed in meaning across individuals. The word "possible" had an interquartile range as large as 43% (Mosteller and Youtz 1990).

A particularly poignant example of how qualitative expressions can be misunderstood comes from a case study of President John F. Kennedy's decision to invade Cuba at the Bay of Pigs. In 1961, Kennedy asked the joint chiefs of staff to assess the plan's feasibility. The chiefs believed the chances of success were roughly 30%, but they conveyed their views verbally by saying, "This plan has a fair chance of success." The report's author, Brigadier General David Gray, later said, "We thought other people would think 'a fair chance' would mean 'not too good.'" However, President Kennedy allegedly interpreted this statement as something more likely. Gray believed that his imprecise language contributed to what was widely viewed as a serious strategic blunder (Wyden 1979, 88–90), a blunder that quantitative terminology might have avoided. Fifty years later, quantitative estimates are still the exception, not the norm.

Tournaments to the Rescue

In recent years, IARPA (the Intelligence Advanced Research Project Activity), the research wing of the U.S. intelligence community, has funded scientists to discover how to better predict unique events. From 2011 to 2015, IARPA sponsored a program called ACE (Aggregative Contingent Estimation), comprising four massive geopolitical forecasting tournaments conducted over the span of four years. They supported five university teams to find optimal ways of eliciting beliefs from crowds and aggregating them.

Questions in the tournaments ranged from pandemics and global leadership change to international negotiations and economic shifts. For example, a question released on September 9, 2011, asked, "Who will be inaugurated as President of Russia in 2012?" Our team, The Good Judgment Project, studied over a million forecasts provided by thousands of volunteers who attached numerical probabilities to over 500 such events (Mellers et al. 2014; Tetlock et al. 2014).

In the ACE tournaments, IARPA carefully defined predictive success using a metric called the Brier scoring rule (the sum of squared deviations between forecasts and outcomes, where outcomes were 0 and 1 for the nonoccurrence and occurrence of events, respectively; Brier 1950). Consider the question, "Will Bashar al-Assad be ousted from Syria's presidency by the end of 2016?" For this question, outcomes were binary; Assad either stayed or left. Suppose a forecaster predicted that Assad had a 60% chance of staying and a 40% chance of being ousted. If, at the end of 2016, Assad remained in power, the participant's Brier score would be $[(1-0.60)^2 + (0-0.40)^2] = 0.16$. If Assad was ousted, the forecaster's score would be worse $[(0-0.60)^2 + (1-0.40)^2] = 0.36$. With Brier scores, lower values mean greater accuracy, and zero is a perfect score. The winning university group had the lowest Brier scores, averaged over individuals, days, and questions.

The Good Judgment Project won the ACE tournaments by a wide margin each year by being faster than the competition at finding ways to push probabilities toward 0 for things that did not happen and toward 1 for things that did happen. Five drivers of accuracy accounted for our team's success. They were identifying talent, training forecasters in probabilistic reasoning, putting forecasters in teams, placing the best forecasters in elite teams to work with each other, and aggregating forecasts using new algorithms (Mellers et al. 2014; Mellers et al. 2015a; Mellers et al. 2015b). We will briefly discuss each driver and then add another.

Identifying Talent

Our team investigated the psychological traits, cognitive abilities, and political knowledge of thousands of forecasters to understand who they were and what factors correlated with their performance (Mellers et al. 2015a). Better forecasters had more political knowledge and greater intelligence (both crystalized and fluid), as measured by the Raven's Advanced Progressive Matrices (Arthur et al. 1999; Balboni, Naglieri, and Cubelli 2010); the Shipley-2 abstraction test (Shipley, Gruber, Martin, and Klein 2009); the cognitive reflection test (Frederick 2005); an extended version of the cognitive reflection test (Baron et al. 2015); and questions from two numeracy scales (Lipkus, Samsa, and Rimer 2001; Peters et al. 2006).

Cognitive styles also correlated with performance. Better forecasters had a competitive streak, a greater appetite for intellectual challenges, and a stronger tendency to change their minds in response to new evidence (Mellers et al. 2015a). They scored high on a test of "actively open-minded thinking," which implied that they searched for and took into consideration information that ran counter to their prior beliefs (Haran, Ritov, and Mellers 2013). Finally, they had greater "need for cognition" (Cacioppo and Petty 1982; Cacioppo, Petty, and Kao 1984). They enjoyed analytic problems, complex puzzles, and intellectual challenges.

The most successful forecasters in the Good Judgment Project believed that forecasting ability was not an innate, God-given ability. Everyone knows the old joke about how to get to Carnegie Hall: practice, practice, practice. They viewed highly skilled performance as something they could do only after intense, focused, long-term commitment. Ericsson, Krampe, and Tesch-Romer (1993) argued that expert performance comes from deliberate practice or grit (Duckworth 2016). More successful forecasters were more engaged and showed greater effort and perseverance. Frequency of belief updating turned out to be the strongest single behavioral predictor of accuracy.

The very top performers—a group called "superforecasters"—had many of these characteristics and more (Mellers et al. 2015b; Tetlock and Gardner 2015). They were more inclined to embrace a secular, agnostic/atheistic worldview that treats everything as subject to deterministic laws of science. This worldview predisposed them to treat their beliefs more like testable probabilistic propositions than sacred possessions—and to be more cautious about over interpreting coincidences by attributing them to supernatural mechanisms such as fate.

Training Forecasters in Probabilistic Reasoning

The Good Judgment Project developed a training module in probabilistic reasoning to help guide participants through the forecasting process. Psychologists have tried for decades to discover methods of improving probability judgments. Promising approaches include statistical training (Fong, Krantz, and Nisbett 1986), feedback (Benson and Önkal 1992), exposure to multiple perspectives (Ariely et al. 2000; Herzog and Hertwig 2009), exposure to historical analogies (Lovallo, Clarke, and Camerer 2012), decomposition of the problem into subsets (Fischhoff, Slovic, and Lichtenstein 1977), and explicit consideration of contradictory evidence (Koriat, Lichtenstein, and Fischhoff 1980).

The Good Judgment training module contained a variety of forecasting recommendations. It gave practical tips about where to find professional and amateur forecasts on the internet. It instructed forecasters to consider multiple reference classes before taking into account information that was specific to the event. It suggested that when forecasters had multiple estimates of the same event from polls, models, or expert opinions, they should average the estimates. Forecasters were also told to imagine possible futures, use decision trees, and avoid judgmental biases such as overconfidence and base-rate neglect (Kahneman, Slovic, and Tversky 1982). The module was interactive, with questions and answers that checked participants' understanding of the concepts.

Placing Forecasters in Teams

Numerous studies have shown that crowd predictions are frequently better than those of a single expert (e.g., Page 2007; Soll and Larrick 2009). But how should the crowd interact in order to generate the most accurate aggregate forecasts? Should they work independently without communicating? Or should they collaborate in teams that promote cooperation within the group and competition across groups? The Good Judgment Project used randomized control conditions to test the effects of independent forecasts versus forecasts based on team interactions.

The case for working alone is statistical. Independent forecasts will often have uncorrelated errors, and, in the aggregate, they should cancel out (Surowiecki 2004). The case for working collaboratively is that groups can be more accurate than individuals when they are cohesive, engaged and share a mental model of the task (Levine and Moreland 1990; Kerr and Tindale 2004). Social interactions can inspire those who wish to perform well in the presence of others. Team members can share information, answer each other's questions, and encourage those who are less involved. The Good Judgment Project found that teams performed significantly better than individuals working alone (Mellers et al. 2014), and this result was replicated four years in a row.

Placing Top Forecasters in Elite Teams

A large literature on peer effects in the classroom suggests that students benefit from working in cohorts of similar ability levels (see Epple and Romano 2011, for a review). The Good Judgment Project reasoned that superforecasters (the top 2% of forecasters at the end of each year) might also enjoy an advantage if they worked with those of similar skill. But any beneficial effects of tracking would depend on the extent to which geopolitical forecasting was attributable to skill versus luck. If forecasting accuracy was mostly luck, superforecasters should regress to the mean after their initial success. If forecasting accuracy was primarily skill, superforecasters should continue their superior performance and possibly do even better in a richer intellectual environment. Defying expectations of regression toward the mean, superforecasters maintained high accuracy across hundreds of questions and a wide array of topics, year after year (Mellers et al. 2015b). This intervention shows the astonishing potential of dedicated, talented forecasters as they tried to keep getting better.

Aggregation of Forecasts

The Good Judgment Project tried many aggregation rules, but the most successful was a relatively simple one, with a single estimated parameter. Predictions were combined using the geometric mean of the log odds (Baron et al. 2014; Satopää et al. 2014a; Satopää et al. 2014b). An empirically estimated exponent was applied to the mean. It is well known that individuals are frequently overconfident in their beliefs, but the mean of multiple forecasts may underestimate the total knowledge of the group. If the estimated exponent is greater than 1, the aggregate forecast is shifted toward the nearest end of the probability scale (0 or 1) as if the aggregate has more information than is reflected in the mean. Similarly, when the exponent is less than 1, the aggregate is shifted away from the nearest end of the scale, as if the aggregate has less information than the mean reflects. The exponent "recalibrates" the geometric mean. The algorithm also discounted older forecasts and differentially weighted individuals based on their previous accuracy and/or effort. This aggregation rule outperformed other methods each year for four years (Mellers et al. 2014). Almost a million aggregate forecasts from the Good Judgment Project were on the right side of maybe 86% of the time. This algorithm outperformed the simple mean of forecasts in a control condition by as much as 60%. In short, we discovered that the human forecasts of unique events could not only be predicted, but they could be predicted with a surprising degree of accuracy.

How Do Professional Intelligence Analysts Make Forecasts?

The 2004 Intelligence Reform and Terrorism Prevention Act requires that analysts "properly caveat and express uncertainties or confidence in analytic judgments." Yet there is no consensus on what it means to properly caveat. The intelligence community uses both qualitative and quantitative methods to express doubt. Common qualitative approaches include verbal terms (i.e., "we judge," "we estimate"), confidence levels (expressed as low, medium, or high), or uncertainty phrases (i.e., "unlikely," "possible," and "probable") (Friedman et al. 2017).

This form of expression may seem reasonable at first glance, but the meaning of such phrases is far from clear (Beyth-Marom 1982; Mosteller and Youtz 1990; Wallsten and Budescu 1995). Researchers have found between-subject and within-subject differences in the meaning of uncertainty phrases. When the same uncertainty phrases were associated with different events, the same subjects assigned different levels of probability. "A good chance" of being

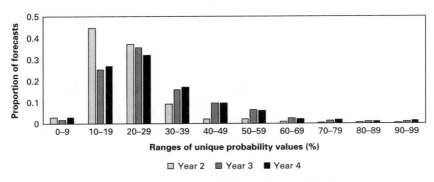

Figure 12.1. The proportion of unique probability values used by forecasters.

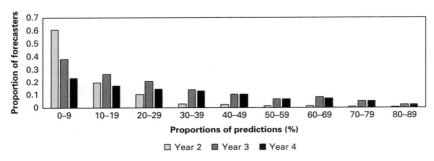

Figure 12.2. The proportion of forecasters using different percentages of more precise predictions (not multiples of 5% or 10%).

assaulted sounded greater to most people than "a good chance" of rain tomorrow. The meaning of probability phrases depended on the desirability of the event (Cohen 1986), the severity of the event (Weber and Hilton 1990), and the base rate of the event (Wallsten, Fillenbaum, and Cox 1986).

Intelligence analysts are currently asked to use a hybrid scale in which they express their beliefs using a numerical rating that is tied to a verbal phrase and a range of probabilities. In November 2015, the National Intelligence Council recommended a seven-point scale, with each phrase anchored to unequal-sized bins of probabilities (Office of the Director of National Intelligence 2015). Numbers were labeled as "Remote," "Very unlikely," "Unlikely," "Even chance," "Likely," "Very likely," and "Almost certainly."

Rating scales such as these represent a compromise between quantitative and qualitative measures. Such measures are typically defended on the basis of what decision theorists call the "congruence principle," or the idea that probability assessors should use a level of precision that reflects their ability to justify and express their beliefs, but no more (Budescu and Wallsten 1987). In areas of high-risk decision-making, it goes without saying that one should not communicate uncertainty in a manner that suggests greater knowledge than one actually has. But is an uncertainty scale with seven categories enough for analysts to convey their beliefs? Is this the best measure for maximizing predictive accuracy?

Using data from the Good Judgment Project, we could answer these questions by tackling three smaller ones (Friedman et al. 2017). How many distinctions along the probability scale do forecasters typically make? How many categories of uncertainty do forecasters actually *need*? And what predicts the tendency to make more granular probability judgments? Answers will tell us whether current methods for expressing uncertainty used in the intelligence community are sufficiently precise.

Distinctions That Forecasters Make

There are several ways to investigate categories of uncertainty that people are able to use. One way is to count the number of unique probability values forecasters use during the course of a given tournament year. Figure 12.1 shows such data from the last three years of the Good Judgment Project. The first year was not included because additional analyses, discussed later, required superforecasters, and they were not identified until the end of the first year. The proportion of forecasters who used different numbers of unique probabilities (shown as bins of 0 to 9, 10 to 19, 20 to 29, etc.) appear for years 2, 3, and 4. Most forecasters used 10 to 29 unique values of probability for the questions they faced during the year. Average numbers of unique values were 22, 30 and 30, in years 2, 3, and 4 respectively. If forecasters expressed their uncertainties in multiples of 10%, they would be making 11 distinctions. If distinctions were in all multiples of 5%, they would be making 21 distinctions. Values of 22, 30, and 30 suggest that, in year 2, people were using multiples of 5% on average, and in later years, they used more distinctions.

A second way to ask how many levels of uncertainty people can distinguish is to examine which percentages they use. To what extent did forecasters submit beliefs such as "19%" and "53%" versus "20%" and "50%"? Friedman et al. (2017) examined instances in which forecasters made predictions that were *not* multiples of 5% or 10%. Results are shown in Figure 12.2, with proportions of forecasts that were not multiples of 5% and 10% (in binned intervals). In the second year, more than half of the forecasters made relatively few such predictions (e.g., 23% or 88%, 9% or fewer). As the years went on, forecasters made a greater number of more precise predictions. Both figures show that there are widespread individual differences in the distinctions of uncertainty that forecasters make across the entire probability continuum.

Distinctions That Forecasters Need

On the surface, one might conclude that more granular probabilities convey more information. Yet, in practice, it is unclear whether more precise responses have additional information or whether they simply reflect a desire on the forecaster's part to *appear* more precise. If differences are purely superficial, one might be safe in assuming that people don't need to express as many distinctions as they are actually making. On the other hand, if more precise forecasts are actually more accurate forecasts, then the intelligence community should allow analysts to use more categories to express their beliefs.

To find out whether more precise forecasts were associated with greater accuracy, Mellers et al. (2015b) rounded the predictions of superforecasters to the nearest 0.10, and 0.33 (corresponding to probability scales with 11 distinctions and 4 distinctions, respectively). In both cases, the rounding of superforecasters' predictions significantly decreased accuracy. That is, Brier scores computed on the rounded predictions were less accurate than original Brier scores. Although these analyses don't speak to cognitive processes directly, they are consistent with the hypothesis that superforecasters were capable of reliably making *at least* 12 distinctions on the probability continuum.

Friedman et al. (2017) used a similar, but more extensive method to estimate the number of categories forecasters could reliably use. They drew on more than 750,000 predictions from over 1,700 forecasters, each of whom had made predictions on 25 or more questions in the last three years of the tournament. Each forecaster's predictions were rounded to the midpoint of equal-sized bins (b), where b ranged from 2 to 101 categories. Friedman et al.

Table 12.1. Rounding forecasts to seven categories: Original Brier scores for different groups and percentage of errors added with rounding

Groups of forecasters	Original Brier scores	Seven categories, unequal intervals	Seven categories, equal intervals
Untrained	Mean: 0.1890	0.5%**	0.5%
individuals	Median: 0.162	0.6%**	0.2%**
Trained teams	Mean: 0.1360	0.8%**	3.3%*
	Median: 0.1000	0.9%**	2.4%**
Superforecasters	Mean: 0.093	6.1%**	10.4%**
	Median: 0.032	1.7%**	10.2%**

Note: * $p < 0.05$; ** $p < 0.001$.

recomputed Brier scores after each rounding and compared them to the original Brier scores. Then they looked at the change in the Brier score after rounding.

Table 12.1 shows mean and median percentages of accuracy associated with three groups from the Good Judgment Project (untrained individual forecasters, trained team forecasters, and superforecasters), as well as abbreviated statistical results concerning the impact of rounding of forecasts. After groups, the table presents unrounded Brier scores for each group. Superforecasters had the lowest Brier scores. Columns to the right show the percentage changes in Brier scores due to rounding. Both columns represent uncertainty scales with seven categories, reflecting the current scale used by the intelligence community. We show two different ways of operationalizing the scales. In the first case, the seven categories were associated with equal-sized intervals, and in the second case, they were unequal intervals. Rounding of forecasts to each number of categories was done by using the midpoints of the interval. Means of rounded and original scores were compared with two-sided t tests, and medians were compared with two-sided Wilcoxon signed-rank tests.

Positive percentages shown in the last two columns in Table 12.1 indicate the percentage increase in Brier scores after rounding (less accuracy). Although these changes are not large for untrained individual forecasters or trained team forecasters, differences are statistically significant when compared to the original Brier scores. Decreases in predictive accuracy are much greater for superforecasters than any other groups. Superforecasters tended to make more granular predictions, and as Friedman et al.'s results demonstrate, their precision often conveyed valuable information.

Table 12.1 tells us that the category rating scales for expressing uncertainty used in the intelligence community do not give forecasters—especially the very best forecasters—enough latitude to convey all of the information they actually have. Forecasters using those scales cannot make the precise predictions that would have maximized their accuracy. Accuracy suffered.

Who Makes Finer Distinctions?

Friedman et al. (2017) developed an index of the granularity, or implicit precision, of each individual's forecasts. They calculated the number of bins, b, for which rounded Brier scores were not statistically different from unrounded Brier scores. The minimum number of categories was interpreted as an indirect measure of the fewest distinctions an individual was reliably capable of making. To explore the correlates of this granularity index, Friedman et al. conducted exploratory regressions using predictor variables such as forecasting accuracy, motivation, training, education, cognitive abilities, and cognitive styles.

Forecasting accuracy was the strongest predictor of the estimate of forecasters' precision. Those who made more distinctions along the probability continuum also tended to be more accurate. These individuals also tended to have training in probabilistic reasoning and were more engaged in the tournament (i.e., updated their forecasts more frequently and attempted to address more forecasting questions). Those whose forecasts were more precise also tended to have more experience by participating in the tournaments for a longer period of time.

These results imply that intelligence analysts and other professional forecasters can increase their accuracy by learning to be more precise. Analysts are full-time professionals whose job it is to assess uncertainty on a daily basis over many years. They have more opportunities and incentives to refine and revise their forecasts in light of new information than did forecasters in the Good Judgment Project, who were largely participating for fun.

Variables that did not predict the granularity index, perhaps surprisingly, included education, numeracy, cognitive ability, and cognitive styles (Friedman et al. 2107). These factors represent more innate variables that are harder to change or manipulate, whereas incentives for effort, engagement, and training in probabilistic reasoning are interventions that organizations could make without huge investments in time and money. In sum, the ability to make more precise predictions appears to be something that forecasters can learn to do with the proper guidance and incentives.

Improving Current Practices

Our results show that standard methods of expressing uncertainty with seven-point rating scales as done in the intelligence community are simply too coarse. As discussed in Friedman et al. (2017), this finding did not depend on the use of extreme probability estimates, questions with shorter time horizons, questions of different types (e.g., military, economic, health-related), or different categories of strictly proper scoring rules. Additionally—and perhaps most importantly—it was the superforecasters who took the greatest hit to predictive accuracy when their response scales were constrained. Given their remarkable accuracy, we suggest that, if anything, superforecasters should have the loudest voices when events are uncertain, information is ambiguous, the stakes are high, or the consequences dire.

Some scholars and practitioners oppose the use of numerical probabilities on grounds that the extra "precision" is essentially noise (e.g., Fingar 2011). The National Intelligence Council (Office of the Director of National Intelligence 2007) also says that "assigning precise numerical ratings to [probabilistic] judgments would imply more rigor than we intend." Others say that numerical probabilities would impose additional mental costs on analysts. Although there may indeed be a learning period, this hypothesis requires empirical testing.

Our message here is simple. We know much more than we did a decade ago about how to accurately estimate the chances of unique events. Some methods are demonstrably better than others. The Good Judgment Project found five ways of improving accuracy. With these drivers, intelligent lay people could make forecasts that were 30% more accurate than those of professional intelligence analysts, even in instances where analysts had access to additional, classified information (Goldstein et al. in press).

Better forecasts require identifying, training, teaming, and tracking forecasters, and optimally aggregating their forecasts. First, getting the right people is essential. Better forecasters tend to take an analytical approach to predictions and to enjoy intellectual challenges. They search for evidence that runs counter to their favored beliefs and maintain open minds. Second, training helps. People can learn to be better forecasters when they are instructed to use best practices for probabilistic reasoning. Third, geopolitical forecasters are more accurate when working in teams than when working independently. The shared information, encouragement and comradery introduced by the team structure in ACE demonstrably outweighed the potential for herding or groupthink. Fourth, accuracy gets an enormous boost when top performers are allowed to work together in elite teams. The added commitment and desire to not disappoint one's teammates proves to be a stronger incentive than we could have imagined. Finally, simple algorithms that incorporate the discounting of old forecasts, the differential skills of forecasters, and the degree of information overlap among the crowd are far superior to simple averages. These factors show that it is the combination of statistical and psychological insights that improve the predictive accuracy of unique events.

Data from the Good Judgment Project allowed us to test another driver of accuracy—the degree of precision intelligence analysts require in their expressions of uncertainty in order to maximize accuracy. Standard methods are seven-point category rating scales of uncertainty. A comparison of forecasters' original accuracy scores to accuracy scores after rounding to seven categories showed that inaccuracy grows if forecasters are constrained to express their beliefs using only seven categories. Even worse, it is top performers whose accuracy suffers the most when forced to communicate with restricted probability scales. This driver is, by far, the easiest one for the intelligence community to implement.

Unfortunately, it is still the norm that intelligence analysts express uncertainties with vague verbiage. What does it mean when a pundit asserts that a military operation is "likely" to succeed? Is the probability just above 55% or is it closer to 90%? Or, what if an expert says that a crisis is "unlikely" to escalate? Does that mean the probability is 10% or 40%? Despite the uncertainty and subjectivity inherent to policy debates, evidence from the Good Judgment Project suggests that there are valid grounds for asking analysts to assess uncertainty numerically using the entire probability scale; greater accuracy will be the result.

Although findings in one domain may not carry over into others, it is worth considering the notion that other professions might be systematically sacrificing predictive accuracy by using qualitative expressions of probability. Qualitative expression of uncertainty is commonly used in regulatory policy (Sunstein 2104), medicine (Nakao and Axelrod 1983), and climate science (Budescu et al. 2014). These are all areas where risk and uncertainty play a crucial role in decision-making. Our research provides a methodological template for addressing this question in a principled way, with the first and foremost ingredient being to keep score.

Any organization that strives for the clearest communication of risks should extract as many useful signals from its people and its environment as possible. The Good Judgment Project has tested a variety of methods scientifically and found ways to bolster accuracy. The world is a messy place, and accurate predictions are unquestionably hard. But when the stakes are high—with billions of dollars or thousands of lives on the line—even small increases in predictive accuracy can translate into enormous benefits to society.

References

Ariely, D., Au, W. T., Bender, R. H., Budescu, D. V., Dietz, C. B., Gu, H., . . . & Zauberman, G. (2000). The effects of averaging subjective probability estimates between and within judges. *Journal of Experimental Psychology: Applied, 6*(2), 130.

Arthur, W., Jr., Tubre, T. C., Paul, D. S., & Sanchez-Ku, M. L. (1999). College-sample psychometric and normative data on a short form of the Raven Advanced Progressive Matrices Test. *Journal of Psychoeducational Assessment, 17*(4), 354–361.

Balboni, G., Naglieri, J. A., & Cubelli, R. (2010). Concurrent and predictive validity of the Raven Progressive Matrices and the Naglieri Nonverbal Ability Test. *Journal of Psychoeducational Assessment, 28*(3), 222–235.

Baron, J., Mellers, B. A., Tetlock, P. E., Stone, E., & Ungar, L. H. (2014). Two reasons to make aggregated probability forecasts more extreme. *Decision Analysis, 11*(2), 133–145.

Baron, J., Scott, S., Fincher, K., & Metz, S. E. (2015). Why does the Cognitive Reflection Test (sometimes) predict utilitarian moral judgment (and other things)? *Journal of Applied Research in Memory and Cognition, 4*(3), 265–284.

Benson, P. G., & Önkal, D. (1992). The effects of feedback and training on the performance of probability forecasters. *International Journal of Forecasting, 8*(4), 559–573.

Berry, D. A. (1993). A case for Bayesianism in clinical trials. *Statistics in Medicine, 12*(15–16), 1377–1393.

Beyth-Marom, R. (1982). How probable is probable? A numerical translation of verbal probability expressions. *Journal of Forecasting, 1*(3), 257–269.

Brier, G. W. (1950). Verification of forecasts expressed in terms of probability. *Monthly Weather Review, 78*(1), 1–3.

Budescu, D. V., Por, H. H., Broomell, S. B., & Smithson, M. (2014). The interpretation of IPCC probabilistic statements around the world. *Nature Climate Change, 4*(6), 508.

Budescu, D. V., & Wallsten, T. (1987). Subjective estimation based on precise and vague uncertainties. In G. Wright and P. Ayton (Eds.), *Judgmental forecasting.* New York: Wiley.

Cacioppo, J. T., & Petty, R. E. (1982). The need for cognition. *Journal of Personality and Social Psychology, 42*(1), 116.

Cacioppo, J. T., Petty, R. E., & Kao, C.-F. (1984). The efficient assessment of need for cognition. *Journal of Personality Assessment, 48*, 306–307.

Cohen, B. L. (1986). *The effect of outcome desirability on comparisons of linguistic and numerical probabilities* (unpublished MA thesis). University of North Carolina at Chapel Hill.

Daniels, R., Ketti, D., and H. Kunreuther (Eds). 2006. *on risk and disaster: Lessons learned from Hurricane Katrina.* Philadelphia: University of Pennsylvania Press.

Duckworth, A. (2016). *Grit: The power of passion and perseverance.* New York: Simon & Schuster.

Epple, D., & Romano, R. E. (2011). Peer effects in education: A survey of the theory and evidence. In *Handbook of social economics* (Vol. 1b, pp. 1053–1163). Amsterdam: North-Holland.

Ericsson, K. A., Krampe, R. T., & Tesch-Römer, C. (1993). The role of deliberate practice in the acquisition of expert performance. *Psychological Review, 100*(3), 363–406.

Fingar, T. (2011). *Reducing uncertainty: Intelligence analysis and national security.* Stanford, CA: Stanford University Press.

Fischhoff, B., Slovic, P., & Lichtenstein, S. (1977). Knowing with certainty: The appropriateness of extreme confidence. *Journal of Experimental Psychology: Human Perception and Performance, 3*(4), 552–564.

Fong, G. T., Krantz, D. H., & Nisbett, R. E. (1986). The effects of statistical training on thinking about everyday problems. *Cognitive Psychology, 18*(3), 253–292.

Frederick, S. (2005). Cognitive reflection and decision making. *Journal of Economic Perspectives, 19*(4), 25–42.

Friedman, J. A., Baker, J. D., Mellers, B. A., Tetlock, P. E., & Zeckhauser, R. (2017). The value of precision in probability assessment: Evidence from a large-scale geopolitical forecasting tournament. *International Studies Quarterly, 62*, 410–422.

Gill, J. (2015). *Bayesian methods: A social and behavioral sciences approach* (3rd ed.). Boca Raton, FL: CRC Press.

Goldstein, S., Hartman, R., Cornstock, E., & Baumgarten, T.S. (in press). Assessing the accuracy of geopolitical forecasts from the US intelligence community's prediction market. *Journal of Forecasting.*

Haran, U., Ritov, I., & Mellers, B. A. (2013). The role of actively open-minded thinking in information acquisition, accuracy, and calibration. *Judgment and Decision Making, 8*(3), 188.

Herzog, S. M., & Hertwig, R. (2009). The wisdom of many in one mind: Improving individual judgments with dialectical bootstrapping. *Psychological Science, 20*(2), 231–237.

Kahneman, D., Slovic, P., & Tversky, A. (Eds.). (1982). *Judgment under uncertainty: Heuristics and biases.* Cambridge: Cambridge University Press.

Kerr, N. L., & Tindale, R. S. (2004). Group performance and decision making. *Annual Review of Psychology, 55*, 623–655.

Keynes, J. M. (1937). The general theory of employment. *Quarterly Journal of Economics, 51*(2), 209–223.

Koriat, A., Lichtenstein, S., & Fischhoff, B. (1980). Reasons for confidence. *Journal of Experimental Psychology: Human Learning and Memory, 6*(2), 107–118.

Levine, J. M., & Moreland, R. L. (1990). Progress in small group research. *Annual Review of Psychology, 41*(1), 585–634.

Lipkus, I. M., Samsa, G., & Rimer, B. K. (2001). General performance on a numeracy scale among highly educated samples. *Medical Decision Making, 21*(1), 37–44.

Lovallo, D., Clarke, C., & Camerer, C. (2012). Robust analogizing and the outside view: Two empirical tests of case-based decision making. *Strategic Management Journal, 33*(5), 496–512.

Mellers, B., Stone, E., Atanasov, P., Rohrbaugh, N., Metz, S. E., Ungar, L., . . . & Tetlock, P. (2015a). The psychology of intelligence analysis: Drivers of prediction accuracy in world politics. *Journal of Experimental Psychology: Applied, 21*(1), 1.

Mellers, B., Stone, E., Murray, T., Minster, A., Rohrbaugh, N., Bishop, M., . . . & Ungar, L. (2015b). Identifying and cultivating superforecasters as a method of improving probabilistic predictions. *Perspectives on Psychological Science, 10*(3), 267–281.

Mellers, B., Ungar, L., Baron, J., Ramos, J., Gurcay, B., Fincher, K., . . . & Murray, T. (2014). Psychological strategies for winning a geopolitical forecasting tournament. *Psychological Science, 25*(5), 1106–1115.

Mill, J. S. (1882). *A system of logic* (8th ed.). New York: Harper.

Mosteller, F., & Youtz, C. (1990). Quantifying probabilistic expressions. *Statistical Science, 5*(1), 2–12.

Nakao, M. A., & Axelrod, S. (1983). Numbers are better than words: Verbal specifications of frequency have no place in medicine. *American Journal of Medicine, 74*(6), 1061–1065.

Office of the Director of National Intelligence. (2007). Intelligence community directive 203: Analytic standards.

Office of the Director of National Intelligence. (2015). Intelligence community directive 203: Analytic standards.

Page, S. (2007). *The difference: How the power of diversity creates better groups, firms, schools, and societies*. Princeton, NJ: Princeton University Press.

Peters, E., Västfjäll, D., Slovic, P., Mertz, C. K., Mazzocco, K., & Dickert, S. (2006). Numeracy and decision making. *Psychological Science, 17*(5), 407–413.

Satopää, V. A., Baron, J., Foster, D. P., Mellers, B. A., Tetlock, P. E., & Ungar, L. H. (2014a). Combining multiple probability predictions using a simple logit model. *International Journal of Forecasting, 30*(2), 344–356.

Satopää, V. A., Jensen, S. T., Pemantle, R., Mellers, B. A., Tetlock, P. E., & Ungar, L. H. (2014b). Probability aggregation in time-series: Dynamic hierarchical modeling of sparse expert beliefs. *Annals of Applied Statistics, 8*, 1256–1280.

Shipley, W., Gruber, C., Martin, T., & Klein, M. (2009). *Shipley-2 manual*. Torrance, CA: Western Psychological Services.

Soll, J. B., & Larrick, R. P. (2009). Strategies for revising judgment: How (and how well) people use others' opinions. *Journal of Experimental Psychology: Learning, Memory, and Cognition, 35*(3), 780.

Sunstein, C. R. (2014). *Valuing life: Humanizing the regulatory state*. Chicago: University of Chicago Press.

Surowiecki, J. (2004). *The wisdom of crowds: Why the many are smarter than the few and how collective wisdom shapes business, economies, societies and nations*. New York: Doubleday.

Tetlock, P. E., & Gardner, D. (2015). *Superforecasting: The art and science of prediction*. New York: Random House.

Tetlock, P. E., Mellers, B. A., Rohrbaugh, N., & Chen, E. (2014). Forecasting tournaments: Tools for increasing transparency and improving the quality of debate. *Current Directions in Psychological Science, 23*(4), 290–295.

Wallsten, T. S., & Budescu, D. V. (1995). A review of human linguistic probability processing: General principles and empirical evidence. *Knowledge Engineering Review, 10*(1), 43–62.

Wallsten, T. S., Budescu, D. V., Rapoport, A., Zwick, R., & Forsyth, B. (1986). Measuring the vague meanings of probability terms. *Journal of Experimental Psychology: General, 115,* 348–365.

Wallsten, T. S., Fillenbaum, S., & Cox, J. A. (1986). Base rate effects on the interpretations of probability and frequency expressions. *Journal of Memory and Language, 25*(5), 571–587.

Weber, E., & Hilton, D. (1990). Contextual effects in the interpretations of probability words: Perceived base rate and severity of events. *Journal of Experimental Psychology: Human Perception and Performance, 16,* 781–789.

Wyden, P. (1979). *Bay of Pigs: The untold story.* New York: Simon & Schuster.

CHAPTER 13

Efficient Warnings, Not "Wolf or Puppy" Warnings

Lisa A. Robinson, W. Kip Viscusi, and Richard Zeckhauser

Warnings are a major instrument that the government employs to control losses from risks. On an everyday basis, we will see, for example, warning labels on cigarettes, notices of the carcinogenic potential of items we are likely to encounter, posted signs when we are in falling rock zones, and if watching television, a litany of side effects that accompany ads for prescription drugs.

Although warnings for widely used products are now quite common, that was not always the case. Warnings requirements initially focused on exposures that posed immediate and toxic hazards. The 1927 Federal Caustic Poison Act required that a dozen of the most toxic chemicals, such as sulfuric acid, be labeled "poison." A decade later, the Federal Food, Drug, and Cosmetic Act required the first warnings for food and drugs, where the focus was on imminent hazards and misbranding. Product labeling rules for over-the-counter drugs did not arrive until 1960. The only other prominent warnings requirements at that time were for insecticides and herbicides under the Federal Insecticide, Fungicide, and Rodenticide Act in 1947. The first warnings regulations for products that did not pose a risk of immediate harm came in 1966, when risk warnings became required for cigarette packs. In 1977, Congress required warnings on products containing saccharin, a product that posed minimal dangers relative to products that had required warnings to date. It was not until the 1980s, when occupational hazard communication efforts and environmental right-to-know policies were implemented, that warnings became a more widespread phenomenon.

An academic literature on warnings also began to emerge at that time. Some observers opposed the use of the warnings approach, claiming that it could never promote safety and that direct regulation was preferable.[1] Other studies took a more favorable view of warnings and focused on criteria that would make them an effective regulatory tool.[2] These latter studies stressed the importance of providing new information in a convincing manner, avoiding label clutter, and using a standardized warnings vocabulary. The academic literature also began to recognize the potential risks should warnings proliferate. Such warnings about warnings have had little effect, as the warnings phenomenon has grown rapidly.

Warnings policies, which are less intrusive than command and control regulations, were dubbed "smart disclosure" policies in 2011 by the Office of Information and Regulatory Affairs, then led by Cass Sunstein of *Nudge* fame (written with Richard Thaler).[3] Information provision, in theory, offers significant advantages over the predominant government approach to risk control, namely regulations that specify what can be done and what cannot. With the latter, for example, the Food and Drug Administration (FDA) determines what drugs are allowed on the market. The Environmental Protection Agency (EPA) determines what levels of various pollutants can be dumped in rivers or the atmosphere.

Information provision via the government offers three main advantages: First, given that information is a public good, it is efficient to have a central agent secure that information and then distribute it to others. Second, a major element of risk control entails risk avoidance by individuals. Given that, a one-size-fits-all approach makes no sense. However, given the information on risk provided by the government, individuals, in theory, will be empowered to make wise decisions for themselves. Thus, individuals who highly value a somewhat risky product can choose to purchase it despite its risks. Individuals who value it less will know to avoid it. Individuals will also be at different risk levels, and if effectively informed, high-risk individuals will know to avoid an exposure that low-risk individuals might accept. Third, some decisions by their very nature are decentralized and cannot be readily monitored by the government, such as how a pesticide is used, or whether a prescription drug is taken with food as recommended.

Information provision as a regulatory strategy breaks down, however, if individuals cannot effectively process the information, in which case more prescriptive regulations may be warranted. In some cases, the government simply prohibits a product, as opposed to giving information, presumably because it thinks that no individual, or at least very few individuals, should purchase it. That is the impetus behind the FDA approach for drugs, or for that matter, making marijuana illegal.

If consumers are relatively heterogeneous, however, the prohibition approach has the strong disadvantage of not securing the benefits of private choice. Thus, it is not surprising that nearly half of U.S. states have recently decided to allow marijuana use for medical purposes, presumably because they think that for an identifiable group of individuals, the benefits of use well outweigh the costs (a few states have made marijuana legal for all.)

For many products, prohibition is too blunt an instrument, and so too is defining certain categories of permissible users. The latter approach fails because within any category that is easily defined, there will be some who if fully informed would like to use the product, and some who would not. To be effective, such categories need to be defined by characteristics such as age or health conditions that can be easily recognized by both the individuals affected and by those enforcing the policies. The difficulties of creating such categories are exemplified by the debate over what constitutes permissible medical use of marijuana or conditions under which individuals may be accompanied by emotional support animals.

Does this not therefore suggest that the government should simply employ a strategy requiring that numerical information be posted, as it does, for example, in identifying caloric or fat content on food labels? The answer would be a confident "yes" if individuals could readily process that information, ascertain their risk levels, assess their benefits, and then make an informed risk-benefit decision. Alas, for all but an exceptional few, utilizing information effectively in this way would be all but impossible. Thus, in many cases the government has chosen neither to provide quantitative risk information directly because it would be too hard for individuals to process, nor to prohibit products because some individuals should be using or consuming them. Instead, it turns to a third strategy: it issues warnings about the risks or, more commonly, requires private parties to post warnings on their products.

In theory, warnings could function in much the same way as information. Individuals, alert to the risks, could make intelligent decisions about whether their personal benefits warranted taking the risk. Before proceeding, we should note the potential nudge feature of warnings. On being alerted that a product brings dangers, but not having its potential benefits highlighted, a warning with respect to the risks of consuming a product or participating in an activity by itself tends to function as a nudge against consumption. For example, cigarette warnings both convey information and indicate government disapproval of smoking.

Efficient Warnings

A warning inevitably creates benefits and costs. We take a benefit-cost approach to assessing efficiency. Other approaches may lead to qualitatively similar results.

The Anatomy of Warnings

To simplify at the outset, posit that there is only one level of warning. For simplicity, we focus on warnings regarding the discrete decision to use or not use a product. Warnings also may serve a function of providing information with respect to precautions undertaken during product use. In a world where most people think most products are safe, and where they have little ability to distinguish among levels of risk, a warning would simply say: "Be careful, this product contains risks above the norm." Posit as well that the government could precisely determine the risk per use of every product. It would then presumably set an optimal cutoff risk level, r^*, above which a product would have to carry a warning label. The terminology of the warning—that is, whether it says "above the norm," "very dangerous," or whatever—would be calibrated to the group of products receiving the warning. Such designations might be specific to the product class, as, for example, the risk level that is above the norm for drain opener might differ significantly from the risk level for denture adhesive, allowing benefits to be taken into account. For simplicity, we focus on a single warning threshold across all products.

A well-informed public, having had experience with this system, would then know that any product with a warning label carries a risk, say risk per use, at r^* or above. If there was substantial variability in the risk level of products getting a label, individuals might have a hard time, since they would not know whether the product was just at the r^* threshold or perhaps many times as risky.[4]

Just as individuals have limited ability to effectively interpret information about risks, they may have difficulties responding effectively to warnings. First,

Table 13.1. Net benefits from warning

	Stop consuming	Continue consuming
Net negative individual	1. B_N (+); m_1	2. W_N (−); m_2
Net positive individual	3. B_P (−); m_3	4. W_P (−); m_4

we identify what the ideal response to a warning would be. Alerted to the potential risk, individuals would first assess their personal level of risk from consuming another unit of the product. That marginal risk level could depend on factors such as their age, health condition, and the amount of the product to be consumed, positing that incremental risk increases with dose. Second, they would quantify their benefits from a marginal unit of consumption. Those for whom the net benefit from another unit of consumption is negative (positive) will stop (continue) consumption.

For simplicity, we shall leave aside secondary considerations, such as reducing consumption, and assume that all individuals would consume one unit of a product absent a warning, and after the warning, each individual would consume either no units or one unit. We define four categories that depend on whether the individual chooses to stop consuming the product as a result of the warning and on whether he or she accrues net benefits from this decision.

Table 13.1 shows the elements of a benefit-cost analysis of a warning. Let B be the (possibly negative) net benefits an individual gets from using the product, W the loss due to the warning for individuals who continue to consume (and may feel anxious or otherwise discomfited as a result), subscripts N and P respectively represent net negative and net positive benefit individuals. Let (+) or (−) then show the sign of the payoff for people in each group. Finally, let m be the number of people falling in each of the four categories. Thus, $m_1 + m_2$ is the number of net negative individuals, and $m_3 + m_4$ is the number of net positive individuals. To illustrate, an individual in category 3 (B_P (−); m_3) might be an individual who gives up fish completely, despite the presence of beneficial omega-3 fatty acids, because of a warning about mercury in some types of seafood.

To tally the total payoff from the warning, T, we simply multiply the payoff in each box by the numbers in each box, and then sum. It is thus,

$$T = B_N{}^*m_1 + W_N{}^*m_2 + B_P{}^*m_3 + W_P{}^*m_4. \qquad (1)$$

The first term in equation (1) represents the intended response of the warning: individuals with negative net benefits who forego consumption. This represents a positive payoff. The other three terms are negative. Leave aside for the moment the second and fourth terms, say because (as seems plausible) the losses from an ignored warning are small in absolute value relative to the benefits from a properly heeded warning, B_N, or the losses due to an inappropriately heeded warning, B_P. That is, $|W_N| \ll |B_N|$ and $|W_P| \ll |B_P|$. Then, the key implication of equation (1) is that a warning will be more worthwhile the greater the fraction of individuals who should stop consuming, the greater the response of such individuals to the warning,[5] and the smaller the fraction of individuals who shouldn't stop consuming who inappropriately do stop in response to the warning.

Warnings come in many flavors, with different intensities. Thus, listing an ingredient on a food label, as with fats or calories, could indicate concern. Text warnings can vary in the extent of the threat they indicate. And rotating threat warnings across packages, as is done with cigarettes in the United States, recognizes that for any particular label there are limits on what people will process, but multiple warnings indicate that consumption brings many dangers. Canada, Australia, and the United Kingdom go further with highly disturbing graphic warnings for cigarettes. Presumably, equation (1) could guide the choice among alternative forms of warning for a product. The warning providing the highest net benefits should be chosen.

For warnings to be efficient, clearly benefit-cost analysis must be brought into play. The key questions involve preferences and elasticities. Under preferences, we must know what benefits and costs are incurred by those who do and do not respond to a warning. The elasticity answer tells us how strongly different groups respond to warnings. We shall illustrate the importance of preferences and elasticities in our analysis of graphic cigarette labels and FDA's trans fat label.

Graphic Cigarette Labels, Preferences and Elasticities

The 1964 U.S. Surgeon General's report on smoking, which indicated that it causes lung cancer, is generally credited as the major milestone in U.S. efforts to decrease cigarette consumption. Since that time, policy interventions have been diverse and numerous, ranging from educational campaigns to taxes, and involving all levels of government. As a leading cause of preventable deaths, smoking is one of the most well-studied public health problems but also one of the most complex, given the effects of addiction, heterogeneity in preferences, and other factors.[6]

We focus here on federal requirements for placing warning labels on cigarette packages. These labels were first required by law in 1965 to be on cigarette packs in 1966, then subsequently modified to indicate specific health outcomes. The labels in use today were introduced by law in 1989. They include four rotating statements: (1) "SURGEON GENERAL'S WARNING: Smoking Causes Lung Cancer, Heart Disease, Emphysema, and May Complicate Pregnancy"; (2) "SURGEON GENERAL'S WARNING: Quitting Smoking Now Greatly Reduces Serious Risks to Your Health"; (3) "SURGEON GENERAL'S WARNING: Smoking by Pregnant Women May Result in Fetal Injury, Premature Birth, and Low Birth Weight"; and (4) "SURGEON GENERAL'S WARNING: Cigarette Smoke Contains Carbon Monoxide."

More recently, the 2009 Family Smoking Prevention and Tobacco Control Act required FDA to issue regulations mandating the addition of color graphics, along with nine revised text warnings.[7] FDA finalized such regulations in 2011 (Food and Drug Administration 2011). Some of the potential impacts of graphic warnings can be illustrated by returning to our model above. Consider categories 1 and 4 of Table 13.1. When these warnings lead more net negative beneficiaries from smoking to stop or reduce consumption, that is beneficial. However, when the graphic health warnings do not alter such individuals' consumption, their enjoyment from smoking is reduced because of the anxiety or disgust triggered by the warnings; that is detrimental. It is also detrimental if warnings lead to exaggerated risk beliefs, which in turn discourage positive-net-benefit smokers.

Several tobacco companies sued FDA on the basis that the 2011 regulations violated the First Amendment and served no constructive role in informing consumers. FDA argued that the warnings visualized factual information. The companies countered that the graphics were not purely factual—they were designed to provoke an emotional response. The U.S. Court of Appeals for the District of Columbia ruled that the graphic warnings that have been developed thus far did not serve an informational function. In its 2012 decision in *R.J. Reynolds Co. v. Food and Drug Administration*, the Court concluded: "FDA has not provided a shred of evidence—much less the 'substantial evidence' required by the APA [Administrative Procedures

Act]—showing that the graphic warnings will 'directly advance' its interest in reducing the number of Americans who smoke." FDA is now reconsidering the regulations.

How greatly any graphic labels policy might further reduce smoking rates is unclear. Existing policies now have likely dissuaded those who are less interested in smoking. Current smokers may persist because they find that the pleasures of smoking outweigh the costs, or because of erroneous decisions that are difficult to remedy through informational efforts. An appropriate benefit-cost analysis will tally the welfare effects of graphic labels on those who continue smoking, whether they fall into category 2 or category 4.

There is substantial debate about the effectiveness of the types of graphics included in FDA's 2011 proposals, quite apart from their legal standing (Viscusi 2011). Whether graphic warnings are desirable depends on whether, given the actual risks posed by cigarettes, the benefits associated with leading net negative smokers to stop smoking and nonsmokers to never start smoking outweigh the costs from requiring continuing smokers to view gruesome images.

Trans Fat in Food: Industry Responds to Consumer Warnings

Under the Federal Food, Drug, and Cosmetic Act, FDA can require certain types of food labeling to aid consumers in maintaining healthy diets. After many years of consideration, FDA issued regulations in 2003 requiring that nutrition labels indicate the amount of trans-fatty acids present in foods and dietary supplements (Food and Drug Administration 2003). The regulation was followed by local bans that also addressed restaurant food, as well as court cases targeting particular companies (Unnevehr and Jagmanaite 2008).[8]

Though fats are just listed on the nutritional labels for foodstuffs, alongside beneficial nutrients such as protein, most consumers do know that they are considered a bad element as a result of the accompanying informational campaigns. However, few individuals know much about the levels and characteristics of risks associated with different quantities of each type of fat, or even what levels are high or low. Thus, unlike other information required by the government, such as calories or miles per gallon for autos, merely having fat content on a nutritional label serves as an undifferentiated warning for most people who note that information. Informational content works just like a warning when individuals know that an ingredient or feature carries risk, but they have little ability to process the information beyond seeing that a risk is present.

The 2003 regulation, which became effective in 2006, requires that manufacturers add a separate line to the nutrition label that indicates the grams of trans fat, following the "saturated fat" listing under the "total fat" heading. While the label includes a percent of daily value for total fats and for saturated fats, no percentage is provided for trans fats. These daily values indicate the amount of each nutrient that should be consumed as part of a healthy diet. However, FDA stated that it lacked the data needed to develop such a daily value for trans fat. Products containing less than 0.5 grams per serving can list trans fat content as zero. If the amount reported is zero, manufacturers can also declare the absence of trans fat on the front of the package. FDA provides some exemptions to this labeling requirement, generally for products that report zero grams of trans fat and do not make claims about their low fat, fatty acid, or cholesterol content.

On its own, listing trans fat on the label provides information, not a warning. After all, nutrition labels list both healthful and unhealthful ingredients. What gives it warning status is the associated information dissemination efforts (by FDA, public interest groups, and others) on the dangers of trans fat consumption. The effectiveness of the labeling is thus dependent on individuals' awareness and understanding of the risk information provided, as well as their attentiveness to the reported trans fat content.

Trans fats are associated with increased risk of coronary heart disease, as well as possibly other health conditions such as diabetes and some cancers. They bring benefits as an inexpensive approach to increasing shelf-life and improving taste and texture, particularly in pastries, margarine, and snacks such as cookies, crackers, and chips. Reformulation to remove them is generally technically feasible and may involve the substitution of saturated fats in some cases. While saturated fats bring health risks, they are believed to be well below the risks brought by trans fats.

Many analyses of warnings take the risk environment as given and consider only responses by consumers. However, producers may also respond when a warning about risk is provided for their product. First, a government information effort may lead them to recognize that a risk is much greater than they thought. Second, producers may have been aware of the risk level, but have been capitalizing on consumer ignorance. Once the information is made available in the market, the jig is up. Third, they may feel that potential litigation over risk imposition has become more likely.

We will focus on a fourth factor: Once producers can get credit for a lower risk product, competitive considerations may make risk reduction worthwhile. Equation (1), in essence, revolved around the elasticity of demand in response to a warning for net negative and net positive individuals. Let's say that after a warning, sales would be 15% higher if a risk were reduced sufficiently to avoid the warning. If avoiding risk is costly, it may not be worthwhile to avoid risk if it would merely boost demand by 15%. A monopolist would think in such terms. But in a market where there was reasonable competition, hence meaningful cross-elasticity of demand, avoiding the warning would be much more consequential to a producer. If other producers kept to their risk levels, the risk-avoiding producer might gain sales of, say, 40%. If most others did reduce, a producer who did not might experience a 60% drop. Of course, the producers are in a form of prisoners' dilemma. If all reduce, they will be back to roughly prewarning market shares, but with a more costly but lower risk product.

Indeed, the trans fat case suggests that observed elasticities of consumption can be due more to producer than to consumer actions. In its economic analysis of the 2003 regulation, FDA conservatively estimated the resulting health benefits, underestimating these effects. It assumed that consumers would choose to decrease their intake by 0.1% and that manufacturers would decrease the trans fat content of margarine by 10% (in addition to margarine reformulation already underway). Using these conservative assumptions, FDA estimated that the labeling requirement would prevent 600 to 1,200 cases of coronary heart disease and 240 to 480 deaths per year, thus providing benefits with a present value of $13 billion to $27 billion over 20 years, compared to costs of $139 million to $275 million (3% discount rate, dollar year not reported). In addition to underestimating the health-related benefits, FDA likely underestimated the negative consequences, although intuition suggests that these costs may be relatively small. The cost estimates focused on the one-time effects of reformulation; the longer term impacts on prices and on supply and demand conditions more generally were not quantified. Nor did FDA quantify the value consumers would place on averting changes in product attributes such as taste and texture. Although FDA believed that reformulation of other products was likely, it lacked the evidence needed to quantify the effects on trans fat intake.

Subsequent research suggests that reformulation was substantial (e.g., Unnevehr and Jagmanaite 2008; Mozaffarian, Jacobson, and Greenstein 2010;

Rahkovsky, Martinez, and Kuchler 2012; Van Camp, Hooker, and Lin 2012). However, it is unclear how much credit goes to the labeling requirements as opposed to the increasing evidence on risk, court cases, local bans, and associated publicity. FDA estimates that between 2003 and 2012, consumption of trans fat decreased by about 78% (Food and Drug Administration 2015). How much of the reduced consumption is attributable to consumer behavior rather than producer decisions is uncertain. For example, one study (Howlett, Burton, and Kozup 2008) suggests that high-risk populations may be confused about the importance of limiting trans fat consumption.

The producer response likely reflects the economic calculus discussed above: producers could cost-effectively reduce trans fat levels without significantly hurting their net revenues or market share. "No trans fat" claims on the front of the package might even increase net revenues. While the producer response limited consumer choice, it is unclear how much consumers valued the advantages conferred by trans fats. A complete benefit-cost analysis would start by assessing individual preferences for both the benefits and harms associated with consuming trans fats.

More information is required before we can make a definitive assessment of the desirability of graphic warnings on cigarette packages or of FDA's dictates on trans fats.

"Wolf or Puppy" Warnings

Every child knows the tale of crying wolf: raising an alarm often when there really is no wolf leads the population to complaisance; it thus ignores the legitimate cry of wolf. This problem hardly afflicts the warning system in most nations.[9] However, a different problem afflicts many such systems. They impose the same warnings on many little dangers that they do on big dangers. Wolves are a dangerous wild animal. When they are about, they deserve a warning. Puppies too could bite you. However, a system that sounded the same alarm—say "Wolf or Puppy About"—when either a wolf or a puppy was in the vicinity would be of little value. People would quickly learn to ignore the warning, since puppies are many times more common than wolves, and represent very little danger. We shall argue that a wolf or puppy warning system provides an apt metaphor for many existing warning systems, where large numbers of products, some imposing very modest dangers and others great dangers, get the same warning labels. In similar fashion, overinclusive warnings by an overcautious parent may induce a child to take more, not fewer, serious risks.

The potential for cancer, which generally heads the public's list of dread diseases, is often the concern for such labels, as it is with California's Proposition 65, discussed below. More than 800 different chemicals were on the list as of 2018. The risks created by exposure to these chemicals differ by orders of magnitude. Not surprisingly, individuals homogenize abundant warnings, and often fail to respond to the small minority that impose grave risks. In a quite different context, companies launching initial public offerings and responding to strictures of the U.S. Securities and Exchange Commission list large numbers of risk factors, making it virtually impossible for investors to discern what the major risks are or how significant overall rates may be.

Mercury in Seafood: Confused Responses to Competing Messages

In 2001, FDA issued an advisory targeted on women who are pregnant and others of childbearing age that encouraged them to avoid eating fish containing potentially high levels of mercury (particularly shark, swordfish, king mackerel, and tilefish), while noting that seafood (here used interchangeably with fish) is an important part of their diet. In 2004, FDA and EPA issued an updated advisory that included similar warnings but placed a greater emphasis on the beneficial impact of overall fish consumption on health.[10] These competing messages were worse than the mixing of puppies and wolves on warnings. Beneficial seafood got confused with detrimental seafood. After substantial study, the agencies eventually issued a new advisory in 2017 that attempts to correct this problem.

Mercury is a neurotoxin associated with developmental delays in young and unborn children, typically measured as reductions in IQ. At the same time, seafood is an important source of healthful omega-3 fatty acids, which may reduce the risk of heart disease and stroke, while also benefiting the neurological development of the young and unborn. The policy goal in this case is to encourage vulnerable individuals to reduce their consumption of those fish species that are high in mercury, while increasing the general population's overall consumption of other seafood types.[11]

The net health benefits of these advisories are likely to be positive if consumers comply with them as intended; however, the available evidence suggests that historically the advisories may have instead led to decreases in overall seafood consumption and health-related losses. The complexity of the messages appears to lead to confusion and misinterpretation, with overattention to potential losses in comparison to potential gains.

For example, Cohen et al. (2005) consider the risk-risk tradeoffs associated with three scenarios. Their "optimistic" scenario assumes women of childbearing age follow the advisory, shifting consumption from high to low mercury seafood. Their "middle" scenario assumes that only women of childbearing age respond to the advisory, but they reduce their overall consumption of seafood rather than changing the mix of seafood consumed. Their "pessimistic" scenario assumes that all members of the population reduce their seafood consumption, rather than solely those targeted by the advisory.[12] Not surprisingly, Cohen et al. (2005) find that following the advisory under the optimistic scenario leads to a large net gain in health. If women of childbearing age reduce all seafood consumption under the middle scenario, the gain is smaller. Under the pessimistic scenario, if the full population reduces their consumption, the health losses are significant.[13] The researchers also consider the health gains associated with increasing, rather than decreasing, seafood consumption and find that they are substantial.

Shimshack and Ward (2010) explore the effects of the January 2001 FDA advisory using scanner data on seafood purchases. They find that the at-risk group reduced their intake of both mercury and omega-3 fatty acids due to a decline in all seafood consumption. Using standard monetary values for lost IQ points and mortality from EPA analyses, the authors estimate that the value of the associated health losses was about $30 per household. They also estimate the gains that would accrue if these households had instead behaved in accordance with Cohen et al.'s (2005) "optimistic" scenario, finding benefits of $587 per at-risk household. Rheinberger and Hammitt (2014) extend this analysis and consider the welfare losses in a dynamic framework. They find that accounting for longer term effects may substantially increase the losses associated with unintended responses to the policy.

In 2017, after substantial study, FDA and EPA issued a new advisory. It provides an easy-to-read, concise chart listing what types of fish should and should not be consumed by women of childbearing age and young children, including specifying the acceptable number of servings and portion sizes. We hope that future research will find that this innovation reduces inappropriate responses without significantly curtailing appropriate ones. The goal is to avoid conflicting or competing messages, thus enabling individuals to be better able to calculate their net benefits, and thereby place themselves in the correct category in Table 13.1.

California Proposition 65—A True "Wolf or Puppy" Warning System

A ballot referendum led to the enactment of California Proposition 65, which is the Safe Drinking Water and Toxic Enforcement Act of 1986. The Proposition's main focus was to establish warning requirements for carcinogens and reproductive toxicants. However, it was confusingly described, and few voters expressed awareness of the warning provisions. Most simply thought that its goal was to protect water supplies/keep them clean, to control toxic chemicals and where they are dumped, to bring toxins under control, and more generally, to protect the environment (Field 1986).

Product warnings have two possible general functions: (1) to influence the discrete decision of whether to use the product, and (2) to influence the manner in which the product is used by, for example, altering precautionary behavior. Proposition 65 warnings are of the first type; they are designed primarily to alert consumers to carcinogens and reproductive toxicants. They do not, for example, indicate how much of a product a person should consume or whether it can be consumed with other products. Even within the narrowly defined objective of informing the discrete product use decision, Proposition 65 warnings flunked the test of providing accurate or useful information to consumers. Only recently has the State of California begun to address the problems that it created.

The risk levels that trigger these warnings historically have been quite low. In the case of carcinogens, the safe harbor risk level below which no warning is required is an exposure that leads to a risk below a lifetime probability of 1/100,000 of incurring a cancer based on a 70-year lifetime of exposure (OEHHA 2013). By way of comparison, the cancer risk of smoking is over 10,000 times greater than this risk level. The safe harbor risk level for reproductive toxicants is a no observable effects standard. This safe harbor value is the amount of exposure for which 1,000 times that exposure has no observable effects on the growth of the fetus, whether these effects are beneficial or adverse.

Until recently, the example of acceptable on-product wording for carcinogens was: "WARNING: This product contains a chemical known to the state of California to cause cancer." The counterpart wording for reproductive toxicants was: "WARNING: This product contains a chemical known to the state of California to cause birth defects or other reproductive harms."

Do such warnings provide accurate information, or do they exemplify the "Wolf or Puppy" warnings discussed above? Survey data on how adult consumers view this warning are instructive (Viscusi 1988). Because the survey testing the warnings language was run in Illinois, the wording of the warning was identical to that for California except that the name of the state was changed. Suppose that the warning language appeared on a consumer product such as breakfast cereal. Most consumers viewed a Proposition 65 warning on cereal as conveying a risk comparable to that of cigarettes. Overall, 69% of consumers believed that the Proposition warning was about a risk equal to that implied by the 1966 cigarette warning ("Caution: Use of this product may be hazardous to your health"), and 48% believed that it was comparable to a variant of the 1969 cigarette warning ("Warning: The state of Illinois has determined that this product is dangerous to your health"). The remaining respondents divided between thinking that the Proposition 65 wording was weaker or stronger than that for cigarettes.

The respondents also considered a linear risk scale and rated the product relative to three different risk anchors. A minority of the sample, 21%, rated a product bearing a Proposition 65 warning as being between zero and the risk of one 12-ounce saccharin cola, 44% rated the risk as being between that of a saccharin cola and a pack of cigarettes, and 35% rated the risk as being between one pack of cigarettes and five packs of cigarettes. Taking cigarettes as the benchmark for wolves, the Proposition 65 warnings are largely about puppies.

Perhaps in part because of the stringency of the warnings language, companies sought to reformulate numerous products so as to avoid the labels. At the time of its implementation, California had about one-eighth of the national market share for grocery products. Among the products that were found requiring warnings were Liquid Paper (correction fluid) and some types of power cables. Liquid Paper was reformulated; the power cords are now labeled.

Warnings for products are not ubiquitous in California because many risks have been exempted from the requirements. These special exceptions carved out in the implementation of Proposition 65 also tend to undermine its usefulness even from the standpoint of "warning wolf" on a consistent basis. In deference to California's agricultural industry, natural carcinogens that are present in food or occur as part of the handling and shipping of the product are exempt from the carcinogen calculations. Thus, carcinogens in peanuts such as aflatoxins are exempt from the lifetime risk threshold. The absence of a warning consequently doesn't necessarily imply that the product poses less cancer risk than does a product for which a warning is required. It would also be potentially deleterious to the California wine industry to have wine from California bear a warning of carcinogenicity and reproductive toxicity that goes beyond what is required nationally.[14] As a result, there is no California requirement for on-product warnings for alcohol, only a placard in the store with a warning such as the following: "WARNING: Drinking distilled spirits, beer, coolers, wine and other alcoholic beverages may increase cancer risk, and, during pregnancy, can cause birth defects" (OEHHA n.d.). There are similar postings in restaurants. There are also postings for environmental exposures at locales such as gasoline stations.

Potatoes have received one of the more bizarre Proposition 65 warnings. When potatoes are fried or baked, not boiled, acrylamide is formed. Because acrylamide is listed by the state of California as both a carcinogen and a reproductive toxicant, the warnings requirement is triggered. Customers at McDonald's would see a posting noting that acrylamide is not added to the potatoes by McDonald's but is present after cooking, and is also present at lower levels once hamburger buns are browned. This warning also appears on products such as potato chips. The behavioral guidance implied by the warning is murky at best, since consumers who seek to avoid the risk by baking potatoes at home will create similar risks, though without any attendant warning. Similarly, the acrylamide that is produced when coffee beans are roasted leads to a Proposition 65 warning at Starbucks and its competitors.

The Proposition 65 experience imparts three principal lessons. First, stamping any product as hazardous will lead consumers to put it in the same class as other mass-marketed products meriting such warnings, such as cigarettes, if their attention is drawn to the warnings. However, if such warnings proliferate, their sheer abundance may lead to their being ignored. Second, the decision to require a warning and the wording of the warning should be designed in a manner that will lead consumers to at least roughly assess the accurate risk level. Using cigarette warning language is seldom desirable because cigarettes are so much more dangerous. Third, warnings should be designed to enable people to make sensible decisions regarding whether to use the product and, if so, what precautions to take.

The state of California has begun to address some of these concerns. For example, as of August 2018 the warnings have been changed to provide more information on the chemical present and the associated risks (OEHAA 2018a). California is also now proposing to remove the warnings requirement for coffee (OEHAA 2018b). However, these changes do not seem to address key issues. For example, rather than better tailoring the warning to the level and type of risk, the new requirements may heighten fear by adding a yellow triangular warning symbol containing an exclamation point. Consumers are directed to a website for more information. Accessing this information, understanding the implications, balancing the risks with the benefits of consumption, and comparing risks and benefits across products is likely to require substantially more time than most are willing to spend on such tasks. Those who take the time to review the information will likely find it to be burdensome. The initiatives also do little to restrain the number of products requiring warnings. Providing warnings that fail to discriminate among risks of differing magnitudes neither fosters efficient risk decisions by consumers nor provides the basis for effective risk-averting behaviors.

Conclusion

The success of informational policies, and their preservation of individual choice, has created substantial support for warnings policies over the past several decades. Our increased understanding of the importance of behavioral factors has provided additional impetus to the adoption of informational approaches. The legitimate economic objective of warnings is to provide accurate information that will assist people—particularly those experiencing high consequences—in making better informed decisions. The principal policy objective should be to lead more people to make correct choices. Based on the true probabilities, ideally we want people for whom the net benefits are positive to consume the product and those for whom the net benefits are negative to avoid or curtail consumption. The benefit-cost calculation for a warning thus has to attend to elasticities of response by the two groups, and their benefits from stopping or continuing consumption.

Many warnings policies, alas, are of a grab bag variety, a feature exemplified by California's Proposition 65. Warnings policies should recognize that wolves are not puppies and that seafoods are not cigarettes. Regulations that are dramatically misplaced tend to undermine the legitimacy of well-targeted regulations.

As we look forward, what is the future of risk and what is the future of warnings, the two being closely entwined? There are many possible strands to the answer. We provide four: warnings proliferation, weaknesses of extant warning systems, the heightened role of intended harms, and newly emerging dangers.

This analysis took an implicit benefit-cost approach to warnings for specific products. It introduced the notion that for individuals who consume despite receiving warnings, the warning will impose a cost: the consumption will be less attractive. Society has been on a warnings spree for the past few decades. Legislatures and agencies do not like to give up their right to warn, in part because on the surface it appears to be a low-cost approach to dealing with the difficult challenges associated with addressing many risks. Thus, there is no letup in sight, much less any curtailment. And there is no check to restrict the emergence of warnings that may serve to divert attention from warnings for more significant hazards. Given this vast proliferation, it is also important to extend cost-benefit considerations across products. It is reasonable to speculate that each additional warning makes individuals less likely to attend to prior warnings. Think of the mother who gives her child a hundred warnings, from "look both ways before you cross the street" to "never play in puddles." The puddle warning, though possibly avoiding exacerbating cold symptoms and the discomfort and hassles of wet clothing, may prove an expected net negative for health and safety if the street-crossing warning gets slightly less attention. So it is with prospectuses for financial investments, where the listing of a few dozen risk factors makes it hard to know which, if any, are important. Our warnings makers must beware of even a weak Cassandra effect. Cassandra issued many prophecies on future dangers, all proved true, but virtually all were ignored.

Psychologists and economists—the major contributors to this volume—have become strange bedfellows in the march toward more warnings, one variant of nudges. Unfortunately, there has been virtually no progress in developing systems that readily differentiate big from little dangers in ways that can effectively inform citizens. Thus, a product imposing some carcinogenic risk, once identified, unless prohibited, secures a warning that proves equivalent for virtually all consumers whether it imposes a 1-in-a-million risk or 1 in 10. The undifferentiated warning problem exists, even when numerical scoring is possible. The Doomsday Clock of the Bulletin of the Atomic Scientists, which indicates the likelihood of global catastrophe, has never moved further than 10 minutes before midnight since 1998. Groups that issue warnings are hesitant to ever state that risks are only moderate, much less minimal. In time, none believe those who continuously cry wolf. Recognizing that our future is one of widespread warnings, significant research is needed on how to make critical warnings more salient than others.

Since the 9/11 calamity, most individuals have felt greater threats from intended harms, notably terrorism, than from mere collateral risks of everyday life, such as dying in an auto accident. That is true even though auto accidents kill many more Americans every year than have been killed by terrorists throughout history. The U.S. Department of Homeland Security (DHS) used to have a color-coded warning system, based on the successful system for forest fires. However, it is far more difficult to assess terrorism risks than forest fire risks. The absence of base rates, the ability of terrorists to adapt to any new protective measures, and the distinctive nature of different terrorist attacks foil predictive methods. It is also hardly clear what benefits warnings would have. It is almost impossible to stay out of vulnerable locales, and political leaders usually tell us to go about our business; otherwise the terrorists have won. DHS ultimately gave up its color-coded warning system and replaced it with more informative advisories.

Some massive emerging risks are clear; others remain cloudy. Both are stimulating the activities of various warnings masters. Climate change is the clearest future risk. The strong scientific consensus is that climate change is real, man-made, and will be highly consequential. Most warnings about it are intended to get societies to do more to control greenhouse gases, though the consensus is also strong that it is probably too late to avoid significant temperature increases and associated climate change. The ability of governments to get together to provide a public good for the world at large is also in question. Perhaps the warning should be that climate change warnings will mostly be ignored.

Emerging technologies are also ringing alarm bells in important quarters. Prominent sources of concern today are gene therapy, artificial intelligence, and solar geoengineering to prevent climate change. Revolutionary technologies almost always raise such concerns. Warnings tend to slow but rarely stop their progress. The warnings, which invariably come from selective quarters, have almost always turned out to be excessive in the past. And should a doomsday technology ever come into being, warnings will have proved to be insufficient. Revolutionary technologies often bring puppy dangers alongside their benefits. At times, they impose wolf dangers. Let's hope our warnings are sufficient when their dangers are dragons.

The major challenge to our densely populated nonsystem of warnings is to find ways to separate puppies from wolves from dragons.

Notes

1. Adler and Pittle (1984) provide such a skeptical view of warnings, which is noteworthy since David Pittle was a commissioner of the Consumer Product Safety Administration.

2. For a review of these policies and economic and behavioral principles for warnings, see Viscusi and Magat (1987); Magat and Viscusi (1992); American Law Institute (1991); Viscusi and Zeckhauser (1996).

3. See Thaler and Sunstein (2008) for articulation of the rationales for "nudge" policies. The information disclosure aspects of this approach were incorporated into U.S. policy in Sunstein (2011).

4. Informing the public about the average risk of labeled products receiving warnings would still suffer the problem of applying the identical label to products representing dramatically different risk levels.

5. This conclusion assumes, as seems plausible, that enough individuals who should stop consuming do stop to make the warning worthwhile for this group alone.

6. See, for example, U.S. Department of Health and Human Services (2014); Jin et al. (2015); Cutler et al. (2015) for more discussion.

7. Sunstein (2014) discusses such warnings from the perspective of "nudge" policies.

8. In 2015, FDA determined that partially hydrogenated oils (the primary dietary source of industrially produced trans fats) are not generally recognized as safe for use in food, effectively banning them.

9. Of course, there are independent organizations that issue warnings about products (or individuals) that pose little or no threat, often for self-serving or political purposes. Our focus is on government operated, imposed, or induced warning systems.

10. More information on these advisories and their evolution is available at https://www .fda.gov/Food/ResourcesForYou/Consumers/ucm393070.htm and https://www.epa.gov/fish -tech/2017-epa-fda-advice-about-eating-fish-and-shellfish

11. For a broader discussion of the risks and benefits of fish consumption, see Oken et al. (2012).

12. The reduction in fish consumption assumed under the middle and pessimistic scenario was 17%, based on previous research on the effects of the 2001 advisory (Oken et al. 2003), which did not discriminate between high and low mercury fish.

13. The findings are aggregated using quality-adjusted life years (QALYs); the optimistic scenario leads to a gain of 49,000 QALYs, the middle scenario leads to a gain of 9,700 QALYs, and the pessimistic scenario leads to a net loss of 41,000 QALYs.

14. The federally required warning reads: "GOVERNMENT WARNING: (1) According to the Surgeon General, women should not drink alcoholic beverages during pregnancy because of the risk of birth defects. (2) Consumption of alcoholic beverages impairs your ability to drive a car or operate machinery, and may cause health problems."

References

Adler, R. S., & Pittle, R. D. (1984). Cajolery or command: Are education campaigns an adequate substitute for regulation? *Yale Journal on Regulation, 1*, 159.

American Law Institute. (1991). *Enterprise responsibility for personal injury: Reporters' study.* Philadelphia: American Law Institute.

Cohen, J. T., Bellinger, D. C., Connor, W. E., Kris-Etherton, P. M., Lawrence, R. S., Savitz, D. A., . . . & Gray, G. M. (2005). A quantitative risk–benefit analysis of changes in population fish consumption. *American Journal of Preventive Medicine, 29*(4), 325–334.

Cutler, D. M., Jessup, A., Kenkel, D., & Starr, M. A. (2015). Valuing regulations affecting addictive or habitual goods. *Journal of Benefit-Cost Analysis, 6*(2), 247–280.

Field, M. (1986, October 16). Prop. 65 getting increased voter attention with supporters having big edge. *California Poll*, Release No. 1366. Retrieved from http://ucdata.berkeley.edu/pubs/CalPolls/1366.pdf

Food and Drug Administration. (2003). Food labeling: Trans fatty acids in nutrition labeling, nutrient content claims, and health claims: Final rule. *Federal Register, 68*(133), 41433.

Food and Drug Administration. (2011). Required warnings for cigarette packages and advertisements: Final rule. *Federal Register, 76*(120), 36628.

Food and Drug Administration. (2015, June). *The FDA takes step to remove artificial trans fats in processed foods* (News release).

Howlett, E., Burton, S., & Kozup, J. (2008). How modification of the nutrition facts panel influences consumers at risk for heart disease: The case of trans fat. *Journal of Public Policy & Marketing, 27*(1), 83–97.

Jin, L., Kenkel, D., Liu, F., & Wang, H. (2015). Retrospective and prospective benefit-cost analyses of U.S. anti-smoking policies. *Journal of Benefit-Cost Analysis, 6*(1), 154–186.

Magat, W. A., & Viscusi, W. K. (1992). *Informational approaches to regulation.* Cambridge, MA: MIT Press.

Mozaffarian, D., Jacobson, M. F., & Greenstein, J. S. (2010). Food reformulations to reduce trans fatty acids. *New England Journal of Medicine, 362*(21), 2037–2039.

OEHHA. (2013). Proposition 65 in plain language. Office of Environmental Health Hazard Assessment, California Environmental Protection Agency. Retrieved from https://oehha.ca.gov/proposition-65/general-info/proposition-65-plain-language

OEHHA. (2018a). New Proposition 65 warnings. Office of Environmental Health Hazard Assessment, California Environmental Protection Agency. Retrieved from https://www.p65warnings.ca.gov/new-proposition-65-warnings

OEHHA. (2018b). Proposed adoption of new section under Article 7 no significant risk levels section 25704 exposures to listed chemicals in coffee posing no significant risk. Office of Environmental Health Hazard Assessment, California Environmental Protection Agency. Retrieved from https://oehha.ca.gov/proposition-65/crnr/proposed-adoption-new-section-under-article-7-no-significant-risk-levels-section

OEHHA. (n.d.). Alcoholic beverages. Office of Environmental Health Hazard Assessment, California Environmental Protection Agency. Retrieved from https://www.p65warnings.ca.gov/products/alcoholic-beverages

Oken, E., Choi, A. L., Karagas, M. R., Mariën, K., Rheinberger, C. M., Schoeny, R., . . . & Korrick, S. (2012). Which fish should I eat? Perspectives influencing fish consumption choices. *Environmental Health Perspectives, 120*(6), 790.

Oken, E., Kleinman, K. P., Berland, W. E., Simon, S. R., Rich-Edwards, J. W., & Gillman, M. W. (2003). Decline in fish consumption among pregnant women after a national mercury advisory. *Obstetrics & Gynecology, 102*(2), 346–351.

Rahkovsky, I., Martinez, S. W., & Kuchler, F. (2012). *New food choices free of trans fats better align U.S. diets with health recommendations* (EIB-95). U.S. Department of Agriculture, Economic Research Service.

Rheinberger, C. M., & Hammitt, J. K. (2014). The welfare value of FDA's mercury-in-fish advisory: A dynamic reanalysis. *Journal of Health Economics, 37,* 113–122.

Shimshack, J. P., & Ward, M. B. (2010). Mercury advisories and household health trade-offs. *Journal of Health Economics, 29*(5), 674–685.

Sunstein, C. R. (2011, September 8). *Informing consumers through smart disclosure.* Memorandum for the heads of executive departments and agencies from the administrator, Office of Information and Regulatory Affairs, Washington, DC.

Sunstein, C. R. (2014). *Simpler: The future of government.* New York: Simon & Schuster.

Thaler, R. H., & Cass R. Sunstein, C. R. (2008). *Nudge: Improving decisions about health, wealth, and happiness.* New Haven, CT: Yale University Press.

Unnevehr, L. J., & Jagmanaite, E. (2008). Getting rid of trans fats in the U.S. diet: Policies, incentives and progress. *Food Policy, 33*(6), 497–503.

U.S. Department of Health and Human Services. (2014). *The health consequences of smoking—50 years of progress: A report of the Surgeon General.* Atlanta, GA: U.S. Department of Health and Human Services.

U.S. Surgeon General. (1964). *Smoking and health.* Advisory Committee on Smoking and Health and U.S. Public Health Service.

Van Camp, D., Hooker, N. H., & Lin, C. T. J. (2012). Changes in fat contents of U.S. snack foods in response to mandatory trans fat labelling. *Public Health Nutrition, 15*(6), 1130–1137.

Viscusi, W. K. (1988). Predicting the effects of food cancer risk warnings on consumers. *Food Drug Cosmetic Law Journal, 43*(2), 283–307.

Viscusi, W. Kip. (2011). *Statement: U.S. Food and Drug Administration Docket No. FDA-2010-N-0568, RIN-0910-AG41, Required warnings for cigarette packages and advertisements.* Comments prepared at the request of R. J. Reynolds Tobacco Company, Lorillard Tobacco Company, and Commonwealth Brands, Inc.

Viscusi, W. K., & Magat, W. A. (1987). *Learning about risk: Consumer and worker responses to hazard information.* Cambridge, MA: Harvard University Press.

Viscusi, W. K., & Zeckhauser, R. J. (1996). Hazard communication: Warnings and risk. *Annals of the American Academy of Political and Social Science, 545*(1), 106–115.

PART IV

Role of Risk Mitigation, Risk-Sharing,
and Insurance

CHAPTER 14

Threats to Insurability

Carolyn Kousky

Introduction

Estimates of the average annual costs of natural disasters ranged between $94 billion and $130 billion between 2000 and 2012 (Kousky 2013a). These losses, in inflation-adjusted terms, have been growing over time (e.g., Kunreuther and Michel-Kerjan 2007). Due to three land-falling hurricanes and devastating wildfires, 2017 broke records in the United States, with losses over $300 billion (Smith 2018). Much of the increase in damages is due to growth in exposure: more people and capital—and more valuable capital—located in risky locations (e.g., Pielke et al. 2003; Miller et al. 2008; Barthel and Neumayer 2012; Aon Benfield 2013). Climate signals are also emerging in some loss data (e.g., Sander et al. 2013) and losses are projected to increase as the climate warms (e.g., Ranson et al. 2014). The largest share of disaster costs—at roughly 85%—comes from weather-related events (Cutter and Emrich 2005; Gall et al. 2011); they are the events most likely to be impacted by climate change. These changes in natural disaster risk may require changes in our approaches to risk reduction and risk transfer.

Insurance is an important risk management tool for dealing with the costs of natural disasters. Insurance can protect people against risks that have a small probability, but which could be financially devastating. Insurance often provides larger and timelier payouts than disaster aid, which, in the United States at least, can be quite limited and delayed for households—contrary to popular perceptions (Kousky and Shabman 2012). For example, following Hurricane Harvey in 2017, average Individual Assistance grants from the Federal Emergency Management Agency averaged only $4,300, whereas the average flood insurance payment averaged $115,000 (FEMA 2018, n.d.). When households and businesses are insured, they are more likely to rebuild (Turnham et al. 2011), which can limit negative economic multiplier effects in a community. Also, by limiting the exposure of firms or households to certain risks, insurance can allow beneficial economic activity to occur that might otherwise not be undertaken. Disaster insurance can thus promote household and community resiliency by limiting financial costs to insureds, speeding recovery, and potentially providing incentives to invest in hazard mitigation through price discounts (Kousky and Shabman 2016).

Natural disasters, however, are challenging to insure and breakdowns in disaster insurance markets are not uncommon. Low take-up rates for disaster insurance are observed, from flooding to earthquakes (e.g., Palm 1995; Dixon et al. 2006; Kousky et al. 2018). In some locations and for some perils, private insurance companies have ceased to write policies or otherwise limited their underwriting (e.g., Stroud 2012). In response, governments have intervened in these markets in a wide variety of forms around the world, including writing disaster policies directly, acting as a reinsurer, backstopping disaster losses, and providing disaster assistance, among other types of interventions (e.g., Swiss Re 2011; Kousky and Kunreuther 2018).

Insurance may become even more challenging for natural disasters, as a result of many converging trends. Climate change altering weather-related extreme events is one, along with new technologies being deployed at a rapid rate, increasing integration of supply chains, vast mobility of the population, and capital continuing to concentrate in risky areas. As the world grows hotter, more integrated, and more crowded, we may need to rethink our risk management approaches and invest in a more thoughtful and targeted way in risk mitigation. This, in turn, can improve the insurability of the residual risk. A new, integrated approach to risk reduction and risk transfer will require responsibilities and complementary efforts by both the public and private sectors.

This chapter discusses the conditions that make a risk more or less easy to insure. It then outlines several emerging challenges to the insurability of disaster risks: (1) greater dependence between risks, particularly in the tails; (2) fat-tailed damage distributions, getting fatter; and (3) larger systemic risks. The fourth section offers suggestions on improving the insurability of disasters, discussing hazard mitigation, novel insurance products, and government policies. The fifth section concludes. Even as natural disaster risks change and, in many cases, worsen, public-private partnerships designed to both reduce and effectively transfer risk can promote resilience of people, communities, and countries to changing and emerging threats.

The Insurability Spectrum

Insurance is a form of risk transfer. A risk-averse entity is willing to pay more than the expected loss to transfer a risk to another entity better able to spread the risk. For risk transfer to be possible, several conditions must be met; these are often presented as ideal conditions for insurability. Some are straightforward. The loss must be uncertain and, to some extent, random. It is not possible to insure an event known to occur with certainty or over which the insured has full control. The loss distribution must be known to a reasonable degree to make underwriting possible. In addition, for indemnity based insurance, such as homeowners' policies in the United States, losses must be, to a large extent, measurable and verifiable after a disaster event.

The risk should not be subject to high levels of adverse selection or moral hazard. These terms refer to the information and incentives of the insured. Adverse selection occurs when the insured knows more about their risk than the insurance company, so the firm cannot price differentiate. If only higher-risk households insure, it can drive up costs and prevent the company from obtaining a broader pool. Moral hazard occurs when an insured fails to take actions to reduce their risk, or actively seeks a risk, since damages will be compensated by the insurance company. Both adverse selection and moral hazard drive up the costs of insurance—in the extreme, to levels that make providing it impossible.

In addition, ideal insurance conditions include that the loss distribution be sufficiently thin-tailed and claims be independent. What do these two conditions mean? The first is that the probability of a loss becomes negligible at extreme values. For instance, height is thin-tailed: at greater heights the probability of occurrence becomes negligible. That is, we do not see 10-foot people. Independent risks imply that when one person suffers a loss, others do not necessarily suffer a loss, as well. For example, when an individual gets in a car accident, it does not mean that their neighbors will also be in accidents. These conditions are what make risk pooling beneficial. When risks are thin-tailed and independent, thanks to the law of large numbers and the central limit theorem, the average claim approaches the expected value and the aggregate distribution becomes thin-tailed or normally distributed. As an insurer writes more policies, then, this lets them charge a pure premium (that is, absent any necessary loadings), closer to the expected value. Finally, risks will only be insured if there is a price that is profitable for the insurance company and which the insured is willing and able to pay. The market must clear.

Natural disasters can violate all of the last criteria. Damages from many disasters are decidedly fat-tailed (e.g., Holmes, Prestemon, and Abt 2008; Wildasin 2008). With fat-tailed losses, the probability of damage falls slowly relative to the severity. This means the most severe event observed can be many multiples of the second most severe event. For instance, some common estimates of the costliest hurricanes in the United States (in inflation-adjusted dollars), indicate that Hurricane Katrina—the most damaging hurricane to date—caused over twice as much damage as the second costliest, Hurricane Andrew (this excludes Sandy, which was not classified as a hurricane at landfall). Imagine the next most-extreme hurricane: it could be multiples of the damage caused by Katrina. Damages from disasters are also spatially correlated, such that when one house suffers damage, it is likely all its neighbors did, too. Natural disasters hit entire communities, not just individual houses.

This combination of fat tails and spatial correlation will make losses much more volatile from year to year, and in some years, very severe losses will occur. For catastrophe risks, therefore, insurance firms must solve an intertemporal smoothing problem of trying to match regular premium payments, insufficient in any given year to cover a large loss, with the need for enormous sums of capital in the catastrophe years (Jaffee and Russell 1997). Given this, firms managing to keep the probability of insolvency below a certain level (value-at-risk requirements) will be required to charge large premiums to cover catastrophic risks. They need these premiums to build a reserve, purchase reinsurance, or invest in other securities to guarantee access to capital to pay claims in high loss years. This can lead to the violation of the last insurability criterion: this high price may not be one at which there is any demand for insurance (Kousky and Cooke 2012). The high cost of catastrophe insurance may mean that homeowners do not think it is worth buying or they may not have the budget to do so.

Insurability of risks, though, is a spectrum. Some are easy to insure, like auto accidents, while some present so many challenges, they will not be insured at all by the private sector, such as the risk of a nuclear terrorist attack.

There are many strategies that insurance companies can employ to make a risk more insurable. Insurance companies insure themselves through reinsurance, which is able to achieve better diversification across geographic regions and perils. Firms may limit their exposure through selective underwriting; for example, limiting the number of certain policies in certain locations. News articles have reported, for example, on companies writing fewer policies in the most hurricane-prone areas of the United States. Insurance contracts may be modified, such as through higher deductibles or caps on coverage. For example, in many places in the United States that are subject to hurricanes, insurance policies contain a "hurricane deductible," which is larger than standard deductibles for other included perils and usually set at a percentage of the home. Insurability is also a dynamic concept, changing over time (Swiss Re 2005). Risks change, economic conditions change, new technologies emerge, and new information becomes available, all of which could impact the insurance market (Kousky 2013b).

Emerging Threats to Insurability

This section discusses three emerging threats to insurability: (1) greater dependence between claims, particularly in the tails; (2) loss distributions with fattening tails; and (3) the emergence or strengthening of systemic risks. All of these threats increase the likelihood of catastrophic loss years.

Dependence in Claims

Natural disasters can generate many types of dependence across insurance claims. First, as mentioned, there can be simple spatial correlation in losses. When a disaster event occurs, it impacts an entire community or region. More troubling, dependence can concentrate in the tails, referred to as tail dependence. Tail dependence can be defined as the probability that one variable takes on an extreme value conditional on another variable taking on an extreme value. Some insurance lines have been found to be tail dependent. For example, automobile, health, property, and life insurance claims may usually be fairly independent, but in a severe disaster event, they all experience losses simultaneously, as observed after severe storms (RMS 2005; Lescourret and Robert 2006).

It is possible that climate change could introduce or strengthen dependencies between risks, including tail dependence (Kousky and Cooke 2009). This could be a simple function of more frequent or more severe disaster events that are more likely to have multiple impacts. For example, extreme heat is projected to increase as the climate warms and we know that heat waves can have a range of negative outcomes. The 2003 heat wave in France, for example, led to uninsured crop losses, fires, loss of nuclear power, higher electricity prices, rockfalls, and excess mortality from the heat and higher ground-level ozone (De Bono et al. 2004; Schär and Jendritzky 2004; Stedman 2004). Thus, in normal conditions, crop losses and mortality might not be correlated, but both become high during an extreme heat event.

Concentration of exposure in hazardous areas can also increase dependence in claims arising from the occurrence of natural disasters. For example, the severe 2011 floods in Thailand highlighted correlations in contingent business interruption losses due to a concentration of manufacturing in the floodplains of a single country. Many companies were not even aware of this risk in their supply chain and (re)insurance companies saw claims come in from around the world as the business interruption cascaded, particularly through the technology and automotive manufacturing sectors. The event also led to claims being filed for much longer than usual as all the interconnections in supply chains were slowly revealed (Holbrook 2013).

Failure to recognize dependencies can lead to a failure of risk management. While there is a saying in finance that in a time of crisis, all things are correlated, those possible tail correlations need to be adequately assessed ex ante if they are to be managed and insured. Yet assessing the dependencies between risks can be quite challenging, particularly for tail dependence where many observations of extremes are required to statistically identify the relationship. Some observers have argued that a failure to appreciate the increased complexities in the financial markets was partially responsible for the economic crisis (Goldin and Vogel 2010). Recently, structured expert judgment has been brought to bear on improving modeling of dependence (Cooke and Goossens 2000; Morales, Kurowicka, and Roelen 2008). Risk Management Solutions, a catastrophe modeling firm, has also noted there may be triggers, which they refer to as phase transitions, where a system moves from roughly independent damages to highly correlated damages. One example they give is a forced evacuation, after which properties deteriorate, there is a lack of personnel for response and operation of critical facilities, and rebuilding costs rise (RMS 2005). Clearly, more work is needed in identifying and quantifying tail dependence, when it emerges, and how it may be changing in response to climate, demographic, or technological trends.

Fatter Tails

As already noted, many disasters have been found to be fat tailed. Climate models predict that the frequency, magnitude, location, and/or duration of many extreme events may be changing (IPCC 2012). These climate changes may be shifting the distribution of disaster losses to the right, leading to more extreme events (U.S. Climate Change Science Program 2008). There is also concern that the distribution of disaster impacts may not just be shifting, but the tails may also be getting fatter. Initial evidence of this has been found in flood insurance claims, where the causes are unknown but likely to involve concentrations of development in high risk areas (Cooke, Kousky, and Michel-Kerjan 2014). As another example, hurricane strength may be increasing in response to warmer sea temperatures (Knutson et al. 2010).

Other global changes may be fattening the tails of disaster loss distributions, as well. As one example, the dramatic increase in the mobility of the population, as well as commodities, worldwide has implications for the spread of disease (Institute of Medicine 2006). Mobility changes are coupled with climate changes that are allowing diseases to enter regions where they were previously not found. These coupled trends mean that previously localized disease outbreaks may more easily become global pandemics. That is, more extreme negative consequences are possible.

As another example, leaner and more integrated supply chains potentially produce economic gains, but also can increase society's vulnerability. Food supply chains have moved toward much smaller inventories, concentrated among a smaller number of suppliers, bringing in food from around the globe instead of locally (Mahanta 2013). This means that there is a greater chance for disruption in the supply chain and when a disruption does occur, it has a bigger impact since there is very little cushion. Essentially, there has been a move toward elimination of redundancy in supply chains in the name of efficiency. While potentially improving earnings in stable periods, this can lead to an escalation of damages when a system is stressed or faced with a threat. A similar push to eliminate "idle" capital and to seek leverage from capital, even if reserved for risk management, could have contributed to the financial crisis of 2008 (Goldin and Vogel 2010). If systems have a "buffer," it can lower damages when an extreme event occurs. The challenge is that such buffers appear wasteful in non-disaster times.

Both tail dependence and fatter tails can increase the "probable maximum loss" (PML) of an insurance company. The PML is an estimate of the worst-case losses that an insurance company could face, either for a policy or for an entire portfolio. Increases in the PML will require increases in capital or will increase the solvency risk insurers face. Such increases would require higher insurance premiums, which, as already stated, could lead to policies costing more to write than insureds are willing or able to pay.

Larger Systemic Risks

Systemic risks—a term generally used to refer to a system-wide risk in which an event affects all entities simultaneously—are, by definition, non-diversifiable and thus not insurable. For example, a company cannot purchase insurance against a global recession. This, in and of itself, is nothing new. What is concerning is the possibility that we are introducing more systemic risks across sectors. There have been efforts to tease lessons from managing systemic risks across fields (e.g., National Research Council 2007), which could inform such changes.

Different definitions of systemic risk are found in the literature. In general, however, there seem to be two types of systemic risks: (1) a very large event that by its magnitude affects all or most entities in a system, and (2) an event of any size that sets in motion a cascade or chain reaction of negative consequences that ultimately impacts most or all of a system (e.g., Kaufman and Scott 2003). In a sense, these are the extreme of the two challenges just discussed—fat tails and dependence—in the former, if an event is fat tailed enough, then an occurrence could be large enough to impact the entire system, and in the latter, if risks are highly dependent, negative consequences could cascade and again the effect could be systemic. Both types of systemic risk may be evolving with recent global trends.

Regarding the first type of systemic risk, scientists are concerned, for example, that climate change could lead to tipping points in the earth system, or other catastrophic impacts, which would induce global, that is systemic, losses (e.g., AAAS and RFF 2014; Schneider 2004). Consider a collapse of the thermohaline circulation in the Atlantic, or a melting of a section of the West Antarctic Ice Sheet, which would cause at least four feet of global sea-level rise (Joughin, Smith, and Medley 2014; Rignot et al. 2014). This sea-level rise is not insurable as it is inevitable and global (albeit with some local variation). Regarding the second type of systemic risk, there is also the possibility that climate change could lead to cascading consequences which would turn a localized event into a global one (e.g., Kousky et al. 2009). For example, a group of retired U.S. admirals and generals found that climate change could be a "threat multiplier" and lead to instability in volatile regions (CNA Corporation 2007).

Of course, what constitutes a systemic risk depends on the system under study. For a small insurance company writing policies in only one region, a single hurricane could be a systemic risk. Consider the small, state-based, so-called "take-out" companies in Florida that have been paid to remove policies from the state wind pool. There is concern these firms, with such concentrated exposure, could not withstand a large hurricane; indeed, many failed even absent a hurricane (Olorunnipa 2013). For a global reinsurance company, however, it would take a global event to reach systemic levels. Global diversification is thus an important tool for managing smaller scale impacts, but some threats, as discussed, stress even the global reinsurance sector and it is those that could prevent the use of insurance as a risk management tool.

Can We Make the Uninsurable Insurable?

Targeted Hazard Mitigation

When the risk of extremes is lower, insurance is more feasible and less costly. A natural first response to challenges of insurability, then, is to examine the possibility for investments in hazard mitigation that could thin the tail of the loss distribution and decouple dependent risks. This possibility drove the creation of the Manufacturers Mutual Fire Insurance Company in 1835. The company only covered properties that had engaged heavily in risk reduction measures and offered lower rates to those properties as a result (Swiss Re 2005). This ultimately became the firm FM Global, which still employs this strategy.

Can we also identify interventions that could prevent cascading consequences or contagion effects? For example, are there "circuit breaker" climate adaptation or hazard mitigation strategies (Kousky et al. 2009) that could be employed to manage systemic threats? Similarly, could we identify investments that decrease problematic correlations? For example, take the 1906 earthquake in San Francisco. This event showed the tail dependence between earthquakes and fires (Steinberg 2006). Breaking this dependence involves the design and installation of gas and water pipes that can withstand extreme earthquakes. Another example is President Obama's suggestion to designate utility workers as first responders. This is an official designation from the Federal Emergency Management Agency that would allow access to disaster sites. Power outages can prevent important relief and repair work or even exacerbate damages and lead to cascading losses. Designating lineworkers as first responders can help bring the power back faster and reduce damages. A similar expansion could be made for those who help restore internet connectivity or other communication networks.

Risk reduction often must be a partnership between the public and private sectors. Insurance could provide some incentive for individuals and businesses to invest in hazard mitigation. If premiums are lowered when risks are reduced, actions that cost less than this difference will be financially attractive for the insured (assuming they have the necessary upfront capital or available financing). As noted by Woo (1999), however, insurance may not be the best driver of hazard mitigation, since in soft market conditions, when prices are low, it can discourage risk reduction, and when prices are high, many people forgo disaster insurance entirely. There is also a large literature suggesting individuals may not evaluate risks as an expert would and thus may fail to adopt cost-effective mitigation measures. Government, in its capacity to regulate land use, enact building regulations, and fund large structural and nature-based infrastructure investments may need to participate in risk reduction through funding and regulation, thus helping making the residual risk insurable.

Models Beyond Traditional Insurance

In recent decades, several innovative risk transfer mechanisms have emerged that could complement traditional insurance in providing cover for difficult-to-insure risks and/or access the capital in financial markets. After Superstorm Sandy, the New York City Metropolitan Transit Authority faced high insurance prices and opted instead for a $200 million catastrophe bond. The bond relies on a parametric trigger—the height of storm surge at tide gauges. More entities may opt for this type of disaster financing, as it can provide more flexible and possibly cheaper access to capital. The risk of parametric based products, however, is that the actual loss will not perfectly match the payout: it may be higher, but it could also be lower. This is termed "basis risk." Basis risk, however, does create an incentive for hazard mitigation since payouts above actual losses sustained can be kept.

As has been recommended for covering flood events in the United States (Michel-Kerjan and Kunreuther 2011), taking a layered approach to disaster risks could prove most effective. For the first layer of losses, the individual or business would retain the risk and self-insure. To lower the costs of insurance, this deductible could be as high as the entity can comfortably manage. For firms, this could involve creating a captive insurance company to be able to set aside capital to cover disaster events, and for individuals could involve the use of disaster savings accounts. The next layer of losses could be covered by standard insurance or through pools of similar entities, such as municipal pools in the United States. After this, losses can be reinsured and/or placed in the financial markets using insurance-linked securities. Finally, for the most severe events, the government can act as a backstop. This could also involve a layer of government reinsurance, such as is done in the United States for terrorism, particularly for higher levels of loss where tail dependence is problematic. However structured, a layered approach would divide up losses among entities best able to handle the given level of risk.

Government Insurance Programs

In the United States and around the world, the challenges with insuring disasters have already led to myriad government interventions in these markets. Many government policies can help the private disaster insurance market function more effectively. This can include regulating land use in hazardous areas, adopting stricter building codes, allowing insurers to price at risk-based levels, and providing financing for property-level investments in hazard mitigation. Still, beyond this, many governments, on their own or in some form of partnership with the private sector, have felt it necessary to create (quasi-)public insurance programs, usually with the goals of increasing the "availability" and "affordability" of disaster insurance.

Such insurance programs have taken a wide variety of forms: federal writing of first-line policies (National Flood Insurance Program), federal reinsurance or formal backstop programs (Terrorism Risk Insurance Program), state residual markets and pools (e.g., state wind pools, California Earthquake Authority), and state reinsurance (Florida Hurricane Catastrophe Fund). In the face of the threats discussed in the last main section, such policy interventions may become increasingly politically popular. They may become more necessary, as well, if the alternative is low take-up rates for disaster insurance and the policy objective is increasing resilience to changing extreme events.

That said, we can be more thoughtful in how we design such public-private insurance programs. How programs are structured will depend critically on the policy objectives. If the goal is to help private sector companies better manage extreme risks, government programs to cover losses in the tail of the distribution, as is done in the Terrorism Risk Insurance Program, for example, could be the approach taken. If the goal is to make disaster insurance available, even if underpriced, to encourage widespread take-up and thus resilience, government programs may write policies directly and include price discounts for certain groups. These programs themselves, however, will not be immune to the nature of catastrophe losses and so will require a financial structure for paying extreme losses, which could include purchasing private reinsurance or taxpayer forgiveness of losses above some threshold.

The cost of insurance for catastrophes is only one part of the challenge in these markets, however. The other is that consumers may not be inclined to insure against disasters due to lack of information on the risks, being overly optimistic about their risk, dismissing low probability risks, failing to understand insurance and the role it plays in recovery, or other decision-making biases. When failing to insure can harm others—such as getting in a car accident and not being able to pay the damage you caused to someone else or having your home burn and not being able to repay the bank—governments (or lenders) have mandated coverage. Government could consider requiring disaster coverage. This is currently the case in the United States for residents of 100-year floodplains with a mortgage from a federally regulated lender, but could be expanded.

Conclusion

As a changing climate and increasingly interconnected economy combine to create the potential for greater extreme events, traditional insurance markets could potentially become stressed for particular perils or in particular regions. Governments around the world have already taken a variety of approaches to helping disaster insurance markets, from offering coverage, to providing reinsurance, to simply regulating building in a way that minimizes losses. Insurability of risks is not a yes-no proposition, but a continuum, and there are many actions that can be taken to make risks more insurable by all sectors. Partnerships between the public and private sectors to continue to manage changing risks will continue to be critical to promoting resilience at a range of scales.

Note

An initial version of this chapter was written in advance of an event at Resources for the Future that the author introduced and moderated titled "Limits to Securitization." The panel discussion is available for online viewing: http://www.rff.org/events/event/2014-06/limits -securitization-future-insurance. I would like to thank the panelists in that event for sharing their insights: Roger Cooke, Andrew Castaldi, Bob Kopp, Bob Litterman, and Peter Nakada.

References

AAAS & RFF. (2014, November 12). *The economic and financial risks of a changing climate: Insights from leading experts: Workshop report*. American Association for the Advancement of Science and Resources for the Future. Washington, DC: Resources for the Future.

Aon Benfield. (2013). *Annual global climate and catastrophe report impact forecasting—2012*. Chicago: Impact Forecasting.

Barthel, F., & Neumayer, E. (2012). A trend analysis of normalized insured damage from natural disasters. *Climatic Change, 113*(2), 215–237.

CNA Corporation. (2007). *National security and the threat of climate change*. Alexandria, VA: CNA Corporation.

Cooke, R. & Goossens, L. J. H. (2000). *Nuclear science and technology: Procedures guide for structured expert judgment* (EUR 18820EN). Luxembourg: European Commission.

Cooke, R., Kousky, C., & Michel-Kerjan, E. (2014, April 24). Flood insurance claims: A fat tail getting fatter. Blog post retrieved from Resources for the Future website: http://www.rff .org/blog/2014/flood-insurance-claims-fat-tail-getting-fatter

Cutter, S. L., & Emrich, C. (2005). Are natural hazards and disaster losses in the U.S. increasing? *Eos Transactions American Geophysical Union, 86*(41), 381–389.

De Bono, A., Peduzzi, P., Kluser, S., & Giuliani, G. (2004). Impacts of summer 2003 heat wave in Europe. *Environment Alert Bulletin, 2* (United Nations Environment Programme).

Dixon, L., Clancy, N., Seabury, S. A., & Overton, A. (2006). *The National Flood Insurance Program's market penetration rate: Estimates and policy implications*. Santa Monica, CA: RAND Corporation.

FEMA. (2018, September 6). Significant flood events. Retrieved from Federal Emergency Management Administration website: https://www.fema.gov/significant-flood-events

FEMA. (n.d.). Texas Hurricane Harvey (DR-4332). Retrieved from Federal Emergency Management Administration website: https://www.fema.gov/disaster/4332

Gall, M., Borden, K. A., Emrich, C. T., & Cutter, S. L. (2011). The unsustainable trend of natural hazard losses in the United States. *Sustainability, 3*(11), 2157–2181.

Goldin, I., & Vogel, T. (2010). Global governance and systemic risk in the 21st century: Lessons from the financial crisis. *Global Policy, 1*(1), 4–15.

Holbrook, E. (2013). A world of supply chain risks. *Risk Management, 60*(3), 6.

Holmes, T. P., Prestemon, J. P., & Abt, K. L. (Eds.). (2008). *The economics of forest disturbances: Wildfires, storms, and invasive species.* New York: Springer Science & Business Media.

Institute of Medicine. (2006). *The impact of globalization on infectious disease emergence and control: Exploring the consequences and opportunities: Workshop summary.* Washington, DC: National Academies Press.

IPCC (Intergovernmental Panel on Climate Change). (2012). *Managing the risks of extreme events and disasters to advance climate change adaptation: Special report of the Intergovernmental Panel on Climate Change.* Cambridge: Cambridge University Press.

Jaffee, D. M., & Russell, T. (1997). Catastrophe insurance, capital markets, and uninsurable risks. *Journal of Risk and Insurance, 64*(2), 205–230.

Joughin, I., Smith, B. E., & Medley, B. (2014). Marine ice sheet collapse potentially under way for the Thwaites Glacier Basin, West Antarctica. *Science, 344*(6185), 735–738.

Kaufman, G. G., & Scott, K. E. (2003). What is systemic risk, and do bank regulators retard or contribute to it? *Independent Review, 7*(3), 371–391.

Knutson, T. R., McBride, J. L., Chan, J., Emanuel, K., Holland, G., Landsea, C., . . . & Sugi, M. (2010). Tropical cyclones and climate change. *Nature Geoscience, 3*, 157–163.

Kousky, C. (2013a). Informing climate adaptation: A review of the economic costs of natural disasters. *Energy Economics, 46*, 576–592.

Kousky, C. (2013b). *Revised risk assessments and the insurance industry* (RFF Discussion Paper 13-35). Washington, DC: Resources for the Future.

Kousky, C., & Cooke, R. M. (2009). *Climate change and risk management: Challenges for insurance, adaptation, and loss estimation* (RFF Discussion Paper 09-03). Washington, DC: Resources for the Future.

Kousky, C., & Cooke, R. (2012). Explaining the failure to insure catastrophic risks. *Geneva Papers on Risk and Insurance: Issues and Practice, 37*(2), 206–227.

Kousky, C., & Kunreuther, H. (2018). Risk management roles of the public and private sector. *Risk Management and Insurance Review, 21*(1), 181–204.

Kousky, C., Kunreuther, H., Lingle, B., & Shabman, L. (2018, July). *The emerging private residential flood insurance market in the United States.* Philadelphia, PA: Wharton Risk Management and Decision Processes Center.

Kousky, C., Rostapshova, O., Toman, M., & Zeckhauser, R. (2009). *Responding to threats of climate change mega-catastrophes* (Policy Research Working Paper No. 5127). Washington, DC: World Bank. Retrieved from http://documents.worldbank.org/curated/en/504001468313505132/Responding-to-threats-of-climate-change-mega-catastrophes

Kousky, C., & Shabman, L. (2012). *The realities of federal disaster aid* (RFF Issue Brief). Washington, DC: Resources for the Future.

Kousky, C. & Shabman, L. (2016, July 29). The role of insurance in promoting resilience. *BRINK*. Retrieved from http://www.brinknews.com/the-role-of-insurance-in-promoting -resilience/

Kunreuther, H. C., & Michel-Kerjan, E. O. (2007). *Climate change, insurability of large-scale disasters and the emerging liability challenge* (NBER Working Paper No. 12821). Cambridge, MA: National Bureau of Economic Research.

Lescourret, L., & Robert, C. Y. (2006). Extreme dependence of multivariate catastrophic losses. *Scandinavian Actuarial Journal, 2006*(4), 203–225.

Mahanta, S. (2013, October 21). New York's looming food disaster. Retrieved from the City-Lab website: https://www.citylab.com/equity/2013/10/new-yorks-looming-food-disaster /7294/

Michel-Kerjan, E., & Kunreuther, H. (2011). Redesigning flood insurance. *Science, 333*(6041), 408–409.

Miller, S., Muir-Wood, R., & Boissonnade, A. (2008). An exploration of trends in normalized weather-related catastrophe losses. In H. F. Diaz and R. J. Murnane (Eds.), *Climate extremes and society* (pp. 225–247). Cambridge: Cambridge University Press.

Morales, O., Kurowicka, D., & Roelen, A. (2008). Eliciting conditional and unconditional rank correlations from conditional probabilities. *Reliability Engineering & System Safety, 93*(5), 699–710.

National Research Council. (2007). *New directions for understanding systemic risk: A report on a conference cosponsored by the Federal Reserve Bank of New York and the National Academy of Sciences.* Washington, DC: National Academies Press.

Olorunnipa, T. (2013, June 3). Despite no hurricanes, many "takeout" insurers fail. *Miami Herald.*

Palm, R. (1995). The Roepke lecture in economic geography catastrophic earthquake insurance: Patterns of adoption. *Economic Geography, 71*(2), 119–131.

Pielke, R. A., Jr., Rubiera, J., Landsea, C., Fernández, M. L., & Klein, R. (2003). Hurricane vulnerability in Latin America and the Caribbean: Normalized damage and loss potentials. *Natural Hazards Review, 4*(3), 101–114.

Ranson, M., Kousky, C., Ruth, M., Jantarasami, L., Crimmins, A., & Tarquinio, L. (2014). Tropical and extratropical cyclone damages under climate change. *Climatic Change, 127*(2), 227–241.

Rignot, E., Mouginot, J., Morlighem, M., Seroussi, H., & Scheuchl, B. (2014). Widespread, rapid grounding line retreat of Pine Island, Thwaites, Smith, and Kohler glaciers, West Antarctica, from 1992 to 2011. *Geophysical Research Letters, 41*(10), 3502–3509.

RMS (Risk Management Solutions). (2005). *Hurricane Katrina: Profile of a super cat: Lessons and implications for catastrophe risk management.* Newark, CA: Risk Management Solutions, Inc.

Sander, J., Eichner, J. F., Faust, E., & Steuer, M. (2013). Rising variability in thunderstorm-related U.S. losses as a reflection of changes in large-scale thunderstorm forcing. *Weather, Climate, and Society, 5*(4), 317–331.

Schär, C., & Jendritzky, G. (2004). Climate change: Hot news from summer 2003. *Nature, 432*(7017), 559.

Schneider, S. H. (2004). Abrupt non-linear climate change, irreversibility and surprise. *Global Environmental Change, 14*(3), 245–258.

Smieth, A. (2018, January 8). 2017 U.S. billion-dollar weather and climate disasters: a historic year in context. Retrieved from Climate.gov website: https://www.climate.gov/news

-features/blogs/beyond-data/2017-us-billion-dollar-weather-and-climate-disasters -historic-year

Stedman, J. R. (2004). The predicted number of air pollution related deaths in the UK during the August 2003 heatwave. *Atmospheric Environment, 38*(8), 1087–1090.

Steinberg, T. (2006). *Acts of God: The unnatural history of natural disaster in America* (2nd ed.). Oxford: Oxford University Press.

Stroud, M. (2012, April 11). As weather gets biblical, insurers go missing. Retrieved from Reuters website: https://www.reuters.com/article/us-insurance-disasters/as-weather-gets -biblical-insurers-go-missing-idUSBRE83911S20120411

Swiss Re. (2005). Innovating to insure the uninsurable. *Sigma, 2005*(4), 19–32.

Swiss Re. (2011). State involvement in insurance markets. *Sigma, 2011*(3).

Turnham, J., Burnett, K., Martin, C., McCall, T., Juras, R., & Spader, J. (2011, August). *Housing recovery on the Gulf Coast, Phase II: Results of property owner survey in Louisiana, Mississippi, and Texas.* Washington, DC: Department of Housing and Urban Development, Office of Policy Development and Research.

U.S. Climate Change Science Program. (2008, June). *Weather and climate extremes in a changing climate: Regions of Focus: North America, Hawaii, Caribbean, and U.S. Pacific Islands* (Synthesis and Assessment Product 3.3). Washington, DC: U.S. Climate Change Science Program.

Wildasin, D. E. (2008). Disaster policies: Some implications for public finance in the U.S. federation. *Public Finance Review, 36*(4), 497–518.

Woo, G. (1999). *The mathematics of natural catastrophes.* London: Imperial College Press.

CHAPTER 15

The Role of Insurance in Risk Management
for Natural Disasters

Back to the Future

Howard Kunreuther

Insurance has a dual role to play in reducing future losses from natural disaster: encouraging those at risk to invest in loss reduction measures by reducing the premiums they pay, while at the same time providing claims payments to these same individuals should they suffer damage from a natural disaster. To meet these two objectives, insurance premiums need to be based on risk so that residents and businesses are aware of the hazards they face and have economic incentives to undertake cost-effective mitigation measures to reduce the likelihood of disaster.

The factory mutual insurance companies of the 1800s used insurance in exactly this manner to encourage safer facilities. Inspections were undertaken prior to issuing an insurance policy and were continued on a regular basis while coverage was in force. Premiums reflected risk and were reduced for factories that instituted additional risk reduction measures; companies where risks increased significantly over time had their policies canceled. In many cases, factory mutual companies would provide coverage only to firms that adopted specific loss prevention methods. To illustrate, the Spinners Mutual only insured risks where automatic sprinkler systems were installed.

One of the first mutual insurance companies providing fire insurance coverage to textile mills was the Boston Manufacturers. Following a mill inspection in 1865, Edward Manton, president of the Boston Manufacturers, provided a report to the company regarding their insurance status that contained the following information: "Renew at same if an additional force pump is added. If not, renew for $10,000 at 1¼" (Bainbridge 1952, 112). This meant that the mill would have to pay an additional 1.25 cents per $1 of coverage without the additional force pump. Given that they had $10,000 in coverage, the extra annual premium would have been $125. The Boston Manufacturers also worked with lantern manufacturers to encourage them to develop safer designs and then advised all policyholders that they had to purchase lanterns from those companies whose products met their specifications. Similarly, the Manufacturers Mutual in Providence, Rhode Island developed specifications for fire hoses and advised mills to buy only from companies that met these standards (Bainbridge 1952). Today FM Global works closely with its policyholders to reduce risk threats by undertaking cost-effective loss prevention measures.

This chapter proposes how insurance can return to its nineteenth-century roots in dealing with the risks facing property owners in hazard-prone areas. More specifically, I will address the following question: What role can the private and public sectors play in reducing losses from future natural disasters, recognizing the limitations of individuals in dealing with low-probability, high-consequence (LP-HC) events and the challenges the insurance industry faces in providing coverage against these risks?

To answer this question it is helpful to understand why residents in hazard-prone areas often ignore future disasters and why private insurers are reluctant to provide protection against extreme events. I begin by reviewing the history of flood insurance to highlight the challenges on both the demand and supply sides of insurance. After providing insight into behavior of both insurers and homeowners due to cognitive biases and simplified decision rules, a set of guiding principles are specified for evaluating strategies that involve insurance coupled with other policy instruments for dealing with LP-HC events over the long-term. The chapter then proposes a program for making insurance coverage against extreme events such as floods more widely available, and encouraging or requiring those at risk to protect themselves against future losses. It concludes with suggestions for future research and empirical studies.

Flood Insurance

The history of flood insurance is an instructive example of the absence of a viable market for protection against this risk.[1] In 1897 an insurance company in Illinois offered coverage against flood damage to property along the Mississippi and Missouri Rivers inspired by the extensive damage from flooding of these two rivers during the previous two years. But in 1899, severe flood damage exceeded the premiums and the net worth of the company, and even washed away the home office (Manes 1938).

The next attempt by insurers in providing flood coverage was in the mid-1920s, but following the catastrophic losses suffered by insurers from severe flooding in 1927 and 1928, every responsible insurer discontinued coverage. There was a widespread belief among private insurance companies that the flood peril was uninsurable by the private sector for the following reasons: (1) adverse selection would be a problem because only particular areas are subject to flood-related losses; (2) risk-based premiums in these parts of the country would be so high that no one would be willing to pay them; and (3) flood losses could be so catastrophic as to cause insolvencies or have a significant impact on surplus (Overman 1957; Gerdes 1963; Anderson 1974).

This lack of coverage by the private sector triggered significant federal disaster relief to victims of Hurricane Betsy in 1965 and led to the creation of the National Flood Insurance Program (NFIP) in 1968. The NFIP is a public-private partnership designed to reduce flood disaster losses by restricting the sale of flood insurance to communities that make a commitment to control the location and design of future construction in the floodplain by land-use regulations and well-enforced building codes. In return, existing properties in the floodplain were provided with flood insurance coverage at highly subsidized rates; new construction was charged premiums reflecting risk. Today, private insurers market coverage under their own name and process claims in return for a portion of the premium to cover their marketing and administrative costs. The Federal Emergency Management Agency (FEMA) is responsible for covering the flood-insured losses from inundation of rivers and storm surge from hurricanes.

In July 2012 (three months before Hurricane Sandy), Congress passed and President Obama signed the Biggert-Waters Flood Insurance Reform Act of 2012 (BW12), that applied the tools of risk management to the increasingly frequent threat of flooding. Among its many provisions, the legislation required that the NFIP produce updated floodplain maps, strengthen local building code enforcement, remove insurance subsidies for certain properties, and move toward charging premiums that reflected flood risk.

Soon after becoming law, BW12 faced significant challenges from some homeowners who had reason to complain that the new flood maps overestimated their risk. These residents and others in flood-prone areas felt that the proposed premium increases were unjustified and that they could not afford the increased costs of their flood insurance. In March 2014, Congress passed the Homeowner Flood Insurance Affordability Act (HFIAA14) that delayed the implementation of risk-based premiums until after FEMA had drafted an affordability framework based on the recommendations of a National Academy of Sciences study on the topic. The two-part study was completed in 2015 (National Research Council 2015a, 2015b). FEMA is currently addressing the affordability issue in anticipation of the renewal of the NFIP.

Even though premiums on existing properties were highly subsidized when the NFIP was passed in 1968, relatively few homeowners purchased coverage voluntarily. This led Congress to pass the Flood Disaster Protection Act of 1973. This bill required all properties holding federally backed mortgages to purchase flood insurance. As of July 2018, the NFIP had sold more than 5.1 million policies in 22,000 communities and provided more than $1.3 trillion in coverage. However, many property owners subject to this hazard still do not have flood insurance today, although data are unavailable to estimate the actual number. We do know that only 20 percent of New York City households in the area inundated by Hurricane Sandy, all of which were eligible to purchase flood insurance, had coverage at the time of the disaster (City of New York 2013).

How Decision-Makers Behave When Faced with LP-HC Events

A large body of cognitive psychology and behavioral decision research over the past 30 years has revealed that individuals and organizations often make decisions under conditions of risk and uncertainty by combining *intuitive* thinking with *deliberative* thinking. In his thought-provoking book *Thinking, Fast and Slow*, Daniel Kahneman characterizes the differences between these two modes of thinking (Kahneman 2011). *Intuitive thinking* (System 1) operates automatically and quickly with little or no effort and no voluntary control. It is often guided by emotional reactions and simple rules of thumb that have been acquired by personal experience. *Deliberative thinking* (System 2) allocates attention to effortful and intentional mental activities where individuals undertake tradeoffs and recognize relevant interdependencies and the need for coordination.

Individuals normally make good decisions when they have considerable past experience to choose between alternative actions. The same cannot be said with regard to decisions in response to extreme events, where by definition decision-makers have limited data on which to base their choices. There is a tendency to either ignore a potential disaster or overreact to a recent one. For example, after a disaster, uninsured individuals are likely to want to purchase insurance even at high prices, while insurers often consider restricting coverage or even withdrawing from the market. In these situations, both parties focus on the losses from a worst-case scenario without adequately reflecting on the likelihood of this event occurring in the future.

Consumer Decision-Making

Empirical studies reveal that when considering whether to purchase flood or earthquake insurance, homeowners often exhibit cognitive biases. A common bias is *availability*, where the judged likelihood of an event depends on its salience and memorability (Tversky and Kahneman 1973). A related error that arises is the *optimism bias*, where people believe that they are more immune to threats than others (Weinstein 1980). Taken together, these two biases lead to a tendency to ignore rare risks until after a catastrophic event occurs. This is a principal reason why it is common for individuals at risk to purchase insurance only *after* experiencing damage from a large-scale disaster and receiving limited disaster relief to pay for their losses. If homeowners have not suffered damage after several years, there is a tendency to feel that the premiums were wasted and hence to cancel their insurance policy.

To illustrate this point, an in-depth analysis of the entire portfolio of the National Flood Insurance Program in the United States revealed that the median tenure of flood insurance was between two and four years, while the average length of time in a residence was seven years. For example, of the 841,000 new policies bought in 2001, only 73% were still in force one year later. After two years, only 49% were in force, and eight years later only 20%. Similar patterns were found for each of the other years in which a flood insurance policy was first purchased (Michel-Kerjan, Lemoyne de Forges, and Kunreuther 2012).

Similar behavior has also been observed with respect to the purchase of earthquake insurance by homeowners in California. The Northridge earthquake of January 1994 led to a significant demand for earthquake insurance. For example, more than two-thirds of the homeowners surveyed in Cupertino County had purchased earthquake insurance in 1995 (Palm and Carroll 1998). There have been no severe earthquakes in California since Northridge and only 10% of those in seismic areas of the state have earthquake insurance today. If a severe quake hits San Francisco in the near future, the damage could be as high as $200 billion, and it is likely that most homeowners suffering damage will be financially unprotected (Risk Management Solutions 2014).

One reason why individuals cancel their policies is that they view insurance as an investment rather than a protective activity. As noted above, many purchase coverage after experiencing a loss from a disaster but feel they wasted their premiums if they have not made a claim over the next few years. Individuals should celebrate not having suffered a loss over a period of time rather than canceling their policy because they have not made a claim. A challenge is how to convince residents in hazard-prone areas that *the best return on an insurance policy is no return at all.*

Failure to undertake protective measures for reducing losses is another example of short-term thinking. Homeowners normally do not engage in deliberative thinking by comparing the upfront costs of the investment in mitigation with the expected discounted benefits over the life of the structure. There are three principal reasons that residents in hazard-prone areas have limited interest in mitigation measures: (1) they underestimate the risk and perceive the likelihood of a disaster to be below their threshold level of concern; (2) the household feels that it cannot afford the high cash outlay due to budgetary constraints; and (3) individuals are myopic and focus on short time horizons. Decision-makers' resistance is likely to be compounded if they are concerned that should they relocate in the next few years, the value of their home will not reflect the expected benefits from investing in loss reduction measures because the new owner will not be concerned about the risk of a disaster (Kunreuther, Meyer, and Michel-Kerjan 2012).

Insurer Decision-Making

Insurers, both in the private market and public sector, are also prone to biases when it comes to LP-HC events, as highlighted by their behavior with respect to offering earthquake insurance coverage in California. In 1985, the California legislature passed a law requiring insurers writing homeowners' policies on one- to four-family units to offer earthquake insurance to these residents. The owners did not have to buy this coverage; the insurers only had to offer it to them. At the time and still today, banks and financial institutions do not require earthquake insurance as a condition for a mortgage. The Northridge earthquake caused insured losses of $12.5 billion (in 1994 prices), primarily to commercial structures (Roth 1988).

In the three years following Northridge, demand for earthquake insurance by homeowners increased by 19% in 1994, 20% in 1995, and 27% in 1996, leading private insurance companies in California to reevaluate their seismic risk exposures (California Department of Insurance 1997–1998). Insurers concluded that they would not sell any more earthquake policies on residential property as they were concerned about the impact of another catastrophic earthquake on their balance sheets, without considering its likelihood of occurrence.

The California Insurance Department surveyed insurers and found that up to 90% of them had either stopped or had placed restrictions on the selling of new homeowners' policies after the Northridge earthquake. This led to the formation of a state-run earthquake insurance company, the California Earthquake Authority in 1996, that is providing most earthquake coverage to homeowners today, although there are some private insurers offering homeowners in California earthquake policies.

Guiding Principles for Evaluating Policies

A set of guiding principles provides a framework for developing and evaluating strategies involving insurance in concert with other policy tools for reducing risks and paying insurance claims. These principles fall into two categories: (1) *information principles* to foster the availability of risk data necessary to implement good policy; and (2) *policy design principles* given that risk data are available.

Information Principle 1: Accurate risk assessments. It is desirable to characterize the likelihood and consequences of specific events and the uncertainties surrounding these estimates. This information should ideally be made available to all participants in insurance markets; no party should have any special informational advantage.

Information Principle 2: Adjusting strategies to reflect actual behavior. As shown in the previous section, consumers and insurers are likely to exhibit cognitive biases and utilize simple decision rules in dealing with extreme events. Policymakers should know the causes of their behavior and take them into account when developing strategies.

Policy Design Principle 1: Premiums should reflect risk. Insurance premiums should be based on risk in order to warn individuals about the hazards they face, and to encourage them to engage in cost-effective mitigation measures to reduce their vulnerability to catastrophes. State regulations that allow insurers to charge premiums based on risk also encourages them to supply coverage when they otherwise might not do so.

Policy Design Principle 2: Define equity and apply it consistently. Subsidies should be made available to individuals deserving special treatment (e.g., low-income homeowners residing in hazard-prone areas) so that individuals can purchase coverage from any insurance firm, just as those who use food stamps can shop at any grocery store. Proposals to improve equity should specify why some groups of buyers deserve special treatment and indicate who will bear the cost of that treatment.

Developing Long-Term Strategies for Dealing with Extreme Events

This section proposes strategies for applying the above guiding principles so that insurance in combination with other policy tools can reduce future losses from extreme events. The proposed risk management strategy involves:

- *Choice architecture* to frame the problem so that the risks are transparent and key interested parties recognize the importance of purchasing and maintaining insurance while also undertaking protective measures to reduce their losses from the next disaster.

- *Public-private partnerships* to assist those who cannot afford to invest in protective measures and provide financial protection against catastrophic losses for risks that are considered uninsurable by the private sector alone.
- *Multiyear insurance* to provide premium stability to policyholders, lower marketing costs to insurers, and a reduction in the cancellation of coverage by those at risk.

Choice Architecture

If those residing in hazard-prone areas perceive the likelihood of losses to be below their threshold level of concern, they will have no interest in purchasing insurance or investing in loss reduction measures. One way to address this problem is to recognize that decisions depend in part on how different options are framed and presented—that is, the use of *choice architecture* (Thaler and Sunstein 2008; Johnson et al. 2012). In the context of LP-HC events, *framing* refers to the way in which likelihoods and outcomes of a given risk are characterized.

Probability is more likely to be a consideration if it is presented using a longer time frame. People are more willing to wear seat belts if they are told they have a 1-in-3 chance of an accident over a 50-year lifetime of driving, rather than a 1-in-100,000 chance of an accident on each trip they take (Slovic, Fischhoff, and Lichtenstein 1978). Similarly, a homeowner or manager considering earthquake protection over the 25-year life of a home or factory is far more likely to take the risk seriously if told that the chance of at least one severe earthquake occurring during this time period is greater than 1 in 5, rather than 1 in 100 in any given year (Weinstein, Kolb, and Goldstein 1996). A recent controlled experimental study revealed that extending the time horizon by presenting the cumulative probability of loss across time (e.g., a 26% chance of flood over 30 years instead of 1% per year) increased the likelihood that study participants would opt for a small but sure loss (paying a premium for insurance) over the possibility of a catastrophic loss (Chaudhry, Hand, and Kunreuther 2018).

Studies have shown that even just multiplying the single-year risk so the numerator is larger, for example presenting it as 10 in 1,000 or 100 in 10,000 instead of 1 in 100, makes it more likely that people will pay attention to the event (Slovic, Monahan, and MacGregor 2000), and that comparisons of risks—rather than just specifying the probability of a loss or an insurance premium—are much more effective in helping decision-makers assess the need for purchasing insurance (Kunreuther, Novemsky, and Kahneman 2001).

Another way to frame the risk so that individuals pay attention is to construct a worst-case scenario about the financial consequences of being uninsured if they were to suffer severe damage from a flood or earthquake. One could then provide information on the likelihood of the event occurring over the next 30 years rather than just next year. In the case of insurers who construct worst-case scenarios, they should determine the likelihood of these disasters occurring before deciding that the risk is uninsurable.

Public-Private Partnerships

If people pay attention to the risk of an LP-HC event, then insurance coupled with other policy tools can incentivize property owners to invest in loss reduction measures. Risk-based premiums will give property owners accurate signals as to the degree of the hazards they face and will provide them with financial incentives to invest in cost-effective mitigation measures in the form of premium reductions that reflect the lower expected claims payments from future disasters.

To deal with problems of affordability, the public sector could provide low interest loans or grants to encourage mitigation, and some type of subsidy to assist low-income residents whose risk-based insurance premiums have increased significantly.

MITIGATION GRANTS AND LOANS

FEMA created the Flood Mitigation Assistance program in 1994 to reduce flood insurance claims. The program is funded by premiums received by the NFIP to support loss reduction measures, such as elevation or relocation of property, floodproofing commercial structures, or demolition and rebuilding of property that has received significant damage from a severe flood.

In July 2014, Connecticut initiated its Shore Up CT program designed to help residential or business property owners elevate buildings or retrofit properties with additional flood protection, or to assist with wind-proofing structures on property that is prone to coastal flooding. This state program, the first in the United States, enabled homeowners to obtain a 15-year loan ranging from $10,000 to $300,000 at an annual interest rate of 2.75%.

More generally, long-term loans to homes and businesses for mitigation would encourage individuals to invest in cost-effective risk reduction measures. Consider a property owner who could pay $25,000 to elevate a coastal property from 3 feet below base flood elevation to 1 foot above to reduce storm surge damage from hurricanes. If flood insurance is risk based, then the annual premium would decrease by $3,480 from $4,000 to $520. A 15-year loan for $25,000 at an annual interest rate of 2.75% would result in annual payments of $2,040, so the savings to the homeowner each year would be $1,440 (that is, $3,480 minus $2,040).

MEANS-TESTED VOUCHERS

One way for insurance premiums to be risk based and at the same time address affordability issues is to provide means-tested vouchers to cover the costs of protecting one's property. Several existing public sector programs could serve as models for developing such a voucher system: the Supplemental Nutrition Assistance Program (formerly known as "food stamps"), the Low Income Home Energy Assistance Program, and the Universal Service Fund. The amount of the voucher would be based on current income or wealth using a specific set of criteria that are outlined in recent reports on affordability of flood insurance by the National Research Council (2015a) and FEMA (2018). As a condition for the voucher, the property owner could be required to invest in mitigation. If the property owner were offered a multi-year loan to invest in mitigation measure(s), the voucher could cover not only a portion of the resulting lower risk-based insurance premium, but also the annual loan cost. An empirical study of homeowners in Ocean County, New Jersey reveals that the amount of the voucher is likely to be reduced significantly from what it would have been had the structure not been mitigated, as shown in Figure 15.1 for property in a 100-year coastal hazard flood area (the V zone) and a 100-year inland hazard area (the A zone) (Kousky and Kunreuther 2014).

CATASTROPHE COVERAGE

As indicated above, insurers' withdrawal from certain markets due to lack of sufficient reinsurance capacity and other risk transfer instruments (for

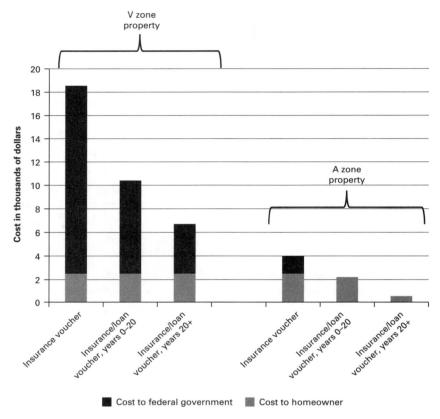

Figure 15.1. Cost of program to the federal government and a hypothetical homeowner. Kousky and Kunreuther (2014).

example, catastrophe bonds) has led to the establishment of government-backed programs such as the National Flood Insurance Program and the California Earthquake Authority.

If insurers were permitted to charge risk-based premiums, they would very likely want to market coverage against earthquakes and floods as long as they were protected against catastrophic losses. State reinsurance facilities could play an important role in this regard if premiums were risk based using data provided by catastrophe models, as illustrated by the Florida Hurricane Catastrophe Fund. It was established in 1993 following Hurricane

Andrew to supplement private reinsurance and reimburse all insurers for a portion of their losses from catastrophic hurricanes.

Lewis and Murdock (1996) proposed that the federal government offer catastrophe reinsurance contracts that would be auctioned annually to private insurers in order to provide them with more capacity to handle truly extreme events. The design of such contracts would have to be specified, and a more detailed analysis would have to be undertaken to determine the potential impact of such an auction mechanism on the relevant stakeholders.

REQUIRING INSURANCE

Given the reluctance of individuals to voluntarily purchase insurance, one should consider requiring catastrophe coverage for all individuals who face risk. Social welfare is likely to be improved under the assumption that individuals would have wanted insurance protection had they perceived the risk correctly.

WELL-ENFORCED BUILDING CODES

Following Hurricane Andrew in 1992 when one-third of the damage could have been averted had building codes been enforced, Florida reevaluated its building code standards, and coastal areas of the state began to enforce new high-wind design provisions for residential housing. As depicted in Figure 15.2, homes that met the wind-resistant standards that were enforced beginning in 1996 had a 42% reduction in average claim severity compared to homes that were built prior to that year. The average reduction in claims from Hurricane Charley to *each* damaged home in Charlotte County built according to the newer code was approximately $20,000 (Institute for Business & Home Safety 2007).

Homeowners who adopt cost-effective mitigation measures could receive a seal of approval from a certified inspector that the structure meets or exceeds building code standards. A seal of approval could increase the property value of the home by informing potential buyers that damage from future disasters is likely to be reduced because the mitigation measure is in place. Evidence from a July 1994 telephone survey of 1,241 residents in six hurricane-prone areas on the Atlantic and Gulf coasts provides supporting evidence for some type of seal of approval. Over 90% of the respondents felt that local home builders should be required to adhere to building codes,

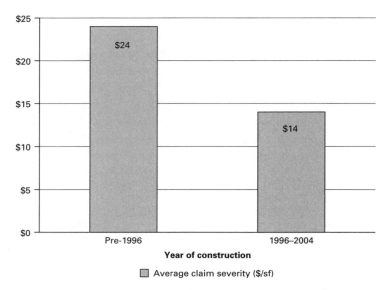

Figure 15.2. Average claim severity by building code category from Hurricane Charley. $/sf = dollars per square foot. *Source:* Institute for Business & Home Safety (2004).

and 85% considered it very important that local building departments conduct inspections of new residential construction (Insurance Institute for Property Loss Reduction 1995).

Multiyear Insurance

As a complement to property improvement loans, insurers could consider designing multiyear insurance contracts of three to five years. The insurance policy would be tied to the structure rather than the property owner, and carry an annual premium reflecting risk that would remain stable over the length of the contract. Property owners who canceled their insurance policy early would incur a penalty cost in the same way that those who refinance a mortgage have to pay a cancellation cost to the bank issuing the mortgage. With multiyear contracts, insurers would now have an increased incentive to inspect the property over time to make sure that building codes are enforced, in the spirit of the factory mutuals of the nineteenth century.[2]

A Strategy for Insuring Low-Probability, High-Consequence Events

For the private sector to want to market coverage against large-scale natural disasters such as floods and earthquakes, the public sector will have to deal with issues of affordability and catastrophic losses, and develop standards and regulations that are well enforced. Such a program for residential property in hazard-prone areas would involve the following features:

- Premiums would be risk based using accurate hazard maps and damage estimates so that private insurers would have an incentive to market coverage.
- Means-tested vouchers provided by the public sector would be used to address the affordability issue for those who undertook cost-effective mitigation measures.
- Premium discounts would be given to homeowners to reflect the reduction in expected losses from undertaking cost-effective mitigation measures. Long-term loans for mitigation would encourage these investments.
- Well-enforced building codes and seals of approval would provide an additional rationale to undertake these loss reduction measures. Land-use regulations could restrict property development in high hazard areas.
- A multiyear insurance policy with stable annual premiums tied to the property would prevent policyholders from canceling their policies.
- Private reinsurance and risk-transfer instruments marketed by the private sector would cover a significant portion of the catastrophic losses from future disasters.
- Federal reinsurance would be provided to private market insurers to protect them against extreme losses.

The benefits of this proposed program would be significant: less damage to property and potentially higher property values, lower costs and peace of mind to homeowners knowing they are protected against a future disaster, more secure mortgages for banks and financial institutions, and less disaster relief assistance by the public sector borne by the general taxpayer.

The National Flood Insurance Program provides a target of opportunity for taking steps to move in the direction of a more effective private-public partnership. As noted earlier, guidelines for modifying the NFIP so that the private sector can be more involved were discussed in two reports by the National Research Council (2015a, 2015b). A recent study on the role of private insurers in marketing flood coverage highlights the role that public-private partnerships can play in this regard (Kousky et al. 2018). Changes in the NFIP could serve as a model for dealing with other extreme events by adopting the guiding principles discussed above.

Future Studies and Research Needs

Future research is needed to understand how choice architecture can be applied to LP-HC events. Field and controlled experiments in behavioral economics reveal that consumers are more likely to stick with the default option rather than going to the trouble of opting out in favor of some other alternative. Many examples of this behavior are detailed in *Nudge* (Thaler and Sunstein 2008). To date, this framing technique has been applied to situations where the outcome is either known with certainty, or when the chosen option (such as a recommended 401(k) plan), has a higher expected return than the other options (Madrian and Shea 2001; Thaler and Benartzi 2004). It is not clear whether people who fail to purchase insurance coverage would reverse course if having insurance against an extreme event were the default option, given the intuitive thinking that individuals employ for these types of risks.

To determine the price of risk-based premiums, there is a need for more accurate data. In the United States, FEMA is now updating its flood-risk maps as recommended in a study by the U.S. Government Accountability Office (2008) and by the recent federal legislation on the NFIP discussed above. The impact of changing climate patterns on future damage from flooding due to sea-level rise and more intense hurricanes also needs to be taken into account.

Studies are also needed as to ways that other policy tools, such as well-enforced building codes to encourage good construction practices, can complement insurance. In this regard, Chile passed a law that requires the original construction company to compensate those who suffer any structural damage from earthquakes and other disasters if the building codes were not followed. Furthermore, the original owner of a building is held responsible for damage to the structure for a decade, and a court can sentence the owner to prison (Useem, Kunreuther, and Michel-Kerjan 2015).

The case for making communities and their residential property more resilient to natural disasters by investing in loss reduction measures is critical given increased economic development in hazard-prone areas (National Research Council 2012). For insurers to be part of such a strategy in the spirit of the factory mutuals, there is a need for support from other key interested parties. These include real estate agents, developers, banks and financial institutions, and residents in hazard-prone areas as well as public sector organizations at the local, state, and federal levels.

Notes

This chapter draws on material in Kunreuther (2015). The section "Guiding Principles for Evaluating Policies" draws from Chapter 10 of Kunreuther, Pauly, and McMorrow (2013).

1. For more details on the history of flood insurance and recent developments, see Michel-Kerjan (2010); Michel-Kerjan and Kunreuther (2011); Knowles and Kunreuther (2014); Kousky (2016).

2. For more details on the advantages and challenges of multiyear insurance, see Jaffee, Kunreuther, and Michel-Kerjan (2010) and Kunreuther and Michel-Kerjan (2015).

References

Anderson, D. R. (1974). The national flood insurance program. Problems and potential. *Journal of Risk and Insurance, 41*(4), 579–599.

Bainbridge, J. (1952). *Biography of an idea: The story of Mutual Fire and Casualty Insurance.* Garden City, NY: Doubleday.

California Department of Insurance. (1997–1998). *California earthquake zoning and probable maximum loss evaluation program.* Los Angeles, CA: California Department of Insurance.

Chaudhry, S. J., Hand, M., & Kunreuther, H. (2018). *Extending the time horizon: Elevating concern for rare events by communicating losses over a longer period of time* (Wharton Risk Management and Decision Processes Center working paper #2018-05). Philadelphia, PA: University of Pennsylvania.

City of New York (2013). *PlaNYC: A stronger, more resilient New York.* New York: Mayor's Office of Long-Term Planning and Sustainability.

FEMA. (2018, April 17). *An affordability framework for the national flood insurance program.* Retrieved from Federal Emergency Management Agency website: https://www.fema.gov/media-library-data/1524056945852-e8db76c696cf3b7f6209e1adc4211af4/Affordability.pdf

Gerdes, V. (1963). Insuring the flood peril. *Journal of Insurance, 30*(4), 547–553.

Institute for Business & Home Safety. (2004, August 13). *Hurricane Charley: Nature's force vs. structural strength.* Tampa, FL: IBHS.

Institute for Business & Home Safety. (2007). *The benefits of modern wind-resistant building codes on hurricane claim frequency and severity: A summary report.* Tampa, FL: IBHS.

Insurance Institute for Property Loss Reduction. (1995). *Homes and hurricanes: Public opinion concerning various issues relating to home builders, building codes and damage mitigation.* Boston: IIPLR.

Jaffee, D., Kunreuther, H., & Michel-Kerjan, E. (2010). Long-term property insurance. *Journal of Insurance Regulation, 29*(7), 167–187.

Johnson, E. J., Shu, S. B., Dellaert, B. G., Fox, C., Goldstein, D. G., Häubl, G., . . . & Wansink, B. (2012). Beyond nudges: Tools of a choice architecture. *Marketing Letters, 23*(2), 487–504.

Kahneman, D. (2011). *Thinking, fast and slow.* New York: Farrar, Straus, & Giroux.

Knowles, S. G., & Kunreuther, H. C. (2014). Troubled waters: The national flood insurance program in historical perspective. *Journal of Policy History, 26*(3), 327–353.

Kousky, C. (2016). Financing flood losses: A discussion of the National Flood Insurance Program. *Risk Management and Insurance Review, 21*(1), 11–32.

Kousky, C., & Kunreuther, H. (2014). Addressing affordability in the national flood insurance program. *Journal of Extreme Events, 1*(01), 1450001.

Kousky, C., Kunreuther, H., Lingle, B., & Shabman, L. (2018). *The emerging private, residential flood insurance market.* Philadelphia, PA: Wharton Risk Management and Decision Processes Center, University of Pennsylvania.

Kunreuther, H. (2015). The role of insurance in reducing losses from extreme events: The need for public-private partnerships. *Geneva Papers on Risk and Insurance, 40*, 741–762.

Kunreuther, H., Meyer, R., & Michel-Kerjan, E. (2012). Overcoming decision biases to reduce losses from natural catastrophes. In E. Shafir (Ed.), *The behavioral foundations of public policy* (pp. 398–413). Princeton, NJ: Princeton University Press.

Kunreuther, H., & Michel-Kerjan, E. (2015). Demand for fixed-price multi-year contracts: Experimental evidence from insurance decisions. *Journal of Risk and Uncertainty, 51*(2), 171–194.

Kunreuther, H., Novemsky, N., & Kahneman, D. (2001). Making low probabilities useful. *Journal of Risk and Uncertainty, 23*(2), 103–120.

Kunreuther, H. C., Pauly, M. V., & McMorrow, S. (2013). *Insurance and behavioral economics: Improving decisions in the most misunderstood industry.* Cambridge: Cambridge University Press.

Lewis, C. M., & Murdock, K. C. (1996). The role of government contracts in discretionary reinsurance markets for natural disasters. *Journal of Risk and Insurance, 63*(4), 567–597.

Madrian, B. C., & Shea, D. F. (2001). The power of suggestion: Inertia in 401(k) participation and savings behavior. *Quarterly Journal of Economics, 116*(4), 1149–1187.

Manes, A. (1938). *Insurance: Facts and problems.* New York: Harper.

Michel-Kerjan, E. O. (2010). Catastrophe economics: The national flood insurance program. *Journal of Economic Perspectives, 24*(4), 165–86.

Michel-Kerjan, E., & Kunreuther, H. (2011). Reforming flood insurance. *Science, 333*, 408–409.

Michel-Kerjan, E., Lemoyne de Forges, S., & Kunreuther, H. (2012). Policy tenure under the U.S. national flood insurance program (NFIP). *Risk Analysis, 32*(4), 644–658.

National Research Council. (2012). *Disaster resilience: A national imperative.* Washington, DC: National Academies Press.

National Research Council. (2015a). *Affordability of national flood insurance program premiums: Reports 1 and 2.* Washington, DC: National Academies Press.

National Research Council. (2015b). *Tying flood insurance to flood risk for low-lying structures in the floodplain*. Washington, DC: National Academies Press.

Overman, E. S. (1957). The flood peril and the Federal Flood Insurance Act of 1956. *Annals of the American Academy of Political and Social Science, 309*(1), 98–106.

Palm, R., & Carroll, J. (1998). *Illusions of safety: Culture and earthquake hazard response in California and Japan*. Boulder, CO: Westview Press.

Risk Management Solutions. (2014). *When the "big one" hits*. Retrieved from http://rms.com /images/loma-prieta/pdf/WhenTheBigOneHits.pdf

Roth, R., Jr. (1998). Earthquake insurance in the United States. In R. J. Roth, Sr., & H. Kunreuther (Eds.), *Paying the price: The status and role of insurance against natural disasters in the United States* (pp. 67–96). Washington, DC: Joseph Henry Press.

Slovic, P., Fischhoff, B., & Lichtenstein, S. (1978). Accident probabilities and seat belt usage: A psychological perspective. *Accident Analysis & Prevention, 10*(4), 281–285.

Slovic, P., Monahan, J., & MacGregor, D. G. (2000). Violence risk assessment and risk communication: The effects of using actual cases, providing instruction, and employing probability versus frequency formats. *Law and Human Behavior, 24*(3), 271.

Thaler, R. H., & Benartzi, S. (2004). Save More Tomorrow™: Using behavioral economics to increase employee saving. *Journal of Political Economy, 112*(S1), S164–S187.

Thaler, R., & Sunstein, C. (2008). *Nudge: The gentle power of choice architecture*. New Haven, CT: Yale University Press.

Tversky, A., & Kahneman, D. (1973). Availability: A heuristic for judging frequency and probability. *Cognitive Psychology, 5*(2), 207–232.

Useem, M., Kunreuther, H., & Michel-Kerjan, E. (2015). *Leadership dispatches: Chile's extraordinary comeback from disaster*. Stanford, CA: Stanford University Press.

U.S. Government Accountability Office. (2008). *Flood insurance: FEMA's rate-setting process warrants attention* (GAO-09-12). Washington, DC: U.S. Government Accountability Office.

Weinstein, N. D. (1980). Unrealistic optimism about future life events. *Journal of Personality and Social Psychology, 39*(5), 806.

Weinstein, N. D., Kolb, K., & Goldstein, B. D. (1996). Using time intervals between expected events to communicate risk magnitudes. *Risk Analysis, 16*(3), 305–308.

CHAPTER 16

Improving Individual Flood Preparedness
Through Insurance Incentives

W. J. Wouter Botzen

Every year we are exposed to news with images of severe flood events that occur around the world. Each flood event is unique, in terms of particular flooding conditions, impacted community, number of casualties, and economic costs. Nevertheless, the storylines that these events share are often very similar. Floods are destructive acts of nature that cause massive human suffering and economic consequences. Even though the impacted areas were designated as potentially flood-prone years ago, people continued to build and live in high-risk areas near rivers and the coast. The flood comes as a shock and people are badly prepared for it. Many have not purchased flood insurance nor taken measures to protect their house or belongings against flood waters. Afterward there are feelings of regret about being badly prepared. Moreover, there is pressure to repair damage quickly so that life can continue the way it was before the disaster, while knowing that a next flood can again damage the properties that are being rebuilt. A main challenge that these flood-prone regions face is how to design policies that help people better prepare for flood disasters. This chapter addresses this question by focusing on the role insurance can play in encouraging risk reduction.

During the last decades, the economic losses caused by natural disasters have increased around the world and floods are among the most costly hazards in these disaster records (IPCC 2012). Examples are the flooding caused by Hurricane Sandy in 2012, with about $19 billion of losses in New York City alone (City of New York 2013), and the 2013 floods in Germany and neighboring states that resulted in $16 billion of property damages (Munich Re 2013). Expectations are that flood risks will increase as a result of climate change and socioeconomic developments, such as population and economic growth in floodplains (IPCC 2012, 2014). As an illustration, a recently developed probabilistic risk model of all main European rivers predicts that current average annual flood losses in the European Union are bound to increase more than fourfold by 2050, if no additional measures to reduce risk are taken (Jongman et al. 2014).

These trends in flood risk highlight the need for investments in flood-protection infrastructure to reduce the likelihood of flooding as well as in measures that limit damage of future flood events. Nevertheless, even after cost-effective investments in limiting flood risk are made, a residual flood risk will remain. The reason is that reducing flood risk to zero is either technically infeasible or too costly relative to the benefits of avoided flood damage. This means that there is an important role to play for insurance in covering this residual risk. Insurance arrangements can spread flood risks over many policyholders, give peace of mind to residents of flood-prone areas, and speed up the recovery process after a flood disaster (Botzen 2013). However, insurance should not act as a substitute for the investments required to limit the expected increase in flood risk. The challenge is thus to design flood insurance arrangements that give incentives that encourage risk reduction. This is especially important because large adaptation efforts are needed to limit trends in flood risk caused by climate change.

Kunreuther (1996), and others, have proposed that flood insurance with risk-based premiums can encourage policyholders to invest in cost-effective flood risk mitigation measures. For example, homeowners who "flood-proof" their home can be rewarded for this by receiving a discount on their flood insurance premiums There are only a few examples of natural disaster insurance arrangements incentivizing risk reduction (Surminski 2014). For instance, the National Flood Insurance Program (NFIP) in the United States charges lower premiums to homeowners with elevated homes, but these discounts insufficiently reflect the lower risk, partly because many NFIP premiums are not truly risk based. Proposals have been made to reform the NFIP and to strengthen the link between premiums and risk reduction activities by policyholders (Michel-Kerjan 2010; Michel-Kerjan and Kunreuther 2011).

Similar reforms have been proposed for flood loss compensation schemes in other countries, like the Netherlands (Botzen 2013). Households in the Netherlands have been able to insure flood losses in recent years through a separate flood insurance policy that differentiates premiums according to the risk a policyholder faces. This insurance offers premium discounts to policyholders who take measures that limit flood damage. However, the uptake of the flood insurance is low due its relatively high premiums compared with risk. This implies that the large majority of households relies on ad hoc compensation for flood damage by the government in the event that a flood disaster occurs. This government arrangement for flood loss compensation does not incentivize flood risk reduction, and there has been a debate as to whether to establish a broad flood insurance coverage with risk-based premiums.

However, it is not evident that insurance can effectively promote risk reduction. In this respect, it is important to note that the way that the economics literature views relations between insurance coverage and individual risk reduction efforts has changed over the last decades. Seminal theoretical papers from the 1970s assumed fully informed rational agents who make decisions about purchasing insurance and engaging in other risk reduction activities on the basis of financial returns and self-interest. The theoretical prediction that follows from this work is that insurance and risk reduction are substitutes (Ehrlich and Becker 1972; Arnott and Stiglitz 1988). This can lead to moral hazard when people invest less in risk reduction after they have purchased insurance, and if financial incentives for policyholders to limit risk are insufficient. For example, moral hazard can arise when insured individuals expect that the insurance company will compensate damage regardless of their risk mitigation efforts, and premiums insufficiently reflect risk reduction from mitigation. Furthermore, adverse selection can occur when it is mainly high-risk individuals who choose to purchase insurance. Moral hazard and adverse selection can lead to problems for the insurance company when, due to information asymmetries, the higher risks of the insured (either through selection into the insurance, or moral hazard after the policy is bought) are not completely reflected in the insurance premiums (Akerlof 1978; Rothschild and Stiglitz 1978).

The literature on behavioral economics developed subsequently has stressed that individuals are often not fully rational and are instead "boundedly rational," which means that they act upon their own beliefs even though these may be inaccurate, such as perceptions of risk which deviate from expert assessments or objective risk. Moreover, behavioral characteristics of individuals may drive decision-making in addition to financial interests, such as social norms and their feelings about risk, like minimizing worry. More recent theoretical work has shown that if one accounts for such behavioral drivers, the opposite of moral hazard and adverse selection may arise, for instance, because behavioral mechanisms, like high risk aversion, cause people to both purchase insurance and invest in risk reduction (de Meza and Webb 2001).

Few studies have empirically examined relationships between flood insurance and flood risk mitigation by policyholders. Lindell and Hwang (2008) found that correlations between flood risk mitigation measures and flood insurance purchases were small for a sample of households in Texas. Thieken et al. (2006) observed that insured households in Germany take more flood risk mitigation measures than households without flood insurance. These results suggest that moral hazard may not pose serious problems for flood insurance markets, but more solid empirical evidence is needed to support this claim.

In this chapter I will highlight some key findings of recent research I conducted with colleagues about empirical evidence of the relationship between flood insurance coverage and individual flood risk mitigation measures in the United States and Germany. This evidence suggests that there are opportunities to encourage risk mitigation with insurance incentives and that moral hazard effects of flood insurance coverage may be minor. Before presenting this evidence, this chapter will discuss the rationale for stimulating flood risk reduction through insurance, and also provide experiences in this regard with insurance products other than for flood. After presenting our empirical evidence, we take a broader perspective than the individual and provide a discussion of how insurance can influence flood risk reduction efforts at the community level. A final section concludes and discusses directions for future research in this area.

The Rationale for Stimulating Flood Risk Reduction Through Insurance

Shifts Toward Integrated Flood Risk Management

In many countries, flood risk management has traditionally relied on engineering approaches that aim to reduce the likelihood of flooding by building flood protection infrastructure, such as dikes and storm surge barriers. This has been gradually changing to integrated flood risk management approaches that, in addition to flood protection, include (building level) measures that limit potential flood damage. This change has been motivated by the expected increase in the flood hazard from climate change and an increased recognition that flood protection infrastructure is not failure proof (Kabat et al. 2005). Integrated flood risk management implies that there is an important role for households in floodplains to take measures that limit flood damage to their property. An emerging evidence base shows that individuals experience significantly lower damage during floods if they have implemented "dry-proofing" measures that aim to prevent flood waters from entering their home or "wet-proofing" measures that aim to limit damage once water has entered (Kreibich et al. 2005; Kreibich and Thieken 2009; Bubeck et al. 2012; Hudson et al. 2014; Poussin, Botzen, and Aerts 2015). Cost-benefit analyses have demonstrated the cost-effectiveness of implementing flood damage mitigation measures in areas with a high flood hazard (Kreibich, Christenberger, and Schwarze 2011; Aerts et al. 2014; Poussin, Botzen, and Aerts 2015). Nevertheless, the evidence base for the effectiveness of specific flood damage mitigation measures is small since empirical estimates are made by only a handful of studies that use data from a few countries. There is a need for further research about how much flood damage can be saved by implementing specific flood damage mitigation measures under a variety of possible flooding conditions.

Individual Flood Preparedness Decisions

Unfortunately many floodplain inhabitants insufficiently prepare for flooding and do not take flood damage mitigation measures, even when these are cost-effective. Explanations for why individuals do not invest in reducing low-probability/high-impact risk can be found in the literature on behavioral economics. Individuals can be characterized as being "boundedly rational," which means that they act upon their own beliefs, while they are not fully informed about the risk they face and may not acquire such information because of (intangible) search costs (Kunreuther and Pauly 2004). Low individual perceptions of flood risk imply that individuals underestimate the benefits of measures that mitigate flood risk, which reduces their demand for such measures (Botzen and Van Den Bergh 2012). Several decision-making heuristics can explain underestimation of low-probability disaster risk. For instance, a survey conducted by Botzen, Kunreuther, and Michel-Kerjan (2015) of flood risk perceptions of ~1,000 homeowners who live in flood-prone areas in New York City shows that most respondents underestimate the damage that they would suffer from a future flood. That study found that underestimation of flood damage occurs among individuals who have not experienced damage during past flood events; think that the flood probability is below their threshold level of concern; have a high trust in government flood risk management; and worry less about the flood hazard. For these individuals, insurance could play a useful role in helping them to make better flood preparedness decisions. Pricing flood insurance according to the risk that policyholders face sends a price signal that can correct for low perceptions of flood risk. Moreover, insurance companies can give premium discounts to reward policyholders who reduce their flood risk, for example, by elevating newly built properties in the flood zone.

Experience from Other Insurance Products
Stimulating Risk Reduction

Linking insurance coverage with risk reduction is not only relevant for flood risk, and there are relevant experiences from other insurance products contributing to risk reduction. For instance, as described by Freeman and Kunreuther (1997) in the case of fire insurance, insurance companies have a long history of combining insurance coverage with incentives for risk reduction. Since the early years of provision of fire insurance, insurance companies did assess the risk of companies when they applied for fire coverage (Bainbridge 1952). Companies with a high risk were not allowed to get fire insurance coverage unless fire mitigation measures were implemented, like sprinkler systems. Policyholders who had taken measures to limit their fire risk were eligible for lower premiums. Using these financial incentives, as well as by providing advice about fire risk mitigation measures, insurance companies were a driving force behind the large improvements in fire safety that occurred over time (Freeman and Kunreuther 1997).

Other examples in the context of natural disaster insurance are earthquake insurance systems in California and Japan (Paudel, Botzen, and Aerts 2012). The California Earthquake Authority (CEA) is a publicly managed, but privately funded, organization which covers earthquake risk in California. CEA policies are sold by private insurance companies. The CEA sets premiums on the basis of risk zones and kinds of insured building. Efforts of the CEA to mitigate risk include raising risk awareness and providing premium discounts to policyholders who retrofit their houses in an earthquake-resilient way. Moreover, additional compensation is available to policyholders for bringing damaged properties into compliance with earthquake-resistant building codes. Another example is the Japanese earthquake reinsurance scheme in which private insurers can participate for offering earthquake coverage as an extension of regular property insurance. Financial incentives for risk mitigation are provided through risk-based premiums, while in addition construction is regulated using earthquake-resistant building codes. An important lesson from these earthquake insurance systems is that a combination of incentives at the policyholder level and broader applicable building codes can be an effective mix for achieving risk reduction.

Empirical Evidence of Relations Between Flood Insurance Coverage and Individual Flood Risk Mitigation Activities

Key Empirical Findings

This section highlights key findings of recent research I conducted with colleagues about empirical relationships between flood insurance coverage and flood risk mitigation activities by policyholders.

> Key findings: General relations between flood insurance coverage and flood risk mitigation measures implemented by policyholders show that insured individuals engage in more risk mitigation activities than the uninsured, even when they are not rewarded for this by premium discounts. This evidence suggests that moral hazard effects of flood insurance coverage are minor.

This finding is supported by two recent studies that will be discussed next: namely, a study about relations between flood insurance coverage and risk mitigation measures implemented by households in Germany and several areas in the United States by Hudson et al. (2017), and a study that examined such relations for homeowners who live in flood zones in New York City by Botzen, Kunreuther, and Michel-Kerjan (2016). It should be noted that these empirical studies did not focus on insurance products that stimulate risk mitigation using premium discounts. These studies examine whether, in the absence of such incentives, insured individuals engage in more or less risk reduction than uninsured individuals. This information is useful for identifying potential moral hazard effects of insurance coverage. Alternatively, insured individuals can be more careful and engage in more risk mitigation than those without insurance, which has been called advantageous selection (de Meza and Webb 2001).

In the first study I collaborated with Paul Hudson, Jeffrey Czajkowski, and Heidi Kreibich (see Hudson et al. 2017). This study examined how the implementation of a variety of household-level risk mitigation measures differs between individuals with, and without, flood insurance coverage in Germany. For this study we used data from surveys by Kreibich et al. (2005) and Kreibich, Christenberger, and Schwarze (2011) of about 2,000 flood-prone households that were conducted in the Elbe and Danube river catchments after flood events occurred in 2002, 2005, and 2006. Among many other variables, this database includes household-level information on implemented flood risk mitigation measures, flood insurance purchases, damage suffered during the last flood event, and flood hazard characteristics, such as experienced inundation depth during flood events. Using this data, we estimated simple probit models of relations between having insurance and implementation of flood risk mitigation activities, while controlling for other relevant explanatory variables.

The results show that individuals with flood insurance coverage in Germany are significantly more likely to have employed mobile flood barriers that keep flood water out of their home, while other measures (flood-proofing homes and adapting building use to flooding) were equally often implemented by insured and uninsured individuals (Hudson et al. 2017). These findings suggest that a moral hazard effect of insurance coverage is absent since households with flood insurance prepare more for floods. Moreover, the absence of a moral hazard effect is confirmed by further analyses that show that the flood damage suffered by insured households does not significantly differ from uninsured households, if it is taken into account that the flood hazard experienced (inundation depth) is more severe for the insured (Hudson et al. 2017). Additional analyses indicate that the better flood preparedness among the insured is related to the seeking of information about flood risk, which can signal that the insured are more risk averse and for that reason take flood risk mitigation measures as well.

Furthermore, Hudson et al. (2017) present similar analyses for windstorm and flood insurance coverage in the United States. The data originate from field surveys conducted by Meyer et al. (2014) that measured risk preparedness activities of about 1,700 coastal residents when three hurricanes—Irene (in 2011), Isaac (in 2012), and Sandy (in 2012)—approached the United States during the 2011 and 2012 hurricane seasons. Results of these analyses also show that individuals with windstorm and flood insurance coverage are more likely to engage in activities that reduce the risk they face of these hazards. It appears that this higher risk mitigation by the insured is not triggered by the insurance deductible. The majority of the individuals in the sample were not aware of their deductible level and for those who did know their deductible, it had only a small, if any, effect on their risk mitigation activities (Hudson et al. 2017). These findings from the United States suggest that it is the higher risk aversion of the insured that is triggering them both to purchase flood insurance and engage in other risk reduction activities.

In the second study that supports the aforementioned key findings, I collaborated with Erwann Michel-Kerjan and Howard Kunreuther. To gain insight into flood preparedness decisions by residents of flood-prone areas in New York City, we implemented a detailed phone survey of more than 1,000 homeowners with a ground floor (Botzen, Kunreuther, and Michel-Kerjan 2016). Respondents were carefully selected to ensure that they lived in an area that was prone to flooding. This survey was implemented six months after large parts of New York City were flooded by Hurricane Sandy. Respondents were asked about a hundred questions with respect to the following topics: flood risk perceptions, motivations for flood preparedness activities, flood insurance purchases, implemented flood risk mitigation measures, and their sociodemographic characteristics. The completion rate of the survey was 73%. Figure 16.1 shows the percentage of respondents who implemented specific flood risk mitigation measures. A distinction is made between homeowners who voluntary purchased flood insurance and those who chose not to purchase flood insurance. This distinction hardly matters for the elevation of homes, which is not surprising since the elevation of residential homes in the 1/100-year floodplain in New York City is subject to building code requirements. The other flood risk mitigation measures are voluntary activities. It is clear from Figure 16.1 that homeowners who voluntary purchased flood insurance were also more likely to have implemented these

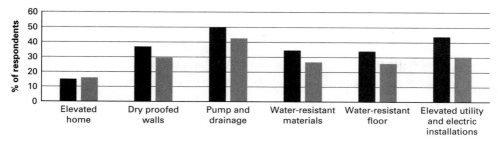

Figure 16.1. Percentage of homeowners in flood-prone areas in New York City who have implemented specific flood risk mitigation measures, distinguishing between those who purchased flood insurance voluntarily and those who have not purchased flood insurance. *Source:* Botzen, Kunreuther, and Michel-Kerjan (2016).

flood risk mitigation measures than homeowners without flood insurance coverage. With further statistical analyses (not reported here), we aim to identify reasons behind the higher levels of flood preparedness among the insured.

Other Related Research

There are several studies about other insurance markets than flood insurance that support the findings that insured individuals have a higher interest in engaging in risk mitigation. Carson, McCullough, and Pooser (2013) use survey data to examine the relationship between windstorm insurance and the implementation of measures that reduce windstorm risk in the My Safe Florida Home Program in the United States. They find a positive relationship, suggesting that households with windstorm insurance engage in more risk mitigation activities. Petrolia et al. (2015) present a similar analysis for windstorm insurance and risk reduction by households along the U.S. Gulf Coast. They find a positive relationship between the decisions to purchase insurance and mitigate risk, which may be interpreted as advantageous selection. Lindell, Arlikatti, and Prater (2009) find small positive correlations between earthquake insurance purchases in the United States and a variety of measures that households have taken to limit earthquake risk. Furthermore, a variety of studies about U.S. health insurance markets show that an individual's health coverage is positively related with activities that reduce health risk (e.g., Finkelstein and McGarry 2006; Cutler, Finkelstein, and McGarry 2008). This does not mean that these findings of the absence of a moral hazard effect always hold. Cohen and Siegelman (2010) provide a review of empirical studies of moral hazard effects in a large diversity of insurance markets (excluding natural disaster insurance), and show that results are mixed. This implies that separate investigations per insurance product are needed, as presented in this chapter for flood insurance.

The results concerning positive relations between flood insurance coverage and flood risk mitigation activities are obtained for flood insurance products with premiums that are not fully risk based, because policyholders did not receive premium discounts for employing the risk mitigation measures. Actively stimulating household investments in flood-proofing of homes using premium incentives could have resulted in a higher implementation of flood risk mitigation measures. However, to my knowledge, the effectiveness of such financial incentives in stimulating risk reduction has hardly been studied empirically. An exception is Botzen, Aerts, and Van Den Bergh (2009), who conducted a survey of about 500 homeowners in flood-prone areas in the Netherlands to examine their (hypothetical) willingness to take specific flood risk mitigation measures in exchange for incentives from their insurer. It turns out that a majority of Dutch homeowners are willing to take measures that flood-proof their home, like installing water barriers, if they receive a reward in the form of a premium discount. Although this finding suggests that insurance incentives can be effective in improving flood preparedness, future research should examine whether these results translate into actual decision-making in the field.

Stimulating Community-Level Flood Risk Mitigation Using Insurance

In addition to the incentives that insurance can provide to stimulate risk reduction at the individual level, insurance can be used to target flood risk mitigation at the community level. This can be done through regulation, such as zoning and building code policies, or by providing incentives such as premium discounts to policyholders who live in communities that invest in risk mitigation. Such community-level regulations and incentives can be complementary to those that encourage mitigation at the policyholder level for the following two reasons. First, a certain minimum level of flood-proofing to mitigate flood damage can be economically efficient for all buildings in a specific flood zone. However, due to behavioral biases in flood-preparedness decisions (considered earlier) not all individuals will voluntary invest in this level of flood-proofing. In that case, imposing minimum building code standards that make flood-proofing compulsory can be economically efficient. Second, some flood risk management measures, like providing information about risk mitigation options and local flood protection infrastructure, are best taken at the community level due to their public good characteristics. Rewarding communities for such measures by providing their policyholders with lower insurance premiums can also make sense from the insurer's perspective because expected claims on policies decline.

The National Flood Insurance Program in the United States is an interesting example of how flood risk mitigation at the community level can be stimulated through regulation that imposes minimum construction standards, and through financial incentives provided by the Community Rating System. Communities can voluntarily decide whether they want to participate in the NFIP, but once they join they have to comply with minimum construction standards which apply to a flood zone that is expected to be flooded once in 100 years on average. These standards prohibit new construction in floodways. Moreover, new buildings and buildings that are substantially renovated have to be elevated above the potential flood water level that a 1-in-100-year flood event would cause. It has been shown that, overall, these minimum requirements have substantially saved flood damage to new constructions in flood zones (Sarmiento and Miller 2006). However, NFIP mitigation policies have done little to limit vulnerability of existing buildings to flooding and have been ineffective in limiting the continued development in high-risk flood zones over time (Aerts and Botzen 2011). These problems may be overcome by providing incentives at the individual policyholder level by charging risk-based flood insurance premiums that discourage building in high-risk areas as well as reward flood-proofing of existing buildings with lower premiums (Michel-Kerjan and Kunreuther 2011).

Communities that have joined the NFIP can voluntarily decide to participate in the Community Rating System. This system rewards communities which engage in flood risk management activities with premium discounts to policyholders who live in the community. These discounts range from 5% up to 45% depending on the kind of flood risk management activities the community undertakes. Most NFIP policies fall under this system. An assessment shows that communities in Florida mainly undertake low-cost measures to earn premium discounts, like information provision, and invest less in more expensive flood risk mitigation measures, like dam infrastructure (Brody et al. 2009). Nevertheless, participation in the Community Rating System has been found to limit flood risk since it is associated with lower claims (Michel-Kerjan and Kousky 2010).

Conclusions and Agenda for Future Research

The expected increase in economic losses from flood disasters as a result of climate change and continued development in floodplains requires large investments in flood protection infrastructure and measures that limit damage from future floods. This integrated approach to flood risk management entails that households should implement cost-effective measures to limit flood damage to their homes. In practice, flood preparedness is suboptimal when many floodplain inhabitants do not invest in flood risk mitigation measures, for example, because they underestimate the flood risk that they face. It has been argued that flood insurance could play a useful function of incentivizing policyholders to take flood risk mitigation measures in addition to providing financial coverage of flood risk. On the other hand, insurance could result in a moral hazard effect when insured individuals engage in fewer risk reduction activities, because they expect that the insurance company will cover their damage anyway if a flood occurs. Few studies have examined empirically the relationship between flood insurance coverage and flood risk mitigation activities of individuals. This chapter presented two recent studies I conducted with colleagues that find that general relations between flood insurance coverage and flood risk mitigation measures implemented by policyholders show that insured individuals engage in more risk mitigation activities. This evidence suggests that moral hazard effects of insurance coverage are minor.

The aforementioned key findings as well as those from other related research discussed in this chapter provide a basis for future research about how flood insurance arrangements can provide incentives that help policyholders better prepare for flood disasters. The existing evidence originates from a few flood insurance markets and countries, and future research could examine whether these results hold in other country and market contexts. As also argued by Lindell, Brody, and Highfield (2016), the literature on behavioral economics and behavioral decision theory should be taken as a starting point for examining why there appears to be a disparity between economically rational behavior and what people actually do in terms of preparing for natural disasters in practice. Economic experiments and field surveys could aim to identify what behavioral mechanisms explain the higher interest in risk mitigation among individuals with flood insurance. Furthermore, future research is needed to understand how effective financial incentives by insurance, such as risk-based premiums, are in incentivizing policyholders to invest in cost-effective risk mitigation measures. Economic experiments could be conducted to obtain such insights, and ideally this topic will be examined in field studies about actual decision-making in practice. Moreover, there may be opportunities for using insurance as a mechanism for stimulating risk reduction at the community level, but a thorough evaluation of the effectiveness of such mechanisms as the Community Rating System in the United States is in order. The research presented in this chapter can provide a starting point for a future research agenda on these themes.

Acknowledgments

This research received financial support from the Netherlands Organisation for Scientific Research (NWO).

References

Aerts, J. C. J. H., & Botzen, W. J. W. (2011). Flood-resilient waterfront development in New York City: Bridging flood insurance, building codes, and flood zoning. *Annals of the New York Academy of Sciences, 1227*(1), 1–82.

Aerts, J. C. J. H., Botzen, W. J. W., Emanuel, K., Lin, N., de Moel, H., & Michel-Kerjan, E. O. (2014). Evaluating flood resilience strategies for coastal megacities. *Science, 344*(6183), 473–475.

Akerlof, G. A. (1978). The market for "lemons": Quality uncertainty and the market mechanism. In P. Diamond & M. Rothschild (Eds.), *Uncertainty in economics: Readings and exercises* (pp. 235–251). New York: Academic Press.

Arnott, R. J., & Stiglitz, J. E. (1988). The basic analytics of moral hazard. *Scandinavian Journal of Economics, 90*, 383–413.

Bainbridge, J. (1952). *Biography of an idea: The story of Mutual Fire and Casualty Insurance.* Garden City, NY: Doubleday.

Botzen, W. J. W. 2013. *Managing extreme climate change risks through insurance.* New York: Cambridge University Press.

Botzen, W. J. W., Aerts, J. C. J. H., & Van Den Bergh, J. C. J. M. (2009). Willingness of home-owners to mitigate climate risk through insurance. *Ecological Economics, 68*(8–9), 2265–2277.

Botzen, W. J. W., Kunreuther, H., & Michel-Kerjan, E. (2015). Divergence between individual perceptions and objective indicators of tail risks: Evidence from floodplain residents in New York City. *Judgment and Decision Making, 10*(4), 365–385.

Botzen, W. J. W., Kunreuther, H., & Michel-Kerjan, E. (2016). *Flood insurance coverage and flood risk mitigation by policyholders.* Working manuscript, Vrije Universiteit Amsterdam and the Wharton School.

Botzen, W. J. W., & Van Den Bergh, J. C. J. M. (2012). Monetary valuation of insurance against flood risk under climate change. *International Economic Review, 53*(3), 1005–1026.

Brody, S. D., Zahran, S., Highfield, W. E., Bernhardt, S. P., & Vedlitz, A. (2009). Policy learning for flood mitigation: A longitudinal assessment of the community rating system in Florida. *Risk Analysis, 29*(6), 912–929.

Bubeck, P., Botzen, W. J. W., Kreibich, H., & Aerts, J. C. J. H. (2012). Long-term development and effectiveness of private flood mitigation measures: An analysis for the German part of the River Rhine. *Natural Hazards and Earth System Sciences, 12*, 3507–3518.

Carson, J. M., McCullough, K. A., & Pooser, D. M. (2013). Deciding whether to invest in mitigation measures: Evidence from Florida. *Journal of Risk and Insurance, 80*(2), 309–327.

City of New York. (2013, June). *PlaNYC: A stronger more resilient New York.* New York: Mayor's Office of Long-Term Planning and Sustainability. Retrieved from https://www1.nyc.gov/site/sirr/report/report.page

Cohen, A., & Siegelman, P. (2010). Testing for adverse selection in insurance markets. *Journal of Risk and Insurance, 77*(1), 39–84.

Cutler, D. M., Finkelstein, A., & McGarry, K. (2008). Preference heterogeneity and insurance markets: Explaining a puzzle of insurance. *American Economic Review, 98*(2), 157–162.

de Meza, D., & Webb, D. C. (2001). Advantageous selection in insurance markets. *RAND Journal of Economics, 32*(2), 249–262.

Ehrlich, I., & Becker, G. S. (1972). Market insurance, self-insurance, and self-protection. *Journal of Political Economy, 80*(4), 623–648.

Finkelstein, A., & McGarry, K. (2006). Multiple dimensions of private information: Evidence from the long-term care insurance market. *American Economic Review, 96*(4), 938–958.

Freeman, P. K., & Kunreuther, H. (1997). *Managing environmental risk through insurance.* Boston: Kluwer.

Hudson, P., Botzen, W. J. W., Czajkowski, J., & Kreibich, H. (2017). Moral hazard in natural disaster insurance markets: Empirical evidence from Germany and the United States. *Land Economics, 93*(2), 179–208.

Hudson, P., Botzen, W. J. W., Kreibich, H., Bubeck, P., & Aerts, J. C. J. H. (2014). Evaluating the effectiveness of flood damage mitigation measures by the application of propensity score matching. *Natural Hazards and Earth System Sciences, 14*(7), 1731–1747.

IPCC (Intergovernmental Panel on Climate Change). (2012). *Managing the risks of extreme events and disasters to advance climate change adaptation: Special report of the Intergovernmental Panel on Climate Change.* Cambridge: Cambridge University Press.

IPCC (Intergovernmental Panel on Climate Change). (2014). *Climate change 2014: Impacts, adaptation, and vulnerability. Part A: Global and sectoral aspects. Contribution of Working Group II to the Fifth Assessment Report of the Intergovernmental Panel on Climate Change.* Cambridge: Cambridge University Press.

Jongman, B., Hochrainer-Stigler, S., Feyen, L., Aerts, J. C.J. H., Mechler, R., Botzen, W. J. W., ... & Ward, P. J. (2014). Increasing stress on disaster-risk finance due to large floods. *Nature Climate Change, 4*(4), 264–268.

Kabat, P., Van Vierssen, W., Veraart, J., Vellinga, P., & Aerts, J. (2005). Climate proofing the Netherlands. *Nature, 438*(7066), 283–284.

Kreibich, H., Christenberger, S., & Schwarze, R. (2011). Economic motivation of households to undertake private precautionary measures against floods. *Natural Hazards and Earth System Sciences, 11*(2), 309–321.

Kreibich, H., & Thieken, A. H. (2009). Coping with floods in the city of Dresden, Germany. *Natural Hazards, 51*(3), 423–436.

Kreibich, H., Thieken, A. H., Petrow, T., Müller, M., & Merz, B. (2005). Flood loss reduction of private households due to building precautionary measures: Lessons learned from the Elbe flood in August 2002. *Natural Hazards and Earth System Science, 5*(1), 117–126.

Kunreuther, H. (1996). Mitigating disaster losses through insurance. *Journal of Risk and Uncertainty, 12*(2–3), 171–187.

Kunreuther, H. C., & Pauly, M. (2004). Neglecting disaster: Why don't people insure against large losses? *Journal of Risk and Uncertainty, 28*(1), 5–21.

Lindell, M. K., Arlikatti, S., & Prater, C. S. (2009). Why people do what they do to protect against earthquake risk: Perceptions of hazard adjustment attributes. *Risk Analysis, 29*(8), 1072–1088.

Lindell, M. K., Brody, S. D., & Highfield, W. E. (2016). Financing housing recovery through hazard insurance: The case of the National Flood Insurance Program. In A. Sapat and A.-M. Esnard (Eds.), *Coming home after disaster: Multiple dimensions of housing recovery* (pp. 49–66). Boca Raton, FL: CRC Press.

Lindell, M. K., & Hwang, S. N. (2008). Households' perceived personal risk and responses in a multihazard environment. *Risk Analysis, 28*(2), 539–556.

Meyer, R. J., Baker, J., Broad, K., Czajkowski, J., & Orlove, B. (2014). The dynamics of hurricane risk perception: Real-time evidence from the 2012 Atlantic hurricane season. *Bulletin of the American Meteorological Society, 95*(9), 1389–1404.

Michel-Kerjan, E. O. (2010). Catastrophe economics: The National Flood Insurance Program. *Journal of Economic Perspectives, 24*(4), 165–86.

Michel-Kerjan, E. O., & Kousky, C. (2010). Come rain or shine: Evidence on flood insurance purchases in Florida. *Journal of Risk and Insurance, 77*(2), 369–397.

Michel-Kerjan, E., & Kunreuther, H. (2011). Redesigning flood insurance. *Science, 333*(6041), 408–409.

Munich Re. (2013). Natural catastrophe statistics online: The new NatCatSERVICE analysis tool (NatCatSERVICE database). Retrieved from https://www.munichre.com/en/reinsurance/business/non-life/natcatservice/index.html

Paudel, Y., Botzen, W. J. W., & Aerts, J. C. J. H. (2012). A comparative study of public-private catastrophe insurance systems: Lessons from current practices. *Geneva Papers on Risk and Insurance: Issues and Practice, 37*(2), 257–285.

Petrolia, D. R., Hwang, J., Landry, C. E., & Coble, K. H. (2015). Wind insurance and mitigation in the coastal zone. *Land Economics, 91*(2), 272–295.

Poussin, J. K., Botzen, W. J. W., & Aerts, J. C. J. H. (2015). Effectiveness of flood damage mitigation measures: Empirical evidence from French flood disasters. *Global Environmental Change, 31,* 74–84.

Rothschild, M., & Stiglitz, J. (1978). Equilibrium in competitive insurance markets: An essay on the economics of imperfect information. In P. Diamond & M. Rothschild (Eds.), *Uncertainty in economics: Readings and exercises* (pp. 257–280). New York: Academic Press.

Sarmiento, C., & Miller, T. R. (2006). *Costs and consequences of flooding and the impact of the National Flood Insurance Program.* Calverton, MD: Pacific Institute for Research and Evaluation.

Surminski, S. (2014). The role of insurance in reducing direct risk: The case of flood insurance. *International Review of Environmental and Resource Economics, 7*(3–4), 241–278.

Thieken, A. H., Petrow, T., Kreibich, H., & Merz, B. (2006). Insurability and mitigation of flood losses in private households in Germany. *Risk Analysis, 26*(2), 383–395.

CHAPTER 17

Strong and Well-Enforced Building Codes as an Effective Disaster Risk Reduction Tool

An Evaluation

Jeffrey Czajkowski

Often, the most vivid images presented in the wake of a natural disaster involve buildings. Intense winds from Hurricane Andrew in 1992 leveled homes in South Florida. Flood waters from Hurricane Katrina in 2005 submerged homes in New Orleans, Louisiana. Tornadoes devastated Moore, Oklahoma—in the heart of tornado alley—in 1999 and again in 2013. While some buildings manage to survive an event due to being built properly beforehand, more often property owners lose everything.

What these poignant examples illustrate is that even in areas of high natural disaster risk with previous experience of significant events, typically not enough is done in advance to mitigate and reduce this known property damage potential. Of course, given the particular hazard intensity of the event, some of the damage is unavoidable, but certainly not all. For example, Hurricane Andrew

blew the roof off decades of shoddy building practices in South Florida, exposing support columns filled with wadded-up newspapers instead of concrete, and knocking down walls made with cheap particle board that crumpled like cardboard in the driving wind and rain. Roof beams that should have been tied down with steel straps were found, after the storm lifted them up, up and away, to have been tied down by nothing. There were more extreme examples, like Styrofoam used as the most substantial material in porch pillars and cement that dissolved in the rain, as mile after mile of devastation from the hurricane revealed a standard of construction and inspections that people would have laughed at if they had not been standing in the ruins of their homes. (Bragg 1999)

This experience is sadly not unique; it persists after many devastating events across the United States. And in a world of steadily increasing costs and frequency of natural disasters (UNISDR 2015) the implementation of effective natural disaster risk reduction strategies is crucial today and into the foreseeable future.

Risk to buildings—as well as to the people inhabiting them—can be reduced through building codes.[1] Having strong building codes in place is frequently touted as a key disaster risk reduction strategy, directly effective in reducing total property damage and loss of life due to natural disaster occurrence, as well as making communities overall more resilient (Mills, Roth, and Lecomte 2006; Kunreuther and Useem 2010; McHale and Leurig 2012; Vaughan and Turner 2013; Rochman 2015). There are a number of other additional benefits to strong building codes, including the potential for spurring technological and engineering innovation given three-year model code review cycles (Vaughan and Turner 2013), the mandatory adoption of disaster protection that might not otherwise happen without the codes in place (Kunreuther et al. 2011), and the avoidance of negative externalities in a community stemming from economic dislocations that would otherwise occur when disaster strikes (Kunreuther et al. 2011). Also, as building codes apply primarily for new construction, the additional building costs to new construction stemming from code implementation are lower at the margin than they would otherwise be for retrofit natural disaster mitigation. Finally, given the increased disaster risk and uncertainty facing the insurance industry moving forward, with growing numbers of property exposures becoming potentially more uninsurable by the private market (Kousky, Chapter 14 in this volume), the broad risk reduction aspect of building codes is noteworthy.

However, despite all of these benefits, a number of issues remain regarding the effective and consistent implementation of building codes in the United States, most pointedly in areas of high disaster risk. Firstly, the United States does not have a single national building code for all states to follow. Rather, building code adoption and enforcement is a bottom-up process left to individual state and even locality discretion. Consequently, across the country there is a wide spectrum of building code implementation in terms of who is responsible for code adoption (the state, localities, or mix in-between) as well as the actual code in use (e.g., adopted 2000 edition of national model code vs. adopted 2015 edition of national model code). Moreover, the implementation of a stringent building code provision is ultimately dependent upon proper enforcement at the local jurisdiction through the permitting and inspection process (Schmith 1999; AIR Worldwide 2010; Deryugina 2013; Vaughan and Turner 2013). Thus, it is always an open question as to how well a code is maintained and enforced at the local level, even for a relatively strong adopted statewide code.

Adopted building codes in a jurisdiction are a form of mandatory regulation that do impose additional costs on new construction even if completed in the most cost-effective way (Kunreuther 2006). Therefore, the value of new codes needs to be demonstrated to and consequently supported by consumers (i.e., property owners) for their adoption, which may be challenging in parts of the country oriented to limited government, which view regulation as an impingement on the workings of the private market. Correspondingly, although the adoption of building codes is a bottom-up democratic process that is meant to be broadly inclusive in who participates in the process, as well as transparent in nature (Vaughan and Turner 2013), there are concerns that certain industry sectors such as homebuilders are overly represented in the process and consequently limiting the adoption of more stringent codes (Shapiro 2016). As increased costs of construction are often the key argument against more stringent codes (Shapiro 2016), issues of affordability should be accounted for in the building code adoption process along with the economic effectiveness of the codes.

In this chapter, I provide an evaluation of building codes as an effective natural disaster risk reduction tool in the United States by providing a snapshot of the wide spectrum of adoption and enforcement of residential building codes, and highlighting the clear room for improvement in building code adoption and enforcement. Indeed, approximately one-third of states in the United States do not adhere to a uniform statewide residential building code standard, with less than half of states and localities using the most up-to-date edition of the code. Additionally, only 7% of states, when rated on the strength and enforcement aspects of their adopted code, are achieving the most favorable ratings. An overview of the research demonstrates how effective building codes have been in reality in reducing natural disaster losses relatively recently. The findings from this research, while primarily based on Florida windstorm losses, are indeed encouraging. Significant reductions in windstorm losses due to stronger building codes have been demonstrated in a number of studies, with loss reductions typically on the order of 40–60%. And the associated existing evidence on the economic effectiveness of these stronger codes is likewise encouraging, with more than 4 dollars in losses saved to every 1 dollar spent on new construction. But do consumers support stronger codes, and further, what is the role the insurance industry in attempting to generate demand for more disaster-resistant buildings? While here the evidence is limited, it does demonstrate that nearly two-thirds of consumers when surveyed are in favor of a proposed building code referendum, and that this type of hypothetical support has been verified in real market transactions, with homes built under new codes selling for a 10% premium compared to those built under a less strict code. Lastly, I outline a number of avenues for future research including playing a role in demonstrating the value of effective codes across a variety of disasters, with learnings applicable from a number of other related regulatory contexts.

Variation of Existing U.S. Residential Building Codes

In the United States, building code adoption and enforcement is left to individual state and sometimes local discretion, although states and local jurisdictions do have national model codes that they can follow and adopt as their own. However, prior to 1994 there was no single national model code to follow, as regional model codes were developed and maintained separately. From 1915 to 1940 three regional organizations developed, creating their corresponding regional model codes: the Building Officials and Code Administrators International, Inc.—East Coast and Midwest; the International Conference of Building Officials—West Coast and Midwest; and the Southern Building Code Congress International, Inc.—Southeast. However, in the mid-1990s these organizations formed the International Code Council (ICC) to develop a national model code. These model codes are developed and updated every three years by independent standards organizations, such as the International Residential Code (IRC) developed by the ICC which is specific to the minimum requirements for natural disaster design and construction of one- and two-family dwellings and townhomes.[2] Consequently, across the country there is wide variation of building code implementation in terms of who is responsible for code adoption (the state, localities, or mix in-between) as well as the actual code edition in use.

For example, as of May 2016[3] there are eight states that have the IRC adopted by local governments (Alaska, Delaware, Illinois, Kansas, Mississippi, South Dakota, Vermont, Wyoming); one state where the IRC is adopted by the state for local implementation (Texas); eight states that have the IRC adopted at a statewide level but with limitations (Arizona, Colorado, Iowa, Missouri, Nebraska, Nevada, North Dakota, Oklahoma); and one state with no adoption of the IRC at any state or local level (Wisconsin). All other 32 states have the IRC building code in place that is effective statewide. In other words, 36 percent of states do not adhere to uniform statewide residential building code standards. Of the 45 states with information on which code edition is in use, as of May 2016, 40% of these states are using the 2009 IRC edition or earlier, with only 22% of the 45 states using the most recent 2015 edition of the IRC. Similarly, only 22% of the 32 states with a statewide IRC code in place are using the most recent 2015 edition of the IRC. As per May 2018, these values continue to hold overall with 24% of all states having zero, one, or multiple state or local jurisdictions adopting an edition of the IRC, but it is not used as a standard for all buildings. Likewise, while 49% of the 39 states with information on which IRC code is in use are using the 2015 edition of the IRC, the remaining 51% are using an IRC edition that is at least six years old.[4]

However, even for a relatively strong and up-to-date adopted statewide code, the implementation of a stringent building code provision is ultimately dependent upon proper enforcement at the local jurisdiction through the permitting and inspection process (Schmith 1999; AIR Worldwide 2010; Deryugina 2013; Vaughan and Turner 2013).

To provide some insight on building code enforcement in the United States, our research utilizes the Building Code Effectiveness Grading Schedule (BCEGS°) rating data (ISO 2014, 2015). Since 1995 the Insurance Services Office (ISO) has administered the BCEGS ratings for more than 16,700 jurisdictions serving more than 25,000 communities.[5] The BCEGS program delivers an overall classification for a jurisdiction representing a combination of elements related to the strength of code, level of code enforcement, quality of code administration, and the interaction of these features. Key components in the development of the strength of code include the edition of the code adopted and any significant amendments. The enforcement section includes elements that provide insight into the level of plan review, inspection, and personnel. Each jurisdiction/community is classified on a scale of 1 to 10, with a class 1 representing exemplary enforcement of a model code and a class 10 indicating the jurisdiction has earned very few points on many evaluation criteria. Classifications of 1 to 3 are considered to be the most favorable ratings, receiving the highest credit.

Of the 45 states with BCEGS ratings in place in at least one community in the state, only 7% achieve a BCEGS state average rating of 3 or better (ISO 2015). While 80% of the 45 rated states have a BCEGS state average from 4 to 6, the remaining 13% of states have a BCEGS state average that is 7 or worse (ISO 2015). Given that these ratings are for the communities in each state that are actually self-selecting and participating in the BCEGS rating program, one can conclude from this rating data that there is room for improvement in terms of adoption and particularly enforcement of effective codes at the local level (Sutter 2009; Shapiro 2016). Of further concern is the lack of financial and technical resources for building code enforcement officials to do their job well, which is only magnified by increasing population sizes (Shapiro 2016). The average population serviced per certified building code official in any one state ranges from a minimum population of 1,875 to a maximum population of 11,034, with a mean of the average population serviced being 5,484 (ISO 2015). Figure 17.1 illustrates how the average populations serviced per certified building code official range across the average BCEGS state classifications. Here we can see that while the largest average populations serviced may have the most favorable scores (7% of states with average BCEGS rating of 3 and mean population serviced of 7,002), there are also large populations serviced with less favorable scores, such as the 6,691 mean population for the 4% of states with an average BCEGS rating of 9.

Lastly, all states regardless of their building code implementation or BCEGS classification are at risk from some form of natural disaster, including earthquake, flood, hail, hurricane, snow, tornado, wind, and wildfire (ISO 2015). In regard to hurricane risk, the Insurance Institute for Business and Home Safety (IBHS) ranks the residential building codes adopted in 18 states along the Atlantic and Gulf coasts most vulnerable to hurricane damage on a scale of 0 (worst) to 100 (best), with the ranking accounting for each state's code strength and enforcement, building official certification and training, and contractor licensing. IBHS scores range from a low of 17 and 27 in Delaware and Alabama respectively, to a high of 95 and 94 in Florida and Virginia respectively. Nine of the 18 states scored had a score below 80, with 6 of these 10 scoring below a 60 (IBHS 2018). Similarly, a recent concept paper aimed

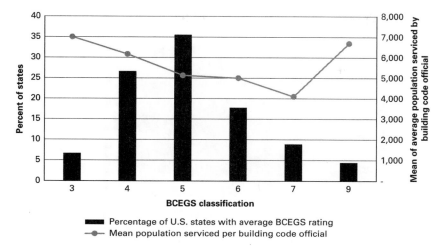

Figure 17.1. Percentage of U.S. states with average BCEGS rating and population serviced per building code official.

at providing community resiliency indicators based on national data finds that as of 2015, out of the 23,569 total individual jurisdictions in the United States that are subject to one or more of seismic, hurricane, or flood hazards, only 60% have adopted a building code with disaster provisions (Mitigation Framework Leadership Group 2016). Or, more than one-third of jurisdictions at risk from these hazards likely have insufficient disaster resistant building codes in place. Figure 17.2 provides a state-by-state view of this disaster resistant building code variation. While we do see, for example, a number of states along the east coast and Gulf of Mexico that are subject to at least hurricane risk among possible other hazards with statewide individual jurisdiction percentages greater than 79 (Florida, Louisiana, New York, South Carolina), there are a significant number of states with percentages between 57 and 79 (Alabama, Georgia, Maryland, Maine, North Carolina, Texas, Virginia), and a fair amount with percentages from 0 to 57 (Connecticut, Delaware, New Jersey, Rhode Island, Massachusetts, Mississippi).

Clearly, there is significant variation across states in the United States as to which level of government is responsible for building code adoption, how current the code adopted is, and how well the adopted codes are enforced, even in areas of high natural disaster risk. Given that all states have populations at risk from at least one natural hazard (ISO 2015), demonstrating the

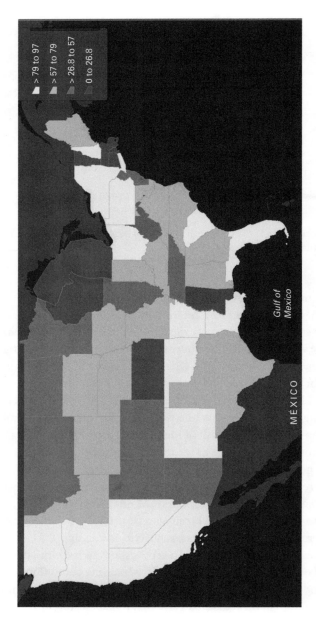

Figure 17.2. State-level percentage of reporting communities that are subject to one or more hazards (seismic, hurricane, or floods) that have adopted building codes with disaster resistance provisions. *Source:* Mitigation Framework Leadership Group (2016).

value of strong and well-enforced codes is ultimately critical for their community adoption and support.

Existing Evidence of Building Code Effectiveness in Reducing Natural Disaster Losses

A number of research studies have identified the significant reduction in windstorm losses—typically on the order of 40–60% less—due to stronger building codes, utilizing event-based realized loss or insurance claim data. In order to demonstrate a reduction in windstorm losses due to stronger building codes from the realized loss data, these studies capture the differences in losses from properties constructed before and after the implementation of a new and stronger building code.[6] Given Florida's significant windstorm risk, value of property exposure at risk, and strong building code adoption, the majority of studies are focused here.

Fronstin and Holtmann (1994) in their analysis of 1992 Hurricane Andrew damage in southeast Florida find that older homes built prior to the 1960s suffered less damage on average than those built after 1960 due to an eroding building code over time. Post-Andrew, the catastrophic hurricane seasons of 2004 and 2005 in Florida provided a natural opportunity to test how well the implemented Florida Building Code (FBC) performed. A study by IBHS following Hurricane Charley in 2004 found that homes built after 1996, had lower claim frequency (60% less) and severity (42% less) as compared to homes built before 1996 (IBHS 2004). This suggests the trend of an eroding building code, reversed after Hurricane Andrew. Applied Research Associates (2008) investigated policy-level claim data from eight different insurance companies following the 2004 and 2005 hurricane seasons and found similar results, with post-2002 homes showing significant loss reduction results compared to pre-2002 homes. They further found that overall losses were reduced according to year built from the mid-1990s onward. Simmons, Czajkowski, and Done (2018) expanded and further verified these Florida Building Code loss reduction results by using windstorm loss differences between properties whose year of construction (YOC) was pre and post 2002, given the fully effective implementation of the statewide FBC that year. Although only indirectly associated with actual damage incurred, stronger building codes reduced post-storm federal disaster spending in 795 unique Florida ZIP codes impacted at least once by the 2004 hurricanes Charley,

Frances, Ivan, and Jeanne as well as Tropical Storm Bonnie (Deryugina 2013). However, contrary to these overall successful building code loss reduction results, Dehring and Halek (2013) find that for the 264 residential properties in a coastal building zone in Lee County following Hurricane Charley, there is no evidence of less damage for homes built after the revised 1992 Florida Building Code.

As new building codes primarily apply to new construction, demonstrating windstorm loss reductions via YOC loss differences that correspond to a code change (e.g., post-2002 YOC for the FBC) captures the value of an improved building code at the extensive margin, that is, the number (extent) of new residential properties built under the new code. Yet, the implementation of a stringent building code provision is again ultimately dependent upon proper local jurisdiction enforcement (Schmith 1999; AIR Worldwide 2010; Deryugina 2013; Vaughan and Turner 2013). The question arises: What is the intensity of building code implementation at the local level and how much does this matter? Czajkowski, Simmons, and Done (2017) show that both extensive and intensive components provide value in reducing windstorm losses in Florida, with the extent of the statewide code being the dominant effect reducing losses on the order of 72%. Although not as substantial in terms of its loss reduction magnitude, intensively implementing building codes at the local level by ensuring codes are properly administered and enforced at this scale provides additional loss reduction value on the order of 15–25%. Czajkowski and Simmons (2014) have shown similar results for both strong and well-enforced building codes in reducing hail-related losses in the state of Missouri by the order of 10–20% on average.

Although the reduction in windstorm damage due to enhanced codes has been demonstrated in a number of cases (but not all), the economic effectiveness of the improved building codes has not been as well documented. The report of the Multihazard Mitigation Council (MMC) on savings from natural hazard mitigation activities (MMC 2005; Rose et al. 2007) concluded that a benefit-cost ratio of 4 dollars saved for every 1 dollar spent was appropriate for mitigation grant spending related to improved building codes.[7] In December 2017, a new interim report was released which updated and expanded the 2005 MMC study, finding a benefit-cost ratio of 5 dollars saved to every 1 dollar spent for wind mitigation as well as construction of new buildings to exceed the 2015 I-code standards (MMC 2017). Englehardt and Peng (1996) conducted an economic assessment on adopted revisions to the

Florida Building Code in the 1990s for 10 related counties and determined that the net present value of the revisions was $7 billion, or benefit-cost ratio greater than 1. Importantly though, this study did not have access to actual building code damage reduction data to utilize in the analysis. In 2002, Applied Research Associates conducted a benefit-cost comparison study stemming from the enactment of the FBC for three related housing types (Shimberg Center and ARA 2002). Loss reductions were estimated by evaluating how the three types of FBC-built houses would perform in probabilistic hurricane scenarios compared to the same houses built under the previous code. Given the probabilistic nature of the analysis, average annual losses were generated that demonstrated post-FBC housing having loss reductions 54% less on average (ranged from 26% to 61% less). These loss reductions were then compared to their estimated cost impacts of the FBC for these housing types with at least break-even benefit-cost ratio results (= 1) determined in the less hurricane intensive areas of the state, and above break-even benefit-cost ratio results (> 1) for the more high-risk hurricane areas. Simmons, Czajkowski, and Done (2018) find that the FBC passes the benefit-cost ratio test on the order of 6 dollars in losses saved to every 1 dollar spent on new construction, with a payback period for the investment of stronger codes estimated at approximately 10 years.

In summary, the existing research confirms that building codes are not only effective in reducing natural disaster losses but also do this in an economically effective way, with the benefits of avoided losses outweighing the additional costs of the new code.

The question then becomes: How well do consumers understand and support the value of the stronger building code (Vaughan and Turner 2013)? This is especially relevant as additional costs of the code may impose affordability concerns on the housing market, even if they are economically effective in their implementation. For example, it has been prescribed that a $1,000 increase in the cost of housing drops more than 200,000 potential homeowners out of the housing market (Shapiro 2016).

Support and Demand for Disaster Resistant Buildings

There are two main ways to gauge consumer understanding and support for stronger building codes: (1) ask them directly through surveys; and (2) infer this value through revealed preference choices such as housing purchases. Both have been utilized, albeit not very extensively.

Vaughan and Turner (2013) refer to a 2012 national study of more than 5,000 adults conducted by the Consumers Union and Building Codes Assistance Project. Findings from this survey indicate an overwhelming percentage of survey respondents "placed a high value on strong building codes" (14). While this result indicates consumers understand and value a strong building code, it is only one study and that from a national perspective. In areas of the country which view regulation as an impingement on the workings of the private market, support for building codes may be more challenging. Ripberger et al. (2018) evaluate this proposition in the conservative-oriented state of Oklahoma.

In the spring of 2015, we asked 2,201 homeowners in Oklahoma the following as part of a survey:

In hurricane-prone regions of the United States, building codes often require that new homes are equipped with a number of wind-protective components when they are constructed. Suppose that through a statewide referendum, the state of Oklahoma was considering a law that would mandate similar building codes in Oklahoma. This law would require that all new homes in the state are equipped with a set of components that would protect the structure of the home from the majority of high-wind events that occur in Oklahoma, including most EF0 [65–85 mph], EF1 [86–110 mph], and EF2 [111–135 mph] tornadoes. On average, installing these components during construction would increase the price of new homes in the state by $[RANDOMIZE: 2,000/3,000/4,000]. Because this is a statewide referendum, you would have an opportunity to directly cast a vote for or against this law.

Would you vote for or against this law in Oklahoma? As you think about your answer, remember that if this law were to pass, it would cost more to build a home in Oklahoma.

1 Definitely Against—I would definitely vote against this law
2 Probably Against—I would probably vote against this law
3 Not sure—I am not sure how I would vote
4 Probably For—I would probably vote for this law
5 Definitely For—I would definitely vote for this law

Almost two-thirds (62.3%) of the homeowners in our sample said that they would probably (35.3%) or definitely (27%) vote in favor of the building code referendum. By contrast, only 19.4% said that they are not sure how they would vote, 11.4% said that they would probably vote against the referendum, and 7% said that they would definitely vote against it. These results are inconsistent with a hypothesis that most homeowners in a limited government state would not support the adoption of building codes, and more in line with the support found in the national study reported in Vaughan and Turner (2013).

A common issue with these types of survey responses, however, is that they are hypothetical in nature. Respondents may say one thing in a survey but act differently with a real market choice. Revealed preference techniques, such as hedonic pricing, are one way to avoid this potential hypothetical bias issue. Here, value is inferred from real market choices that indirectly capture the good to be valued, in this case, building codes. For example, do homes built under stronger codes sell for more than homes built prior to the implementation of the code, all else being equal? Dumm, Sirmans, and Smersh (2011) investigate this in Florida and find that Miami-Dade County homebuyers do in fact value homes built under the new stronger code regime. They find that in the high-risk coastal area, homes built under the new code sell for about 10% more than those built under the less strict code. From their literature reviewed, this is opposite to the expectations that homebuyers would likely not place additional value on building mitigation, similar to the survey findings of Ripberger et al. (2018) in Oklahoma. An additional study by Awondo et al. (2016) finds a similar result in that switching from a conventional construction standard to an IBHS Fortified designation increases the value of a home by nearly 7%. Although these studies are limited in number, they do provide evidence that consumers do see value in disaster resistant building codes.

The insurance industry is taking a lead in translating this underlying value into actual demand for disaster resistant buildings. One such example is IBHS's Fortified Home™ program. Under the Fortified program, new or existing homeowners can strengthen their home against natural disasters following the Fortified building standards. Homes are officially evaluated and if standards are met, designated as a Fortified Home, eligible for insurance premium discounts such as those provided by the Alabama, Mississippi, and South Carolina wind pools. And the Fortified effort is now being promoted not only in coastal areas but also in the central United States, where a

Fortified home for high wind and hail is being built in Tulsa, Oklahoma (Leberfinger 2016). Given property insurers' history as primary developers of modern building codes and their continued engagement over the years (Vaughan and Turner 2013), this is not unexpected.

The insurance industry's role in this area is critical given the broad risk reduction aspect of building codes and the fact that there is a growing concern that many properties (homes and businesses) in high hazard areas are becoming uninsurable via the private insurance market (Vaughan and Turner 2013; Kousky, Chapter 14 in this volume). For example, Vaughan and Turner (2013) cite that the value of properties insured by the U.S. government and subject to hurricane wind risks has increased to nearly a trillion dollars ($885 billion), a 15-fold increase since 1990. This concern is especially acute in the high hurricane risk state of Florida, where Citizens Property Insurance Corporation, the state-run residual market wind pool,[8] had insured nearly 1.5 million policyholders (as of 2012), representing a statewide market share of nearly 25%, and has become the primary underwriter of new insurance policies in the state (Florida Catastrophic Storm Risk Management Center 2013). While the number of Citizens policies has been reduced to about one-third of this 1.5 million amount, they still represent relatively substantial market share in Florida (Heritage Insurance n.d.).

Conclusion and Future Research Directions

The existing evidence reviewed here demonstrates that stronger and well-enforced building codes are effective in reducing natural disaster losses, typically on the order of 40–60% less. Moreover, while additional costs are imposed on new construction to meet these standards, the new codes have also been shown to be economically effective, with the avoided losses being greater than the imposed construction costs. Despite the demonstrated value and economic effectiveness of stronger building codes, uniform adoption of strong codes across the country as well as optimal enforcement at the local level have not been achieved, even in high-risk natural disaster areas. Clearly there is room for improvement on both fronts, with evidence (albeit limited) of consumer support for stronger and well-enforced codes. And there are precedents in other industries—uniform regulations for automobiles in terms of minimum safety standards—that would imply that these types of regulations can be achieved and thought valuable by consumers (Shapiro 2016).

Research can continue to play an important role in this regard. Many of the research studies demonstrating the value of building codes in reducing natural disaster losses have been conducted in Florida and related to hurricane risk. More research aimed at other significant natural hazards such as flood, tornado, and hail located in other parts of the country would be useful. Czajkowski and Simmons (2014) have investigated this in Missouri in regard to hail damage. Recently, the city of Moore, Oklahoma, in the aftermath of the two major tornadoes noted above, enacted a number of codes designed to protect residential structures from high wind events, and Simmons, Kovacs, and Kopp (2015) have demonstrated the economic effectiveness of these enacted building code measures. But much more can be done to quantify the value of improved building codes across the country and for various hazards, as was identified by the Applied Technology Council (2015) as a key recommendation in their report on strategies to encourage state and local adoption of disaster resistance codes and standards to improve resiliency. Importantly, the variation in building code adoption across and within states provides a nice natural experiment setting to undertake this research.

Similarly, while local enforcement is critical for the ultimate effectiveness of the adopted code, little is known about what key factors drive building code enforcement at the local level. The extensive BCEGS rating data provide an opportunity for further study, similar to the research on community rating system participation for the National Flood Insurance Program (Brody et al. 2009; Landry and Li 2012; Sadiq and Noonan 2015). In a state-level analysis on the percentage of communities in a state participating in the BCEGS program, the percentage of communities in a state rated 1 to 3, and the mean BCEGS rating of all communities (participating and nonparticipating) in a state, Sutter (2009) found little linkage between hazard risk and more effective codes, with the strongest effects resulting from states with more urban populations having more effective codes and more corrupt states having less effective codes. It is plausible that the decision to implement effective building codes at the local level may not be determined on a building code economic effectiveness basis alone, but may come down to other (non-economically) based rationales. Shapiro (2016) discusses in detail the political realities surrounding more effective building code implementation. Thus, this type of research effort is important to start to identify local building code rationales for participation and intensity of implementation, potentially beyond economic efficiency, in order to better inform policymakers and ultimately target policies that enable further building code risk reduction.

While there have been a handful of studies on consumer support for improved building codes—either via surveys or revealed preference techniques—much more research can be done here as well. Particularly useful from a consumer support perspective would be analyses focused on the affordability issue of improved building codes. While the notion that a $1,000 increase in costs to new construction leads to over 200,000 being excluded from the housing market (Shapiro 2016) has become conventional wisdom, research should be directed toward validating these figures, especially in light of the number of external benefits stemming from the implementation of building codes. Also, further insights on the value of codes embedded in housing prices would be relevant, especially for those homes that have been deemed to be disaster resistant such as the IBHS Fortified homes (Awondo et al. 2016).

Finally, other research has been focused on the value of codes in terms of their energy efficiency savings as opposed to disaster resilience loss reductions (see Jacobsen and Kotchen 2013; or Levinson 2016 as examples). As in the long run these two notions likely converge—more energy efficient buildings lead to lower carbon emissions leading to lower (or less intense) natural disaster frequency in the future—learning from both research strands should be combined, especially since issues of variation in adoption and enforcement as well as consumer and political support cut across both building code purposes.

Notes

1. Note that this chapter focuses on building codes in regard to their direct natural disaster risk reduction capabilities. Codes also "ensure structural integrity; electrical, plumbing and mechanical system safety, as well as accessibility and practical and achievable levels of energy efficiency" (Vaughan and Turner 2013, 4). It is feasible that energy-efficient building codes that simultaneously achieve carbon emission reductions might have the further impact of reducing future extreme event occurrences due to these lower emission levels, thereby also indirectly reducing future disaster risk (Shapiro 2016).

2. Other codes oriented to natural disaster design include the International Building Code for all buildings and structures other than one- and two-family dwellings, and the International Existing Building Code for existing buildings.

3. IRC data obtained from the ICC at https://www.iccsafe.org/wp-content/uploads/State -Local-Code-Charts.pdf. Note that for Alabama I classified this is as effective statewide given its coding of XA15 where X = effective statewide, A = adopted but may not yet be effective; for Mississippi I classified this as adopted by local governments given its coding of A15, L where A = adopted but may not yet be effective and L = adopted by local governments.

4. See https://www.iccsafe.org/wp-content/uploads/Master-I-Code-Adoption-Chart-May-Update.pdf.

5. Material in regard to the ISO BCEGS ratings is sourced from ISO's Building Code Effectiveness Grading Schedule (BCEGS®). For more detailed information on the BCEGS ratings please see the description on their website (ISO 2014). In the states of Hawaii, Idaho, Louisiana, Mississippi, and Washington, an independent rating bureau administers the BCEGS program.

6. Other studies have empirically demonstrated the value of effective building codes through a probabilistically based catastrophe model framework that has been validated and/or calibrated with historical claim data (see Shimberg Center & ARA 2002; Kunreuther et al., 2011; AIR Worldwide 2010).

7. Mitigation grant spending was for process activity grant which is defined as follows: "A grant for a process activity yields a benefit primarily when it results in a 'spin-off,' a type of 'synergistic activity' defined as a mitigation activity not directly funded by FEMA that is the direct result (an action that would have not otherwise taken place) or indirect result (an action that is accelerated in timing, but would have taken place eventually) of FEMA hazard mitigation grant support" (MMC 2005).

8. Although Citizens was originally designed as a residual market entity for when a policyholder was rejected in the private market, it now writes both residual and nonresidual market policies (Florida Catastrophic Storm Risk Management Center 2013).

References

AIR Worldwide. (2010). *Mississippi Insurance Department: Comprehensive hurricane damage mitigation program: Cost benefit study.* Boston: AIR Worldwide.

Applied Research Associates, Inc. (2008). *2008 Florida residential wind loss mitigation study.* Retrieved from http://www.floir.com/siteDocuments/ARALossMitigationStudy.pdf

Applied Technology Council (2015). *Strategies to encourage state and local adoption of disaster-resistant codes and standards to improve resiliency* (ATC-117). Report prepared for the Federal Emergency Management Agency.

Awondo, S., Hollans, H., Powell, L., & Wade, C. (2016). *Estimating the effect of FORTIFIED Home™ construction on home resale value.* Retrieved from https://culverhouse.ua.edu/uploads/ckeditor/attachments/31/FORTIFIEDReport_V2__2_.pdf

Bragg, R. (1999, May 27). Storm over South Florida building codes. *New York Times.*

Brody, S. D., Zahran, S., Highfield, W. E., Bernhardt, S. P., & Vedlitz, A. (2009). Policy learning for flood mitigation: A longitudinal assessment of the community rating system in Florida. *Risk Analysis, 29*(6), 912–929.

Czajkowski, J., & Simmons, K. M. (2014). Convective storm vulnerability: Quantifying the role of effective and well-enforced building codes in minimizing Missouri hail property damage. *Land Economics, 90*(3), 482–508.

Czajkowski, J., Simmons, K. M., & Done, J. M. (2017). Demonstrating the intensive benefit to the local implementation of a statewide building code. *Risk Management and Insurance Review, 20*(3), 363–390.

Dehring, C. A., & Halek, M. (2013). Coastal building codes and hurricane damage. *Land Economics, 89*(4), 597–613.

Deryugina, T. (2013). *Reducing the cost of ex post bailouts with ex ante regulation: Evidence from building codes.* Retrieved from https://papers.ssrn.com/sol3/papers.cfm?abstract_id=2314665

Dumm, R. E., Sirmans, G. S., & Smersh, G. (2011). The capitalization of building codes in house prices. *Journal of Real Estate Finance and Economics, 42*(1), 30–50.

Englehardt, J. D., & Peng, C. (1996). A Bayesian benefit-risk model applied to the South Florida building code. *Risk Analysis, 16*(1), 81–91.

Florida Catastrophic Storm Risk Management Center. (2013). *The state of Florida's property insurance market: 2nd annual report: Released January 2013 for the Florida Legislature.* Retrieved from http://www.stormrisk.org/sites/default/files/2nd%20Annual%20Insurance%20Market%20Rpt-FSU%20Storm%20Risk%20Center.pdf

Fronstin, P., & Holtmann, A. G. (1994). The determinants of residential property damage caused by Hurricane Andrew. *Southern Economic Journal, 61*(2), 387–397.

Heritage Insurance. (n.d.). Citizens Insurance is nearly under 500,000 policies. Retrieved from https://www.heritagepci.com/blog/citizens-insur00000-policies/

IBHS. (2004). *Hurricane Charley: Nature's force vs. structural strength. Executive summary.* Insurance Institute for Business and Home Safety. Retrieved from http://disastersafety.org/wp-content/uploads/hurricane_charley.pdf

IBHS. (2018). *Rating the states: 2018: An assessment of residential building code and enforcement systems for life safety and property protection in hurricane-prone regions.* Insurance Institute for Business and Home Safety. Retrieved from http://disastersafety.org/wp-content/uploads/2018/03/ibhs-rating-the-states-2018.pdf

ISO. (2014). ISO's Building Code Effectiveness Grading Schedule (BCEGS˚). Insurance Services Office. Retrieved from https://www.isomitigation.com/bcegs/

ISO. (2015). *National Building Code assessment report: ISO's building code effectiveness grading schedule.* Insurance Services Office. Retrieved from https://www.isomitigation.com/downloads/ISO-BCEGS-State-Report_web.pdf

Jacobsen, G. D., & Kotchen, M. J. (2013). Are building codes effective at saving energy? Evidence from residential billing data in Florida. *Review of Economics and Statistics, 95*(1), 34–49.

Kunreuther, H. (2006). Disaster mitigation and insurance: Learning from Katrina. *Annals of the American Academy of Political and Social Science, 604*(1), 208–227.

Kunreuther, H. C., Michel-Kerjan, E. O., Doherty, N. A., Grace, M. F., Klein, R. W., & Pauly, M. V. (2011). *At war with the weather: Managing large-scale risks in a new era of catastrophes.* Cambridge, MA: MIT Press.

Kunreuther, H., & Useem, M. (Eds.). (2010). *Learning from catastrophes: Strategies for reaction and response.* Upper Saddle River, NJ: Prentice Hall.

Landry, C. E., & Li, J. (2012). Participation in the community rating system of NFIP: Empirical analysis of North Carolina counties. *Natural Hazards Review, 13*(3), 205–220.

Leberfinger, M. (2016, May 1). Nonprofit organization rolls out plan for disaster-resistant homes in Tornado Alley. Retrieved from AccuWeather website: https://www.accuweather.com/en/weather-news/nonprofit-organization-rolls-out-plan-for-disaster-resistant-homes-tornado-alley-of-us/56980104

Levinson, A. (2016). How much energy do building energy codes save? Evidence from California houses. *American Economic Review, 106*(10), 2867–94.

McHale, C., & Leurig, S. (2012). *Stormy future for U.S. property/casualty insurers: The growing costs and risks of extreme weather events.* Boston: CERES.

Mills, E., Roth, R. J., Jr., & Lecomte, E. (2006). Availability and affordability of insurance under climate change: A growing challenge for the United States. *Journal of Insurance Regulation, 25*(2), 109–149.

Mitigation Framework Leadership Group. (2016, June). *Draft interagency concept for community resilience indicators and national-level measures.* Published for stakeholder comment. Retrieved from http://www.fema.gov/media-library-data/1466085676217-a14e229a461adfa574a5d03041a6297c/FEMA-CRI-Draft-Concept-Paper-508_Jun_2016.pdf

MMC (Multihazard Mitigation Council). (2005). *Natural hazard mitigation saves: An independent study to assess the future savings from mitigation activities.* Washington, DC: National Institute of Building Sciences.

MMC (Multihazard Mitigation Council). (2017). *Natural hazard mitigation saves: 2017 interim report: An independent study.* Washington, DC: National Institute of Building Sciences.

Ripberger, J., Jenkins-Smith, H., Silva, C., Czajkowski, J., Kunreuther, H., & Simmons, K. (2018, July). Tornado damage mitigation: Homeowner support for enhanced building codes in Oklahoma. *Risk Analysis.* doi:10.1111/risa.13131

Rochman, J. (2015, July 8). Commentary: Stronger building codes make communities more resilient. *Claims Journal.* Retrieved from http://www.claimsjournal.com/news/national/2015/07/08/264405.htm

Rose, A., Porter, K., Dash, N., Bouabid, J., Huyck, C., Whitehead, J., . . . & Tobin, L. T. (2007). Benefit-cost analysis of FEMA hazard mitigation grants. *Natural Hazards Review, 8*(4), 97–111.

Sadiq, A. A., & Noonan, D. S. (2015). Flood disaster management policy: An analysis of the United States community ratings system. *Journal of Natural Resources Policy Research, 7*(1), 5–22.

Schmith, S. (1999). Memorandum from the Florida Department of Community Affairs, Office of the General Counsel. Retrieved from http://www.floridabuilding.org/fbc/legal/legal_opinions/state_agency_op/agency_enf_maint.PDF

Shapiro, S. (2016). The realpolitik of building codes: Overcoming practical limitations to climate resilience. *Building Research & Information, 44*(5–6), 490–506.

Shimberg Center & ARA (2002). *Florida building code cost and loss reduction benefit comparison study.* Shimberg Center for Affordable Housing & Applied Research Associates, Inc. Retrieved from http://www.floridabuilding.org/fbc/publications/demo_report/Main_report.pdf

Simmons, K. M., Czajkowski, J., & Done, J. M. (2018). Economic effectiveness of implementing a statewide building code: The case of Florida. *Land Economics, 94*(2), 155–174.

Simmons, K. M., Kovacs, P., & Kopp, G. A. (2015). Tornado damage mitigation: Benefit–cost analysis of enhanced building codes in Oklahoma. *Weather, Climate, and Society, 7*(2), 169–178.

Sutter, D. (2009). Public sector quality assurance and building codes. *Journal of Public Finance and Public Choice, 27*(2–3), 155–169.

UNISDR (2015). *Making development sustainable: The future of disaster risk management. Global assessment report on disaster risk reduction.* Geneva: United Nations Office for Disaster Risk Reduction (UNISDR).

Vaughan, E., & Turner, J. (2013). *The value and impact of building codes.* Retrieved from http://www.eesi.org/files/Value-and-Impact-of-Building-Codes.pdf

PART V

Government and Risk Management

CHAPTER 18

Getting the Blend Right

Public-Private Partnerships in Risk Management

Cary Coglianese

Pollsters have long asked Americans if they think the United States has *too much* or *too little* government regulation. Only a minority of Americans ever report thinking that the country has too little regulation; most believe the government imposes either too much or "about the right amount" of regulation (Dugan 2015).[1] Such a Goldilocks-style poll question can surely prove informative to public opinion researchers interested in tracking patterns of political ideology in a two-party American system that divides into competing progovernment and promarket camps. But such a question turns out not to be very relevant to public and private sector decision-makers when they confront concrete real-world problems and need to know how to structure the interaction between business and government to solve those problems. The question for decision-makers is not one of *more* or *less* government regulation in general; the key question is *how* government should relate to and interact with the private sector in the specific context confronting decision-makers. In other words, the issue is really one of how to build effective relationships—or partnerships—between the government and the private sector to solve problems and deliver meaningful public value to society. When trying to solve major risk management problems, such as those stemming from climate change and its effects, the most vital challenge lies with getting the right blend between business and government in specific settings, not worrying about the overall "amount" of governmental intervention.

In the context of concrete problems, effective risk management necessitates the finding of the appropriate type of public-private relationship or partnership to solve those problems. Exactly *how* should government interact with business to deliver improved conditions in the world? Sometimes the appropriate terms of a public-private partnership will put government and business at arm's length with each other, even potentially in an adversarial relationship. Many other times, though, society will be best served when the public and private sectors work in tandem, in cooperative partnerships. What defines each relationship or partnership, as well as affects its ultimate success, can be captured by four core factors that I will describe here as *interface, incentives, information*, and *institutions*. Making public-private partnerships effective—that is, getting the blend, or interface, right between business and government—will depend on choosing and designing, for each problem, the governmental and private sector institutions that will ensure the best information will come forward and that relevant actors' incentives will be suitably aligned to solve the underlying public problem.

The Growth and Appeal of Public-Private Partnerships

For the past several decades, innovative government leaders have recognized the value of public-private partnerships, particularly when it comes to improving the environment and managing risk (see Freeman 1997; Pongsiri 2002).[2] Starting in the 1990s, the language of "partnership" enveloped the government reinvention movement, with the Clinton administration's National Performance Review eventually even being renamed the National Partnership for Reinventing Government (Kamarck 2013). At that time, the U.S. Environmental Protection Agency (EPA) launched a series of programs that sought to facilitate voluntary improvements through the creation of public-private partnerships, with some of the earliest being the agency's 33/50 Program (designed to encourage the voluntary reduction of designated toxic chemicals by 33% and ultimately 50% of current levels) (Arora and Cason 1995) and the Common Sense Initiative (promising to cut red tape and develop sector-based public-private partnerships to redesign environmental regulation) (Coglianese and Allen 2005). The now well-known Energy Star program was also established around that same time to offer a wide range of manufacturers of consumer products the possibility of earning a governmental energy efficiency designation for their products (Brown,

Webber, and Koomey 2002). Over the years, the EPA has created dozens of other so-called partnership programs (Borck, Coglianese, and Nash 2008). For example, the agency's nine-year flagship partnership program known as the National Environmental Performance Track offered private facilities public recognition and regulatory relief if they demonstrated various beyond-compliance commitments (Coglianese and Nash 2014). The EPA's Burn Wise program currently offers consumers financial incentives to replace old, highly polluting wood-burning stoves used in residential buildings (EPA 2018a). These and dozens of other similar innovative programs established by the EPA and the Department of Energy have charted a way toward what has sometimes been called a "next generation" approach to environmental protection and energy conservation in the United States (Chertow and Esty 1997; see also Gunningham and Sinclair 2002).[3]

A similar emphasis on partnership has figured prominently in recent risk management responses to climate change. For example, although the Obama administration's EPA made a number of high-profile efforts to initiate traditional forms of regulation to address climate change, such as its Clean Power Plan aimed at regulating energy efficiency and emissions in the electric utility sector, the agency also continued to sponsor a variety of voluntary partnership programs designed to encourage businesses to make progress in reducing carbon and methane emissions.[4] The Obama administration also launched a series of new public-private partnerships to improve infrastructure resilience in response to climate change, such as the Department of Energy's Partnership for Energy Sector Climate Resilience (U.S. Department of Energy 2015), the Resilience AmeriCorps program (AmeriCorps 2015), Climate Services for Resilient Development (White House 2015), and other similar programs.

Presumably a "business friendly" Trump administration prefers these kinds of so-called voluntary initiatives over the conventional forms of regulation that the administration has targeted for repeal or modification. Not only has the Trump administration undertaken efforts to repeal or replace various conventional environmental regulations, but its EPA has established a new Smart Sectors program modeled on the Common Sense Initiative (Joselow 2018). The EPA describes Smart Sectors as "a partnership program that provides a platform to collaborate with regulated sectors and develop sensible approaches that better protect the environment and public health" (EPA 2018b).

This pervasive and continuing interest in public-private partnerships is understandable, especially in an era of continued legislative gridlock. With one main exception, Congress last passed major U.S. environmental legislation over a quarter-century ago.[5] Looking forward, legal uncertainty will likely continue to surround the use of the Clean Air Act to address climate change (or to reverse course and rescind the Clean Power Plan), and there seems to be no realistic prospect of any new, major national climate change legislation on the horizon in the United States.[6] As a result, those seeking to respond to climate change—or any other emerging or unaddressed public risk management problem—have understandably turned to other tools, in particular voluntary partnerships. It is telling that, just a day after President Trump announced his intention to withdraw the United States from the Paris Agreement on Climate Change, former mayor Michael Bloomberg announced "a partnership among American cities, states, and businesses" to honor and fulfill the U.S. commitment under the Paris Agreement (Bloomberg 2017; see also Stokols 2017).

A renewed interest in partnerships is only likely to be reinforced by the federal government's continued fiscal constraints. The kinds of investments needed to adapt the nation's vital infrastructure and prepare communities to withstand the effects of climate change will depend, by necessity in an era of government austerity, on leveraging private sector resources, including those from private foundations and major corporations.

In addition to these various operational constraints and strategic considerations that have made public-private partnerships attractive in recent decades, it bears noting that the very term and concept of "partnership" generates its own warm glow. Especially in an era of partisan polarization and seemingly intractable policy conflict, the idea of creating partnerships offers something refreshing and positive, enhancing its appeal to policymakers and citizens alike. Moreover, because partnerships are voluntary, they skirt all the negative criticisms of excessive burdens and costs associated with mandatory risk regulation. When private firms get involved in public-private partnerships, they presumably do so because they believe the costs of their participation are justified by the benefits.[7]

Why Risk Management Requires Public-Private "Partnership"

Contemporary policy discussions typically treat the concept of a "public-private partnership" as having a very specific meaning, namely government initiatives aimed at leveraging, on a voluntary basis, the efforts or resources of private sector firms to achieve public goals (see, e.g., Coglianese and Nash

2006). However, decision-makers can yield value from taking a broader perspective and conceiving of the entire domain of risk management as necessitating a reliance on public-private partnerships—although of widely differing kinds. Seeing all risk management as a "partnership" may seem at first glance to be an unjustifiably expansive claim, but in fact virtually every effort to manage risk in society involves some interaction between the public and private sectors.[8] Even if we do not immediately perceive such interaction in some instances to look like a "partnership," in reality, if any risk management intervention is to be effective, it must be based on an optimal relationship or balance between the public and private sectors.[9] That public-private relationship may well need in some cases to be adversarial, built on coercion by state authority in the form of regulation—a type of relationship that might seem anathema to the concept of a "partnership." But even within the domain of risk regulation, there remain vital ways in which cooperative interactions between the public and private sectors enhance public value.

When seeking to impose regulations on the private sector, for example, government officials depend on the involvement and cooperation of the private sector in developing new regulations and ensuring compliance with them, even if we do not usually see that type of interaction as a kind of partnership. Or if business-government cooperation over regulation is viewed as a partnership, it usually is understood to be an undesirable one of lobbyists "capturing" government officials to advance their own special interests. Still, it cannot be ignored that for decades the federal rulemaking process in the United States has been self-consciously designed to provide numerous opportunities for private sector firms to work with government regulatory authorities in the development of regulation, whether minimally by submitting public comments or more significantly through participation in federal advisory committees (Coglianese 2006). Government regulators' need for information has provided the longstanding justification for participation by private actors in public rulemaking processes. Regulatory officials based in Washington, DC, after all, generally know much less than private sector firms do about the risks those firms create or the strategies for mitigating those risks; hence, effective regulation depends vitally on public sector regulators gaining access to and learning from information held by private sector firms (Coglianese, Zeckhauser, and Parson 2004; Coglianese 2007).

In addition, public sector regulators rarely have the capacity to monitor compliance by every firm and must depend extensively on the "voluntary" compliance of regulated entities. In many cases, those regulated entities are responsible for the very testing and conformity assessment efforts upon which public sector authorities rely. For example, private pharmaceutical companies conduct the safety tests mandated by the Food and Drug Administration before a new drug can be approved for marketing. Likewise, automobile manufacturers subject their vehicles to the emissions testing requirements imposed by the Environmental Protection Agency. To be sure, as the recent Volkswagen crisis makes plain (Gates et al. 2017; see generally Coglianese and Nash 2017), reliance by public authorities on private implementation of regulations can at times be abused, but nevertheless the regulatory system in the United States (and elsewhere) depends to an unmistakably large degree on the expectation that businesses will comply with rules even if the prospects for detection of noncompliance are remote.

The main point is that, even with regulation, risk management depends in vital ways on productive, even though at times optimally adversarial, relationships between the public and private sectors and on how those relationships are managed. Much the same point can be made with respect to other types of risk management responses. Move to the other end of the public-private spectrum and consider a seemingly completely free-market risk management tool: private insurance markets. Not only do private insurance contracts provide for compensation in the face of losses, but the pricing of premiums in insurance markets can be a tool to induce sound risk management measures without any seeming intervention of the public sector (see, e.g., Ben-Shahar and Logue 2012; Coglianese and Kunreuther 2016). Insurers, after all, do not make money if they price premiums below expected losses, so a competitive insurance market exerts pressures on purchasers of insurance to manage their risks and thereby earn or maintain lower premiums. Private insurance companies may also impose their own private "regulatory" standards on their insured companies—for example, when they will not insure facilities that do not install or operate specified risk controls—and they may also offer technical risk management assistance to their customers (Freeman and Kunreuther 1997).

All of this socially valuable effort on the part of private insurance companies inducing positive risk management by private sector companies might seem to undermine the claim that all risk management depends on a public-private partnership. But here, too, the partnership claim is valid once we step back and look more carefully. For one thing, all markets depend on some background support from government to maintain the viability of contracts and the kind of rule-of-law stability that makes any economic market possible, including an insurance market. In addition, insurance markets are themselves regulated markets, which means that getting government regulation of these markets right is absolutely vital to ensuring that the insurance mechanism works well as a risk management strategy.

With respect to a variety of important problems, the successful deployment of insurance as a risk management strategy will also depend on public intervention in the form of regulatory mandates to purchase insurance (see, e.g., Moore and Viscusi 2014). If only hazardous drivers purchased automobile insurance, and if only older individuals or those with health problems bought health insurance, insurance companies would be unable to spread risk. In a similar vein, risk-rated premiums for property insurance will only induce optimal land development patterns and risk mitigation efforts that reduce property damage and loss of life from floods and wildfires if all property owners need to buy insurance and if those requirements are adequately enforced (Kunreuther 2015). If property owners can just drop their insurance coverage instead, the incentive effects of insurance will be lost. Hence, instances of what may at times look like a purely "market-based" approach through insurance will depend ultimately on sound and credibly enforced regulation by public sector institutions.[10]

Essential Components of Effective Public-Private Partnerships

Seeing all risk management—even government regulation and private insurance markets—as different types of public-private partnerships can yield important insights about improving the ways that risks are managed in society, as well as help reveal insights about what can and cannot be reasonably expected from the more limited, contemporary meaning of public-private partnerships reflected in programs such as Energy Star and the Resilience AmeriCorps. (These latter, narrower programs—Energy Star, Resilience AmeriCorps, and the like—are called "partnerships" in the contemporary policy lingua franca, but I will refer to them in this chapter as "P3 initiatives," to distinguish them from the broader category of all possible coordinated public-private interactions or partnerships.)

Thinking broadly, the essential components of any type of effective public-private partnership are: *interface, incentives, information,* and *institutions*—or what I will refer to as the "four *i*'s," as shown in Table 18.1. Let me begin with the first "*i*," interface.

Table 18.1. Essential components of an effective public-private partnership

Interface	How well does the partnership fit with the underlying risk management problem it is intended to solve?
Incentives	How well does the partnership align incentives to encourage optimal behavior by public and private actors?
Information	How well does the partnership leverage the respective informational advantages of businesses and government in identifying and redressing risks?
Institutions	How well do the rules and structures of a partnership support and deliver in terms of interface, incentives, and information?

Interface

Interface refers to the way in which a public-private partnership fits with the specific risk management problem it is intended to help solve. The effectiveness of the interface will be very much a function of the other three *i*'s, but it will also depend on other features of the partnership that relate to the specific problem to be solved. To solve a problem, a public-private partnership, as with any strategy, has to address the underlying causes of that problem. A public-private partnership that promotes childhood literacy might be superbly well designed to improve reading skills, but it will obviously do little to improve the climate resilience of the nation's energy system. Such a program would have a poor interface with the latter problem because it does not address at all the underlying problem of energy sector resilience. However, a program that squarely aimed to improve the climate resilience of the energy grid but which still failed in fact to address the underlying vulnerabilities in the energy system would also prove ineffective. Much the same would apply to a partnership program that aimed to mitigate climate change in the first place but completely ignored carbon dioxide and methane emissions.

The importance of a good interface may seem like plain common sense, but its obviousness can be sometimes lost on policy leaders who want to set up partnership programs. An extensive study that Jennifer Nash and I conducted of the EPA's National Environmental Performance Track indicated that this P3 initiative suffered from a low-quality interface between the program and the underlying problems it sought to solve (Coglianese and Nash

2014). Performance Track sought to recognize and reward facilities for undertaking voluntary efforts to improve their environmental performance. To participate in the program, facilities had to demonstrate a relatively clean compliance track record, make commitments to improve their environmental performance in specific areas, establish and maintain an environmental management system, and engage with their local communities. As initially conceived, the program intended to shift what the EPA called "the environmental performance curve," inducing firms to undertake beyond-compliance actions in order to secure the rewards the EPA offered through the program. Unfortunately, the rewards the EPA offered through this program were not all that significant, so the number of facilities participating was but a tiny fraction of all regulated firms. More importantly, our research indicated that the key feature distinguishing facilities that participated in Performance Track turned out not to be their levels of environmental performance; rather, it was the facilities' managers' propensity to engage in public outreach. In other words, Performance Track tracked more "extroverted" facilities, not necessarily the better performing facilities—a disconnected interface between program and problem.

The Performance Track program illustrates a still more fundamental point: the purpose of public-private partnerships should be to solve real problems, not merely to create certain kinds of public-private partnerships. Sometimes, public officials have reason to create P3 initiatives so as to make it look like they are doing something (what social scientists call "credit claiming"), when they are really not doing much of anything at all. In the 1990s, for example, the EPA devoted much effort and attention to a program it called the Common Sense Initiative (CSI), but without actually accomplishing much of anything for the environment. Part of the CSI focused on the metal finishing sector, but it attracted private-sector participation from only the tiniest fraction of metal finishing firms; as a result, it had remarkably little impact (Coglianese and Allen 2005). Some observers have suggested that CSI and other early EPA voluntary programs were mainly intended to make the EPA appear more "business friendly" and stave off opposition in Congress to conventional environmental regulation, rather than deliver tangible, significant environmental results. If that was true, then perhaps the CSI succeeded. But surely if the core aim of the CSI or any other P3 initiative is to reduce risks or enhance resilience, it needs to effectuate meaningful change in investment or environmental behavior—not just amount to a public relations strategy that makes the government look more cooperative or makes agency officials look like they are doing something meaningful when they are not.

Incentives

The possibility that government officials may, at least on occasion, have incentives to engage in certain types of public-private partnerships as mere symbolic gestures brings us to the next "*i*"—*incentives*. Incentives matter in both public and private behavior generally, as well as specifically with respect to public and private actors' involvement in modern P3 initiatives. Effective public-private sector partnerships need to align incentives to encourage optimal behavior by both public and private actors.

If governmental officials may sometimes act upon suboptimal or narrow incentives to create P3 initiatives for symbolic gain, private actors also can respond to socially suboptimal incentives to participate in these initiatives. Private sector actors may favor P3 initiatives for symbolic reasons too. Participation can make them look good. A positive public image and reputation may advance their private interests, especially if their customers value socially responsible businesses (Reinhardt 2000). Participation in P3 initiatives could also be used strategically by some firms as part of an effort to stave off costlier (even if, from the public's standpoint, more effective) regulatory requirements (Lyon and Maxwell 2004). A further concern is that, if firms' main incentive to participate in P3 initiatives is to get a government agency's seal of approval, these initiatives may prove insufficient to induce deep, sustained behavioral change. Of course, one need not succumb to conspiratorial theories about either public officials or private-sector managers to see the larger point: namely, that incentives matter.

In order to manage risks well, incentives must be carefully analyzed and addressed in taking into account how the relationship between business and government is structured. To the extent that private actors' incentives are misaligned with broader public goals, then a particular kind of public-private partnership—the one called "regulation"—will likely be needed. This is clearly the case when businesses create negative externalities, which by definition are costs that a firm's activities impose on third parties who are not in a direct contractual relationship with the firm. If a business invests in efforts to control these externalities, it reaps benefits for community members, future generations, or others who are not paying for them—but it does not yield equivalent private benefits to the firm itself. In cases of such so-called mar-

ket failure, the public sector needs to adopt clear rules and impose a meaningful possibility of penalties for noncompliance with those rules (Breyer
1984; Viscusi, Harrington, and Sappington 2018). When significant externalities exist, P3 initiatives like the EPA's Performance Track will not be sufficient to provide the kind of incentives firms need to make the necessary
improvements in their environmental performance.

On the other hand, when firms already have some private incentives to
incur costs to deliver goods or services of public value, then regulation may
not be needed. For example, telephone companies, railroads, and energy firms
presumably have some incentive of their own to protect their infrastructure
from natural disasters, for if their services were to be so unreliable that they
broke down following the slightest storm or stress, they would not likely remain in business for very long. Especially when competition is robust, regulation will not be as needed to induce firms to undertake socially valuable
efforts to address climate resilience if the firms have some private interests
to do so already. Of course, the operative word in the preceding sentence may
be "as," because even though private firms have some private incentives to
invest in climate resilience, they still may not have sufficient incentives to engage in the socially optimal level of risk management. This may be especially
true for infrastructure industries that effectively operate natural monopolies
and therefore are protected from competitive pressures.

Nevertheless, the fact remains that incentives matter and that, to be effective, partnership programs must seek to augment whatever existing incentives firms may have to engage in socially desirable behavior. Private firms
today may well already have a greater degree of inherent self-interest in making their operations more resilient to the ravages of climate change than they
did in decades past—or than they do even now in protecting someone else's
health or property from the risks created by local air pollution. For this reason, the twenty-first century's P3 initiatives to promote climate resilience may
well prove more successful than late twentieth century's P3 initiatives aimed
at improving environmental quality, simply because the former may require
fewer additional incentives to be provided by the P3 initiative.

Information

Accurate, relevant information is essential for effective interface—that is,
for ensuring that public-private partnerships actually help solve problems.

Business and government will have varying levels of knowledge about particular problems and their solutions, and the relative degree to which each has informational advantages may vary from problem to problem as well as over time. When it comes to identifying risks caused by business activity, business will often have better information about those risks and their solutions (Coglianese, Zeckhauser, and Parson 2004). Yet this will not always be the case. Small businesses, for example, may not know as much as government does about how to fix problems that the businesses themselves are creating. More generally, businesses of all sizes may have a lower capacity to understand systemic effects, such as flood patterns and other natural disaster risks that might affect their operations.

When government decides it needs to impose regulation on firms, it will be able to do so more effectively if it thinks about what kinds of partnerships it needs to forge with industry in order to gather the information necessary to determine how to design and enforce an effective regulatory scheme (Coglianese 2007). Sometimes that "partnership" in the regulatory context will simply take the form of picking up the phone and calling a manager or representative in the industry to gather relevant information. Sometimes it will entail holding a public hearing or conducting a site visit. Other times, it may well require creating formal P3 initiatives that enable government regulators to forge relationships with leading-edge firms. This latter strategy may be ultimately the most important value the EPA gained from its flagship Performance Track partnership program. Managers at the EPA reported that they learned more about effective environmental management from their engagement with the kinds of outward-facing facilities that participated in Performance Track. If that knowledge fed back into the development of regulations so that they were made more effective and efficient, then the EPA and the public may have gained considerably from Performance Track, notwithstanding the program's small or undeterminable direct impact on the environment (Coglianese and Nash 2014).

Institutions

Although private firms may often have better information about risks than their public sector counterparts, this does not mean they will have sufficient incentives to act on that information to deliver public value. Institutions need to be designed that can provide the appropriate incentives needed to induce required behavioral change. By institutions, I refer to the rules and structures of any public-private partnership—or what is sometimes called "choice architecture."[11] The challenge is often one of structuring the partnership's architecture in a way that shapes incentives so that businesses can either reveal information to government regulators or directly put to use the informational advantage they have.

Up to this point, I have mainly been distinguishing between two types of institutional arrangements: traditional *regulation* and more innovative *P3 initiatives*. But this dichotomy has largely been used for ease of exposition. The reality is that there are not just two institutional forms, but a multitude. Within the category of regulation alone, institutional variation is reflected in the highly diverse forms of regulatory instruments that can be deployed in any regulatory response to public problems: design or specification standards; performance standards; management-based regulation; information disclosure requirements; tradable permits; regulatory taxes; and so forth (see, e.g., Richards 2000; Coglianese 2012; Transportation Research Board 2018).

Just as with regulatory instrument choice, the potential institutional variation across P3 initiatives is widespread as well. The dozens of voluntary programs the EPA has launched since the 1990s have been structured in highly varying ways. Even putting aside the substantive requirements for membership in the EPA's partnership programs, some of these programs have been administratively easy to join while others have imposed quite onerous administrative hurdles for participation. Some have been harder to stay in than others. In addition, the benefits of membership have varied as well. Some programs have offered regulatory relief to members; others have offered technical assistance; still others have only offered public recognition (a product label or even a flag that the business could display at its facility). In one study that Jennifer Nash and I conducted, we found that these kinds of institutional details correlated closely with business participation in different EPA programs (Coglianese and Nash 2009). We found, perhaps not surprisingly, that irrespective of membership benefits, the greater the administrative hurdles for participation in P3 initiatives, the fewer firms participated. Obviously institutions matter.

Conclusion: Implications of Viewing Risk Management as Relational

Putting together the "four *i*'s," it is possible to reach an overarching conclusion about what it takes to make public-private partnerships effective. *Decision-makers need to build institutions that ensure that the best information comes*

forward and that incentives are suitably aligned to induce the behavior needed
to solve the underlying problems that decision-makers intend to solve.

Viewing risk management as a relationship between the public and private sectors helpfully moves beyond thinking just about whether there should be "more" or "less" governmental intervention in the marketplace. The key question is not one of more or less government, but of how business-government relations should be structured. In other words, what is the proper design of risk management's inherent public-private partnership? How should the *relationship* between business and government be structured and managed to ensure it results in meaningful, net-beneficial effects?

In addition to framing these questions more clearly, one more implication follows from what I have been describing as a *relational* view of risk management, a view that all successful risk management requires the right kind of partnership between the public and private sectors. The remaining implication is this: *people matter*. Ordinarily, risk management is viewed as a highly technical enterprise, calling for extensive scientific assessments of risks and rigorous economic analysis. Undoubtedly sound science and careful analysis are essential. Yet an important body of research on the behavioral economics of insurance markets and risk decision-making, much of it produced at the Wharton Risk Management and Decision Processes Center over the last 30 years, has made clear how much human psychology factors into what might otherwise be thought to be a purely expert-based enterprise called risk management (see, e.g., Kunreuther, Meyer, and Michel-Kerjan 2013; Michel-Kerjan and Slovic 2010).

A relational perspective of risk management builds on behavioral research by suggesting that, in addition to human psychology, other aspects of business-government relations matter as well, specifically aspects that might ordinarily be captured under the banner of "politics." Considering the politics of business-government relations demands attention to *incentives*, *information*, and *institutions*, and how they affect the *interface* between problems and their solutions. Politics brings into better focus issues of equity, in addition to effectiveness and efficiency, because politics is driven by how society's pie is divided more than by how large the pie is. Politics matters crucially in "getting the blend right" between public policy and private action because risk management is ultimately about people: their fears, their interests, their futures, and their behaviors.

Managing risk, then, requires managing relationships—that is, building partnerships between actors with different and sometimes misaligned goals and interests. Sometimes those relationships will be by necessity adversarial; many times they will be synergistic or cooperative. In the end, how well risk management succeeds will depend on how the core features of partnerships, as discussed here, are aligned so as to make sure public and private sectors work effectively to deliver more optimal and equitable outcomes for society overall.

Acknowledgments

The author gratefully acknowledges helpful comments and assistance from Ed Blum and Shana Starobin.

Notes

1. According to Gallup's annual Governance survey in 2015, more Americans say government regulation of business is "too much" (49%) than "too little" (21%). In that same year, 27% reported that they thought the amount of regulation just right. A similar pattern has generally existed as long as pollsters have been asking the public about regulation, notwithstanding underlying changes in the numbers and economic impacts of government rules over time. Commenting on polls from the 1930s through the early 1980s, Lipset and Schneider (1983) note that "a majority has consistently opposed increased regulation of business at any given moment. Most people have generally taken the position that the current amount of regulation was about right or too much."

2. The focus in this chapter will be on public-private partnerships for addressing domestic policy problems. Considerable interest has also emerged over the use of partnerships for addressing international governance matters (Linder and Rosenau 2000; Börzel and Risse 2005).

3. Interestingly, the number of such partnership programs is hard to pin down. In a 2007 report, the EPA's Office of Inspector General stated that "Depending on the source, the number of EPA voluntary programs varies between 54 and 133" (EPA 2007).

4. For a current list of "many programs and projects that partner with industry and others to reduce greenhouse gas emissions," see EPA (2017).

5. The recent exception is the passage in 2016 of the Frank R. Lautenberg Chemical Safety for the 21st Century Act which amended the Toxic Substances Control Act of 1976.

6. That said, in December 2015, Congress did renew federal tax credits for investments in solar and wind energy, which will may help significantly encourage movement toward the eventual "decarbonization" of the U.S. energy system (Cusick 2015). Still, legislative debate persists over whether to extend those tax credits further—and the Trump administration has entertained the possibility of providing subsidies for coal and nuclear energy. Perhaps a future federal initiative to expand infrastructure funding might well keep renewable energy tax credits in place or perhaps offer increased subsidies for renewable energy development.

7. Yet just because "partnership" may generate a warm glow, that does not mean public-private partnerships are meaningful or effective merely because of that glow. Reflecting on a four-year field study of America's towns and cities, James and Deborah Fallows (2018) included public-private partnerships on their list of the ten essential ingredients for a thriving city; however, they made a point specifically to say that such partnerships need to be more than just a "slogan."

8. This point bears some affinity with Martha Minow's observation of a "continuum of relationships between government and private groups" (Minow 2003). She notes that, of course, "a more complicated analysis would pursue many dimensions" of public-private partnerships, not just a single continuum. As she explains, "The government may forbid, permit, encourage, subsidize, or establish private entities."

9. As Donahue and Zeckhauser (2006) put it in the context of what they call "collaborative governance," the outcomes for society depend on being able to "fine-tune" the interaction between the public and private sectors so as to "maximize the benefits less the costs." They define "cooperative governance" as "the pursuit of authoritatively chosen public goals by means that include engaging the efforts of, and sharing discretion with, producers outside of government."

10. It bears noting as well, of course, that public sector institutions are themselves often staffed and supported by private sector contractors. For cautionary accounts of the extensive reliance of the federal government on private contractors, see Verkuil (2007) and DiIulio (2014).

11. On institutions, see North (1991). On choice architecture, see Thaler and Sunstein (2009). For a discussion of institutional structure in the specific context of voluntary environmental programs—or partnerships—see Potoski and Prakash (2005).

References

Americorps. (2015, July 9). Public-private partnership launches new AmeriCorps program to help communities build resilience. Corporation for National and Community Service. Retrieved from http://www.nationalservice.gov/newsroom/press-releases/2015/public--private-partnership-launches-new-americorps-program-help

Arora, S., & Cason, T. N. (1995). An experiment in voluntary environmental regulation: Participation in EPA's 33/50 program. *Journal of Environmental Economics and Management, 28*(3), 271–286.

Ben-Shahar, O., & Logue, K. D. (2012). Outsourcing regulation: How insurance reduces moral hazard. *Michigan Law Review, 111*(2), 197.

Bloomberg, M. R. (2017, June 2) Mike Bloomberg to President Macron: Americans don't need Washington to meet our Paris commitment (press release). Retrieved from Bloomberg Philanthropies website: https://www.bloomberg.org/press/releases/bloomberg-following-meeting-president-macron-mayor-hidalgo-us-commitment-paris-agreement/

Borck, J. C., Coglianese, C., & Nash, J. (2008). Environmental leadership programs: Toward an empirical assessment of their performance. *Ecology Law Quarterly, 35*(4), 771–834.

Börzel, T. A., & Risse, T. (2005). Public-private partnerships: Effective and legitimate tools of international governance. In E. Grande & L. Pauly (Eds.), *Complex sovereignty: Recon-*

structing political authority in the twenty-first century (pp. 195–216). Toronto: University of Toronto Press.

Breyer, S. G. (1984). *Regulation and its reform.* Cambridge, MA: Harvard University Press.

Brown, R., Webber, C., & Koomey, J. G. (2002). Status and future directions of the ENERGY STAR program. *Energy, 27*(5), 505–520.

Chertow, M. R., & Esty, D. C. (Eds.). (1997). *Thinking ecologically: The next generation of environmental policy.* New Haven, CT: Yale University Press.

Coglianese, C. (2006). Citizen participation in rulemaking: Past, present, and future. *Duke Law Journal, 55,* 943–968.

Coglianese, C. (2007). Business interests and information in environmental rulemaking. In M. E. Kraft & S. Kamieniecki (Eds.), *Business and environmental policy: Corporate interests in the American political system* (pp. 185–211). Cambridge, MA: MIT Press.

Coglianese, C. (2012, September 17). Regulation's four core components. *Regulatory Review.* Retrieved from https://www.theregreview.org/2012/09/17/regulations-four-core -components/

Coglianese, C., & Allen, L. K. (2005). Building sector-based consensus: A review of the U.S. EPA's Common Sense Initiative. In T. de Bruijn & V. Norberg-Bohm (Eds.), *Industrial transformation: Environmental policy innovation in the United States and Europe* (pp. 65– 92). Cambridge, MA: MIT Press.

Coglianese, C., & Kunreuther, H. (2016). Insurance and the excellent regulator. In C. Coglianese (Ed.), *Achieving regulatory excellence.* Washington, DC: Brookings Institution Press.

Coglianese, C., & Nash, J. (2006). The promise and performance of management-based strategies. In C. Coglianese, & J. Nash (Eds.), *Leveraging the private sector: Management-based strategies for improving environmental performance* (pp. 249–263). Washington, DC: Resources for the Future.

Coglianese, C., & Nash, J. (2009). Government clubs: Theory and evidence from voluntary environmental programs. In M. Potosky & A. Prakash (Eds.), *Voluntary programs: A club theory perspective* (pp. 231–258). Cambridge, MA: MIT Press.

Coglianese, C., & Nash, J. (2014). Performance track's postmortem: Lessons from the rise and fall of EPA's "flagship" voluntary program. *Harvard Environmental Law Review, 38*(1), 1–86.

Coglianese, C., & Nash, J. (2017). The law of the test: Performance-based regulation and diesel emissions control. *Yale Journal on Regulation, 34*(1), 33–90.

Coglianese, C., Zeckhauser, R., & Parson, E. (2004). Seeking truth for power: Informational strategy and regulatory policymaking. *Minnesota Law Review, 89*(2), 277–341.

Cusick, D. (2015, December 21). Renewables boom expected thanks to tax credit. *Scientific American.*

DiIulio, J. (2014). *Bring back the bureaucrats: Why more federal workers will lead to better (and smaller!) government.* West Conshohocken, PA: Templeton Press.

Donahue, J. D., & Zeckhauser, R. J. (2006). Public-private collaboration. In M. Moran, M. Rein, & R. E. Goodin (Eds.), *The Oxford handbook of public policy* (pp. 496–525). Oxford: Oxford University Press.

Dugan, A. (2015, September 18). In U.S., half still say gov't regulates business too much. Retrieved from Gallup website: http://www.gallup.com/poll/185609/half-say-gov-regulates -business.aspx

EPA. (2007). Voluntary programs could benefit from internal policy controls and a systematic management approach. Office of Inspector General, U.S. Environmental Protection Agency. Retrieved from http://perma.cc/QD6E-XNSV

EPA. (2017, January 13). Voluntary energy and climate programs. U.S. Environmental Protection Agency. Retrieved from https://19january2017snapshot.epa.gov/climatechange/voluntary-energy-and-climate-programs_.html

EPA. (2018a, April 24). Burn Wise. U.S. Environmental Protection Agency. Retrieved from http://www.epa.gov/burnwise

EPA. (2018b, September 6). EPA Smart Sectors program. U.S. Environmental Protection Agency. Retrieved from https://www.epa.gov/smartsectors

Fallows, J. & Fallows, D. (2018). *Our towns: A 100,000-mile journey into the heart of America.* New York: Pantheon.

Freeman, J. (1997). Collaborative governance in the administrative state. *UCLA Law Review, 45*(1), 1–89.

Freeman, P. K., & Kunreuther, H. (1997). *Managing environmental risk through insurance.* Boston: Kluwer.

Gates, G., Ewing, J., Russell, K., & Watkins, D. (2017, March 16). How Volkswagen's "defeat devices" worked. *New York Times.* Retrieved from http://www.nytimes.com/interactive/2015/business/international/vw-diesel-emissions-scandal-explained.html

Gunningham, N., & Sinclair, D. (2002). *Leaders and laggards: Next-generation environmental regulation.* Sheffield: Greenleaf.

Joselow, M. (2018, August 31). When industry has concerns, this EPA team's all ears. *Greenwire.* Retrieved from https://www.eenews.net/greenwire/stories/1060095541/feed

Kamarck, E. (2013, June 18). Lessons for the future of government reform. Testimony before the House Committee on Oversight and Government Reform. Retrieved from https://www.brookings.edu/testimonies/lessons-for-the-future-of-government-reform/

Kunreuther, H. (2015). The role of insurance in reducing losses from extreme events: The need for public–private partnerships. *Geneva Papers on Risk and Insurance: Issues and Practice, 40*(4), 741–762.

Kunreuther, H., Meyer, R., & Michel-Kerjan, E. (2013). Overcoming decision biases to reduce losses from natural catastrophes. In E. Shafir (Ed.), *The behavioral foundations of public policy* (pp. 398–413). Princeton, NJ: Princeton University Press.

Linder, S. H., & Rosenau, P. V. (2000). Mapping the terrain of the public-private policy partnership. In P. V. Rosenau (Ed.), *Public-private policy partnerships* (pp. 1–18). Cambridge, MA: MIT Press.

Lipset, S. M., & Schneider, W. (1983). *The confidence gap: Business, labor, and government in the public mind.* New York: Free Press.

Lyon, T. P., & Maxwell, J. W. (2004). *Corporate environmentalism and public policy.* Cambridge: Cambridge University Press.

Michel-Kerjan, E., & Slovic, P. (Eds.). (2010). *The irrational economist: Making decisions in a dangerous world.* New York: PublicAffairs.

Minow, M. (2003). Public and private partnerships: Accounting for the new religion. *Harvard Law Review, 116*(5), 1229–1270.

Moore, M. J., & Viscusi, W. K. (2014). *Compensation mechanisms for job risks: Wages, workers' compensation, and product liability.* Princeton, NJ: Princeton University Press.

North, D. C. (1991). Institutions. *Journal of Economic Perspectives, 5*(1), 97–112.

Pongsiri, N. (2002). Regulation and public-private partnerships. *International Journal of Public Sector Management, 15*(6), 487–495.

Potoski, M., & Prakash, A. (2005). Covenants with weak swords: ISO 14001 and facilities' environmental performance. *Journal of Policy Analysis and Management, 24*(4), 745–769.

Reinhardt, F. L. (2000). *Down to earth: Applying business principles to environmental management.* Cambridge, MA: Harvard Business School Press.

Richards, K. R. (2000). Framing environmental policy instrument choice. *Duke Environmental Law & Policy Forum, 10*(2), 221–285.

Stokols, E. (2017, June 2). Bloomberg-led group plans pledge for Paris Accord. *Wall Street Journal.* Retrieved from https://www.wsj.com/articles/bloomberg-led-group-plans-pledge -for-paris-accord-1496378860

Thaler, R. H., & Sunstein, C. R. (2009). *Nudge: Improving decisions about health, wealth, and happiness.* New Haven, CT: Yale University Press.

Transportation Research Board. (2018). *Designing safety regulations for high-hazard industries.* Washington, DC: National Academy of Sciences.

U.S. Department of Energy. (2015). Partnership for Energy Sector Climate Resilience. Retrieved from https://www.energy.gov/policy/initiatives/partnership-energy-sector-climate -resilience

Verkuil, P. R. (2007). *Outsourcing sovereignty: Why privatization of government functions threatens democracy and what we can do about it.* Cambridge: Cambridge University Press.

Viscusi, W. K., Harrington, J. E., & Sappington, D. E. M. (2018). *Economics of regulation and antitrust* (5th ed.). Cambridge, MA: MIT Press.

White House. (2015, June 9). Fact sheet: Launching a public-private partnership to empower climate-resilient developing nations (press release). Retrieved from https://obama whitehouse.archives.gov/the-press-office/2015/06/09/fact-sheet-launching-public -private-partnership-empower-climate-resilien

CHAPTER 19

The Regulation of Insurance Markets Subject to Catastrophic Risks

Robert W. Klein

Introduction

The regulation of insurance companies and markets is a subject of considerable interest to academic researchers, policymakers, industry practitioners, and others. Researchers have focused primarily on how regulation affects insurance companies and markets and how regulatory systems, policies, and methods should be structured or reformed to best serve the public interest. There also has been some work on the political economy of insurance regulation, for example, what are the factors that determine actual regulatory behavior and policies. This chapter examines several important areas of insurance regulation that can have significant implications for how well insurance markets function and the efficiency of risk management.

Depending on how it is structured and administered, insurance regulation can improve market performance, have no effect, or cause significant problems in insurance markets. One example of how regulation can substantially undermine the efficient functioning of insurance markets is Florida's response to pressures in its homeowners insurance market following the 2004–2005 storm seasons. Florida imposed significant constraints on insurers' efforts to raise their rates and adjust their underwriting. This led to considerable disruption in the state's homeowners insurance market as major insurers substantially reduced their supply of insurance coverage to homes in high-risk areas. The affected homeowners were forced to find coverage from other sources, including single-state companies and the state's residual market mechanism: the Citizens Property Insurance Corporation of Florida. Consequently, the number of policies insured by Citizens grew to an unprecedented level.[1] Additionally, some homeowners who had been previously insured by well-capitalized, large national carriers now had their coverage supplied by small, single-state companies with much less capital and geographic diversification. The ultimate result was a substantial shift of property exposures from the private sector to a government-sponsored insurance mechanism, a significant increase in cross-subsidies flowing from homeowners in low-risk areas to homeowners in high-risk areas, and a decline in the "quality of coverage" for homeowners who were forced to move their policies to single-state companies.[2]

For this chapter, insurance regulation is examined from both a normative perspective (i.e., how should policy in a particular area be structured to maximize social welfare?) and a positive or descriptive economics perspective (e.g., what are the policies that are actually adopted and why?). The chapter focuses on the regulation of insurance markets that are subject to significant catastrophic risks, especially hurricanes. In such markets, significant issues arise with respect to how insurance should be regulated versus how it is regulated.

The regulation of insurance companies and markets can have important implications for the efficiency of risk management. Insurance is one of a set of risk management methods that includes other forms of risk transfer and financing, risk retention, and loss control. Efficient insurance markets facilitate optimal risk management. Insurance not only provides a means to finance risk that it is otherwise not cost-effective to avoid or reduce, it also provides a means to send proper signals regarding the benefits of risk avoidance and control (Kunreuther 2015). Risk-based pricing and underwriting of insurance along with other provisions in insurance contracts encourage insureds to make good decisions in controlling their risk.

The principal findings offered in this chapter are as follows. Insurance regulation can be welfare enhancing when regulators adhere to two basic principles: (1) regulation should address true market failures where it can realistically remedy or ameliorate such failures; and (2) regulatory policies should seek to achieve outcomes consistent with what would be produced by a workably competitive market. When regulators fail to adhere to these principles, for example, when they interfere with risk-based pricing and/or constrain insurers' ability to properly manage their risk exposures, this leads to significant market distortions. These distortions can include a reduced sup-ply of insurance coverage and moral hazard resulting from diminished in-centives for the insured to mitigate their exposure to losses. Political pressure from consumers and other interest groups can cause regulators to implement policies that seek to artificially alter market outcomes but, ultimately, such policies are doomed to fail. The challenge for regulators and other stakehold-ers is to craft policies that are both economically efficient and politically viable under difficult conditions.

The chapter is structured as follows. The next section reviews some basic principles for insurance regulation. This is followed by a discussion of the po-litical economy of insurance regulation due to its relevance to understand-ing the factors that can cause suboptimal regulatory policies. Subsequent sections examine regulatory policies in several key areas: insurance pricing and underwriting, policy provisions, residual market mechanisms, and sol-vency. The chapter ends with some concluding thoughts and suggestions for further research.

Principles for Insurance Regulation

The rationale for why insurance companies and markets should be regulated is based on market failures that arise primarily from information problems and externalities (Munch and Smallwood 1983; Klein 2014). It is difficult for consumers to evaluate the financial condition of insurers as well as under-stand the coverages they offer. Hence, in the absence of regulatory controls, consumers could be misled into buying insurance policies from companies that were in poor financial condition and would be vulnerable to abusive trade practices.[3] Further, there may be negative externalities associated with excessive insurer insolvency risk as the costs of unpaid claims from insurer defaults may be shifted beyond their policyholders to their creditors (Saunders and Cornett 2003).

Regulation, properly structured and implemented, can remedy or ame-liorate these market failures by requiring all insurers to meet laws and regu-lations governing their financial condition and risk along with their market conduct. Solvency regulation should be principally aimed at limiting insur-ers' risk of insolvency and intervening when they encounter financial distress. Market conduct regulation should seek to ensure that insurers do not take unfair advantage of consumers in their marketing, products, pricing, underwriting, and claims adjustment. Hence, in theory, insurance regulation should improve the functioning of insurance markets, which in turn, should contribute to more efficient risk management. However, when regulators pursue other objectives such as imposing tight constraints on insurers' prices in an attempt to make coverage more "affordable," significant problems can result.

The Political Economy of Insurance Regulation

A long strain of scholarship on regulatory behavior is pertinent to the political economy of the regulation of insurance markets subject to catastrophe risk. A seminal work in this strain was written by Stigler (1971), who postulated a theory of economic regulation in which the concentrated interests of firms tend to prevail over the diffused interests of consumers in the transfer of wealth through regulation. Peltzman (1976) subsequently generalized Stigler's model to allow for the regulatory bias between consumers and firms to vary depending upon cost and demand conditions and the relative political sensitivities of consumers to prices and firms to profits.

Political scientists have extended the work of economists in developing constructs that consider a broader range of factors that can influence regulatory behavior.[4] Meier (1985) postulated a multidimensional model in which regulatory policy is influenced by various actors—industry groups, consumer groups, regulatory agencies, and political elites—and then applied this construct to insurance regulation (Meier 1988). The saliency and complexity of regulatory issues also affect the ability of these different actors to affect public policy, according to Meier. Greater complexity tends to increase the influence of those with expertise (e.g., the regulated firms), while greater saliency attracts consumer attention and the intervention of political elites.

Insights can be drawn from this literature that can help us better understand the forces that influence regulatory policies and decisions in insurance markets subject to catastrophe risk.[5] Clearly, various interest groups can be affected by how insurance companies and markets are regulated in the presence of catastrophe risk. In the case of homeowners insurance, these interest groups include homeowners, insurance companies, insurance agents, developers and builders, realtors, and other parties affected by the cost and availability of insurance. The greater and more concentrated the economic interests of a particular group are, the more influence it would be expected to assert in the regulatory process, all other things equal.

Insurance companies, insurance agents, developers and builders, and realtors, among other groups, should have strong and concentrated interests in how homeowners insurance is regulated in hurricane-prone states. Working through their respective trade associations, these groups would be expected to heavily lobby legislators and regulators to adopt policies that most favor their particular interests. The fact that the interests of these groups conflict makes this situation more complex. Presumably, insurance companies will seek to minimize regulatory interference with their activities, while certain other groups would be expected to pressure regulators to adopt measures that they believe will lower the cost and increase the availability of insurance. It is difficult to predict which side will exert greater influence over regulators in a particular state without examining the specific circumstances in that state which go beyond the relative strengths of the competing interest groups.

Among the other relevant factors that may influence regulators' behavior is the complexity and saliency of the issues involved with catastrophe insurance. Arguably, many aspects of insurers' activities are complex and more so when they are exposed to catastrophe losses. For example, the pricing of homeowners insurance in areas subject to hurricanes requires the use of catastrophe models that require considerable technical expertise to evaluate. One might infer from Meier's model of regulatory behavior that such complexity should tend to favor insurers in getting their rates approved, but such an inference would be too simplistic. Over time, regulators have greatly increased their understanding of how these models work. This development, coupled with the fact that model results are highly sensitive to the inputs and assumptions that are used, enable regulators to question the use of a particular model by an insurer that justifies higher rates than that preferred by regulators.

Issues concerning homeowners insurance can also become very salient for consumers in catastrophe-prone areas. Understandably, high insurance premiums can be very disconcerting to homeowners, particularly if they believe their premiums greatly exceed what they believe would be reasonable. Other aspects of insurers' activities such as policy nonrenewals and claims settlements following a catastrophe also can generate considerable discontent. Elected and appointed officials are aware of consumers' concerns and likely feel political pressure to demonstrate that they are doing something to alleviate consumers' pain. Such pressure can push regulators into efforts to lower the price and secure the availability of insurance, as well as take other actions that the public will view as proconsumer. It also could be argued that the information problems that cause people to underestimate catastrophic risks contribute to their perception that homeowners insurance premiums are excessive.[6] This is another factor that could further pressure regulators to constrain insurers' rates and other actions that consumers object to.

In sum, a number of factors can influence the regulation of insurance companies and markets. These factors can cause actual regulatory policies and decisions to diverge from those that economists would argue would promote the most efficient market outcomes. While legislators and regulators might otherwise act in a manner that they believe is most consistent with the public interest, under certain circumstances they must also deal with pressures exerted by interest groups and consumers. Further, what legislators and regulators believe is in the public interest will be subject to their own perceptions and biases in processing mounds of information on complex issues. Understanding the political economy of insurance regulation is critical to understanding why certain regulatory policies are suboptimal and create market distortions.

The Pricing and Underwriting of Insurance

Insurance rates must adhere to regulatory standards in every state; specifically, rates must be adequate, not excessive, and not unfairly discriminatory (Klein 2014). How the regulators in each state interpret and apply these standards varies by state and line of insurance. In a competitive market, insurers would be expected to charge prices that are risk based and no higher than necessary to cover their costs of providing coverage, including their cost of capital (Born and Klein 2015). In areas where there is substantial exposure to catastrophe losses, the cost of risk will be high and this will compel insurers to charge high premiums commensurate with the risk. This can lead to sharp disputes between insurers and regulators over what constitutes adequate but not excessive nor unfairly discriminatory rates (Grace and Klein 2009; Kunreuther et al. 2011). Regulators are much more inclined to attempt to constrain insurers' rates for high-risk areas than low-risk areas. This inclination can be attributed to several factors, including political pressure from homeowners and other affected parties, and regulators' concerns with respect to the affordability of insurance.

Regulators' attempts to constrain insurers' rates cause several problems. Insurers may be willing to accept a "minor" degree of rate inadequacy for a period of time, but severe regulatory rate caps will force insurers into compensating actions (Born et al. 2018). What typically happens is that insurers subject to tight constraints on their rates will no longer be willing to provide coverage for homes for which the premiums they are allowed to charge are substantially below what it costs to insure these homes. This could affect an insurance market in several ways. To the extent that large, well-capitalized, and broadly diversified insurers tighten their underwriting standards and reduce the number of homes they cover, this could result in a shift of homes from these companies to smaller companies with less capital and that are less diversified. Owners of homes that cannot find any insurer that will cover them in the voluntary market will be forced to secure coverage in their state's residual market mechanism (RMM).

Insurers may also tighten their coverage provisions and claims adjustment, but there are limits to what they can do in these areas. Regulators will not allow insurers to significantly reduce the coverage provided by their policies, and insurers are bound by law, regulation, and their own ethics to offer fair claim settlements. This said, insurers may still find ways to reduce the coverage they offer as well as the amounts they pay in claim settlements within the bounds of regulation and law.[7] Additionally, insurers subject to tight constraints on their pricing and underwriting in a state may elect to hold less capital and/or purchase less reinsurance (Klein et al. 2002). This increases the likelihood that some insurers will become insolvent and be unable to meet their claims obligations in the event of one or more severe catastrophes.

Hence, one primary distortion that can be created by severe regulatory constraints on insurance prices is a substantial reduction in the supply of insurance and the shift of homes from the private market into RMMs (Born and Klein 2015; Born et al. 2018). This increases moral hazard when residual markets rates are also inadequate; that is, incentives for the insured to reduce their exposure to catastrophe losses are diminished when they do not pay the full cost of their coverage.[8] The other potential effects of severe regulatory constraints on insurers' prices will effectively reduce the amount or the quality of coverage for insureds. Ultimately, these distortions undermine the objective of efficient risk management, as private insurance markets are not allowed to function properly, high-risk insureds pay inadequate rates, and incentives for the insured to reduce their risk are compromised, resulting in higher catastrophe losses. Further, reductions in the adequacy or quality of coverage could result in more uninsured losses. The effects of rate regulation on homeowners insurance markets is an area that warrants further research.[9]

The states also regulate insurers' ability to use their discretion in accepting new insurance applications or renewing existing policies. Regulators may constrain insurers' preferred actions in this area by limiting the criteria they can use in underwriting or interfering with insurers' attempts to reduce their portfolios of exposures to more manageable levels. For the most part, such restrictions have not been excessive; however, there have been instances where states have imposed restrictions that are more problematic.[10] For example, Florida prohibited insurers from cancelling or not renewing insurance policies from February until May of 2007 and dropping insureds during the "hurricane season" which started on June 1 and ended on November 30, 2007. Beginning in 2008, insurers that sold homeowners insurance in other states were also required to offer it in Florida in order to be allowed to sell other lines of insurance in the state. These restrictions are no longer in place but they illustrate how severe market pressures can result in regulatory constraints on insurers' underwriting that can be problematic.

Policy Provisions

The specific provisions of homeowners insurance policies and their regulation also warrant some discussion. The most significant development following Hurricane Andrew in 1992 was the introduction of specific or "named" windstorm or hurricane deductibles that are higher than the deductibles for other perils. Windstorm/hurricane deductibles can be stated in dollar amounts but the more common approach is to set them as a percentage of the Coverage A (dwelling) limit on a homeowner's multiperil policy. Currently, insurers have mandated or offered higher optional percentage windstorm/hurricane deductibles that range from 1% to 5%, usually with options to buy back broader coverage for an additional premium.[11] Some states allow insurers to offer higher optional windstorm/hurricane deductibles that can range from 5% to 15%.

Depending on a state's law, an insurer may impose a mandatory windstorm/hurricane deductible or a mandatory standard deductible on policyholders in higher risk areas of a state. Higher deductibles allow insurers to better manage their catastrophe risk exposure and losses and also allow homeowners to lower their premiums by accepting higher deductibles.

Windstorm/hurricane deductibles also provide greater risk-sharing between insurers and insureds that increase insureds' incentives to mitigate their exposure. There is the danger, however, that some homeowners might opt for or be forced to accept deductibles higher than the amount they could afford to cover out-of-pocket.

State laws and regulations vary with respect to the size of the windstorm/ hurricane deductibles that insurers either are allowed to offer or require as a condition for providing coverage (Insurance Information Institute 2018a). Although it is understandable that very large optional or mandatory deductibles could be problematic in terms of exposing homeowners to a high amount of retained losses, low regulatory limits on deductibles undermine the supply of insurance and/or require homeowners to pay significantly higher premiums because they are not allowed to opt for higher deductibles than those permitted by law. Additionally, arbitrary limits on deductibles inhibit risk-sharing between insureds and insurers and increase moral hazard.[12]

Issues also arise with respect to insurers' inclusion of anti-concurrent causation (ACC) clauses in their policies. Under an ACC clause, "if an excluded peril contributes directly or indirectly to cause a loss, then coverage is excluded regardless of any other cause or event that contributes concurrently or in any sequence to the loss" (Krekstein and McGowan 2014). For example, under a homeowners insurance policy, if damage to a home is caused by a covered peril, such as wind, and an excluded peril, such as flood, then none of the damage may be covered under the policy. When damage is caused by a covered peril and an excluded peril, the application of an ACC clause essentially hinges on the identification of a "loss." If it is possible to identify damage solely caused by a covered peril then, in theory, that damage should be covered, and the damage that is attributed to the excluded peril would not be covered. However, for many claims, it may be difficult to distinguish the damage caused by covered and excluded perils. In such a situation, the insured typically carries the burden of proof in segregating the damage caused by the covered peril.

Insurers' application of ACC provisions became a matter of significant debate and litigation following Hurricane Katrina in 2005, when many homes suffered losses from both wind and flooding (Kunreuther et al. 2011). These provisions also led to considerable consternation and litigation following Superstorm Sandy in 2012, for which damage caused by flooding was much greater than the damage caused by wind.[13] While the courts have generally upheld insurers' application of their ACC clauses, there have been legislative attempts, albeit unsuccessful to date, to prohibit their use.[14] Nonetheless, at the very least, litigation to overturn insurers' use of ACC provisions in their policies creates uncertainty with respect to what their claims obligations will be following an event with substantial losses arising from a noncovered peril. Insurers base their pricing on the provisions of their policies, and when there is uncertainty about whether these provisions will be upheld, insurers would be expected to respond by increasing their prices and/or insuring fewer homes where coverage disputes may arise.[15]

Hence, outright legislative prohibition of the use of ACC provisions, while appearing to be beneficial to policyholders, would necessarily increase the cost of their coverage and could also reduce the availability of coverage. There is no ideal solution for this issue. Including the flood peril in home-owners insurance policies might seem to some to be a good way to help solve this problem, but is probably not realistic.[16] Alternatively, much stronger efforts could be made to increase the purchase of flood insurance by homeowners in high- and moderate-risk areas. Such efforts could encompass both voluntary and coercive measures. The latter would likely encounter significant political resistance but still warrant consideration, given the alternatives.

Residual Market Mechanisms

There are three basic types of residual market mechanisms that are used for property insurance subject to catastrophic risk: (1) Fair Access to Insurance plans; (2) wind/beach plans; and (3) government-sponsored insurers (Klein 2009).[17] While these mechanisms may serve as short-term safety valves in the event of disruptions in the supply of private insurance, they are generally not intended to serve as long-term sources of coverage for a substantial portion of a state's property exposures.[18] For this reason, most states seek to properly structure and manage these mechanisms and minimize their size by retain-ing or moving as many exposures in or to voluntary markets as possible. Beyond efforts to maximize the supply of voluntary insurance, measures aimed at keeping policies out of the residual market include maintaining re-sidual market rates above voluntary market rates and imposing stringent rules with respect to who is allowed to obtain insurance from the residual market.[19] Efforts to move policies out of the residual market include "take-out" incentives for private insurers, and programs designed to match resid-ual market policyholders with private insurers that are willing to cover them.

Proper administration of RMMs also is important. To that end, a well-managed RMM will charge adequate rates to cover the loss exposures that it insures and will also purchase adequate reinsurance to diversify its exposure to catastrophic losses. Historically, some RMMs failed to employ such measures and, consequently, incurred substantial deficits when they incurred high hurricane losses (Klein 2009). In such instances, insurers are charged assessments to pay for the deficits, most of which they are allowed to pass on to their policyholders. At the very least, these assessments constitute a cross subsidy between voluntary market insureds and RMM insureds. The amount of assessments that insurers are not allowed to pass on to their policyholders must be funded out of their premiums and surplus. This can further chill insurers' willingness to write business on a voluntary basis and increase the size of the residual market, all other things equal.

Florida offers an interesting case study of how it has approached its voluntary market vis-à-vis its RMMs. Florida has been subject to significant market pressure since Hurricane Andrew in 1992, which rose to a much higher level with the 2004–2005 storm seasons. The number of policies in Florida's RMMs spiked precipitously following Hurricane Andrew to 1.403 million in 1996 and then fell to 383,756 by 2001. In 2002, with the creation of the Citizens Property Insurance Corporation of Florida, the number of residual market policies in Florida rose to 685,058 and ultimately increased to an unprecedented level of 1.483 million as of November 30, 2011. Florida's regulatory constraints on private insurers as well as certain actions it took with respect to how Citizens was administered contributed significantly to the growth in its residual market. These actions included allowing homeowners to purchase a Citizens policy if a comparable policy would cost 15% more or higher in the voluntary market, and rolling back Citizens' rates.

In 2009, the Florida legislature began contemplating changes to how Citizens was administered to reduce its size to a more sustainable level. Its rates were subsequently increased and an aggressive depopulation effort was initiated, among other measures. As of July 31, 2018, the Citizens policy count had fallen to 443,204.[20] However, it should be noted that certain aspects of this depopulation initiative have been controversial. Specifically, single-state startup companies have been allowed to select policies they wish to take out of Citizens, and the owners of these policies are required to file a form with Citizens in order to avoid being placed with the company that has selected them. Concerns have been raised that some of the take-out companies will lack sufficient capacity to meet their claims obligations when one or more hurricanes strike the state; the basis for these concerns is discussed below (Hurtibise 2016).

The primary takeaway from this discussion is that regulatory interference with voluntary insurance markets coupled with the mismanagement of RMMs can result in significant underpricing of high-risk properties that can distort insureds' incentives to undertake cost-effective hazard mitigation, resulting in higher than necessary losses when catastrophes occur. This illustrates the interconnection between the various aspects of insurance regulation in determining market outcomes.

Solvency

Catastrophes can pose a significant threat to an insurance company's solvency. High catastrophe losses can push an insurer into financial distress and potentially into bankruptcy. According to a study by A. M. Best (2011), the primary cause of approximately 7% of property/casualty insurer insolvencies occurring over the period 1969–2010 was catastrophes. Nine insurers failed due to Hurricane Andrew and four insurers failed due to losses they incurred from the 2004–2005 hurricane seasons.[21] Consequently, an important element of an insurer's financial management is properly managing its catastrophe risk. This includes charging adequate rates, avoiding high concentrations of exposure in an any given geographic area, holding adequate capital, and purchasing adequate amounts of catastrophe reinsurance and using other financial diversification instruments (e.g., catastrophe bonds), among other measures.

Regulators have the responsibility of ensuring that insurers have adequate catastrophe risk management programs in place. Regulators must have the technical expertise and resources necessary to properly evaluate insurers' catastrophe risk management and be attuned to insurers who may attempt to "game the system." An insurer can be enticed into a strategy of maximizing short-term profits at the expense of their long-term viability. Insurance premiums for catastrophe-exposed properties include a provision for catastrophe losses that can be substantial for properties in high-risk areas. The revenues generated from this provision during periods when there are no hurricanes should be used to bolster an insurer's capital as well as purchase reinsurance. However, there is also the temptation to misappropriate these funds, which can be siphoned off as upstream dividends to parent companies and owners and/or through excessive fees paid to managing general agents. An insurer who employs this strategy will seek to minimize the amount of capital retained within the company, as this capital will be lost when the company becomes insolvent due to one or more catastrophes. In essence, this could be viewed as a form of gambling or using something akin to a put option, where an insurer reaps the upside for as long as there are no catastrophes and most of the downside is effectively transferred to states' guaranty associations and unsecured creditors.[22]

An illustration of this strategy is what happened with the Poe companies in Florida (Grace and Klein 2009). There were three insurance companies within the Poe group that insured a large number of homes in coastal areas of Florida with insufficient capital and reinsurance. As a consequence of the 2004 storm season, the Poe group incurred substantial losses. Rather than scaling back its exposures, Poe did the opposite and increased its exposures in 2005 in hopes of eventually "winning back" the money it had lost. This strategy backfired when Poe was subsequently driven into insolvency due to the additional losses it incurred from 2005 hurricanes.[23] The resulting hit to Florida's guaranty association alone was close to $1 billion.

Arguably, there was a significant regulatory failure here. If Poe had been subject to proper supervision, then it would not have been allowed to place itself in such a precarious financial position. The Florida Office of Insurance Regulation has since tightened its financial regulation of insurance and appears to be strengthening its procedures in reviewing and approving insurers' catastrophe risk management plans. Nonetheless, some observers have expressed a concern that there are more "Poe disasters" waiting to happen.

After Hurricane Andrew in 1992, Florida has been aggressive in encouraging new companies to enter its property insurance markets to assume policies that had been dropped by other insurers and to stem the growth in its RMMs. This activity accelerated after the 2004–2005 storm seasons. Many of the new entrants are "start-up" companies, formed in Florida and only writing business in Florida (Born and Klein 2015). Hence, they do not have the geographic diversification of the large national and regional companies and they hold relatively small amounts of capital. To remain viable, such companies must be very careful in their pricing and underwriting and buy significant amounts of reinsurance. This is likely the case with most of these companies. However, as noted above, there is a concern that at least a few of these companies are at high risk of becoming insolvent as more hurricanes strike Florida.[24]

This illustrates the tension between the regulatory objectives of limiting insolvency risk and promoting the availability and affordability of insurance coverage. Regulators should seek to achieve a proper balance of the tradeoffs associated with these two objectives. Relaxing solvency requirements can be tempting when insurance markets are subject to substantial cost pressure due to catastrophe risk. The "benefits" of relaxed solvency requirements are quickly realized, while its costs do not become apparent until catastrophes strike.

Concluding Thoughts

Insurance plays an important role in the management of many risks. Efficient insurance markets contribute to more efficient risk management. Regulation can play a constructive role in improving how insurance markets function but it can also undermine market efficiency. Reasonable and appropriate regulatory policies aimed at limiting insurers' insolvency risk and protecting consumers against abusive trade practices should help insurance markets work better. On the other hand, when regulators seek to impose outcomes that are different from what would occur in a competitive market, significant disruptions can occur.

Catastrophe risk can create circumstances that will induce regulators to adopt policies that diverge from what would be optimal. Regulatory biases coupled with pressure from certain interest groups and consumers can cause regulators to attempt to artificially lower the price of insurance, impose cross subsidies, and increase the availability of coverage in ways that are counterproductive. More specifically, problems tend to occur when regulators impose arbitrary caps on prices, interfere with insurers' underwriting, prohibit or limit certain policy provisions, mismanage residual market mechanisms, and fail to properly supervise insurers' catastrophe risk management. The adverse consequences of such policies include a reduced supply of insurance coverage and diminished incentives for cost-effective hazard mitigation.

While this chapter focuses on the regulation of insurance markets subject to hurricane risk, similar issues could arise in the future with respect to earthquake and flood insurance. In recent years, earthquake insurance (and its regulation) has not received much attention. This is likely due to that fact that homeowners generally are not required to have earthquake coverage as a condition for obtaining a mortgage and only a small proportion of homeowners buy it.[25] In high-risk areas, earthquake insurance is viewed as greatly overpriced relative to the coverage that is provided (Jaffee 2015b). If lenders were to change their policies and attempt to require mortgage holders to have earthquake insurance, this would likely encounter substantial opposition and raise familiar issues with respect to how earthquake insurance is regulated.

Currently in the United States, flood insurance at a primary level has been underwritten mostly by the National Flood Insurance Program. Although there has been considerable discussion of "privatizing" flood insurance, such a move faces a number of issues. Beyond the issue of whether insurers would be comfortable with adding substantial flood risk to their portfolios, there is the issue of how private flood insurance would be regulated. Insurers would understandably be concerned that they could be subject to the same kinds of regulatory constraints as they face in offering wind coverage for hurricanes in offering flood policies that would provide coverage similar to that currently provided by the NFIP.

There have been several legislative attempts in Congress to facilitate the sale of private flood insurance. Most recently, the House passed H.R. 2874—the 21st Century Flood Reform Act (FRA)—on November 14, 2017, against bipartisan opposition.[26] This bill would enable private insurers to sell policies that could differ significantly from NFIP policies, for example, policies with much higher deductibles. Government-sponsored enterprises (GSEs) and federal agency lenders would be required to accept policies approved by state regulators as an alternative to NFIP policies. While the legislation could make it much more feasible for private insurers to offer flood insurance at prices substantially below those charged by the NFIP in many areas, several groups have expressed concerns that some homeowners would purchase policies with inadequate coverage (see, for example, Consumer Mortgage Coalition 2016).[27] This said, even without legislative help from the Congress, in recent years insurance companies (including non-admitted or surplus lines carriers) have increased their sales of flood insurance underwritten on their "own paper."[28]

There are opportunities for further research that would increase our understanding of the issues involved with catastrophe insurance and its regulation and potential measures that could be employed to address these issues. Further empirical research is needed on the effects of varying regulatory policies on insurance markets affected by catastrophe risk. While there have been a number of case studies in specific states related to this topic, significant insights could be drawn from more analysis across all states for extended periods of time with more refined measures of regulatory policies.[29] More specifically, we need to identify those policies that promote efficient market outcomes and address the problems created by catastrophe risk in a constructive manner, as well as those policies that do more harm than good.

There also is a need for further research on strategies and devices that could help to overcome the informational and behavioral biases that lead property owners to make suboptimal decisions with respect to purchasing insurance and investing in risk mitigation. Such research could be augmented by the development of innovations in the mechanisms available to finance and mitigate catastrophe risk. While such work would not address regulation per se, it could help to alleviate some of the pressures that lead to inefficient regulations.

Finally, we need to develop a much better understanding of the political economy of the regulation of catastrophe insurance. Enhancing our comprehension of the regulatory decision-making process and the factors that affect that process could establish a foundation for developing strategies to promote the adoption of more efficient policies under difficult political and economic conditions. There is also need to gain a better understanding of how insurers navigate and respond to difficult regulatory environments.

The insights drawn from additional research in these areas could be used to advise policymakers on what would constitute best regulatory practices for insurance markets subject to catastrophic risk and how to marshal the political support needed to adopt and implement such practices. The ultimate goal should be the achievement of regulatory policies that promote healthy insurance markets and effective management of catastrophic risks. Social welfare is enhanced when regulation is structured and implemented to enable insurance markets to function as well as possible so that they may provide an efficient source of financing for losses arising from catastrophic events as well as encourage property owners to invest in cost-effective risk mitigation measures.

Notes

1. By November 2011, the number of policies insured by Citizens had grown to 1.483 million—the highest number of policies it had insured in its history.

2. As discussed below, the concern with the single-state companies is that some of these insurers may be at substantial risk of becoming insolvent if they incur large losses from one or

more hurricanes. The substantial growth in Citizens moved Florida legislators to make significant changes in its structure and administration to shift policies back to the private market. Single-state companies have assumed most of these policies.

3. Abusive trade practices could include insurers selling policies with substantial gaps in coverage, the misrepresentation of the insurance policies sold, and insurers failing to pay legitimate claims.

4. Born et al. (2018) provide a more detailed review of the literature on the political economy of insurance regulation.

5. See also Jaffee (2015a, 2015b) for a discussion of how political and economic considerations can affect government intervention in catastrophe insurance markets.

6. Kunreuther (2015) provides a good summary of the literature pertaining to why people tend to underestimate catastrophic risks and also discusses why they tend to underinvest in hazard mitigation. See also Kunreuther, Meyer, and Michel-Kerjan (2013).

7. An insurer is bound by the provisions of its contracts, but this said, they do exercise some discretion in how they adjust and settle claims. For example, in homeowners insurance, insurers may decide to be "less generous" in accepting contractors' estimates for repairs to a home and/or be more rigorous in applying coverage exclusions.

8. Danzon and Harrington (2001) find evidence of the moral hazard effect of excessive rate regulation in workers compensation insurance. Derrig and Tennyson (2011) also find that regulatory caps on auto insurance rates for high-risk drivers increase loss costs.

9. To date, there have been only two published studies of homeowners insurance rate regulation that employ an econometric analysis of pooled cross-sectional data for all states over an extended time period: Born and Klimaszewski-Blettner (2013) and Born and Klein (2015, 2016); the two Born and Klein publications utilize the same econometric analysis. Both studies use a simple measure of rate regulation, specifically whether a state has a prior-approval or a competitive rating system. Born and Klein (2016) and Born et al. (2018) discuss the limitations of this approach and the interest in developing more refined measures of the degree of rate regulatory environment in each state.

10. It is common for states to issue short-term moratoriums (e.g., 90 days) on policy cancellations and nonrenewals following a hurricane.

11. Currently, 19 states and the District of Columbia allow the use of hurricane deductibles (Insurance Information Institute 2018a).

12. There may be future innovations in insurance policies that cover catastrophic risks to which regulators should give fair consideration. An example of such an innovation would be the issuance of fixed-price multiyear insurance contracts, as proposed by Kunreuther and Michel-Kerjan (2015).

13. It is reasonable to surmise that there are disputes over claim settlements arising from damages stemming from Hurricane Harvey due to insurers' application of the ACC clauses in their homeowners policies. This would be expected to occur in areas of Texas where there was substantial damage due to both wind and flooding.

14. To date, the courts in only four states—California, North Dakota, Washington, and West Virginia—have refused to uphold ACC clauses (Krekstein and McGowan 2014).

15. The actions of the Mississippi attorney general to force companies to settle their customers' property insurance claims despite the flood exclusion ultimately resulted in State Farm's decision to withdraw from the state.

16. It would be reasonable to expect that any proposal to automatically include flood risk as a covered peril in standard homeowners insurance policies would face strong resistance from the insurance industry and potentially many homeowners who would object to the associated increase in the cost of their homeowners insurance coverage.

17. There are currently three such insurers: the Citizens Property Insurance Corporation of Florida, Louisiana Citizens Property Insurance Corporation, and the California Earthquake Authority.

18. Even in times when there is an ample supply of insurance in the voluntary market, there may be some properties that meet minimum insurability conditions but are unable to secure voluntary market coverage. Hence, it is common for these mechanisms to insure a relatively small number of homes for extended periods.

19. An example of such a rule is the requirement that a homeowner applying for insurance coverage from an RMM must show one or more declinations from voluntary market insurers.

20. Information on Citizens is available at https://www.citizensfla.com/.

21. Two insurance companies also became insolvent due to their losses from Hurricane Iniki in 1992.

22. Every state has a property/casualty guaranty association that covers some of the claims of insolvent insurers. Homeowners insurance claims are included in guaranty association coverage.

23. At the time when the Poe group was seized by Florida regulators in 2006, it was the second largest homeowners insurer in the state after Citizens, with 320,000 policyholders primarily concentrated along the southeast and southwest coasts.

24. It should be noted that 14 of the companies that were formed after 2005 to take policies out of Citizens have become insolvent even though no major hurricanes struck the state after 2005 until Hurricane Irma in 2017. Despite causing widespread wind damage in Florida (total claims estimated to be $10.5 billion by the Florida Office of Insurance Regulation as of October 13, 2018), no insurance company insolvencies have been attributed to Irma.

25. It is estimated that only 10% of California homeowners also buy earthquake insurance (Insurance Information Institute 2018b).

26. The text of this bill is available at https://www.congress.gov/bill/115th-congress/house-bill/2874/text.

27. The legislation would also enable surplus lines (non-admitted) insurers to sell private flood policies in states that would allow this. Surplus lines insurers are typically subject to much less regulation than licensed insurers and their policyholders are not protected by state guaranty associations if the insurers become insolvent. Among the concerns raised is that some homeowners with these alternative private flood policies could be stuck with large amounts of uninsured losses in the event of a severe flood, leading to greater demands for federal disaster assistance as well as a spike in mortgage defaults.

28. In 2017, direct premiums written for private flood insurance were $570.2 million. For 2016, this figure was $356.6 million. These figures do not include premiums for private flood insurance written by non-licensed companies that do not file their data with National Association of Insurance Commissioners. A recent study by Kousky et al. (2018) examines the developing market for private residential flood insurance.

29. Born et al. (2018) examine the effects of varying degrees of rate regulatory stringency on insurers' loss ratios for homeowners insurance. They found that, in the year following a

catastrophe, more stringent regulation increased insurers' loss ratios. Further research is needed to determine how more stringent regulation affects other aspects of structure, conduct, and performance in homeowners insurance markets.

References

A. M. Best. (2011). *Special report: U.S. property/casualty, 1969–2010 impairment review.* Oldwick, NJ: A. M. Best.

Born, P., Karl, J., & Klein, R. W. (2018). Does state rate regulation matter? An assessment of more stringent regulation on insurers' performance in homeowners insurance. Retrieved from https://papers.ssrn.com/sol3/papers.cfm?abstract_id=3288760

Born, P. & Klein, R. W. (2015). *Best practices for regulating property insurance premiums and managing natural catastrophe risk in the United States* (Issue analysis paper). Indianapolis, IN: National Association of Mutual Insurance Companies.

Born, P., & Klein, R. W. (2016). *Catastrophe risk and the regulation of property insurance markets.* Retrieved from https://papers.ssrn.com/sol3/papers.cfm?abstract_id=2782834

Born, P. H., & Klimaszewski-Blettner, B. (2013). Should I stay or should I go? The impact of natural disasters and regulation on U.S. property insurers' supply decisions. *Journal of Risk and Insurance, 80*(1), 1–36.

Consumer Mortgage Coalition. (2016, June 30). *No more hikes: Small business survival amidst unaffordable flood insurance rate increases.* Testimony before the Senate Committee on Small Business and Entrepreneurship. Retrieved from http://www.consumermortgage coalition.org/fullpanel/uploads/files/cmc-flood-insurance-testimony—06-30-16-.pdf

Danzon, P. M., & Harrington, S. E. (2001). Workers' compensation rate regulation: How price controls increase costs. *Journal of Law and Economics, 44*(1), 1–36.

Derrig, R. A., & Tennyson, S. (2011). The impact of rate regulation on claims: Evidence from Massachusetts automobile insurance. *Risk Management and Insurance Review, 14*(2), 173–199.

Grace, M. F., & Klein, R. W. (2009). The perfect storm: Hurricanes, insurance, and regulation. *Risk Management and Insurance Review, 12*(1), 81–124.

Hurtibise, R. (2016, September 26). Citizens streamlines takeout notification and opt-out process. *SunSentinel.* Retrieved from http://www.sun-sentinel.com/business/consumer/fl -citizens-board-of-governors-20160928-story.html#

Insurance Information Institute. (2018a, June 25). Hurricane and windstorm deductibles. Retrieved from https://www.iii.org/article/background-on-hurricane-and-windstorm -deductibles

Insurance Information Institute. (2018b, September 2). Facts + Statistics: Earthquakes and tsunamis. Retrieved from https://www.iii.org/fact-statistic/facts-statistics-earthquakes -and-tsunamis#Earthquake insurance

Jaffee, D. M. (2015a). Catastrophe insurance. In D. Schwarcz, & P. Siegelman, (Eds.), *Research handbook on the economics of insurance law* (pp. 160–189). Northampton, MA: Edward Elgar.

Jaffee, D. M. (2015b). *Insurance risks and government intervention* (draft conference paper). Retrieved from http://opim.wharton.upenn.edu/risk/conference/pprs/Jaffee_Insurance -Risks-and-Government-Interventions.pdf

Klein, R. W. (2009). *Hurricane risk and residual market mechanisms.* Retrieved from http:// opim.wharton.upenn.edu/risk/library/2009-05-29Klein_ResidualMkt.pdf

Klein, R.W. (2014). *An introduction to the insurance industry and its regulation.* Kansas City: National Association of Insurance Commissioners.

Klein, R. W., Phillips, R. D., & Shiu, W. (2002). The capital structure of firms subject to price regulation: Evidence from the insurance industry. *Journal of Financial Services Research, 21*(1/2), 79–100.

Krekstein, W. & McGowan, E. (2014, February). Anti-concurrent causation clauses in property policies. *Property Matters.* Gen Re Research.

Kousky, C., Kunreuther, H. C., Lingle, B., & Shabman, L. (2018). *The emerging private residential flood insurance market in the United States.* Wharton School of Business, University of Pennsylvania. Retrieved from http://d1c25a6gwz7q5e.cloudfront.net/reports/07-13-18 -Emerging%20Flood%20Insurance%20Market%20Report.pdf

Kunreuther, H. C. (2015). *The role of insurance in risk management for natural disasters: Back to the future.* Wharton School of Business, University of Pennsylvania. Retrieved from http://opim.wharton.upenn.edu/risk/conference/pprs/Kunreuther_Role-of-Insurance -in-Risk-Management.pdf

Kunreuther, H., Meyer, R., & Michel-Kerjan, E. (2013). Overcoming decision biases to reduce losses from natural catastrophes. In E. Shafir (Ed.), *The behavioral foundations of public policy* (pp. 398–413). Princeton, NJ: Princeton University Press.

Kunreuther, H., & Michel-Kerjan, E. (2015). Demand for fixed-price multi-year contracts: Experimental evidence from insurance decisions. *Journal of Risk and Uncertainty, 51*(2), 171–194.

Kunreuther, H. C., Michel-Kerjan, E. O., Doherty, N. A., Grace, M. F., Klein, R. W., & Pauly, M. V. (2011). *At war with the weather: Managing large-scale risks in a new era of catastrophes.* Cambridge, MA: MIT Press.

Meier, K. J. (1985). *Regulation: Politics, bureaucracy, and economics.* New York: Palgrave Macmillan.

Meier, K. J. (1988). *The political economy of regulation: The case of insurance.* New York: SUNY Press.

Munch, P., & Smallwood, D. E. (1983). Theory of solvency regulation in the property and casualty insurance industry. In G. Fromm (Ed.), *Studies in public regulation* (pp. 119–167). Boston: MIT Press.

Peltzman, S. (1976). Toward a more general theory of regulation. *Journal of Law and Economics, 19*(2), 211–240.

Saunders, A. & Cornett, M.M. (2003). *Financial institutions management: A risk management approach.* New York: McGraw-Hill.

Stigler, G. J. (1971). The theory of economic regulation. *Bell Journal of Economics and Management Science, 2*(1), 3–21.

CHAPTER 20

Rethinking Government Disaster Relief
in the United States

Evidence and a Way Forward

Erwann O. Michel-Kerjan

In the fall of 2015, the credit rating agency Standard & Poor (S&P) released its report *Storm alert: Natural disasters can damage sovereign creditworthiness*. Based on a sample of 48 countries, the analysis shows that significant natural disasters (earthquakes, tropical storms, floods, and winter storms), which can be expected once in every 250 years,[1] can weaken sovereign ratings. The top five catastrophes across countries, measured in damages as share of value, could lead to downgrades of around 1.5 notches for the sovereigns affected. In Japan, one of the largest economies in the world, the analysis shows that a 1-in-250-year event could cause a significant economic downturn and a decline in the sovereign rating by at least two notches, with potentially severe economic and financial repercussions for the rest of the world.[2]

The United States might seem to some immune to a downgrade resulting solely from a natural disaster hitting the country. Indeed, Hurricane Katrina in 2005 triggered nearly $150 billion in losses, but this amount—the largest of any disaster in recent U.S. history—represented "only" 1% of the nation's GDP (White House 2007). That said, a series of events happening over a year or so—a long predicted massive earthquake on the west coast combined with major droughts and destructive hurricanes—combined with U.S. looming national debt, could have a different impact.

Moreover, over time, disasters could have a significant impact on the U.S. economy and can have serious ripple effects as well as reconsideration of risk management needs (Michel-Kerjan 2015a). Across the United States as of 2010 there is nearly $10 trillion dollars of insured value located directly along the coastline from Texas to Maine. Much more exposure is *not* insured by either public or private insurance (Kunreuther et al. 2011). Cummins, Suher, and Zanjani (2010) show that the expected exposure of the U.S. government to natural and man-made disasters over the next 75 years could reach a staggering $7 trillion. According to the authors, this amount would be greater than the projected social security shortfall over the same period.

A downgrade of municipality bonds directly resulting from such an extreme event is most likely to occur, unless states and cities are systematically rescued by their general taxpayers. But is this really a sustainable public policy?

This concern is echoed internationally by presidents, prime ministers, and rulers about the exposure of governments to natural disasters and other extreme events. Losses for national governments resulting from major shocks that destroy public assets, lower tax revenues, and increase government-run insurance program claims and disaster relief for uninsured losses can be significant. This issue was put on the agenda of the G20 summit of the world's major economies in 2012 (for the first time, ever), recognizing that as disasters occur more frequently and cost more, we cannot continue to simply rely on governments and taxpayers to foot the bill again and again (Michel-Kerjan 2012; OECD 2012). Given that G20 countries represent two-thirds of the world population and 90% of the global economy, this was a significant admission.

Munich Re, the world's largest reinsurer, estimates that the frequency of what it calls "great natural disasters" has more than doubled from half a century ago. Higher concentrations of population and assets in high risks areas, combined with a changing climate triggering more intense climate disasters, have heralded a new era of catastrophes.

Natural disasters are a growing concern in many economies, as demonstrated by the results of the annual surveys of the World Economic Forum in their Global Risks reports (World Economic Forum 2015, 2016), which a group of us has helped design since their inception in 2004. Extreme weather events, for instance, have consistently ranked among the top five global risks that concern business and public policy leaders from around the world in recent years.

There is also growing concern about the financial protection gap: many households who are exposed to disaster risk are unprotected or not sufficiently protected financially. While the United States is the largest insurance market in the world, data on insurance penetration for flood risk or earthquake risks indicate that coverage still lags. For instance, 90% of residents in California are not insured against earthquake. And 80% of New York City residents in areas inundated by Superstorm Sandy in 2012 had no flood insurance, while 92% of small businesses had not purchased flood insurance, either (City of New York 2013), possibly because they assumed the government would bail them out. In a study we undertook in New York, we found that at least a third of the people there expected to receive such aid after a disaster (Botzen, Kunreuther, and Michel-Kerjan 2015). Expectation of disaster relief has increased in recent decades. For instance, seminal work by Kunreuther et al. in the 1970s showed that disaster relief was not a reason as to why people did not purchase disaster insurance back then (Kunreuther et al. 1978).

In this chapter I will highlight a few findings from recent research specific to disaster relief in the United States: (1) the U.S. federal government has become much more involved in disaster relief in recent years than ever before and the trend is growing, especially for large catastrophes; (2) contrary to what some might think, most of the money goes to local governments to rebuild public infrastructure, not to the victims themselves; (3) but even the relatively small amount going to uninsured victims creates a moral hazard situation: after receiving aid, on aggregate, individuals significantly reduce their demand for disaster insurance, which then results in higher need for future aid when the next disaster strikes. I will then make three proposals to move from the status quo.

A Fast-Growing Federal Disaster Relief Trend in the United States

Federal disaster relief has become a salient political economy issue as, in recent years, post-disaster government relief to aid the uninsured (individuals, businesses, and local governments) has risen to historic levels around the globe (Cummins and Mahul 2008; Moss 2010). In the United States, taxpayers paid $89 billion in relief in response to the 2005 hurricane season (2010 prices); that amount was more than private insurers paid for wind-related insured losses and what the federally run National Flood Insurance Program paid for flood insured losses, combined (Michel-Kerjan 2010). When Hurricane Sandy hit in 2012, Congress voted another $60 billion of appropriation.

Under the current disaster relief system, largely driven by the 1988 Stafford Act, the governor of an affected state can request that the president declare a "major disaster" and offer special assistance if the damage is severe enough. The Act then guarantees that *at least* 75% of the losses to public infrastructures and assets in the states will be paid by the federal government.[3] Depending on the disaster and political will, this portion can actually go higher.

A look at the number of major U.S. presidential disaster declarations from 1953 to 2015 clearly reveals an upward trend (see Figure 20.1, with a simple linear regression over time trend). In the 1950s and 1960s, the average number of such declarations was about 15 per year. But in recent years, that annual *average* was closer to 60 per year.[4] As one would expect with disasters, some years are more active than others. Notably though, as Figure 20.1 also shows, many (although not all) of the peak years correspond to presidential election years. This is consistent with recent research that has shown that election years are a very active time for disaster assistance (all other things being equal). Six salient examples are the Alaska earthquake in 1964 (a presidential election year), Tropical Storm Agnes[5] and the Rapid City Floods in June 1972, Hurricane Andrew in September 1992, the four hurricanes in 2004, and Hurricane Sandy, which occurred just days before election day in 2012. In 1996 and 2008 (both presidential election years), there were 75 presidential declarations. This record number was exceeded in 2010 when there were 81 major disaster declarations, and again in 2011 with 99 declarations. Figure 20.1 also depicts a linear trend over this 1953–2015 period.

This up-trend is a remarkable change over the history of the country. Indeed, Congress provided assistance to the victims of a major fire in New Hampshire as early as 1803, but disaster relief was not generally viewed as an ongoing federal responsibility in the United States until well into the twentieth century.

In fact, there were only 128 specific acts of Congress providing ad hoc relief for the victims of various disasters over the years 1803 to 1947 (Moss 2010). That is 128 times in 144 years . . . or less than once a year on average. Nowadays it is once a week, if not more often (again, as an average over time).

Several explanations, not exclusive from each other, have been proposed. For one, as more people live in harm's way and do not protect adequately,

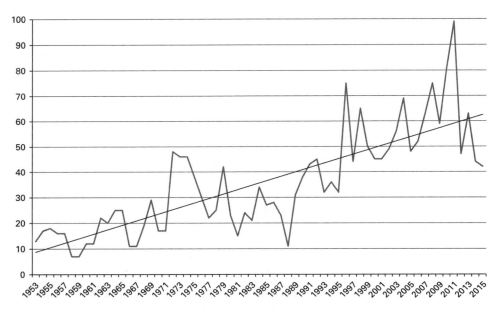

Figure 20.1. Major U.S. disaster presidential declarations per year, 1953–2015.

similar events have more devastating consequences. Consider natural disaster exposure in the United States. From 1970 to 2010, the population of coastal shoreline counties increased by 39%, and of coastal watershed counties by 45% (NOAA 2013). In 2010, 123 million people in the United States resided in counties directly on the shoreline (excluding Alaska), thus subjecting them to damage from floods and hurricanes. Slightly more than half of the total U.S. population lives in counties that drain to coastal watersheds, and are thus subject to flood and/or storm risks (164 million). This urbanization and dense population mean greater concentrations of assets and hence a higher likelihood of catastrophic losses from future disasters. Or consider California: 2016 was the fifth year in a row that the state declared a statewide drought.

Secondly, as shown by Moss (2010) and Eisensee and Strömberg (2007), increasing media coverage of disasters has played a critical role in increasing government relief in the United States over the past decades. Disasters have become media events, often watched live on television. As a result, they become immediate political events as well.

Experience shows that elected officials will have a hard time not being extremely generous when a disaster strikes. Media pressure to help the victims and immediate demand from their constituencies, along with empathy from the general public, are likely to be very high right after the disaster. Should elected officials opt not to provide relief, they run the risk of not being reelected. Irrespective of what political party is in power, not only is the number of presidential disaster declarations higher during election years (as noted above in Figure 20.1), but federal disaster payments are also significantly higher compared to non-election years (Garrett and Sobel 2003; Michel-Kerjan 2010). Four salient examples are the Alaska earthquake (March 1964) Tropical Storm Agnes (June 1972), Hurricane Andrew (September 1992) and the four Florida hurricanes (August–September 2004). In 1996 and 2008 (both presidential election years) there were 75 presidential declarations. The year 2012, another election year, is not associated with a large number of disaster declarations, but still over $60 billion of relief was voted, second only to the amount for Hurricane Katrina. Of note, the White House estimates that the federal government, across all agencies, spent about $105 billion on disaster relief between 2006 and 2015 (White House 2015). But this number needs to be considered along with additional supplemental appropriation, often given when large catastrophes occur. For instance, the supplemental appropriation following Hurricane Katrina in 2005 alone was for another $120 billion; appropriation for Hurricane Sandy in 2012 was $50 billion (Kousky and Shabman 2013).[6]

Finally, there is what I call the "precedents effect." Imagine a new administration has just taken office. Not only are there expectations when a severe and highly mediatized disaster strikes that relief is on the way, but in order to get maximum political reward for its action, the amount of relief that the new administration will push for most likely will be higher than that of the previous administrations for similar disasters.

This creates a spiral of ever-growing disaster relief, without accounting for the indirect consequences this can create, namely, lowering interest in pre-disaster risk reduction measures and insurance coverage, as I show in the next section of the chapter. And it is not just the number of declarations that has significantly increased over time, but also the proportion of federal disaster aid relative to total economic losses for large catastrophes (Michel-Kerjan 2013, 2015b). Figure 20.2 provides striking evidence from five large hurricanes,[7] starting with Hurricane Diane in 1955, for which the federal

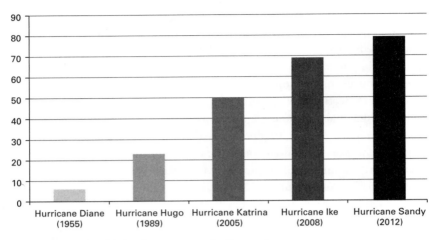

Figure 20.2. Role of federal government in disaster loss payment.

government provided roughly 6% of cost; up through Hurricane Sandy in 2012, when the government paid roughly 80%.[8]

Disaster relief and appropriation has typically not been balanced by budget cuts in other spending by the United States. Successive administrations, Democrat and Republican, finance this extra spending simply by increasing the public deficit. The national debt (that is, the amount owed by the U.S. federal government) is now surpassing $21 trillion, in part due to Katrina and Sandy and the resulting cost of more recent disasters.

The enlarged national deficit, of course, has long-term consequences; the ultimate cost of recovery will be even greater because of the cumulative interest on the additional indebtedness. It also means that future administrations will be less likely to undertake politically unpopular measures: the burden of the cost of recovery would be imposed on future taxpayers.

An interesting counterexample outside of the United States is Chile. In 2010, the country was hit by one of the most powerful earthquakes ever recorded on the planet, which destroyed about 18% of its gross domestic product (Katrina was "only" 1% of the U.S. GDP). The government, which was running a surplus, could have easily decided to finance the uninsured portion of the disaster by issuing debt as had been done in the United States. Instead, the newly elected conservative administration temporarily increased taxes on businesses (after two years, taxes dropped back to pre-disaster levels). Chile was also able to issue a dedicated bond on the international debt markets to finance another portion of the needed federal spending. Take-up rates for earthquake insurance increased in the years that followed (Useem, Kunreuther, and Michel-Kerjan 2015).[9]

This Ever-Growing Relief Environment Has Consequences, But Not All Relief Policy Tools Create Moral Hazard

Since the seminal work by Buchanan (1975) and Coate (1995), economists have been interested in the balance between the social benefits associated with government-provided financial relief and the potential disincentives that this policy might create. In the context of government disaster relief given to individuals, one might ask: Why should people invest in risk reduction measures or purchase insurance coverage if they expect to be bailed out anyway? (This is a form of charity hazard as described by Browne and Hoyt 2000.) As Kunreuther and Miller (1985) already noticed 30 years ago, "although Congressmen and federal agencies have become more concerned with finding ways to help communities struck by severe disasters, there has also been a realization that government has been viewed as the protector of risks in ways that would have been unthinkable 50 years ago." Today, people expect to be helped in a way that was probably not true before.

There have been only a handful of contributions focusing on the economics of disaster relief. Some have focused on the disincentive for purchasing insurance that relief creates (e.g., Raschky and Weck-Hannemann 2007), and others on the negative impact that foreign aid can have on the economic development of the receiving country and lack of proper investments in disaster risk reduction measures ex ante (see Raschky et al. 2013, for a review).

As noted, the irony is that governmental disaster relief is usually earmarked to rebuild destroyed infrastructure, not as direct aid to the victims. To the extent that a large portion of such disaster relief goes to the states, post-disaster assistance also distorts the incentives of state and local governments to prefinance their disaster losses through insurance and other mechanisms. Cities and states are not well incentivized to incur upfront cost to make them more resilient to future disasters.

In a study jointly conducted with Carolyn Kousky and Paul Raschky, we examine the influence of federal disaster aid on individuals' flood insurance purchase decisions over 2000–2009 (Kousky, Michel-Kerjan, and Raschky 2018). We estimate the effect of grants from the Individual Assistance (IA) program of the Federal Emergency Management Agency (FEMA) and low-interest loans to homeowners from the Small Business Administration (SBA). We find that IA grants to individuals, while of fairly limited size, lead to a statistically significant reduction in insurance coverage purchased: a $1,000 increase in the average IA grant per household in a ZIP code decreases average insurance coverage per household by $6,400 in that area the following year. We also find that the moral hazard impact of federal aid is more significant for large disasters. Overall, low-interest SBA loans have no or very limited effect on insurance demand, maybe because borrowers have to pay it back, while IA is "free money."

While relief certainly helps those in need, these individuals would have been better off having their house (often by far the largest asset the family owns) covered by an insurance contract. Insurance, as one of the largest industries in the world and an effective risk transfer mechanism, can play an important role by providing more comprehensive and expedite reimbursement following a disaster. There are, of course, issues about why so many people do not voluntarily purchase such coverage (budget constraints and affordability, misperception of the risk, other spending priorities, etc.) that are important but which I will not discuss here (see Kunreuther, Meyer, and Michel-Kerjan 2013, for a review).

Three Proposals to Move from the Status Quo

Proposal 1: A national initiative is launched to create accessible record-keeping of all government disaster aid and recipients (states, cities, communities, businesses, and households) as an important move toward more transparency, accountability, and ultimately, more responsibility.

It is surprising how little data are publicly available on the amounts of federal aid that victims of disaster actually have received for, say, the disasters that occurred in the past 20 years. Some aggregate numbers per declared disaster are available for specific relief programs, but there is no systematic effort to make an account of the sum of all relief-related money that is being spent by different departments and federal and state agencies. Moreover, no granular accounting of how taxpayers' money is used for disaster relief (that is, how much money went to what city to do what exactly) is publicly available (to the best of my knowledge). As the saying goes, "what gets measured gets managed."

Given today's technology this would not seem to be a herculean task, but rather something that should be done systematically via a uniform tracking system (Michel-Kerjan 2015b).

It is also critical to better communicate information about relief programs that are available to victims of disasters, maximum compensation that recipients can expect, and the conditions and limitations on obtaining such relief (for example, what collateral is required for an SBA loan). Indeed, while relief figures are often high for large disasters, individuals are most likely to discover after being hit by one that they are more or less on their own. The main source for them might be FEMA's individual assistance program, but this is capped at $32,000 (as of 2016) and the majority of beneficiaries only receive a grant in the $4,000 to $5,000 range, which can help in the days following the disaster but will not rebuild. Low-interest loans from the SBA are typically larger but they come with numerous requirements; going through the administrative process of obtaining one of these loans is not easy and can take months. In a recent survey of small businesses affected by Sandy in 2012 that we conducted with the New York Federal Reserve Bank, we found that one-third of firms that began the application process withdrew their application before completing it. Managers at the SBA report that as firms learn more about the program (interest rates, collateral requirements, etc.) through the application process, some choose not to continue. Almost 60% of firms that completed the SBA post-disaster loan application process were rejected by the SBA (Collier et al. 2017).

Proposal 2: The Stafford Act is modified to provide incentives for states to proactively invest in pre-disaster preparedness and risk reduction measures. States that can demonstrate significant risk reduction actions would have access to cost sharing higher than 75%—say 80 or 85%.

While the Act was certainly well intentioned when passed, with the growing number of disaster declarations, it needs to be modified. The federal government working across government agencies, research institutions, and the private sector could establish national standards for resilience-enhancing actions that states can follow. To incentivize broad adoption of these new standards, states adopting them could access higher levels of cost sharing from the federal government when a disaster hits. I would expect this to translate into less payment by taxpayers since the disaster would have a lower impact due to preventive measures in place.

States not adhering to these new standards would either be capped at the current 75%, or at a lower level, even though I recognize that lowering this level would be politically hard to do.

FEMA's recent interest in increasing the financial responsibility of the states is certainly encouraging. One idea that is currently being discussed is for FEMA to increase the current deductible states have to pay before benefiting from federal aid through Public Assistance. FEMA still uses the same 1986-set threshold of $1 per capita, which has not been adjusted for inflation nor modified to reflect different per capita income across states. As of 2015 it stood at about $600,000 in Vermont, $4.5 million in Louisiana, $20 million in New York, and about $39 million in California, our most populous state. Kousky, Lingle, and Shabman (2016) did a back-of-the-envelope calculation on the impact across all states that a uniform deductible threshold would have had on the number of declarations over the period 1998–2015; they found that a $12.5 million deductible would have reduced the number of such declarations by more than 50% (since public assistance aid was below this threshold). More granular analysis must be performed to study the impact, state by state, of future changes, though.

Proposal 3: Public sector entities, cities, and states purchase disaster insurance coverage to speed up their recovery process in the aftermath of a disaster rather than relying on uncertain, limited and slow-to-come federal government relief.

Howard Kunreuther and I have proposed that more cities and states purchase some amount of disaster insurance to protect their public critical infrastructure (Kunreuther and Michel-Kerjan 2013). Insurance, while associated with premium cost, provides some element of certainty that the insured loss will be indemnified and in a rapid manner. Although government relief has increased significantly in recent years, it is not guaranteed, is always a cumbersome administrative process, and it typically takes a lot of time to be disbursed. For instance, two years after Hurricane Sandy hit the east coast, a large portion of the federal aid had still not been spent. In order to develop a much larger insurance market for public critical infrastructure, better risk assessment is needed. Accurate pricing is needed also, in order to evaluate the incentives to encourage infrastructure owners and operators to purchase some amount of coverage. Recent advances in probabilistic risk assessment, scientific data sharing and analytics can help a lot here. This is potentially a massive growth opportunity for insurers and reinsurers. Those firms might also have a vested interest in making this infrastructure more resilient to future disasters, since it will move the insurability frontier in the right direction. As insurers are large asset managers (with over $30 trillion of assets under management, second only to pension funds), it should be a win-win situation if regulators were to support and reward this type of long-term investment more than they currently do.

Conclusion

The question of who will/should pay for catastrophes in the future and how to best organize risk-sharing is likely to become more and more salient as more frequent and costly catastrophes unfold.

I have mainly focused here on natural disasters as a core example, but terrorism threats, technological disasters, large-scale cyberattacks, pandemics, and geopolitical risks, among others, also need to be considered, quantified, managed, and financed, as part of a more holistic and integrated national risk management strategy by Congress and the White House. Businesses have also come to realize that strategic risk management is becoming key to quality growth and competitiveness in a fast changing environment.

Designing and implementing optimal risk-sharing solutions between those at risk, the private sector, and government so one actually enhances resilience, rather than encouraging too much risk-taking, will certainly be a central pursuit for the United States and many other countries in the twenty-first century.

Thirty years ago, the field was nascent, but we have learned a lot since then, which can help design and implement better public policies and business strategies. One key learning is certainly that catastrophes and politics are intertwined. Because of the number of people affected, the scale of the devastation, and the high level of emotion and empathy in the hours that follow a disaster, it is hard for any elected official not to want to help those in need as much as they can.

Disaster relief is no exception, as the historical levels of appropriation by the U.S. Congress in recent disasters has shown. But public policy is also about setting the right direction, longer term. With more than three-quarters of the cost of Sandy in 2012 paid by American taxpayers, it will become harder and harder for the United States or any other market-based economy to go beyond that threshold. At some point, one will have to stand up and break the cycle. But this might be hard to do politically, for reasons discussed above.

As an alternative, I proposed a glide path to get there, which has three prongs:

1. Designing and implementing a national accounting system of how much relief is spent, where the money is coming from, and where it is going, which will provide the necessary data analytics to then propose better policies based on measurable evidence.
2. Not necessarily abolishing, but reforming, the Stafford Act, which today remains the central piece of the entire relief system but unfortunately provides no incentive for states to make risk management a priority, since they are guaranteed that a large proportion of their losses will be paid by others.
3. Newly designed insurance solutions should help provide the necessary financial protection as more risk is retained by those who are actually exposed to it. The insurance gap is significant, in turn creating significant opportunities to make more Americans and businesses adequately financially protected when the next Big One strikes.

In the coming years, I expect all credit rating agencies to take a deeper look at the financial strength of countries faced with the risk of extreme shocks. Soon the attention will also go to states, cities, and businesses (as it has already started to do). One day not far off, the same analysis might be performed for individual credit rating; creating an algorithm that would simulate how anybody's personal credit rating would be impacted after suffering from a disaster loss (taking into account the protection the individual has in place to sustain the shock, or not) is totally feasible given today's digitalization and use of smart data. In the end, this might be a powerful tool to raise the issue of risk management, and trigger actions. Who does not care about their credit score?

Notes

1. This is an average return period. It could be the case that a series of such events hit a country over just two or three years.
2. This is not hypothetical. S&P revised its outlook of Japan's sovereign rating to negative in 2011, in part due to the impact of the large earthquake and resulting tsunami that hit the

country. That same year, New Zealand was also downgraded, a decision partly explained by the required public spending in the aftermath of the significant earthquakes that occurred there.

3. Public infrastructure is primarily rebuilt with federal funds through the Stafford Act, with only 25% percent picked up by state and local governments. Individuals and small businesses can apply for low-interest disaster loans from the Small Business Administration; some individual assistance grants, capped at $32,000 per household, are also available from the Federal Emergency Management Agency to cover uninsured losses.

4. One single major disaster affecting a large area will probably trigger several declarations at once.

5. After Tropical Storm Agnes and the Rapid City floods, Congress effectively converted the disaster loan programs into primarily a grant program where the first $5,000 of each loan was forgiven and the annual interest rate on the remaining portion was 1% (Kunreuther 1973).

6. Several federal programs exist to provide disaster assistance. The Public Assistance (PA) program provides aid to states after a presidentially declared disaster. Kousky et al. (2016) shows that the PA program directs funds to states (applicants) and local governments for emergency protective measures, debris removal, and for public buildings and infrastructure repair. PA spending after major disaster declarations totaled $82 billion from August 1998 to October 2015. Three events account for over half: Hurricane Katrina (over 25% of the total), Hurricane Sandy (18.5%), and the 9/11 attacks (9.4%). Over that period, the average spending on PA per declaration was $87.5 million. Excluding Katrina and Sandy, the average drops to $50 million (Kousky, Lingle, and Shabman 2016).

7. Data from public sources and Cummins, Suher, and Zanjani (2010) based on their analysis of 57 catastrophes after correction for price-level changes and size of the housing stock, so the ratio is not overweighed by the most recent disasters.

8. Based on $60 billion federal relief figure (including the $9.7 billion additional borrowing capacity provided to the federally run National Flood Insurance Program to pay its flood insurance claim liability.

9. In contrast to the United States, earthquake insurance penetration is high in Chile; 90% of residents with a mortgage have earthquake insurance, as it is required by mortgagees in Chile. As a result, about a third of the total economic loss from the 2010 earthquake in Chile had been paid by insurance and reinsurance, mostly from outside the country, providing a large influx of capital to help speed up recovery and reconstruction (Useem, Kunreuther, and Michel-Kerjan 2015).

References

Botzen, W. J. W., Kunreuther, H., & Michel-Kerjan, E. (2015). Divergence between individual perceptions and objective indicators of tail risks: Evidence from floodplain residents in New York City. *Judgment and Decision Making, 10*(4), 365–385.

Browne, M. J., & Hoyt, R. E. (2000). The demand for flood insurance: Empirical evidence. *Journal of Risk and Uncertainty, 20*(3), 291–306.

Buchanan, J. (1975). *The Samaritan's dilemma.* In E. S. Phelps (Ed.), *Altruism, morality, and economic theory.* New York: Russell Sage Foundation.

City of New York. (2013). *PlaNYC: A stronger more resilient New York*. New York: Mayor's Office of Long-Term Planning and Sustainability. Retrieved from https://www1.nyc.gov /site/sirr/report/report.page

Coate, S. (1995). Altruism, the Samaritan's dilemma, and government transfer policy. *American Economic Review, 85*(1), 46–57. Collier, B. L., Haughwout, A. F., Kunreuther, H. C., Michel-Kerjan, E. O., & Stewart, M. A. (2017). *Firms' management of infrequent shocks* (NBER Working Paper No. 22612). National Bureau of Economic Research.

Cummins, J. D., & Mahul, O. (2008). *Catastrophe risk financing in developing countries*. Washington, DC: World Bank.

Cummins, J. D., Suher, M., & Zanjani, G. (2010). Federal financial exposure to natural catastrophe risk. In D. Lucas (Ed.), *Measuring and managing federal financial risk* (pp. 61–92). Chicago: University of Chicago Press.

Eisensee, T., & Strömberg, D. (2007). News droughts, news floods, and U.S. disaster relief. *Quarterly Journal of Economics, 122*(2), 693–728.

Garrett, T. A., & Sobel, R. S. (2003). The political economy of FEMA disaster payments. *Economic Inquiry, 41*(3), 496–509.

Kousky, C., Lingle, B., & Shabman, L. (2016). *FEMA public assistance grants: Implications of a disaster deductible* (policy brief). Washington, DC: Resources for the Future.

Kousky, C., Michel-Kerjan, E. O., & Raschky, P. (2018). Does federal disaster assistance crowd out private demand for insurance? *Journal of Environmental Economics and Management, 87*, 50–164.

Kousky, C., & Shabman, L. (2013). *A new era of disaster aid? Reflections on the Sandy Supplemental* (Issue Brief 13–05). Washington, DC: Resources for the Future.

Kunreuther, H. (1973). *Recovery from natural disasters: Insurance or federal aid?* Washington, DC: American Enterprise Institute.

Kunreuther, H., Ginsberg, R., Miller, L., Sagi, P., Slovic, P., Borkan, B., & Katz, N. (1978). *Disaster insurance protection: Public policy lessons*. New York: Wiley.

Kunreuther, H., Meyer, R., & Michel-Kerjan, E. (2013). Overcoming decision biases to reduce losses from natural catastrophes. In E. Shafir (Ed.), *The behavioral foundations of public policy* (pp. 398–413). Princeton, NJ: Princeton University Press.

Kunreuther, H., & Michel-Kerjan, E. (2013, October 29). A proposal for insuring public facilities and infrastructure against disaster losses. *Huffington Post*.

Kunreuther, H. C., Michel-Kerjan, E. O., Doherty, N. A., Grace, M. F., Klein, R. W., & Pauly, M. V. (2011). *At war with the weather: Managing large-scale risks in a new era of catastrophes*. Cambridge, MA: MIT Press.

Kunreuther, H., & Miller, L. (1985). Insurance versus disaster relief: An analysis of interactive modelling for disaster policy planning. *Public Administration Review, 45*, 147–154.

Michel-Kerjan, E. O. (2010). Catastrophe economics: The national flood insurance program. *Journal of Economic Perspectives, 24*(4), 165–186.

Michel-Kerjan, E. (2012). How resilient is your country? *Nature, 491*(7425), 497.

Michel-Kerjan, E. (2013, March 14). Testimony before the U.S. Senate, Committee on Small Business and Entrepreneurship. Roundtable on Helping Small Businesses Weather Economic Challenges and Natural Disasters. Washington, DC.

Michel-Kerjan, E. (2015a). Effective risk response needs a prepared mindset. *Nature, 517*(7535), 413–414.

Michel-Kerjan, E. (2015b, March 8). Presentation before the U.S. House of Representatives, Committee on Transportation and Infrastructure. Roundtable on What Is Driving the Increasing Cost and Rising Losses from Disasters? Washington, DC.

Moss, D. (2010). The peculiar politics of American disaster policy: How television has changed federal relief. In E. Michel-Kerjan & P. Slovic (Eds.), *The irrational economist* (pp. 151–160). New York: PublicAffairs.

NOAA (National Oceanic and Atmospheric Administration). (2013). *National coastal population report: Population trends from 1970 to 2020*. Washington, DC: U.S. Department of Commerce.

OECD (2012). *G20/OECD methodological framework on disaster risk assessment and risk financing*. Paris: Organisation for Economic Co-operation and Development.

Raschky, P. A., Schwarze, R., Schwindt, M., & Zahn, F. (2013). Uncertainty of governmental relief and the crowding out of flood insurance. *Environmental and Resource Economics, 54*(2), 179–200.

Raschky, P. A., & Weck-Hannemann, H. (2007). Charity hazard: A real hazard to natural disaster insurance? *Environmental Hazards, 7*(4), 321–329.

Standard & Poor (2015). *Storm alert: Natural disasters can damage sovereign creditworthiness.* New York: Standard & Poor's Rating Services.

Useem, M., Kunreuther, H., & Michel-Kerjan, E. (2015). *Leadership dispatches: Chile's extraordinary comeback from disaster*. Stanford, CA: Stanford University Press.

White House (2007). *Economic report of the President*. Washington, DC.

White House (2015). *OMB sequestration update report to the President and Congress for fiscal year 2016*. Washington, DC: Office of Management and Budget, Executive Office of the President of the United States.

World Economic Forum (2015). *Global risks report 2015*. Geneva: WEF.

World Economic Forum (2016). *Global risks report 2016*. Geneva: WEF.

the National Research Council of the National Academy of Sciences, as well as the Department of Homeland Security's Flood Apex research review board. He has participated in policy forums for the Resilient America Roundtable, the Federal Insurance and Mitigation Administration, the Applied Technology Council, and the Engineering for Climate Extremes Partnership. He has also assisted in guiding research direction and findings for the NSF, Environmental Protection Agency, New York Sea Grant, RAND Corporation, and the Verification of the Origins of Rotation in Tornadoes Experiment-Southeast, among others. He holds a BS from Carnegie Mellon University, an MS in environmental and urban systems from Florida International University, and a PhD in economics from Florida International University.

Nate Dieckmann is an Associate Professor at Oregon Health & Science University and a senior research scientist at Decision Research. He conducts basic and applied research in decision-making, risk communication, and applied statistics. His current work is focused on developing and testing methods for the effective presentation of uncertainty in a variety of domains. Other areas of interest include how numerical ability (numeracy) affects judgment and decision-making, and examining lay perceptions of conflicting health information, expert disagreement, and trust in science more generally.

Robin Dillon is a Professor and Area Coordinator for the Operations and Information Management Group in the McDonough School of Business at Georgetown University. Dillon's research specifically examines critical decisions that people have made following near-miss events in situations with severe outcomes, including hurricane evacuation, terrorism, cyber-security, and NASA mission management. She has served as a risk analysis and project management expert on several National Academies committees, including the review of the New Orleans regional hurricane protection projects and the application of risk analysis techniques to securing the Department of Energy's special nuclear materials. She has a BS/MS from the University of Virginia in Systems Engineering and a PhD from Stanford University. From 1993 to 1995 she worked as a systems engineer for the Fluor Daniel Corporation.

Baruch Fischhoff is the Howard Heinz University Professor, Department of Engineering and Public Policy, Institute for Politics and Strategy, Carnegie

Mellon University. A graduate of Detroit public schools, he holds a BS in mathematics and psychology from Wayne State University and an MA and PhD in psychology from the Hebrew University of Jerusalem. He is past president of the Society for Judgment and Decision Making and of the Society for Risk Analysis, and recipient of the latter's Distinguished Achievement Award. He was founding chair of the Food and Drug Administration Risk Communication Advisory Committee and recently chaired the National Research Council Committee on Behavioral and Social Science Research to Improve Intelligence Analysis for National Security, and cochaired the National Research Council Committee on Future Research Goals and Directions for Foundational Science in Cybersecurity and the National Academy of Sciences Sackler Colloquium on "The Science of Science Communication." He is a Fellow of the American Psychological Association (APA) and the Association for Psychological Science and has received APA's Award for Distinguished Service to Psychology. Recent books include *Risk: A Very Short Introduction* and *Counting Civilian Casualties.*

Jeffrey A. Friedman is an Assistant Professor of Government at Dartmouth College. He studies national security decision-making, with an emphasis on understanding how assessments of uncertainty shape major policy choices. He received his PhD (Public Policy) from the Harvard Kennedy School in 2013 and has held fellowships at several interdisciplinary centers, including the Weatherhead Center for International Affairs, the Belfer Center for Science and International Affairs, the Dickey Center for International Understanding, and the Institute for Advanced Study in Toulouse.

Robin Gregory is a Senior Researcher at Decision Research and Director of Value Scope Research, a small consulting firm. Gregory is also an adjunct professor in the Institute for Resources, Environment and Sustainability, University of British Columbia. He leads research projects and workshops for government, industry, and First Nations on structured decision-making, risk management, the conduct of deliberative groups, and techniques for eliciting preferences and addressing difficult tradeoffs. Gregory began his career as an economist (Yale, 1972), interested in choices made by individuals in relation to tradeoffs between economic development and environmental protection. After completing a master's degree in Natural Resource Economics (University of British Columbia, 1974), he worked as a teacher and consultant for several years, focusing on questions relating to the pros and cons of the many hydroelectric developments that at that time were reshaping the societies and economics of the Pacific Northwest.

Robert W. Klein is Associate Professor and Director at the Center for Risk Management and Insurance Research at Georgia State University. Before starting his career at Georgia State in 1996, Klein served as the director of research for the National Association of Insurance Commissioners. He also served as a staff economist for the Michigan Insurance Bureau and the Michigan Senate Fiscal Agency. Klein has written extensively on various topics on insurance and insurance regulation, including the structure and performance of insurance markets, competitive rating, catastrophe insurance problems, urban insurance issues, workers' compensation, international insurance regulation, and solvency regulation.

Carolyn Kousky is Director for Policy Research and Engagement at the Wharton Risk Management and Decision Processes Center at the University of Pennsylvania. Kousky's research has examined multiple aspects of disaster insurance markets, the National Flood Insurance Program, federal disaster aid and response, and policy responses to potential changes in extreme events with climate change. She has published numerous articles, reports, and book chapters on the economics and policy of natural disasters and disaster insurance markets, and is routinely cited in media outlets including NPR, the *New York Times*, the *Washington Post*, *Fortune*, CBS News, and *Business Insurance*, among others. She is the recipient of the 2013 Tartufari International Prize from the Accademia Nazionale dei Lincei. Kousky was a member of the National Research Council Committee on Analysis of Costs and Benefits of Reforms to the National Flood Insurance Program and is a visiting Fellow at Resources for the Future. She has a BS in Earth Systems from Stanford University and a PhD in Public Policy from Harvard University.

Howard Kunreuther is the James G. Dinan Professor; Professor of Decision Sciences and Business and Public Policy at the Wharton School, University of Pennsylvania; and co-director of the Wharton Risk Management and Decision Processes Center. Kunreuther has a long-standing interest in ways that society can better manage low-probability, high-consequence events related to technological and natural hazards and has written numerous papers on these topics. He is a Fellow of the American Association for the Advancement of Science, a Distinguished Fellow of the Society for Risk

Analysis, and twice was recipient of the Kulp-Wright Book Award for the publication that makes the most significant contribution to the literature of insurance. In 2015 he received the Shin Research Excellence Award from the Geneva Association and the International Insurance Society in recognition of his outstanding work on the role of public-private partnerships in mitigating and managing risks.

Craig E. Landry is Professor of Agricultural and Applied Economics, University of Georgia. He is a natural resource economist with expertise in non-market valuation, coastal resources management, and experimental economics. His research agenda includes individual decision-making under risk and uncertainty; risk management, insurance, and mitigation for natural hazards; dynamic optimization models for studying coupled human-natural coastal systems; modeling of recreation demand; and experimental economics for assessing non-market valuation methods and willingness to pay for public goods. Landry has served as review panelist for the National Science Foundation, Environmental Protection Agency, and National Oceanic and Atmospheric Administration Sea Grant programs. He holds master's degrees from the University of Georgia and University of Maryland—College Park. His PhD is in Agricultural and Natural Resource Economics from the University of Maryland–College Park.

Barbara A. Mellers is the I. Georgy Heyman University Professor and Professor of Marketing at the Wharton School, University of Pennsylvania. She was appointed in 2011 as the 11th Penn Integrates Knowledge Professor. Her research examines the factors that influence judgments and decisions, including emotions, self-interest, past mistakes, sensitivities to risk, and perceptions of fairness. Mellers is an author of almost a hundred articles and book chapters, co-editor of two books, and a member of numerous prestigious editorial boards. She served as president of the Judgment and Decision Making Society, was a five-year National Science Foundation Presidential Young Investigator, and has received major research support from the National Science Foundation. She earned a PhD in 1981 and an MA in 1978 in Psychology from the University of Illinois at Urbana-Champaign and a BA in 1974, also in Psychology from the University of California at Berkeley.

Robert J. Meyer is the Gayfryd Steinberg Professor and Co-Director of Wharton's Risk Management and Decision Processes Center. His research focuses on consumer decision analysis, sales response modeling, and decision-making under uncertainty. His work has appeared in a wide variety of professional journals and books, including the *Journal of Consumer Research* and the *Journal of Marketing Research*. He has served as the editor of *Marketing Letters* and currently serves on the editorial review boards of several major journals.

Erwann O. Michel-Kerjan co-edited this book when he was Executive Director of the Risk Management and Decision Processes Center of the Wharton School, University of Pennsylvania, where he taught in the Wharton MBA and executive programs. He is now a Partner at McKinsey. Views expressed in this volume under his name are his own and do not represent the views of his current employer. An authority on strategy, enterprise-risk management, and the financing of extreme events, he has advised heads of state, corporations, and not-for-profit and international organizations. A Young Global Leader of the World Economic Forum, he also served as chairman of the Organisation for Economic Co-operation and Development's High Level Advisory Board on Financial Management of Catastrophes (2008–2017). Recent books include *Leadership Dispatches* (with Michael Useem and Howard Kunreuther); *The Irrational Economist* (with Paul Slovic); and *At War with the Weather* (with Howard Kunreuther), which received the Kulp-Wright award for the most significant contribution to the literature of risk management and insurance.

Robert Muir-Wood is the Chief Research Officer of Risk Management Solutions. He co-founded the London office of RMS in 1996. He has a degree in Natural Sciences and a PhD in Earth Sciences, both from Cambridge University. He is the author of many scientific papers on the analysis of earthquakes, hurricanes, and windstorms, more than 150 articles and six books. He has more than 20 years' experience in developing probabilistic catastrophe models, and has led projects to build models for earthquake, tropical cyclone, windstorm, and flood, in Europe, Japan, North America, the Caribbean, and Australia, and has been the technical lead on a number of catastrophe risk securitization transactions. He has also lectured widely on catastrophe risk and the business response to climate change. He was lead author on Insurance, Finance and Climate Change for the 2007 Fourth Assessment Report of the United Nations Intergovernmental Panel on Climate Change, and is vice chair of the Organisation for Economic Co-operation and Development's High Level Advisory Board of the International Network on the Financial Management of Large Scale Catastrophes.

Mark Pauly holds the position of Bendheim Professor in the Department of Health Care Systems at the Wharton School of the University of Pennsylvania. He is a former commissioner on the Physician Payment Review Commission and an active member of the Institute of Medicine. One of the nation's leading health economists, Pauly has made significant contributions to the fields of medical economics and health insurance. His work in health policy deals with the appropriate design for Medicare in a budget-constrained environment and the ways to reduce the number of uninsured through tax credits for public and private insurance. He is an appointed member of the U.S. Department of Health and Human Services National Advisory Committee to the Agency for Healthcare Research and Quality, and co-editor-in-chief of the *International Journal of Health Care Finance and Economics.*

Lisa A. Robinson is a senior research scientist at the Harvard T.H. Chan School of Public Health, Center for Health Decision Science and Center for Risk Analysis. She focuses on improving the use and usefulness of benefit-cost analysis, particularly for policies with outcomes that cannot be fully valued using market measures. Recently, she has been working on applying these methods to global health and on improving responses to hazard warnings. She was previously a senior fellow at the Harvard Kennedy School of Government's Mossavar-Rahmani Center for Business and Government and is an affiliate fellow of its Regulatory Policy Program. She is also past president of the Society for Benefit-Cost Analysis, and recipient of its Richard O. Zerbe Distinguished Service Award; and a fellow and former councilor of the Society for Risk Analysis, and recipient of its Richard J. Burk Outstanding Service Award. She received her Master in Public Policy degree from the Harvard Kennedy School.

Adam Rose is Research Professor, Price School of Public Policy, and Faculty Affiliate, Center for Risk and Economic Analysis of Terrorism Events (CREATE), University of Southern California. He serves as an advisor on disaster resilience to the United Nations Development Programme. A major focus of his research has been on resilience to natural disasters and terrorism at the levels of the individual business, market, and regional economy.

He is currently working on studies sponsored by the Department of Homeland Security (DHS) on economic consequence analysis of radiological and biological threats, and on the economic impacts of U.S Customs and Border Protection institutions and policies. He recently completed studies sponsored by the National Science Foundation and DHS analyzing the economic consequences of behavioral reactions to terrorism. He has served on a National Research Council panel on Earthquake Resilience, was the lead researcher on the Multihazard Mitigation Council report to the U.S. Congress on the net benefits of Federal Emergency Management Agency hazard mitigation grants, and coordinated eight studies to arrive at a definitive estimate of the economic consequences of 9/11.

Paul J. H. Schoemaker was Research Director for the Mack Center for Innovation Management at the Wharton School, and founder and executive chairman of Decision Strategies International, Inc., a consulting and training firm specializing in strategic management and leadership. The company's clients include several of the largest corporations worldwide, as well as over a hundred of the Fortune 500. Paul is internationally known for his many articles (he ranks in the top 1% of scholarly citations globally) and books on decision-making and strategy, including *Decision Traps*; *Winning Decisions*; *Wharton on Managing Emerging Technologies*; *Profiting from Uncertainty*; *Peripheral Vision*; *Chips, Clones and Living Beyond 100*; and *Brilliant Mistakes*.

Paul Slovic is a founder and President of Decision Research and Professor of Psychology at the University of Oregon, studying human judgment, decision-making, and risk analysis. He and his colleagues worldwide have developed methods to describe risk perceptions and measure their impacts on individuals, industry, and society. He publishes extensively and serves as a consultant to industry and government. Slovic is a past president of the Society for Risk Analysis and in 1991 received its Distinguished Contribution Award. In 1993 he received the Distinguished Scientific Contribution Award from the American Psychological Association. In 1995 he received the Outstanding Contribution to Science Award from the Oregon Academy of Science. He has received honorary doctorates from the Stockholm School of Economics (1996) and the University of East Anglia (2005). Slovic was elected to the American Academy of Arts and Sciences in 2015 and the National Academy of Sciences in 2016.

Philip E. Tetlock is the Leonore Annenberg University Professor of Psychology and Management at the University of Pennsylvania and a Penn Integrates Knowledge Professor with the Wharton School and the Department of Psychology in the School of Arts and Sciences. He is an award-winning scholar of political psychology and organizational behavior. His best-known work, *Expert Political Judgment: How Good Is It? How Can We Know?* (2005), argued that "expert" predictions of political and economic trends are no more reliable than those of non-experts, based on a 20-year study of more than 82,000 predictions by 284 experts. This widely influential book received from the American Political Science Association both the Robert E. Lane Award for Best Book in Political Psychology and the Woodrow Wilson Award for Best Book on Government, Politics or International Affairs. He is a Fellow of the American Academy of Arts and Sciences, and the winner of numerous major professional awards, including, from the International Society of Political Psychology, the Harold Lasswell Award for Distinguished Scientific Contribution in the Field of Political Psychology and the Erik H. Erikson Early Career Award.

Daniel Västfjäll has been a Professor in Cognitive Psychology at Linkoping University since 2011. He has PhDs in Acoustics (2003) and Psychology (2002). His main research interest is in emotion and its effect on everyday behavior, with the goal of helping people make better decisions. This is studied according to four different main themes: prosocial helping/the decision to donate; Homo Heuristicus—how decisions are actually made; neuroeconomics—studies of how the brain and body make decisions; and the effects of music and sound on emotions. He has previously published in the *Journal of Behavioral and Experimental Economics*, *Proceedings of the National Academy of Sciences*, and *Frontiers in Psychology*, among others.

W. Kip Viscusi is Vanderbilt's first University Distinguished Professor, with tenured appointments in the Department of Economics and the Owen Graduate School of Management as well as in the Law School. Viscusi's pathbreaking research has addressed a wide range of individual and societal responses to risk and uncertainty, including risky behaviors, government regulation, and tort liability. He is widely regarded as one of the world's leading authorities on benefit-cost analysis. He has served as a consultant to the U.S. Office of Management and Budget, the Environmental Protection Agency, the Occupational Safety and Health Administration, the Federal Aviation

Administration, and the U.S. Department of Justice on issues pertaining to the valuation of life and health.

Elke U. Weber is Gerhard R. Andlinger Professor in Energy and the Environment, Professor of Psychology and Public Affairs, Princeton University. She is an expert on behavioral models of decision-making under risk and uncertainty, investigating psychologically and neurally plausible ways to model individual differences in risk taking and discounting, specifically in risky financial situations and environmental decisions. Weber is past president of the Society for Mathematical Psychology, the Society for Judgment and Decision Making, and the Society for Neuroeconomics. She has edited two major decision journals, serves on the editorial boards of multiple journals across several disciplines and on advisory committees of the U.S. National Academy of Sciences related to human dimensions in global change, and is a lead author in Working Group III for the Fifth Assessment Report of the United Nations Intergovernmental Panel on Climate Change.

Richard Zeckhauser is the Frank P. Ramsey Professor of Political Economy, Kennedy School, Harvard University. He graduated from Harvard College (summa cum laude) and received his PhD there. He is an elected fellow of the Econometric Society, the National Academy of Medicine (National Academy of Sciences), and the American Academy of Arts and Sciences. In 2014, he was named a Distinguished Fellow of the American Economic Association. Many of his policy investigations explore ways to promote the health of human beings, to help markets work more effectively, and to foster informed and appropriate choices by individuals and government agencies.

NAME INDEX

SUBJECT INDEX

Page numbers in italics refer to figures.

ACA (Affordable Care Act, 2010), 79, 80, 81, 91
  adverse selection and, 86
  individual mandate, 89–91
  mix of subsidies and regulation, 82, 86–87
  See also Health insurance purchasing
Adaptation, 173–176, *178*, 199
Administrative Procedures Act (ADA), 233–234
Adverse selection, 83, 86, 253, 288
Africa, drought in, 116, 121
Aggregative Contingent Estimation, 211, 222
Agriculture, 69, 70
Air-traffic control, false-positive warnings and, 101
Applied Technology Council, 317
Automobile industry, 156, 330

Bangladesh, 117
Barclays Bank, 162, 163
Bayesian probability theory, 67, 159
BCEGS (Building Code Effectiveness Grading Schedule), 307–308, *309*, 317, 319n5
  See also Building codes
Bhopal disaster, 152, 155
Biases, 50, 60
  allocation concealment bias, 57, *58*
  attrition bias, 57, *58*
  availability bias, 271
  blinding bias, 57, *58*
  debiasing studies, 55
  estimation bias, 96
  intervention selection bias, 57, *58*
  methodological audit and, 57, *58*
  optimism, 121–122, 239, 262, 271, 246n13

  pessimism, 96, 121–122, 239, 246nn12–13
  sequence generation bias, 57, *58*
  status quo bias, 79
  See also Decision-making; Deliberative thinking; Intuitive thinking
Biggert-Waters Flood Insurance Reform Act (2012), 269–270
Black swan events, 5, 165
Bloomberg, Michael, 328
Bogle, John, 155
Boston Manufacturers, 267–268
BP Gulf of Mexico oil spill (2010), 151, 166
  See also Deepwater Horizon
Brier scores, 211, 218, 219
Building codes
  Consumers Union and Building Codes Assistance Project, 314
  demand for disaster-resistant buildings, 313–316, 318
  earthquakes and, 282, 292
  Florida Building Code (FBC), 311, 312, 313
  Fortified Home program, 315–316, 318
  future research directions, 316–318
  insurance and, 8, 279–280, 282, 304–306
  natural disaster loss reduction and, 311–313
  variation of existing U.S. residential codes, 306–311, *309*, *310*
  See also BCEGS
Business interruption insurance, 181
Butterfly effects, 165

California, 112, 366
  California Earthquake Authority, 262, 273, 278, 291–292